A Forest of Ideas

Ramblings in Interpretative Frameworks

"Art Therapy, Interpretive Method,
Social Construction, Metaphor,
Phenomenology & All That!"

BLAKE PARKER

Edited by Monica Carpendale, 2014

 www.trafford.com

North America & international
toll-free: 1 888 232 4444 (USA & Canada)
fax: 812 355 4082

Contents

Preface

Blake Parker, a medical anthropologist and performance poet, taught psychoanalytic concepts, symbolic interpretation, culturally-infused views of mental illness, research methods and poetry for many years at the Kutenai Art Therapy Institute (KATI), Nelson, BC. Blake was the life partner of Monica Carpendale, founder and executive director of KATI.

This series of writings emerged as a mixture of poetry, dialogues, book reports and short essays. Blake wrote this series of short little essays to be used by Kutenai Art Therapy Institute (KATI) students as a sort of shorthand to a number of concepts, primarily from sociology & anthropology, which he saw as useful, if not actually essential, for their understanding of the therapeutic process in a social and cultural context. He wrote most of these essays in the last year of his life while he was living with a terminal diagnosis of cancer (2006). As such, he attempted to bring together a number of concepts that seem to be ubiquitous in the context of art therapy education but which do not constitute separate areas of special interest. Blake uses a phenomenological understanding of metaphor in order to throw light upon the process of social construction, creativity and conceptions of mysticism or spirituality.

Blake focused many of the essays on mysticism and spirituality and the book includes some of his personal reflections regarding death, dying, creativity and the meaning of life. The "notes" are essentially a hermeneutic of mysticism, a moving from the parts to the whole and the whole to the parts. This book is a forest of ideas and ramblings in interpretive frameworks that emerged and is presented in a circular spiral.

These essays are a combination of topics, which he used to teach at the Institute and which have been the basis of our ongoing dialogue. The "I" voice is always Blake's unless clearly otherwise specified. He wrote these essays in a very conversational rather than academic style, and they are written very much as he would have spoken in class. The informal, poetic and personal style of writing has been retained as well as his way of writing using & instead of and. The ideas have not been specifically referenced in the body of the writing in an academic way as there was a sense of urgency in Blake's last year when he just wrote and allowed all the connections to just come together. I have decided to publish it in the spirit in which it was written and ask for forgiveness in the informality. The blend is his own and the essays circle around in a hermeneutic spiral inspired by topics that emerged in dialogue with myself, my brother, Jeremy Carpendale, and various friends and students. The bibliography is compiled of his key sources.

The diagrams were created by Blake to provide a visual framework for the concepts being discussed and were intended to be used for teaching. Gail Joy is to be thanked for doing the initial editorial organization of bringing all the pieces into a whole. I worked over the last years on the final structural edit and tried to provide some clarification of ideas, included exercises, and diagrams. The order of notes, essays and diagrams could have been structured in a number of different ways. The reader is encouraged to explore the book in a circular way of reading moving forwards and backwards and not insisting on a linear process.

It is meant to stimulate thinking and there is space for your own notes and diagrams. I am sure that you will find mistakes and things to question as well as insight and inspiration.

Monica Carpendale

Seminar on Interpretation

The purpose of the seminar is to discuss a broad range of topics pertaining to the concept & practice of "interpretation." The stories that we make will be as much as possible "dialogic" in nature. That is, we will all participate in the making of the story. Because of the interlocking nature of the ideas, the discussion may seem to jump around some but that's just in the nature of the game.

Various statements made in these maps will be provocative & by no means reflect settled "knowledge. These statements are meant to be starting points for discussion.

In the seminar there are actually a number of domains or areas of particular interest.

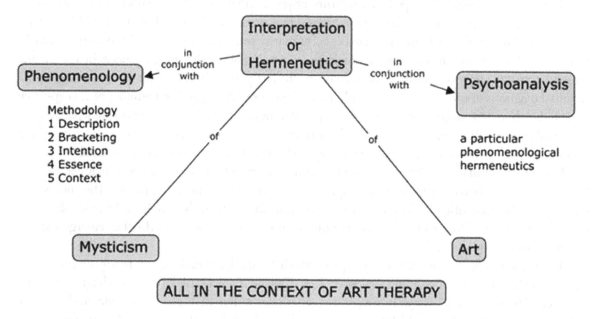

Why Mysticism?

In elaborating a number of elements of my interpretive practice I chose mysticism as the object of interpretation for a number of reasons. The first is that it is a subject I as well as a great number of people are interested in these days & there are certainly elements of mysticism that can be useful to the therapist. (In particular the issue of therapeutic presence). In addition, mysticism poses a particular problem with regard to contemporary language oriented theories of how meaning is formed. Language is central to metaphor theory, social constructivism & phenomenology & while sociological has a similar starting place as mysticism -- namely the illusory nature of the world we create, the 2 disciplines differ greatly beyond that.

Interpretation

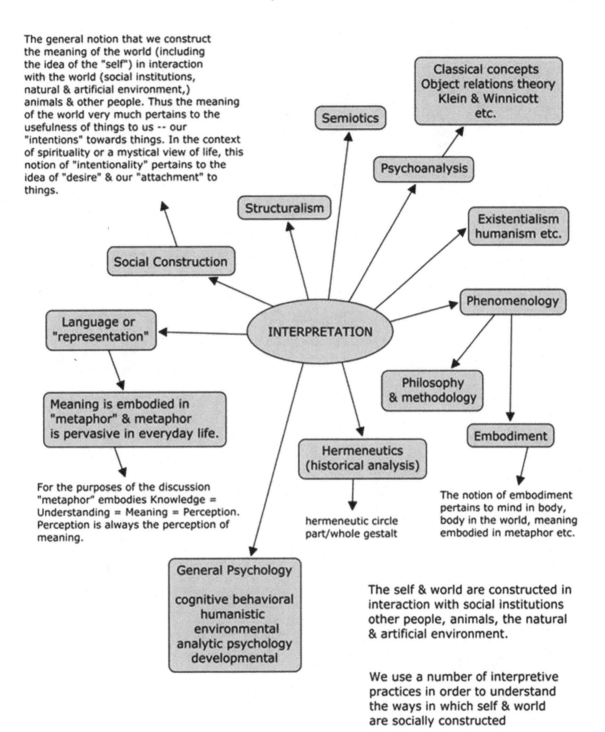

The general notion that we construct the meaning of the world (including the idea of the "self") in interaction with the world (social institutions, natural & artificial environment,) animals & other people. Thus the meaning of the world very much pertains to the usefulness of things to us -- our "intentions" towards things. In the context of spirituality or a mystical view of life, this notion of "intentionality" pertains to the idea of "desire" & our "attachment" to things.

Semiotics

Classical concepts
Object relations theory
Klein & Winnicott
etc.

Psychoanalysis

Structuralism

Existentialism
humanism etc.

Social Construction

Phenomenology

INTERPRETATION

Language or
"representation"

Philosophy
& methodology

Meaning is embodied in
"metaphor" & metaphor
is pervasive in everyday life.

Embodiment

Hermeneutics
(historical analysis)

For the purposes of the discussion
"metaphor" embodies Knowledge =
Understanding = Meaning = Perception.
Perception is always the perception of
meaning.

hermeneutic circle
part/whole gestalt

The notion of embodiment
pertains to mind in body,
body in the world, meaning
embodied in metaphor etc.

General Psychology

cognitive behavioral
humanistic
environmental
analytic psychology
developmental

The self & world are constructed in
interaction with social institutions
other people, animals, the natural
& artificial environment.

We use a number of interpretive
practices in order to understand
the ways in which self & world
are socially constructed

Introduction to a Wander in the Woods

In this following little note, I will lay out the basic territory that I wish to cover in this constellation of short essays or notes. It is perhaps my third attempt at a beginning. I began by writing about mysticism, discovered I needed more at the beginning, or more context, so wrote that, and then later discovered there wasn't enough, so wrote more. I suppose it is just the general difficulty we have in explaining anything at all – how far back do we have to go or how much can we assume our audience already knows. I want these essays & notes to be as accessible as possible & so it seems I will have to go quite far back. My ideal reader I picture as an intelligent but not necessarily well read or well educated person. I don't want to "turn off" those who don't already know some social theory, just as I don't want to turn off those with a different orientation than mine.

In particular I am thinking, in this latter case, of those with a general mystical orientation towards reality & the world. I do have to be careful in this last instance because if I'm not careful I've found a certain dismissive attitude does creep into my writing. I am writing these notes in the context of a return to a more academic discourse and find that certain attitudes have hardened in me since my earlier immersion in the theoretical domain. In general, I find myself now in what often appears to be the "scientific" camp, in an oppositional relation to the "mystic" camp. I do not feel altogether comfortable in the "scientific" category but do have to admit that I have a strong orientation towards the idea of "logical development" in the domain of ideas. I very much like the idea of things making sense to me. It is important to me. Essentially, if things don't logically fit together, then they don't make sense to me. I say this knowing that many of the "mystic persuasion" find "logic" somewhat tiresome and in no way the most important way of gaining or organizing knowledge.

In fact, the mystic way of knowledge does have to do with the circumvention of logic & discourse in general. Its way appears to have to do with the immersion of the self in the totality of all things, or in the godhead. It has to do with "participation" in the sacred world. As I understand it, mysticism doesn't deny the knowledge & activity of the ordinary world conditioned as it is by language, but puts forward the idea that there is another more complete & ultimately more satisfactory way of knowing.

As I said, I don't feel completely comfortable in the "scientific" camp & should perhaps say a few more words about this. First off, where do I feel comfortable? I guess I have to say that I feel the most comfortable in no camp at all. I find science as an institution to be no more comfortable than religion, say. (I understand that mysticism & religion are quite different.) I still remember how satisfied I felt when I came across the observation somewhere that both science & religion had the same belief in an "objective" world. They both thought this world wasn't it, but such a thing was "out there" waiting to be discovered.

In general, I have to say that I feel much more comfortable with the idea that the world as we know it, which means I suppose, the social world, is "created" by us, not discovered. I take it that there is "something" out there that could be called "nature" or "the universe," but essentially, it is unknowable. It is the ground, the background to everything we do, and what we do is create a world -with language.

With language, we tame the wild & dangerous world. With language, we create our gods & in our forgetfulness, we think we have "discovered" them. With language, we create our society &

think that we have discovered the "natural" way to do things. With language, we create the self & make distinctions between the "true" self & the untrue. With language we create the world & then forget we made it, only to have our creations appear years later as natural born entities that we have just "discovered."

This cycle of creativity, forgetfulness, and discovery can be related to the idea of Ideology as the body of ideas reflecting the social needs and aspirations of an individual, group, class, or culture. Ideology often appears to be "natural" precisely because we invented it ourselves but then forgot that we invented it. Years later the familiar ideas return, and it seems we have discovered a "natural order." This is certainly one aspect of a sociological explanation for mystical ideas & occult entities.

Note on "Criticism," Critical Thought & Just Talk

Speaking to a friend today, I realized I need to be really careful in speaking about the "sacred" etc. to not denigrate the "experience" of the sacred. It is important to make sure it is very clear that I am criticizing the ideology of mysticism, the authoritarian structure of groups led by gurus & the abuse of power, not the experience itself. I suppose even concerning the experience itself I am interested in the "why" of the situation rather than its factuality. I was speaking to another friend the other day about homeopathic remedies & at a certain point I was surprised to realize that this friend thought I didn't think homeopathic remedies worked. I responded in my surprise with the statement that everything "works" and it's the question of why things work that interests me. As happens so often in such cases, the friend was not very interested in why it worked just that it did, especially with children. For some reason it still seems important to know if something works in a purely chemical or "materialistic" way or by way of "suggestion" & psychology or even "psychic" reasons.

Objectivity

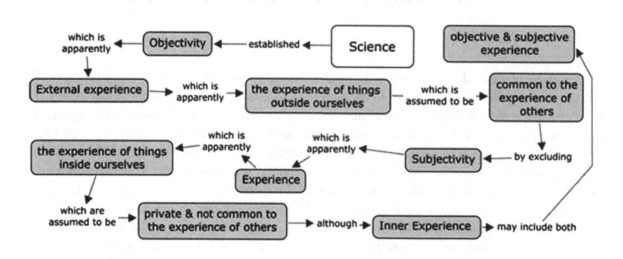

Science created the concept of "subjectivity" at the same moment that it created the concept of "objectivity."

Because of the diminishment of subjectively & "the subject" modern science is generally criticized as a bad influence upon contemporary culture because people come to be treated "objectively" as things or machines & morality is lost. This

Before the advent of modern scientific method & the distinction between objectivity & subjectivity, writing & other symbolic communication in different cultures paid little attention to this distinction & thus the symbolic categories of indigenous psychology, religious & medical writings etc. were a mixture of what we today call subjectivity & objectivity. This had the advantage of always presenting the self in relation to objects & events in the world but had the disadvantage of not being able to separate the self (beliefs, emotions, cultural & personal bias) from what we now call objective "facts."

In reaction to the bias towards science & objectivity & the absence of morality & spirit scientific & technological culture many people today have again become interested in religion & spirituality in general. Again we are finding many discourses that mix subjectivity & objectivity but because of the dominance of science these discourses are mistakenly seen as "objective" but a sort of super objectivity that ordinary science hasn't been able to discover yet. This is common in the so called occult-sciences as they are represented in new-age discourse.

Because of the lack of interest in subject-object distinctions, as understood in the context of rational science, we should then expect to find in pre-modern cultures various admixtures of subjective & objective symbology. We find this in such areas as Chinese medicine & philosophy, European medieval alchemy & so on. Psychology & physiology are freely mingled. As with nature & culture, different culture divide up the pie of "the world" & "things" in different ways. Here also we find the anthropological idea of the pre-modern self distinguished from the modern individual by its "participatory" nature. Before the subject-object distinctions of modern culture & before the birth of the separate individual, the self "participated" in the world in a different way. The boundary between what we call psychology & we call material science was quite different in different cultural contexts.

Phenomenology, Sociology & Mysticism

Merleau-Ponty's Five Key Concepts to Phenomenology

In addition to my linguistic orientation, I also want to use the phenomenological approach to the discovery of meaning. I do not see this approach as conflicting with the structural or post-structural approach because I take language to be intimately bound up with consciousness in general. I use Merleau-Ponty's phenomenological approach comprised of five analytical categories. These are:

1) Description
2) Bracketing. This refers to the "bracketing" out of the taken-for-granted world. This world is essentially the world as it apparently spontaneously appears to us – a meaningful world, where everything is named & in its place, as it were. When looking out at the world we don't have to think up the names of everything, things simply appear to us as "things" – a table is a table without us having to think about it. It just appears before us as a meaningful element of our "given" or "taken-for-granted" world. It is the ordinary world where language is intimately related, but not necessarily on a conscious level, to our perception of the meaningful world.
3) Essence
4) Intentionality
5) The world or context.

My overall interpretive practice then, can be characterized as a "phenomenological hermeneutics." See Monica's essay on these concepts. – Getting to the Underbelly.

Hermeneutics / Interpretation

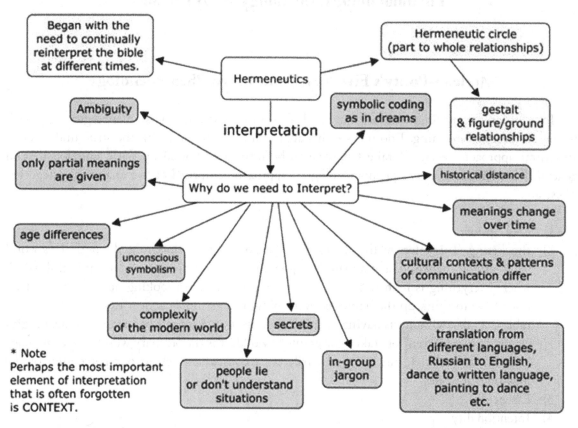

* Note
Perhaps the most important
element of interpretation
that is often forgotten
is CONTEXT.

In this seminar, social constructivism is the general orientation to understanding the social world. This theory holds that the social world is constructed by us primarily with the use of symbolic language in the context of social interaction. The background to this social interaction & the creation of our understanding of the world is human history & the evolutionary interaction between the natural environment & the biological organism. Given that we construct our world with language, it makes sense that we interpret that world as some sort of linguistic system. In the early part of the century, Structuralism was one of the dominant mode of interpretation & it used the individual sign as the basic unit of interpretation. More lately, metaphor theory has come to the fore & the basic unit of interpretation has become.

Metaphor operates by bringing one entity into relationship with another entity. This relationship is one of "similarity" but the nature of this similarity is by no means completely obvious because there are also always elements of "difference" which are included in the metaphor. This means that while a particular metaphor reveals a particular meaning it also conceals or blinds us to other meanings

A strong argument that Metaphor is the appropriate level for analyzing contemporary culture is that because of the complexity of contemporary culture, meaning is continually being "hidden."

* Note: See the CMap entitled "Interpretation" for a constellation of interpretive practices.

Language

I want to link these ideas of "meaning" to language but I aware at this point that I have neglected to give an adequate description or explanation of what I really mean by language. Rather than attempt to go back & try to find the "right place" to put in this explanatory description, I will do it now & hope that this suffices. Saying this I am also aware that very often there is a backwards & forewords shifting focus in the reading process itself. As the reader, I hope you can take what I give you now with regard to the nature of language & place it back somewhere else in the reading if not the writing & arrive at the appropriate knowledge. Causal sequence is very much identified with "ordinary consciousness" & so if I hope to actually show the complementary nature of the two modes of consciousness perhaps I can be forgiven departing from the causal sequence & depend upon the readers' intuitive mode of knowing. But I go on.

By language, I mean a very much expanded notion of what we ordinary think of as language – that is "written" or "spoken" language made up of mostly arbitrary sound units called words. These words are organized in sequential units called sentences guided by various "rules" of grammar. My use of the term language is that usage found in semiotics – the general study of "signs." (Signs in conventional language are the arbitrary units or words). In semiotics the sign is any unit at all that can be considered on its own. This might be the picture of a face or the sound of an explosion. The picture & the sound are both signs in a context. In ordinary language the context is the other words in the language & the rules that govern their relationships. In semiology, the context is respectively the whole catalogue of possible pictures (perhaps whittled down to all the pictures of the human body or even the face) & the catalogue of all possible sounds (perhaps limited to "non-musical" sounds.) In any even, when I use the word "language" I mean a very extended use of the term to mean any form of "representation" within which meaning (meaningful relationships) can be formulated. This does not mean that all meaningful relationships are linguistic but rather that all meaning can be understood or analyzed in terms of language. The "language" may be the language of "dressing up" or the visual language of architecture or the language of advertising.

The point is all meaningful human activity may be understood in terms of the relationship between various "units." All languages (as all meaning) will thus have a foreground & a background. The foreground will be comprised of the individual units & their relationships (which capture awareness) while the background will be the more broadly "perceptual" aspect of language – that is to say, the whole context that is brought up & within which the individual units are "situated." This sense of language, then, is not only extended to all sorts of audio-visual & sensual "languages," as forms of representation, it is also language situated "in the real-world." Language as it is used by people in concrete situations. When language is "used" in order to communicate with another person, the image of the world is constantly being evoked. This is true in "ordinary" language as well as in all the other languages. When a word is uttered, a picture appears in the mind – or not, perhaps, a picture, but an "impression" of what is meant by the word. Words make sense in relationship to other words but ultimately they must refer to the world – to real contexts, real situations. Language cannot begin or go on without real-world contexts. In teaching a child to speak, one says the word "nose" & touches one's nose. The child touches my nose & then her nose & imitates my sound – "nose." All first learning takes place in real contexts & with other people. Thus

7

language – the individual units as well as the whole of language have 2 distinct referents: 1) other units, more or less conventionalized in the representation system & 2) the real world as we perceive it with our bodily senses.

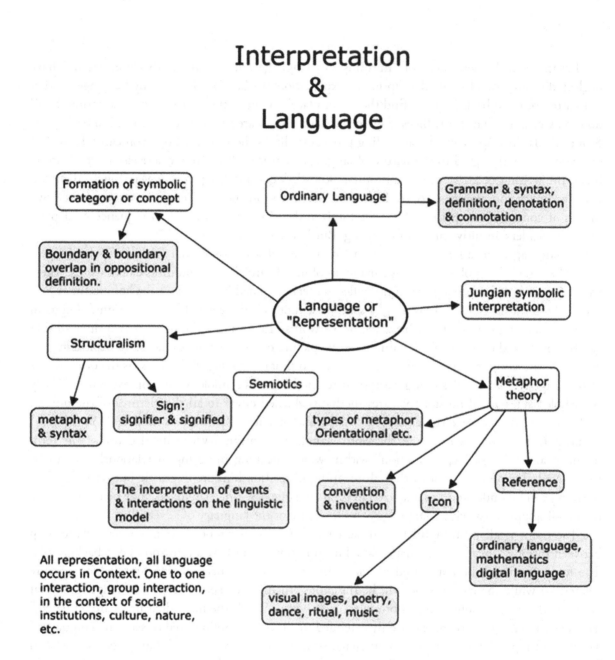

Structuralism and Semiotics

Structuralism & semiotics, the general study of signs which developed from the structuralist program, have a complex theory of the way signs work but, in essence, we may say that the categories of meaning (words) are comprised in a system of binary oppositions: white & black, body & mind, the sacred & the profane, individual & collectivity. We are engaged, then, in the study of signs & sign systems.

Structuralism analyzes society & elements of society via binary oppositions that it sees as essential to the way the brain works. Post structuralism, on the other hand, sees this binary dualism as an aspect of Western thought & not universal. For postmodernism, meaning & the categories of thought are shifting & unstable. While using many of the fundamental ideas in structuralism, I follow the American anthropologist Roy Wagner in using the notion of trope or metaphor in the context of a phenomenology in order to map the unfolding structure of social forms.

Using linguistic sociological tools in an analysis of mysticism & some other relevant subject matter such as magic, sacrifice, ritual initiation, and so on, is difficult for several reasons. One of these is that language & the structure of society were in their origins and development completely entangled in religion and the sacred. It seems that language originally was, by its very nature & power, sacred. In addition, it is pretty clear that secular society developed out of religious society & the secular self-developed out of the "primitive" self which itself was formed in the context of early religious societies.

In addition to, but perhaps arising out of, this historical entanglement between the analytical tools & the object of analysis, there is also the fact that both mysticism & sociology provide a theory of society that is sometimes quite similar. Thus, sociology at times can be shown to have the same insights into the composition of society & the self as mysticism while at other times it provides a critique of the mystical orientation to reality. It is important to keep this fact in mind: sociology & mysticism are two sometimes similar & sometimes different "orientations to reality." It is a given, then, that sociological analysis will sometimes make a person with the mystic orientation uncomfortable. I can certainly say the opposite: that the mystic orientation sometimes makes me uncomfortable, not so much because of its differences, but rather because of its similarities. Because of these similarities, I can sometimes glimpse myself as mystic, a role that at this time in my life I am uncomfortable with.

I'd like to speak briefly, then, of where I'm coming from. I have been interested in mysticism & the occult for pretty much most of my life. Before my academic training began at about age 40, I have to admit that my thinking was pretty much a hodgepodge of thought from all over, elements of the occult mixed with aspects of post-modernism, literary theory mixed with elements of philosophy, & so on. My academic training in sociology & anthropology gave me what I consider to be a fairly cohesive, if eclectic, analytical frame for the study of what I continue to be most interested in, the nature of society & the self.

In the study of society & self, I am primarily interested in the production & understanding of "meaning" & there can be no doubt that meaning in human society is fundamentally created by written & spoken language. But, of course, there are a great many other ways of creating meaning (gesture, architecture, fashion, visual art etc.) but I am happy to say that these may each be treated as some sort of sign system within the context of general semiotics. From the point of view of sociology as well as from the point of view of a poet, I love language. Language, for me, provides the context for my creative life, the life of my family & friends as well as my relationship with the wider community. I understand what I understand primarily (if not totally) through the agency of language. Language provides a way of knowing "about" things & it also provides a way of knowing in itself. There is much to be learned by simply writing.

One could say, in fact, that language is the very water we swim in, & this is perhaps why, in the ordinary course of our common understanding, we tend to ignore it. It is just there, all around us, & all in us too. It is our invisible "social" environment. Many hold that we tend to treat it as badly as the "natural" environment.

For me, then, language is central to the human experience. Thus, there is certainly one aspect of mysticism that makes me uncomfortable. It is precisely mysticism's apparent rejection of language as an adequate way of understanding experience. I am also suspicious of the very idea of dividing a linguistic way of knowing from some other occult way of knowing. Right on the surface of things, the supposed non-dualism of mysticism appears to create a dual world – the un-enlightened world of language & the enlightened world of non-linguistic, unified mystic experience. The notion of a split between "pure experience" & all other language-modified experience is difficult at best.

From the Tao Te Ching, we have the statement 'The path that can be named is not a true path'. In this statement, we have the common mystical understanding that the true ways of mysticism cannot be named & that the mystical path & the mystical experience itself cannot be formed in language. Following from this, we find, in many different texts, the general idea that the ordinary world structured by language is essentially dualistic & thus cannot grasp the essential unity (or monism) of the mystic experience. In this, at least, structuralism & mysticism agree: the ordinary world & language are dualistic.

Now that I've got to this point, I suppose I also should mention that the notion of "non-attachment" is also a little difficult for me. On first glance, it can appear to simply mean "not caring" but, as many have told me, this is not the true meaning of the term. Whether or not this is correct, there is none-the-less a sense that the mystic path in general involves a retreat from the world, its attachments, and responsibilities. There is an essential renunciate element in the mystical program.

Renunciate religions demand the renunciation of selfishness for some higher good or morality defined by the religion. This is a good thing except of course there may be some problem with the image of the higher good, the image of the whole. There may be a masking of power relations in the sense that the religion legitimizes those relations with its system of rewards & punishments.

The Structural Grid

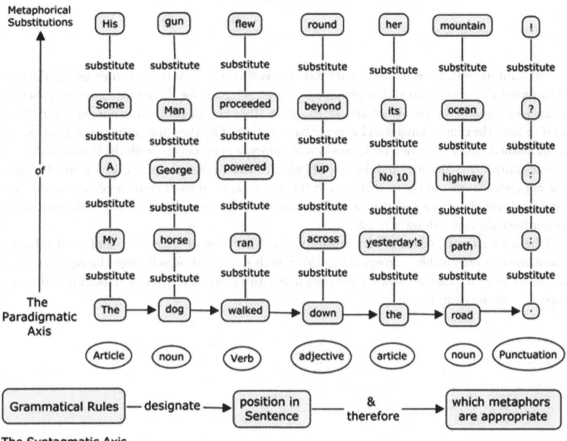

Metaphorical Substitutions

of

The Paradigmatic Axis

His	gun	flew	round	her	mountain	!
substitute	substitute	substitute	substitute	substitute	substitute	substitute
Some	Man	proceeded	beyond	its	ocean	?
substitute	substitute	substitute	substitute	substitute	substitute	substitute
A	George	powered	up	No 10	highway	;
substitute	substitute	substitute	substitute	substitute	substitute	substitute
My	horse	ran	across	yesterday's	path	:
substitute	substitute	substitute	substitute	substitute	substitute	substitute
The →	dog →	walked →	down →	the →	road →	.
Article	noun	Verb	adjective	article	noun	Punctuation

Grammatical Rules — designate → **position in Sentence** — **&** **therefore** → **which metaphors are appropriate**

The Syntagmatic Axis

The Grammar Police enforce the social rules about language. These rules are for the most part internalized like other social rules regarding how to act.

A small note

To want too much is evil, but to want too little is also evil. To want too much breaks the rules in various ways, often to do with individual desire vs. goodness for the whole community, but the renunciate religions are passive & ask for too little. They retreat from conventional reality. They want to leave the conventional world alone & have no part of it. They may ultimately retreat into an acetic aestheticism, a reduction of the world to its simplest components, with the intention that the "inside" mirrors the "outside" and they are likewise reduced to their simplest components. I suppose it is not quite fair to add the aestheticism in this instance, for it would only apply in certain cases when life is ritualized to a high degree: for instance, one might be reduced to "one" cup but it would be just the right cup, a thing of beauty.

The spiritual quest seems to very much require this notion of "retreat" to a place of calmness where one can presumably regroup, get in touch with the sacred, which might be one's own true self, & get ready to face the outside world once more. This desire is very much embodied in the great popularity of the term "retreat."

Diagrammatic Representation

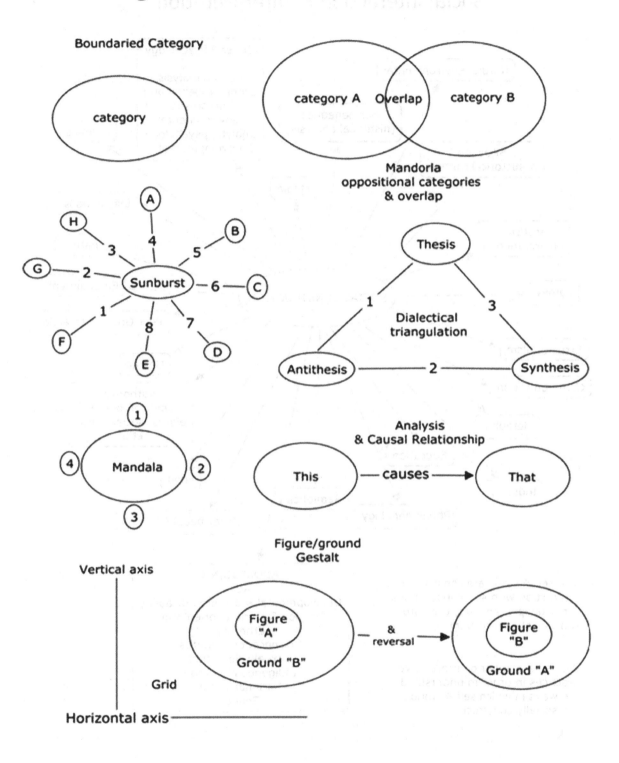

Boundaried Category

category

category A   Overlap   category B

Mandorla
oppositional categories
& overlap

A
H
B
G
3
4
5
2
Sunburst — 6 — C
1
8
7
F
E
D

Thesis

1   3

Dialectical
triangulation

Antithesis ——— 2 ——— Synthesis

1
4   Mandala   2
3

Analysis
& Causal Relationship

This — causes → That

Figure/ground
Gestalt

Vertical axis

Figure
"A"

Ground "B"

&
reversal

Figure
"B"

Ground "A"

Grid

Horizontal axis ————

Social Construction
Social interaction & Interpretation

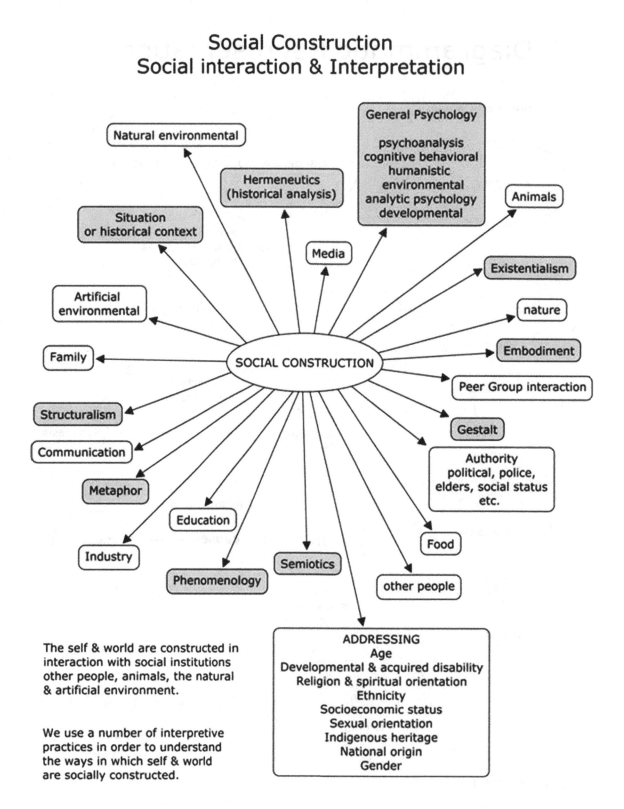

The self & world are constructed in interaction with social institutions other people, animals, the natural & artificial environment.

We use a number of interpretive practices in order to understand the ways in which self & world are socially constructed.

Metaphor & Meaning

A Note on "Meaning"

In the context of semiotics, the "meaning" of a sign comes from its relationship to other signs in the sign system. That is, the meaning of a word or sentence comes from its "role" in the broader meaningful context. Two aspects of meaning that may be given approximate analyses are the *connotative relation* and the *denotative relation*. The connotative relation is the relation between signs and their interpreting signs. The denotative relation is the relation between signs and objects.

Meaning is established originally by the constitution of a name or category, by the establishment of what is "inside" & what is "outside" a category. Thus there are the items that are "inside" the category, say of the "family," & this category is surrounded by other categories which are not in it. The ones closest to the category of the "family" are other categories such as "community" or "tribe" or "unmarried woman" and so forth. These do have some similarities to the first category & yet in some ways they are very different. There are similarities & differences between the categories that in a sense cluster around each other like overlapping rings. In order to make clear cut distinctions; there must be a rigorous establishment of difference at the boundaries of the each category.

The establishment of clear boundaries can be done by a rigorous sorting out of what is in & what is out of the category. There can also be a social suppression or repression of similarities between categories. This happens when the categories themselves do not lend themselves to rigorous separation. These might be categories concerning the emotions, for instance, or especially highly-charged social categories pertaining to religious matters or sexual matters. We can say that our present understanding of the concept "family" is considerably wider & more ambiguous than it used to be. In general "conservative" elements in our society want to keep the category "clear cut" & include only a married couple (that is, a man & a woman) & children. However, we now have single parent families and there is ongoing conflict about homosexual marriage. Certain liberal elements in society are fighting for social change. This fight is very tied up with the establishment of new definitions for old categories. Some of this battle goes on as simple symbolic interaction (talk) while some goes into the language of purposive action -- the organization of political rallies, the establishment of laws & so forth.

The definition and establishment of emotionally highly charged social categories as normative may need to be established by force as well as by persuasion or political action. Those who have control of the "reality concession" (Burroughs) get to establish the normative categories. Such definitions, as part of a mythology, often gloss over points of conflict or tension in the social structure. It is good for those in power if their rules appear to be "natural." There is a very strong tendency for the collective to accept & value that which is natural.

Representation & Interpretation

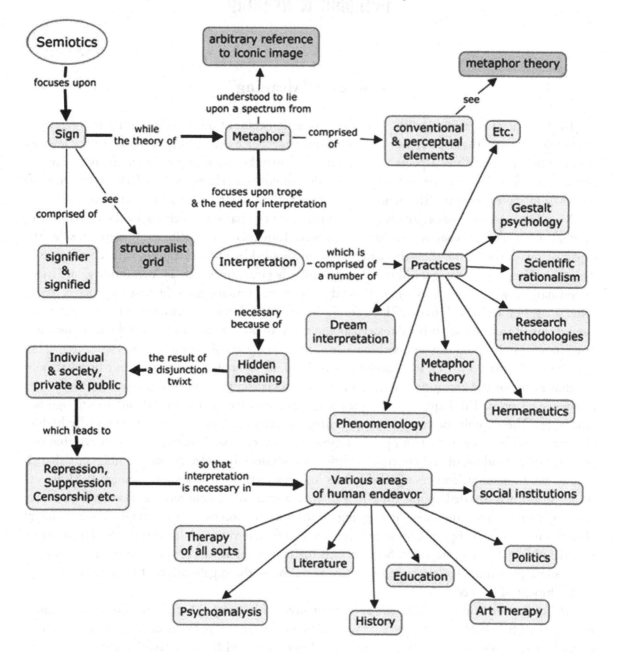

Perception, Meaning and Metaphor

But let's speak for a moment of "meaning" as a perception. We "perceive" meaning. We are in the habit of thinking of perception in terms of the 5 senses. When we speak of perceiving, we think of perceiving a thing or a bunch of things, a room, the sky, the wind, a brass band. But in fact, given our living in the normative every-day ordinary world, we instantly "perceive" the "meaning" of all these things. They don't come to us as meaningless & we don't have to think about what any given thing "is" in linguistic terms. The world presents itself to us in an instantly meaningful way. This sort of instantly recognizable ordinary reality is exactly the reality that is to be "bracketed" out in our phenomenological analysis. We "perceive" meaning.

I would like to examine for a moment the work of the American anthropologist, Roy Wagner. In particular I want to look at his concept of "metaphor" & the "perception" of metaphor. He wants to understand meaning in terms of trope or metaphor rather than in the usual sense of structuralist categories. Trope gathers together two aspects, one understood more than the other. The idea is to get the attributes of the better-known thing to kind of slide off & go over to the not-so-well-known thing. Thus we have a certain meaning (one thing known in terms of another) "embodied" in the form of metaphor.

That's the first part of it. But Wagner is talking in terms of "perception," the perception of meaning. Thus he goes on to speak of the "perception" of "metaphor." What this conceptual move does, actually, is simply situate metaphoric usage in actual living contexts, situate metaphor in the context of the living experience. Thus we are speaking of actual language usage as opposed to the more "dead" language usage that we find, say, in a dictionary. But more importantly, we situate meaning in the "perceptual world." Wagner then proceeds by positing a dialectical relationship between the conventional aspect of the metaphor & the perceptual or experiential aspect. This experiential aspect he terms "iconic" as opposed to the "conventional" symbolism of ordinary language. The "iconic" dimension or image is the perceptual image of the world sans language. It doesn't exist on its own, however, at least as a perception, any more than conventional language can exist on its own *as* a perception. In the instant givenness of the world – in the instant apprehension of meaning -- we have the apprehension of a merging of the iconic dimension & the conventional dimension. We "experience" meaning as a living thing. We "perceive" the meaningful world.

Thus in Wagner's model, we treat the eliciting of meaning at this higher level of construction – the metaphor is constituted as a relationship between lower level categories. Wagner understands social meaning as "unfolding," at this higher level of abstraction, as a series of higher & higher level frames. This "unfolding" process he terms "obviation" because the metaphor at each level is "exhausted" as it unfolds. This metaphoric "unfolding" occurs as a dialectic between the experiential (iconic) part of metaphor & the conventional (arbitrary) part of metaphor.

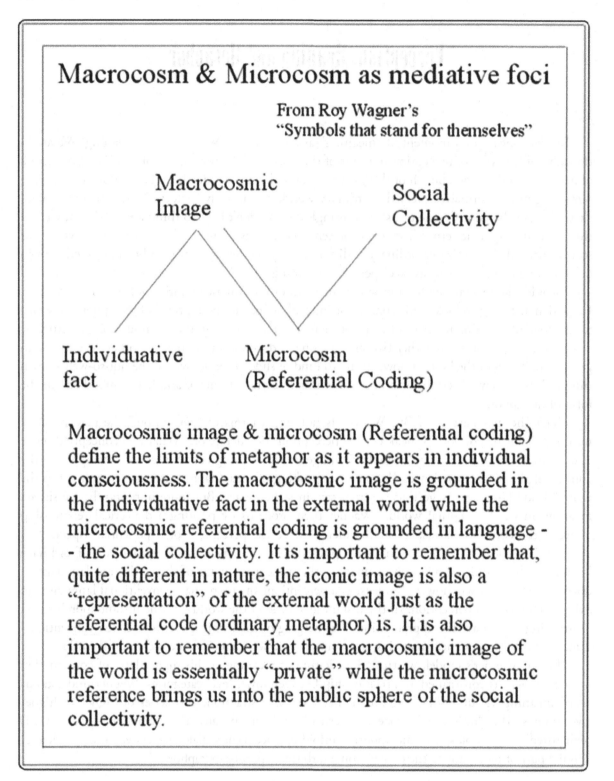

Macrocosm & Microcosm as mediative foci

From Roy Wagner's
"Symbols that stand for themselves"

Macrocosmic
Image

Social
Collectivity

Individuative
fact

Microcosm
(Referential Coding)

Macrocosmic image & microcosm (Referential coding) define the limits of metaphor as it appears in individual consciousness. The macrocosmic image is grounded in the Individuative fact in the external world while the microcosmic referential coding is grounded in language -- the social collectivity. It is important to remember that, quite different in nature, the iconic image is also a "representation" of the external world just as the referential code (ordinary metaphor) is. It is also important to remember that the macrocosmic image of the world is essentially "private" while the microcosmic reference brings us into the public sphere of the social collectivity.

A Note on Metaphor

In general, our conventional understanding of metaphor is that it maps the meaning of one domain that is better known onto a lesser-known domain, the target. This is metaphor as literary trope. In fact, the whole of our language is essentially metaphoric; all of our words have hidden within them, their metaphoric foundation. In the case of individual words, the metaphoric element has worn down & been forgotten so that words seem to be just arbitrary representations of some particular object in the environment.

Although some theorists have tried to prove that all metaphor can be reduced to a literal meaning, this does not really seem possible; metaphor creates its own reality & meaning is always in a sense excessive. Metaphor creates a world where some of the meaning that moves from one domain to the other is similar. This presumably is the reason the metaphor was used in the first place, but there is always an excess that in a sense creates a different context & a fuller meaning. This meaning may or may not be fully intended by the user.

Metaphor is considered by some to be simply the way the brain works. Others think that it is culturally conditioned & that it exemplifies not how the brain works but how language works. As humans, we seem to need to live in a "meaningful" world. Because perceptions are always perceptions "of something," our perceptions are necessarily of a meaningful something. To shorten the equation, perceptions are perceptions of meaning. Because of the way we create & perceive, meaning is essentially metaphorical and one domain is known in terms of another. All perception is the perception of meaningful metaphor. Thus, metaphor is completely integrated with experience. Meaningful experience is pretty much impossible without metaphor or simple "language," given that language is metaphoric from top to bottom.

Given all this, it is clear that our being in the world & all of our experience is conditioned by language or, to put it another way, it's clear that part of all our experience as sentient human beings is the perception of metaphoric meaning. In this sense, we are never exactly where we think we are, or never exactly where we think our bodies are, because we are located in a metaphoric universe of meaning that links & extends all of the world that is in our purview with the larger universe, with things that are absent, things that perhaps only exist in thought. It is also clear that our senses of perception such as sight, hearing, touch, etc. perceive more than intellectual or cognitive meaning. We perceive the world in one way or another as a vast array of "things" – the sky, books, a house, lights, cars, a highway. They simply appear to us in our experience as more or less meaningful or "known objects." Semiologists distinguish, then, between the perceived image of the world & the words or metaphors that attach themselves to that world. The large & detailed image is termed "iconic,"

While the word (or cultural aspect of meaning) is "referential" or simply "conventional," when we perceive the iconic image of a house, for instance, in all its detail, the metaphor "house" is in a way hidden within our perception. We "know" it is a house at the moment we perceive the image of the house without having to say the word to ourselves – meaning, as a perception, just magically appears.

It is clear, then, that our experience is always comprised of this iconic perception & relevant conventional perception (metaphoric language.) Going one step further, we can say that all of our experience is essentially metaphoric: we map one domain (the conventional) onto another domain (the iconic) or vice versa (the iconic domain onto the conventional.) We can even go further & designate the large perceptual image of the world as essentially the natural or "cosmic" world while the conventional aspect of the world is the world of culture, the world of names, "nomos."

Thinking of the nature of our perceptions, we can go further than this. The cosmic iconic image appears to be a continuous stream or flow of information. We do not see any given individual item at one time & then another item, (except when using special lighting to create this situation); everything is connected. It is a continuous world, & in the temporal dimension, there is a continuous flow of information. This effect is even more heightened if we can imagine perceiving the world without any words, hidden or otherwise. This is difficult because without words, the world in its continuity would be essentially meaningless, a meaningless blur of things, things that blur one into the other: a world where there are no boundaries, no edges.

The conventional world, however, presents a different picture. Words, per se, or "categories," are created precisely by creating boundaries, an inside, & an outside. The continuous flow of meaning is continually interrupted. The world of language is a world that is created by a system of inclusions & exclusions, stops & goes. It is a world of separations, one thing mapped onto another, one experience mapped onto another. Sentences. Periods. Commas. Paragraphs. One discrete word after another & following each other according to certain conventional rules called syntax.

Metaphor
(Icon to Reference)

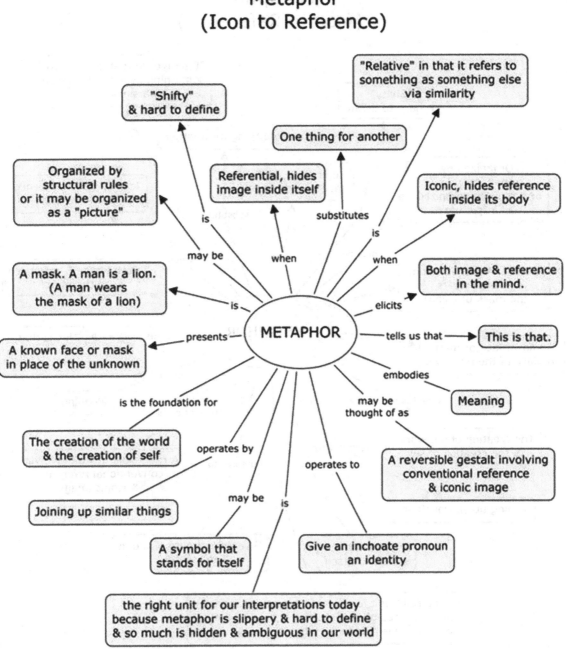

Metaphor
(Icon to Reference)

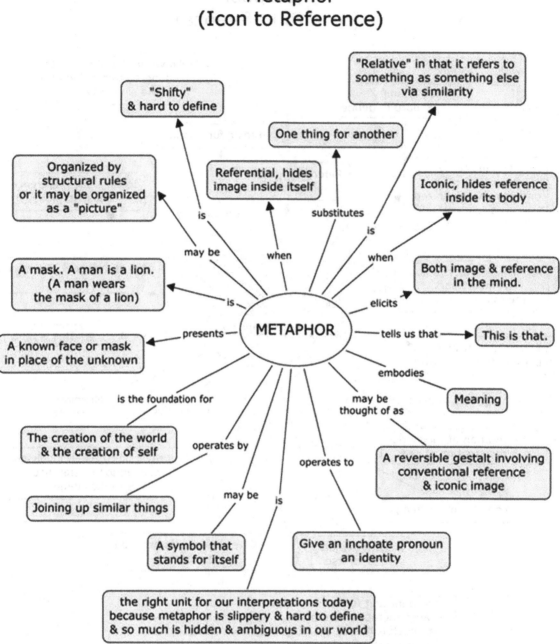

From Sign To Metaphor # 1

In the formation of meaning in language we have the fundamental unit of the "sign" comprised of signifier & signified. Each sign or "category" is defined with regard to what it is not (its polar opposite). Thus categories overlap each other, the overlap representing "similarities" between the two categories & the other parts their differences. In order to make clear distinctions & limit ambiguity, at least some of these similarities tend to be repressed or suppressed. In the case of important cultural ideas, these elements of similarity are designated as taboo. These tabood elements, which are not allowed to be expressed contain a lot of unexpressed energy or meaning. For instance, the category of the conscious is defined in terms of the unconscious & the repressed overlap, being unavailable in everyday life, tends to be expressed in dream.

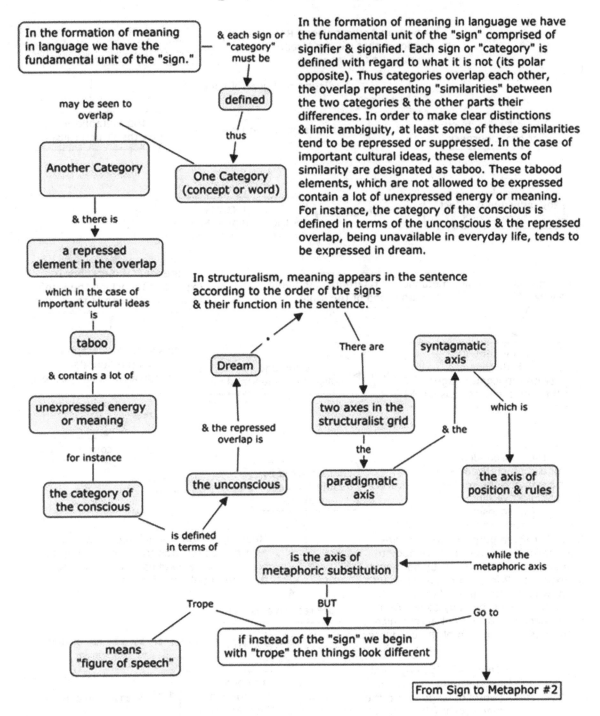

In the formation of meaning in language we have the fundamental unit of the "sign."

& each sign or "category" must be

defined

thus

One Category (concept or word)

may be seen to overlap

Another Category

& there is

a repressed element in the overlap

which in the case of important cultural ideas is

taboo

& contains a lot of

unexpressed energy or meaning

for instance

the category of the conscious

is defined in terms of

the unconscious

& the repressed overlap is

Dream

In structuralism, meaning appears in the sentence according to the order of the signs & their function in the sentence.

There are

two axes in the structuralist grid

the

paradigmatic axis

syntagmatic axis

which is

the axis of position & rules

& the

while the metaphoric axis

is the axis of metaphoric substitution

Trope

means "figure of speech"

BUT

if instead of the "sign" we begin with "trope" then things look different

Go to

From Sign to Metaphor #2

From Sign to Metaphor # 2

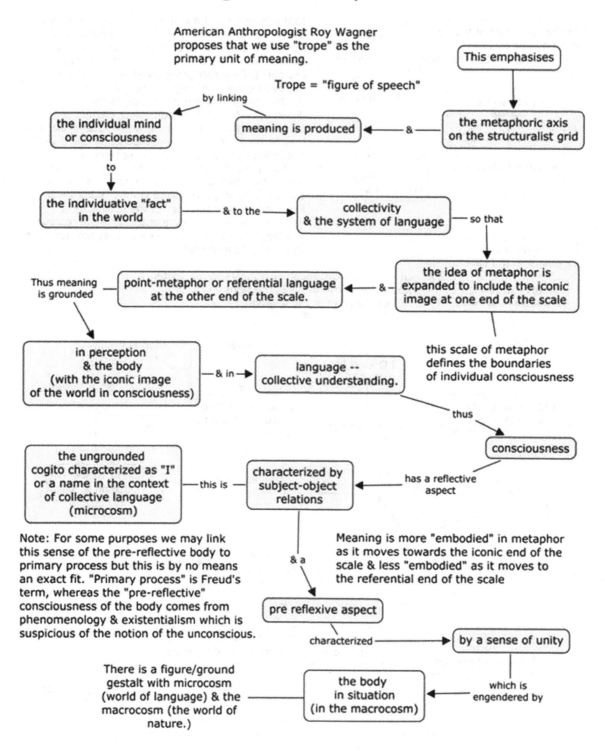

American Anthropologist Roy Wagner proposes that we use "trope" as the primary unit of meaning.

Trope = "figure of speech"

This emphasises

by linking

the individual mind or consciousness

meaning is produced

&

the metaphoric axis on the structuralist grid

to

the individuative "fact" in the world

& to the

collectivity & the system of language

so that

Thus meaning is grounded

point-metaphor or referential language at the other end of the scale.

& —

the idea of metaphor is expanded to include the iconic image at one end of the scale

in perception & the body (with the iconic image of the world in consciousness)

& in

language -- collective understanding.

this scale of metaphor defines the boundaries of individual consciousness

thus

consciousness

the ungrounded cogito characterized as "I" or a name in the context of collective language (microcosm)

this is

characterized by subject-object relations

has a reflective aspect

Note: For some purposes we may link this sense of the pre-reflective body to primary process but this is by no means an exact fit. "Primary process" is Freud's term, whereas the "pre-reflective" consciousness of the body comes from phenomenology & existentialism which is suspicious of the notion of the unconscious.

Meaning is more "embodied" in metaphor as it moves towards the iconic end of the scale & less "embodied" as it moves to the referential end of the scale

& a

pre reflexive aspect

characterized

by a sense of unity

There is a figure/ground gestalt with microcosm (world of language) & the macrocosm (the world of nature.)

the body in situation (in the macrocosm)

which is engendered by

24

Representation
metaphor & sign

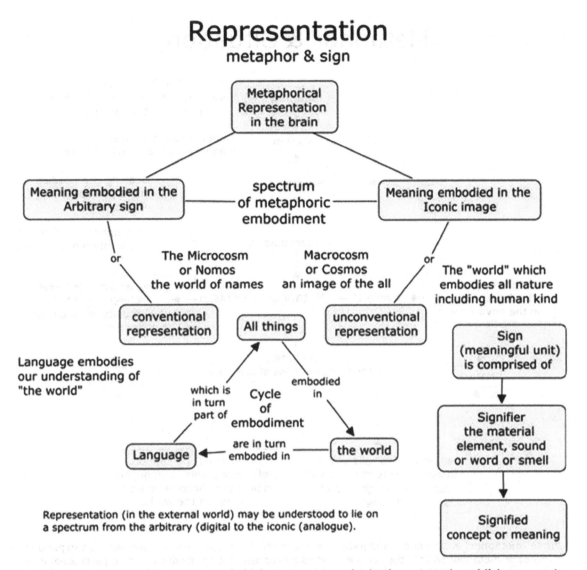

Representation (in the external world) may be understood to lie on
a spectrum from the arbitrary (digital to the iconic (analogue).

The only way we know this spectrum, (which appears to exist in the external world) however, is as a perception of meaning in consciousness. It is important to remember, then, that all perceptions of whatever type are "representations" in the mind & at no point do we have "direct" contact with the external world. While touch, taste, smell all seem to be more direct, more "bodily" & less mental, the meaningful representation given to us by these senses remain in the zone of representation.

There is the intuitive sense, however, that analogue (iconic) imagery is more "direct" than arbitrary representation (usually language.) This is because analogue representation seems to "stand for itself" -- it is what it is - it is what it looks like, etc. while digital linguistic) representation must be referred to a more or less arbitrary system of language in order to be meaningful. There is, however, the felt sense of a pre-reflective "I" which adheres to all our experience. This sense, while meaningful, does not appear to be discursive but only give to us the notion that our experience belongs to us alone & to no one else.

Interestingly, iconic representation, while apparently being more "universal" is also more "private" in the sense that one can never really communicate exactly what one sees or hears. On the other hand, the more arbitrary & coded, language is more public & social & therefore more able to be shared than the "universal" iconic imagery.

Blake Parker

Metaphor & Situation

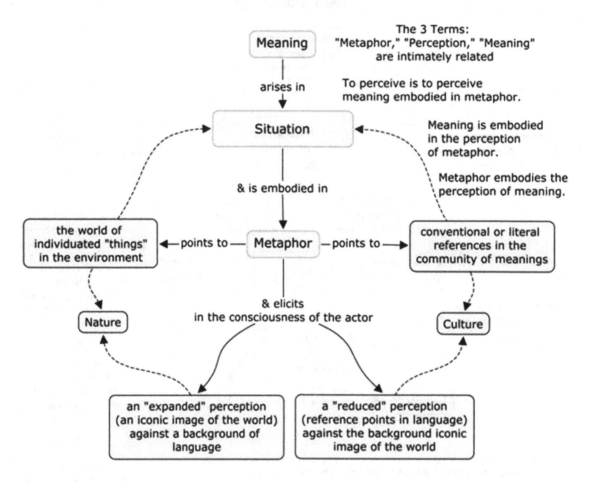

While "metaphor" is commonly understood to mean literary trope, here we are using an expanded concept of metaphor so that the term embodies all representation, from the iconic perceptual image in consciousness to all the words in ordinary language.

The concept of perception seems to imply the direct perception of "the world" (a sensory replication inside of what is out there) but perception actually involves the perception of meaning & meaning always involves representation. We perceive meaningful representation in consciousness. This meaningful representation lies on a spectrum from the iconic image of the world to arbitrary reference in language.

Thus we are interested in the expansion & contraction of perception with regard to representation, continuity & discontinuity pertaining to what is included & what is excluded by the boundaried category (metaphor.) In the creation of meaning we are always interested in the relationship between personal experience & public reference.

26

Exercises for exploring metaphor

- Free writing using a single word or object as a stimulus. A series of words can be written on small pieces of paper and distributed in class. Themes based on kitchen objects, animals, housekeeping or gardening activities have been used. Participants are encouraged to free writing – that is to write without stopping for a given period of time, which could be 1 to 10 minutes. Participants are encouraged to write whatever comes to mind: conventional meanings, nursery rhymes, parables, fairytales, uses, phrases and metaphors.
- After the writing is done, the participants are to read through what they have written to find themes or "meaning units" and to distill the essence into a poem.
- Another exercise would be to take the same or different stimulus words or objects and to write using an "I" voice for the animal or object – to embody the word and to personify the inanimate. Again distilling themes, essence and emerging with a story or poem.
- Another exercise is to write using the stimulus words or objects without naming it – so that what emerges is a description or riddle.
- Photographs or magazine images can be used to write a phenomenological description and to distill significant metaphors that emerge in the perception and writing.

Exercises

Think about the boundary between the important categories listed below. How are these boundaries defined & negotiated in our culture, in some other culture? What are some of the ambiguities and / or suppressed aspects at their boundaries? Think about whether the two categories are at the same level of abstraction or whether they are on different levels. Does one embody or contain the other? What are the implications of this? Think about them in terms of the figure/ground relationship.

1) Clean & Dirty
2) (Eros) Love & Thanatos (Aggression & Anger)
3) Sickness & Health
4) Soul & Spirit
5) Mind & Body
6) Good & Evil
7) Black (Night or darkness) & White (Day or Light)
8) Fight & Flight
9) Nature & Culture
10) Wild & Tame
11) Raw or Cooked
12) High & Low
13) Past & Future
14) Man & Woman
15) Adult & Child
16) Mad & Same
17) Subjective & Objective
18) Science & Art
19) Logic & Intuition
20) Animal & Machine
21) Animal & Human
22) Husband & Wife
23) Exterior (society) & Interior (individual)
24) Attic & Basement
25) Fecundity & Sterility
26) Earth & Sky

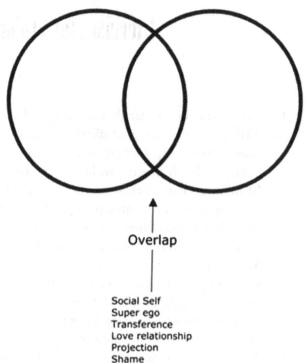

Overlap

Social Self
Super ego
Transference
Love relationship
Projection
Shame

Exercises

1) Make a Mandorla Diagram to show the constitution of oppositional categories & explore the overlapping portion of the two categories as the ambiguous terrority of their relationship. This overlap necessarily partakes of both categories & there is a tension & ambiguity here that is often supressed in public discourse in order that there is a clear definitive boundary between the two. This suppression occurs especially when the two categories are important culturally, essential to the functioning of social life or the maintaining of power for elites. The establish-ment of the boundaries of metaphoric categories often have political ramifications. For instance, in the general sense the delineation of the boundary between the categories of "good & evil" will have implications for the overall structure of social relations in a given culture. So also for the relations in medieval times of king & surf.

In early cultures, the relationship between important categories involving life & death, sexual relations, the wild & tame, the raw & the cooked, included many "taboos" -- in this way strict contnrol was exorcised on the relationship by way of ritualized ways of negotiating the boundaries & repairing difficulties when the taboos were not properly adhered to.

2) Discussion of the figure / ground relaltionship in one of the pictures provided. Pay particular attention to the cultural & personal symbolism of the background both as image & as cultural history.

3) Create a diagram with the centre category as animal or machine & develop a number of metaphors with animal or machine as the source category. Alternately develop metaphors from a particular animal or a particular machine, ie, a "dog" or a "car."

4) Describe an image (either photo or painting) in a phenomenological way, that is paying attention to how the image enters into your consciousness so that you are includings both subjective & objective information but paying attention to understanding your own attitudes & bias (your intentionality.) In particular pay attention to the metaphors that you use in your description.

The polarities accrue

Wild & Tame
Nature & Culture
Enlightenment & Un-enlightenment
Non-ordinary state & Ordinary state of consciousness
Flow of perception & Conventional language
Selflessness & Selfishness
Unity/oneness & Division/isolation
Formlessness & the world of Form
Unity & Separation
Eternity & time
Fearlessness & Fear
Fundamentalism & Experimentalism.
Status Quo & Social Change

This equation can be read as "Wild" is to "Tame" as "Nature" is to "Culture" as "Enlightenment" is to "unenlightened" as "Non-ordinary state of consciousness" is to "Ordinary state of consciousness," et cetera.

We can also have polarities that appear to be properly placed on one side or the other of the larger polarities.

Environment & Organism -- Society & Individual

The former pair would seem to be on the side of Nature, Flow & the Formless while the latter pair should be properly placed on the side of Form, Separation/culture.

In general, the order of business in the mystic program is how to get from the right side of the equation (Separation, Division & Fear) to the left side (Eternity, Unity & Enlightenment.)

Similarities & Differences betwixt Metaphor Theory & Mystic Theory

Stepping into the metaphoric world of the mystical worldview, for a moment, we find the distinction between the un-named world of unified perception & the world of conventional culture. It seems easy enough to map the image of metaphoric experience onto the image of mystical experience. While there are some similarities in the two domains, there are, as in all metaphors, some differences that carry over. It seems easy enough to see that the image of the conventional world is more or less the same; for both, they are conventional, conditioned by language but without going into how language works. From the metaphoric point of view, both sides of the equation are present in all experience – the iconic & the conventional. In some sense, from the mystic orientation, mystic unity is also understood to pervade the ordinary conventional world.

When we look at the image of "cosmos" & the image of "mystic unity" there are also similarities: both apparently give us an image that is unified, in a sense seamless. But it is hard to think that, the wonderful image of seamless perfection that is the nirvana of the mystic experience is the same as the meaningless blur of the nameless flow that, from the point of view of metaphor theory, we find as part of the experiential world. From this point of view, the only way that this meaningless perceptual flow could be changed into the fullness of the mystic experience is by adding "meaning" to the mix, that is, metaphoric meaning & language, but this is precisely what is excluded in the mystic theory. There is a supposed "going beyond" language in the mystic vision.

Either the theory of the mystic experience is mistaken, or there is some other organ of perception or some other different & parallel world that is being experienced. Given the fact that the mystic way is very old combined with the fact that religious, mystic & magical ways of understanding the world are all pretty resistant to change, it doesn't seem too strange that it is not "up" on recent sociological theory or the theory of metaphor. It is quite good, however, in the phenomenological domain – that is, in the ability to "describe" the experience. It is not at all the experience itself that is at issue; such experiences obviously occur & have been occurring for a long, long time. What is at issue, is how & why they occur & what the real makeup of these experiences is.

Metaphor & Mysticism

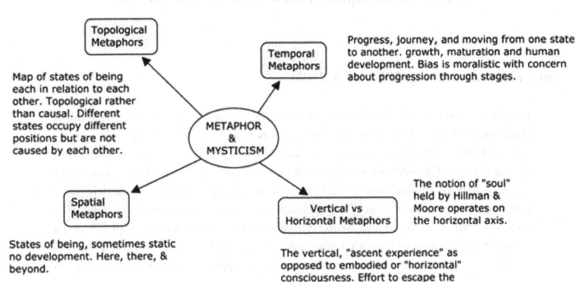

Topological Metaphors

Map of states of being each in relation to each other. Topological rather than causal. Different states occupy different positions but are not caused by each other.

Temporal Metaphors

Progress, journey, and moving from one state to another. growth, maturation and human development. Bias is moralistic with concern about progression through stages.

METAPHOR & MYSTICISM

Spatial Metaphors

States of being, sometimes static no development. Here, there, & beyond.

Vertical vs Horizontal Metaphors

The notion of "soul" held by Hillman & Moore operates on the horizontal axis.

The vertical, "ascent experience" as opposed to embodied or "horizontal" consciousness. Effort to escape the body rather than to work through it.

The paradox is that mystical experience is understood to be above & beyond language & yet there is a great deal of language that purports to express the mystical vision. There are some who hold that mysticism is in fact a literary genre & that a great deal more is actually communicated by language than is usually supposed. The whole rhetoric of "illusion" & "lies" & "falsification" seems to be part & parcel of the experience.

A Note on Metaphor Downloaded from the Net

John Holcombe (LitLangs 2004, 2005, 2006)

But there is the obvious fact that language is built of dead metaphors. As a traditional critic put it: *"Every expression that we employ, apart from those that are connected with the most rudimentary objects and actions, is a metaphor, though the original meaning is dulled by constant use."* Consider the words of that very sentence: an 'expression' is something squeezed out; to 'employ' something is to wind it in (*implicare*); to 'connect' is to tie together (*conectere*); 'rudimentary' comes from the root to root or sprout; an 'object' is something thrown in the way; an 'action' something driven or conducted; 'original' means rising up like a spring or heavenly body; 'constant' is standing firm. 'Metaphor' itself is a metaphor, meaning the carrying across of a term or expression from its normal usage to another." {2}

Metaphors are therefore active in understanding. We use metaphors to group areas of experience (*life is a journey*), to orientate ourselves (*my consciousness was raised*), to convey expression through the senses (*his eyes were glued to the screen*), to describe learning (*it had a germ of truth in it*), etc. Even ideas are commonly pictured as objects (*the idea had been around for a while*), as containers (*I didn't get anything out of that*) or as things to be transferred (*he got the idea across*). {3}

A Note concerning Emotion & Mystic Understanding

It strikes me that I have not spoken directly about emotion & the meaning of emotion in the context of meditation. I have spoken about the notion of withdrawing attention or identification from emotions & thoughts & just letting them flow but I'd like to say a little bit more about anxiety & what has been termed "direct experience" beyond the symbolism of language.

Anxiety in the context of psychoanalysis is understood to arise because of the emergence in consciousness of unacceptable drive energy or unacceptable desires. These desires are denied or repressed but in their place is left a general worry or anxiety concerning these desires & their import for the self. In addition, there is the general existential anxiety (angst) that comes with the knowledge of death – the fact that we all die. Again, what we have is a general miasma of worry or fear. Because the fear of death is omnipresent and anxiety is the result of denial or repression of original fears that appeared early on in childhood, it tends to be "free floating." This free-floating anxiety causes the mind to reach for different reasons for its existence. Thus, there is the sense that anxiety "clings" to one event after another. The problem for the mind is: what exactly am I worried about now? One minute I'm worried about this, the next moment, the worry has shifted to something else. Therefore this problem will always be there without ever getting to the root of the worries & understanding where they come from.

Instead of looking for the root of the problem, as one does in depth psychology, meditation quiets the mind in the sense that one simply "sits" with it. The emotional attachment, often of anxiety, to this or that tends to loosen. After a while, it becomes clear what is going on with this free-floating anxiety & its attachments, & other deeper concerns, emotional as well as cognitive, come to the surface. On the other hand, if one remains attached to the idea of being a "good" person, then one remains attached to "good" moral ideas about oneself. Meditation will then be the arena whereby the emotional attachment to these super-ego messages acts to further repress or split off the id desires from the unconscious. In either case, one is set up for an ongoing practice of meditation.

Let's go back for a moment & consider exactly what an emotion is. This is a difficult subject. There has been a great deal written about emotions, but at the center of these ideas is the notion of "motion" and movement in the body, the movement of energy. This movement of energy is not meaningful on its own. It needs to be interpreted as fear, anger, love, or whatever. Emotion, then, is not separate from the cognitive sphere, but a conjunction of bio-energy & thought. For our purposes, this is probably a good enough definition: emotion is the movement of energy in the body attached to a cognitive interpretation. From this point of view, there is no real debate about whether emotions are "universal" or culturally determined. There are obvious universal existential situations wherein the movement of energy in the human body will be interpreted in very similar ways. Threat of harm to the body is one of them. A loving smile that passes between mother & child is another. On the other hand, certain emotions will be "culturally appropriate" in some situations & not others.

When the claim is made that there is a fundamental underlying state of consciousness beneath our cognitive understanding of the world, it seems likely enough that this state is some sort of an "emotional" state, some sort of state of biological symbolism or symbolic-energy which we have seen does not exist on its own as separate from cognition. As such, it appears as a sort of "atmosphere" or energy envelope that embodies the self & other, the perceiver & the perceived. Cognitive activity will thus appear to go on above or within this general state of being which is emotional. When it is claimed we can make "direct" contact with experience above & beyond language, what is being signified is the direct immersion in & recognition of this emotional state of being. But it is not above & beyond language because, as we have seen, emotion already contains its own interpretation.

Let us go back again. Desire: what is desire? Desire is a strong drive to satisfy some urge that arises in the body or mind – a sexual desire, the desire for food & so forth. When our wants or desires are thwarted, we tend to get aggressive. Both desires & aggressive urges are the focus of repression & of dissociation. The metaphor of repression is vertical with one layer holding down another, while that of dissociation is a horizontal image of splitting. Neuroses is understood generally to be the product of repression while multiple personality is understood to be a product of the splitting off of parts of the self.

The main thing is that desire manifests as a strong emotional pull towards some object in the world. Desire, although it appears to be an "emotion" or biological state like love or hunger, it is always a mixture of biology & cognition, as is aggression.

Freud saw sexuality as the fundamental desire, while Jung saw spiritual aspiration as fundamental. Freud, for his part, saw spiritual aspiration as a secondary misinterpretation of sexual desire while Jung saw sexuality as a secondary overlay & a misinterpretation of spiritual yearning. Which is more fundamental – sexuality or desire for God? It seems in a simplistic way that sexuality arises in the body while the desire for God arises in the mind. The question then is, which came first, the mind or the body? Evolutionary theory is quite clear that the body came first & the mind evolved slowly, but from the spiritual Jungian point of view, it is some sort of cosmic thought that came first. My own view is that mind is an evolution & that this evolution of mind is a moral as well as cognitive development. We as a species are the moral element of nature. The spiritual view is generally that our moral nature came from God or some cosmic entity or entities & that we "fell" into the body in some way. In the beginning was the word. While my preference is clear, there really is no way to "prove" the point one way or the other. For me, one seems more "logical" than the other & I tend to privilege "logic" over "emotion" or "intuition" in this matter. In other matters, such as my own creative writing, I very often privilege emotion, intuition, & the "music" of language over the logical elements.

Let's get back to comparing & contrasting for a moment. The spiritual seems to involve an escape from separation from the world & a merging with it, while the sociological involves an understanding of our separate being in the world. The central image of spirituality is "merging" (the quality of emotion) while the central image of sociology is "interdependence" (emotional & cognitive). It's interesting that the spiritual ideology is always trying to escape the word – cognition & thinking – that was at its origin. Sociology on the other hand, sees mind as an evolution, with cognitive symbolism as the beginning & the very nature of self.

I have been wandering in the realms of desire. Now let's get back to something a little more solid. Let's go back to the notion that emotional knowledge is direct whereas cognitive knowledge is non-direct. What can this mean? Ideas swarm in my head. Which to pick first? The notion of perception? No, the notion of metaphor. No, let's begin with the gestalt. What to do?

We have seen that emotion itself is a conjunction of energy & interpretation, or biology & symbolism. Let's say, then, that we have a figure/ground gestalt. When biology is in the background, our understanding of our "feeling" is controlled by a cognitive interpretation, fleeting as it may be. Reversing the gestalt, we have a field of cognitive understandings that the biological flow of energy will control. In the first case, it is simple: energy flows, there is an interpretation, "I am hungry" or "I am afraid," & appropriate behaviour follows. What of the second case, when the whole field of cognitive symbolism is the background & the biological flow is in control? On the surface of things this sounds exactly like the case where we are told to simply "follow our hearts" – which I take to mean, we should follow our desire. As we saw earlier, desire is a fundamental emotion although it has aspects of biology & interpretation. Desire, then, is already goal directed. To follow one's heart, emotion, or desire means then to impose one's larger desirous schema on things rather than go with the ordinary or conventional interpretation of the event under consideration.

There is a further complication because symbolism or metaphor itself is not singular & purely cognitive; it is comprised of a perceptual part & a conventional part. Of course, the "perceptual" can easily be understood as the "biological" or bodily aspect, while the conventional can easily be understood as the cognitive element. The cognitive & the biological go together to make "meaning." In a similar way, biological flow (of energy) & cognitive symbology go together to make "emotion."

Thus, we have two figure/ground relationships in relationship to each other.

> Emotion = biological energy + cognitive symbolism
> Cognitive symbolism = perceptual flow + conventional symbolism

Both of our elements, Emotion & Cognitive Symbolism, are constituted as figure/ground gestalts. Thus, when we have any given emotion we have to consider two sets of figure/ground relationships; one is bio-energy & cognitive symbolism and the other is perceptual flow & conventional symbolism. One could go on to create some sort of programmatic grid of types of emotions & types of cognitive symbolism & their relationships, but let's let that go for the moment & stick with the simple fact that both emotion & cognitive symbolism are a mixture of each other, even though one appears as "body" & the other as "mind."

The upshot of our consideration, then, is that "direct" contact with a fundamental type of consciousness that underlies cognitive symbolism is a very simplistic way of looking at things. Although this underlying layer appears to be more biological, more "purely" energetic, these elements are not "meaningful" without interpretation. The interpretive practice that appears more "direct" is the emotional one (as opposed to the cognitive), but as we have seen, emotion is already a complex conjunction of biological energy & cognitive convention. There is no way out of "the world." We are in it for good or for ill, for secular or sacred.

Endnote

When discussing the above with Monica, she thought I should elaborate more upon the universal non-cognitive substrate of emotion in early childhood. There is certainly a more or less universal biological aspect to emotion in early childhood. For instance, before language development the infant, when in need of food or a change of diapers, experiences a general bodily discomfort that is often accompanied by tears. One would hope that this behaviour elicits appropriate behaviour from the caregiver. At another time the infant & the mother may "coo" at each other & this emotional exchange is somehow understood in a non-cognitive way. Without going into any detail, it is clear that there is a universal emotional foundation that adult emotion is built upon. It is also clear that there are different culturally developed ways in which to appropriately "express" emotion.

Part of the development of emotion & of the child in general concerns the responses that the infant's behaviour elicits. If, for instance, the infant's behaviour does not elicit appropriate behaviour from the caregiver, & her needs remain unmet, the infant will over time learn to stop that behaviour & try something else. This may ultimately lead to the development of a distorted identity involving a distortion in the emotional & cognitive life. Winnicott has identified the false self and true self construction as developing from patterns of holding and handling in the first years of life.

Monica also pointed out that some psychologists view the first "awareness" that certain behaviour elicits a particular response as the first "creative" act. Of course, this "awareness" cannot be a cognitive reflective awareness & this "creativity" may be seen as the foundation for "agency" or the utility of behaviour.

Some further thoughts arose in a conversation with Monica's brother, Jeremy Carpendale, who is working with Piaget's ideas re early child development. He pointed out that emotion is a presupposition in interaction between the infant & her environment. At the earliest stage, there is no separation of emotion from cognition – there is simply a basic "emotional" orientation to action. There is practical action in which the infant can "do" something & an "awareness." but not a reflective awareness, that this "doing" has an effect in the world. In this sensory-motor stage we presuppose an emotional, that is, intentional orientation towards doing. "Meaning" is present right from the very beginning, but it is a sensory-motor knowledge in the whole body, not a cognitive reflective meaning.

Beyond this, in the process of development, the child engages in all sorts of reflective activity so that in maturity, the person has learned many things about emotions, how to talk about them, appropriate expression of them, their meaning in different contexts & so on. Ultimately, then, it seems that there is some essential core of emotions & an early interactional foundation for the development of one's mature & thoroughly "social" emotional life. The emotions, then, have undergone a symbolic development & in no way can they be "pure." They are born in social interaction & develop within the context of social symbolic action.

It is hard to know what it exactly might mean to regress or return to the early state of sensory-motor awareness before the development of cognitive reflection. I assume it would be some sort of "animal" awareness of intention & practical application. It seems to me that any "going back" to this early stage would involve a sort of "burying" of cognitive understanding so that it would be present but "hidden" beneath this purely early bodily knowing. But perhaps there is some aspect of this state of consciousness that is being indicated by the notion of a "direct" non-symbolic interaction with the world.

A reflective note

I would also like to note & follow up elsewhere the focus on the development of language in the context of triadic interaction. The triad would include two people & some element of the world. Learning takes place when a person points out or indicates some element of the environment for the child, or, even more than this, one demonstrates to the other how one can "transform" the world by "doing." This triadic interaction, where all elements are "present" & there is a practical doing of something with the body, is the foundation for all further learning – the ability to speak of things that are not present at the time, the development of abstract thought & so on.

On reflection it would be good if I had the time or the patience to re-write the main body of this note integrating this aspect of bodily triadic social learning into it & doing away with the simplistic concepts of "biology" & "social convention." I like very much the emphasis upon practical bodily social interaction & the presupposition of a sort of whole-body emotional intentionality as the foundation for thinking about the development of emotion as well as cognition. But, for now I'm afraid the readers will have to allow this endnote to cast its shadow back over the body of the endnote on their own.

Social Construction

The model of phenomenological metaphor I use must be understood in the broader context of "social construction." My basic assumption is that culture itself and the individual selves within it are social constructions. That is to say, while we live in a "natural world" and have "biological bodies" this world and our bodies over time come to have more or less conventionalized meanings. The world we live in is the world as it is presented to us as a set of cultural meanings. The self we create (or have created for us) is created in the context of this social understanding. From this point of view, the self is a set of understandings, ideas, images, feelings, that I identify as myself, my identity. This world is characterized by "difference" – things are boundaried & separate. Unless I go out of my way to create myself in individualistic ways, this self is essentially conventional. I wear conventional clothes or at least I accept the convention of wearing clothes, I take on a gender identity of one sort or another & so forth. This is the "ego" identity that, in the mystic model, constitutes the entrapment of consciousness. In this "ordinary" world where "rationality" is the organizing principle, it is easy to conceive of two fundamentally different types, the conventional person & the creative person. We shall hear more of them soon. Of course, there are many different schemes whereby personality types are identified but these two are of present interest with regard to our chosen topic of mysticism.

In my model of phenomenological metaphor, I understand the social construction of self & society to be accomplished essentially by metaphor. Or rather, given that "meaning" is the main social construction, the "meaning" of self & society is constituted via metaphor, but not just any metaphor, living metaphor. I use the ordinary concept of metaphor as a linguistic device but situate it in a living context. The idea is that in order to understand society & self as a social construction, we must deal with real life experiences. Central to the understanding of "real life," at least for us, is the concept of "embodiment." We are "embodied beings." Furthermore, culture can be understood to "embody" various meanings. Culture (a system of meanings) is constituted by metaphor & metaphor "embodies" meaning. Going further, we, as living breathing selves, on one hand, embody metaphor (our thought) and on the other hand, we are the living embodiment of metaphor (a metaphoric social creation.)

Living metaphor, then, (metaphor in context) is comprised of the conjunction of two elements – the living world of context & the conventional world of culture. Our apprehension of the living contextual world, however, is through our perception. It is, in fact, the world of perception. Thus we can say that living metaphor embodies, on the one hand, the flow of perception – that is to say "the world," not yet conceptualized, the world as it simply is, ongoing & eternal, &, on the other hand, the conventional aspect of our understanding – the world of forms, concepts, thoughts etc. This is "metaphor" understood from a living phenomenological point of view. It is "language" in the broadest sense, language working in the world & including those who make language as well as that of which language is made.

It is important to note, then, that we (as conventional beings) are embodied by cultural metaphor. We are metaphoric creatures, created by culture. On the other hand, we (as creative cultural beings) embody our cultural metaphors. As artists, scientists, mystics, we make & re-make those metaphors & thus society changes.

Metaphor, from the phenomenological point of view, may also be understood as comprised of a figure/ground gestalt whereby one side or the other is in the foreground & "controls" the other. Thus the formless can guide & "control" conventional form, or the world of form (convention) can guide & "control" the formless. Thus, "meaning" or "meaningful experience" for an embodied entity (a person) arises from the living interaction of perception (awareness) in real life situations and our conventional understandings (words.) The conventional word "cow" combines with some sort of experience of the perceptual cosmos with a cow in it, to create the constellation of meanings, denotative & connotative, of the word "cow." The conventional understanding occurs in the context of the natural world (cosmos).

The self is comprised of metaphor. The self is a metaphor, or perhaps a series of unfolding metaphors. It is a system of forms, ideas, objects, & so forth. Culture itself is also a system of metaphors, thoughts, ideas, institutions, and forms.

When we allow the conventional side of metaphor to control the phenomenological (formless) side, then we constitute conventional experience. This is the land of so-called "ego," wherein we are fixated on various elements of illusion we think of as "reality." This is the conventional "everyday" world & we are trapped in a conventional self or "ego." The constitution of "meaning" is conventional. Very often in mystical thought, we hear of our imprisonment being caused by our "identification" with illusions, our fixation on people & things, our "love" and our "hate." In general, from a mystic worldview the real world (cosmos-perception) is understood to be distorted or hidden by our attachment to the emotional life & so on.

If on the other hand, we allow (or set things up in such a way that) the free flow of perception (the formless, the "real" world, the eternal, etc.) is allowed to control conventional cultural meanings, then we are in a "creative state" & we make new metaphors, make ourselves anew, are renewed, revivified with the flowing world, our ego is abandoned, we are free. In order to set up these "creative" conditions we need to "let go" of our conventional understanding (bracket it out) and let the full richness of experience come into our awareness. In meditation, one simply watches the way one's thoughts go, lets the images flow through one, not attaching to one or the other of them.

The realm of the formless is thus an ever-present element of our experience, as are the conventional understandings we call language, thoughts, & so forth. Both the formless world & the world of forms are ever present in the making of meaning. From this way of understanding things, "meaning" is not of the world of forms & not of the formless world. It is comprised of both worlds, the formed & the formless, although, in the everyday world, the fullness of experience and meaning of the cosmic domain remains hidden behind & within all experience.

The mystic understanding of the world very often privileges & gives a higher value to the "formless" world, which is conceived of as the "real" world, the world that is behind, above & beyond the conventional world of forms & human understanding. Thus the path to "enlightenment" leads us towards an understanding of this formless world & its teachers often seem to denigrate the ordinary everyday world of form: "the body," the "ego," "language," & so on. As with any rudimentary polemic, a "straw man" is set up so that it can easily be knocked down. Thus, the mystic knocks down "the mere body" the mere world of forms, the mere ego, etc. On the other hand, the rationalist tends to privilege the conventional world (particularly of science) and has scant understanding of either the artistic or the mystic vision, & sets up & knocks down all sorts of irrational, sick, & mad beings. The world of art & perception are understood to be merely "subjective" & thus not "real."

From the phenomenological view put forward here, the "formless" world is simply part of all human experience; in a sense it is the creative realm, and if it could be "pure" it would be "pure perception" with all thought, all assumptions about the everyday nature of things, bracketed & put aside. However, one cannot dwell only in the formless world of perception any more than one can dwell only in the world of language. As living beings we take our "place" in the world as a set of meanings, living metaphors. However, the "natural world" of perception is the creative world only insomuch as we continually learn from it, from our own ongoing experience in the world.

The terms "perception" & "convention" although they can be thought of as a reversible figure/ground gestalt, are not on the same plane as each other. They are similar to the "nature/culture" dichotomy.

In its "natural" state, perception is understood to be the perception of the transcendent world, the whole, in the sense of the "natural world" – it is thus identified with the fullness of the iconic image & with the large all-encompassing "cosmos." On the other hand, the "natural" state of "convention" is the cultural, social, or linguistic domain, having to do with the small world of "nomos[1]," naming things, the world of conceptions & forms.

Thus in the "natural state" of things, the cultural world of "nomos" is embodied in the larger all-encompassing world of "cosmos." The figure is "nomos" and the ground is "cosmos." This is the natural state of things.

In the "natural" state of affairs, we exist as conventional beings in a conventional world, in the world of forms, "nomos." We are surrounded & have our being in the eternal vastness of the cosmos. In this conventional state, we allow our conventional everyday understandings to shape & control & create meanings of the cosmic world. In a sense, we reduce its vastness to our own size.

On the other hand, when we endeavor to create & re-create our cultural domain, the world of nomos, then we enter into a state of being whereby the gestalt is reversed & the vast eternal flow of nature, cosmos, the fullness of iconic vision as figure comes to create new meanings, new awareness, new types of identity, new art, new selves, new institutions. Also, as we come to dwell in this reversed gestalt, it seems to many that we allow the great cosmic percepts to guide our behaviour so that we attempt to give service to others, promote world peace, act with generosity of spirit and so forth.

---

1   In sociology, a **nomos** is a socially constructed ordering of experience. The term derives from the greek νόμος, and it refers, not only to explicit laws, but to all of the normal rules and forms which people take for granted in their day to day activities.

The first influential writer to use the term in a modern context is Peter L. Berger. Berger writes of human beings fashioning a world by their own activity (1967:5). Berger sees this taking place through a continual three-fold cycle between individuals and society: externalization, objectivation and internalization. The world thus fashioned has an order—a set of principles—which comes to be read onto society by individuals through externalization and objectivation, and also internalized in each individual. This order thus comes to be assumed, spoken of, and placed into social discourse to be treated as common sense. This ordering of the world and experience, which is a corporate and social process as well as an individual one, is a nomos....

In order to be at its most effective the nomos must be taken for granted. The structure of the world which has been created by human and social activity is treated, not as contingent, but as self-evident. 'Whenever the socially established nomos attains the quality of being taken for granted, there occurs a merging of its meanings with what are considered to be the fundamental meanings inherent in the universe.' (1967:24-25). www.wikipedia.org

Although "the creative" & "the good" can be seen to come from a similar state of being, they are in fact somewhat different. This difference probably resides in different understandings of the "nature" of the cosmic, non-dual world. From the point of view of art & the artist, the cosmos is simply that, the large all-encompassing world of the senses. It is neither good nor evil. It is simply there, characterized by an incredible richness of detail & depth. From the point of view of mystic experience and the mystic, the cosmos is experienced as the unified image of God, the divine, the one. What is more, this one, this unified cosmic god is generally understood to be good, provide guidance, instill us with "spiritual" qualities etc. In the mystic state of oneness we leave behind our petty concerns with self and separation. We participate in the eternal process of creation.

In addition, there are certain differences in the state being aimed at. (This is concerned with our "intention" or "intentionality" in general. More on that later.) On the one end of the spectrum we have the creative state of being, but shall we say, still quite reasonable, at the other end of the spectrum, we have the non-ordinary states of reality, the ecstatic state, visions and so on.

Certain other difficulties arise when we move from the objective to the subjective world, that is from understanding the problem as being "out there" & capable of being objectified or conceptualized, to understanding the problem as being "inside" oneself, a living being who experiences the world & is contained within its processes. This is the difference between "ideology" & "experience" described in more detail a little later on.

Another interesting difference that comes up is that between the terms "discovery" & "creation." The mystic is convinced he or she has "discovered" the real world, whereas the artist is quite convinced he or she has "created" it. It's interesting that the mystic is quite like the scientist: both assume there is some sort of knowable objective world out there, even though the mystic will often deny that the world and certain types of mystic experience are knowable except by direct experience. Thus the state of liberation, like the state of the lover, cannot be known unless experienced. It is more, one imagines, then, an emotional state, than an intellectual one, although, again, the mystic is likely to deny that it is an "emotional state" precisely because it cannot be conceived of and "emotions" are in the dualistic world of forms. More likely, our attachment or identification with certain emotions resides in this realm of forms. Emotions as the generalized rush of energy in the body, (sans interpretation) are of the formless world but they cannot be named.)

The artist (or cultural constructionist) acknowledges that there is a "real" world out there somewhere but that we can't know it in any "pure" form. Our knowing is always hybrid, part natural, and part conventional. Our knowing is always metaphoric. On the other hand, the created conventional world also cannot be inhabited in any pure way. It is always changing, always being created and destroyed.

Meaning, Metaphor & Embodiment

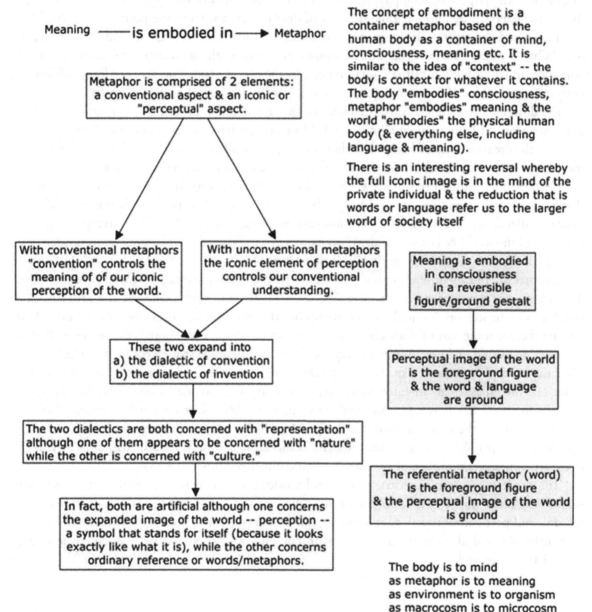

Meaning ———is embodied in——→ Metaphor

Metaphor is comprised of 2 elements: a conventional aspect & an iconic or "perceptual" aspect.

With conventional metaphors "convention" controls the meaning of of our iconic perception of the world.

With unconventional metaphors the iconic element of perception controls our conventional understanding.

These two expand into
a) the dialectic of convention
b) the dialectic of invention

The two dialectics are both concerned with "representation" although one of them appears to be concerned with "nature" while the other is concerned with "culture."

In fact, both are artificial although one concerns the expanded image of the world -- perception -- a symbol that stands for itself (because it looks exactly like what it is), while the other concerns ordinary reference or words/metaphors.

The concept of embodiment is a container metaphor based on the human body as a container of mind, consciousness, meaning etc. It is similar to the idea of "context" -- the body is context for whatever it contains. The body "embodies" consciousness, metaphor "embodies" meaning & the world "embodies" the physical human body (& everything else, including language & meaning).

There is an interesting reversal whereby the full iconic image is in the mind of the private individual & the reduction that is words or language refer us to the larger world of society itself

Meaning is embodied in consciousness in a reversible figure/ground gestalt

Perceptual image of the world is the foreground figure & the word & language are ground

The referential metaphor (word) is the foreground figure & the perceptual image of the world is ground

The body is to mind
as metaphor is to meaning
as environment is to organism
as macrocosm is to microcosm
as nature is to culture

IDENTITY & METAPHOR

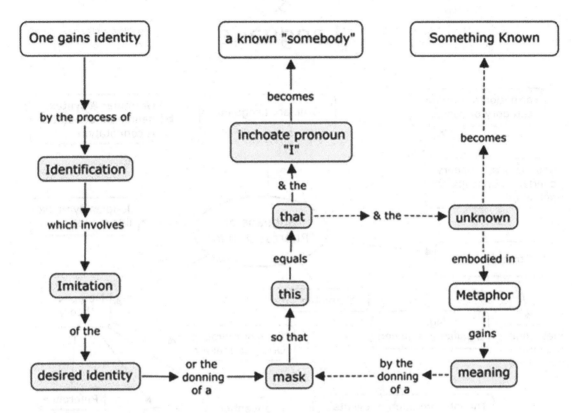

If we view the self as a symbolic entity constituted in language then we could say that identity is accomplished by predication on an inchoate pronoun.

Metaphor is a mask worn by one entity in order to pretend to be another entity.

The donning of a mask accomplishes a metaphoric transformation which is at the root of the shamanic experience. This sort of transformation in the context of ritual & dance is expressive in the iconic mode. Aspects of this transformation certainly point beyond the signifiers in the symbolic language but there is a very real sense in which the symbol points nowhere but to itself I am the mask I wear -- I am a certain sort of animal, or a dragon, or whatever. Interestingly this is exactly what we are fearful of in modern society -- everybody wants to take their masks off -- we say we are not our social role -- we are not the persona we project -- we are something else, something better more pure.

Alan Watts points to the "play" of music, dance & ritual & the whole iconic realm of representation as a more adequate model (the model espoused by Zen) for how to live than the mechanistic model of more referential, analytical & rational language. Of course, referential language that points beyond itself is ideally suited for "work."

As children we often imitate animals in game play. Paul Shephard in his book "Thinking Animals" argues that human identity throughout history has been constructed in dynamic interplay with animals. It is only recently that we have begun to model the self as a machine -- a mechanism with replaceable parts.

Interpretation
&
Language

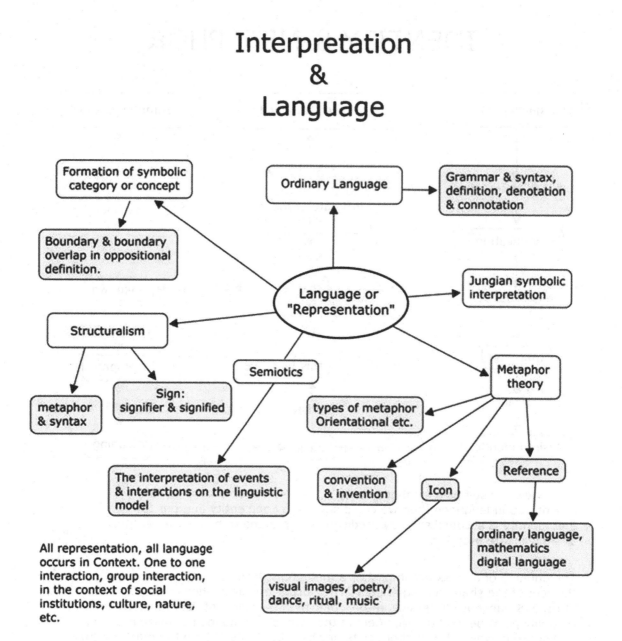

Formation of symbolic category or concept

Boundary & boundary overlap in oppositional definition.

Ordinary Language

Grammar & syntax, definition, denotation & connotation

Language or "Representation"

Jungian symbolic interpretation

Structuralism

metaphor & syntax

Sign: signifier & signified

Semiotics

Metaphor theory

types of metaphor Orientational etc.

The interpretation of events & interactions on the linguistic model

convention & invention

Icon

Reference

ordinary language, mathematics digital language

visual images, poetry, dance, ritual, music

All representation, all language occurs in Context. One to one interaction, group interaction, in the context of social institutions, culture, nature, etc.

Phenomenology & Metaphor Theory re "Mystic" Understanding

I am going to attempt a short essay in which I will use the concept of phenomenological metaphor to "explain" the mystic understanding of the world & the path towards "enlightenment." My model of phenomenological metaphor will be rather skeletal as will be my model of the mystic journey.

The mystic model of the world that I will attempt to explicate is the following: we poor earthlings, trapped in illusion, dwell in a dualistic world of forms that hides the ultimate divine reality of the formless, non-dual world. We experience the non-dual world as "oneness" – it is unified and all embracing & within it there is no separation. We are trapped in this dualistic world because of our "identification" with forms and a fixation on our "ego," our own self-centered interests. These attachments keep us in a world of illusion and unable to see the great pervasive god energy all around us in the mystical realm of oneness where there are no boundaries. We continually mistake one or another concept for the ultimate "truth," (no words can explain or grasp the reality of oneness) & thus we are continually seeking. We move along the path towards freedom & this more real eternal & formless life with the use of meditation & other bodily & mental practices designed to free our minds & bodies from their attachment to illusion (our pain) and our separate boundaried identities. The attainment of enlightenment is the ultimate state of unity with the divine, however it is named. Most mystics, rather than remain in isolation in this state, return to the world & engage in one way or another with the teaching of one "path" or another to reach perfection.

From this point of view, there are two types of people, those trapped in the illusory world & those liberated ones who apprehend the true nature of existence. It can be seen that within the image of the real world as being all "one" & lacking separation, there is an inherent dualism between the sacred realm & the profane, between the enlightened & the non-enlightened.

A Note on the Distinction between "Experience" & "Ideology"

For the most part, I have no problem with the mystic experience per se. It does seem to have some, what could be called, "pure" elements, unmediated by social symbolism. These would include a feeling of selflessness, a feeling of being merged with the totality of the world or cosmos, a rushing in of feelings of love & a lack of fear. These feelings are more or less polar oppositions to feelings in the ordinary world -- feelings of having an individual self (or selfishness), feelings of being a separate entity in the cosmos & perhaps even unconnected to it in any meaningful way, so-called "negative" emotions like anger & hatred, & of course, feelings of fear, anxiety & paranoia. Obviously, the feelings in the mystic realm are "good" whereas those in the ordinary realm are "bad" if not outright evil. Never mind, for the moment, that all of these "good" feelings exist to one extent or another in the "ordinary world," or that it takes an ordinary individual self to experience the mystic realm.

Even as an experiential state, of course, there are a myriad of ways in which social symbolism molds & forms the experience. As in all other realms of life, there is a tendency to experience what one expects to experience. The core emotions or states of being listed above as more or less "pure" are very often modulated by the expectation of reaching a certain "level" of consciousness characterized by certain colours, images and so on. Even outside any organized set of symbolisms such as one finds in different religious groups & cults of one sort or another, the popular media give us any number of images of visionary & non-ordinary states of consciousness. No matter how skeptical one is, one expects one's experience to in some way match what was advertised.

As I said, the mystic realm of experience, no doubt, is experienced by many people & as an experiential state. I have no problem with that. My problem concerns primarily what happens when this state, the feelings & thoughts attached to it & the ways in which one can reach this exalted state are crystallized into an ideology and a social program. This ideology includes the dual worlds (enlightened & non-enlightened, formless & formed etc.), the "ladder" or "path" that joins the two realms & which the student navigates to reach the desired state, & the authoritarian structure of the groups with the "enlightened" teaching at the top, the organized "teaching" of the way.

I am well aware that many gurus & teachers do not see themselves or acknowledge themselves as "enlightened" just as I have come across nobody at all involved in such a system that either acknowledges it as authoritarian or sees anything wrong with such a structure. After all, it is to be expected that the one who knows most (if not all about the main subject) should run the show & those who are mere seekers should do what they are told in order to reach the desired goal. One of the most common answers to anyone who has the temerity to question the teacher's knowledge is simply: you must try it, and see what happens. The admonition is to let "experience" guide one.

On the whole, this is a very good guide. Go through a particular process & then see what happens. The next step in the development of understanding has to do with "why" such & such happened. In fact, a great number of people are not at all interested in "why" something occurs; they are just happy enough that it occurs. This discussion leads to the discussion of the difference between "discovery" & "creation" a discussion about the "purity" of the mystic experience & the degree in which it is molded or "created" by social language.

It also avoids the issue of democracy. In fact, "democracy" is seen to be in the land of forms, the land of social relations, the land of isolation, & by this very fact it is outside the enlightened domain. So, although the spiritual organization appears to be also in the land of forms & isolation, in some sense it is not – because of its enlightened leadership, it remains somewhat outside the realm of democracy & society in general. It is a "special" case because it leads to a special state of superior being. Its authoritarianism is thus seen as "natural" – that is, it belongs to the natural order of things with regard to this special state that cannot be expressed in words. It is "beyond" the ordinary world & thus beyond our ordinary understandings of "healthy relationships" & such concepts as "democracy."

This authoritarian aspect of the mystic program can readily be understood as the link between mystic ideology & fascism proper. Looking up the etymology of "fascism," we find that the word is from the Italian *fascismo,* from *fascio* bundle, fasces, group, from Latin *fascis* bundle & *fasces.* It is a political philosophy, movement, or regime that exalts nation and often race above the individual and that stands for a centralized autocratic government headed by a dictatorial leader, severe economic and social regimentation, and forcible suppression of opposition.

It is clear that the mystic ideology aims to submerge individuality in a cosmic unity (& also in the special group). The idea of "the bundle" or binding together, points to the spiritual unity of the community. In addition, we have the autocratic leadership of the enlightened one as well as the social regimentation & so on.

As I have pointed out earlier, only some groups or cults with a mystic orientation are organized in such an autocratic fashion. Others, with supposedly "real" teachers, do not aim at a dependency of the student on the leader or the group but actually do what they say they will do, that is, promote self-knowledge & the freedom of the individual in society. This "freedom" is essentially a way of being wherein one is not "attached" to the forms of the world, including one's own emotions & so on. That world stays essentially the same but one is "in" it in a different way. But even with the best will in the world and in situations which appear most egalitarian, the very nature of the quest seems to lead to abuse of the powerless by the powerful.

At least part of the problem seems to have to do with the importation of an educational method from an essentially tribal or pre-modern situation where the primary mode of maintaining social order was authoritarian & in which the individual tended to be submerged in the collective. The importation of such forms into our individualistic stratified society is problematic in a number of ways. For one thing, in modern society the individual is expected to have an extensive set of internal controls – morality is essentially seen as an individual thing – whereas in the earlier unstratified societies, the moral order remained essentially an external set of institutional controls. The enlightened leader of the East when the old external controls appear to be missing is at somewhat of a loss. Enlightenment, it would appear, often appears to somewhat context dependent, as is all other knowledge. Western religious organizations still consider the external controls as a necessary way to maintain morality. For the most part, in the Christian religion, the individual is not trusted to control him or herself but is understood to need continual reminding if not actual external controls. Thus, we also have the political right's continual harping on the need for more law & order.

A Note on Value Dualism

Value dualisms involve the creation of two categories, one more valued than the other. The dual categories we are interested in here are the categories of "enlightened" and "non-enlightened," of the "formless world" & the "world of forms, and, of" the world of "underlying unity" & the world of "individuation." Each of these is a value hierarchy whereby the first term is valued over the second. They are treated, in fact, as figure/ground gestalts in which the former term is seen as the larger, spiritual domain and the latter as the more ordinary or conventional one.

Dialectic & the formation of the self

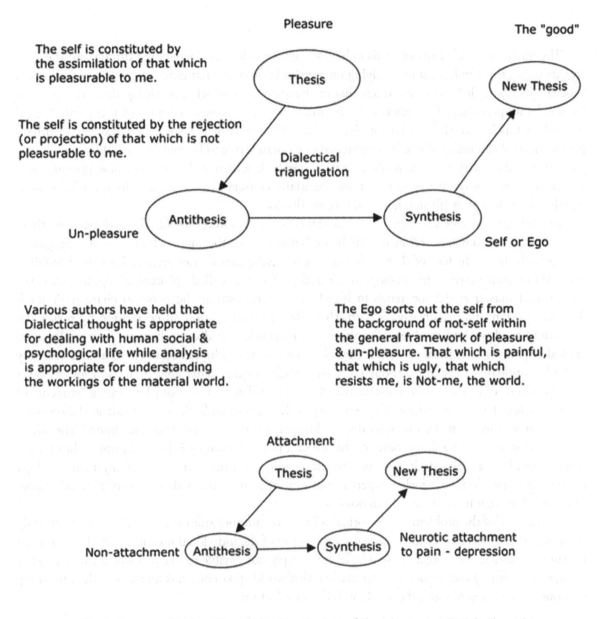

The self is constituted by the assimilation of that which is pleasurable to me.

The self is constituted by the rejection (or projection) of that which is not pleasurable to me.

Pleasure

The "good"

Thesis

New Thesis

Dialectical triangulation

Antithesis

Synthesis

Un-pleasure

Self or Ego

Various authors have held that Dialectical thought is appropriate for dealing with human social & psychological life while analysis is appropriate for understanding the workings of the material world.

The Ego sorts out the self from the background of not-self within the general framework of pleasure & un-pleasure. That which is painful, that which is ugly, that which resists me, is Not-me, the world.

Attachment

Thesis

New Thesis

Non-attachment

Antithesis

Synthesis

Neurotic attachment to pain - depression

Beyond our understanding of the functioning of the pleasure principle there is the idea that "attachment" of any sort is better than no attachment at all.

A Note on Enlightenment: Ideology & Authoritarianism

The image of enlightenment tends to be static with wisdom as unchanging throughout the ages. In this sense, it is fundamentalist, relying on a given body of unchanging (un-evolving) & timeless "ancient wisdom." It is also fundamentalist in the sense that mystic knowledge depends upon the "proper" interpretation of experience & the world by an unquestioned authority (an enlightened person) in touch with the special formless realm (of oneness or the void) in a way that ordinary people aren't. Presumably if one is enlightened one doesn't have to be told, one would simply know. This anti-evolutionary view of wisdom and awareness blocks new knowledge, new insights, new practices, & new ways of being. It is thus essentially conservative & static. The specified goal of mysticism to clear away illusion has bred its own illusion.

In spiritual or mystic ideology, there is a higher world & a lower world. The path between them is a hierarchy of value according to which the better one is, the more selfless one is. The goal is selfless perfection. The fact of there being only a few enlightened ones gives at least the possibility for authoritarian power. The ideological hierarchy of the so-called spiritual disciplines with the enlightened master at the top tends to breed authoritarianism at the personal charismatic level. The very notion of a person who is perfectly selfless & thus beyond all corruption by power (by definition) tends to lead to abuse of authority & corruption. It does so because there really is no critical apparatus in place to question the selflessness of the enlightened one. All abuses can very easily be rationalized because although a master might acquire what appears to be a lot of power & possessions, of course, he is non-attached & so it is different. Once one becomes a "student" of such a master, that whole process of questioning is always thrown back on the student, the one who doesn't know. How can the one who doesn't know question the one who does know? The whole ideological system with a few people on the top of a power hierarchy is by its nature authoritarian. The mystical experience itself may be "timeless" but the whole structure of mystical ideology attempts to crystallize this timeless experience in time & form in the body of the enlightened teacher & the wisdom that he or she is said to possess.

At the root of the problem is a historical reliance on authoritarian systems, & it could certainly be argued that at the root of these systems is the desire of the individual for some sort of stand in for parental authority. For a great many people, it is simply not tenable to live in a world where one has to figure everything out for oneself, especially if this world apparently has no transcendent meaning without some notion of God, the Void, or Selfless perfection.

Karma

Karma is basically a cause & effect type relationship that is extended across the boundary of death, which from the position of the enlightened worldview, is a false separation. The wonderful thing about Karma, of course, is that it cannot ever be checked or verified. It is something to be accepted on faith. Again, it is dependent upon an "authority" to explain why a person is having the difficulties that we all have. One's difficulties, of course, always pertain to our attachment to the limited world of self-interest. The notion of an enlightened authority combined with the idea of Karma, and the idea of the rising & lowering of status due to experience in past lives creates a closed system where almost anything can be rationalized. In fact, it would appear that the mystical ideological system is absolutely made for the psychological defenses of rationalization, projection, repression, splitting, etc.

Analysis
& Causal Relationship

There can be many metaphorical substitutions for the pronouns "this" or "that"
but each substitution while creating identity only does so in relation to the other.

Evolution

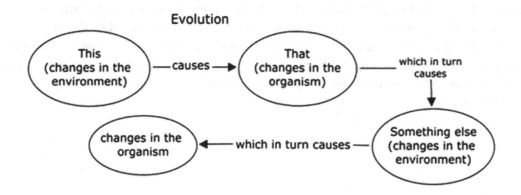

Analytical, rational or scientific representation give us a mechanistic understanding of the world. Problems occur when such analytical modes are applied to humans. It tends to turn human beings into "things." Alternately when dialectics are applied to the external world, then the world itself appears to be alive from top to bottom. There are many on both sides of this issue who want to treat all things according to their preference for dialectics or analytical thought.

Analytic language gives us a mechanistic understanding of the world. Problems occur when such analytical modes are applied to the human world. This tends to turn human beings into "things." Alternately when dialectics are applied to the external world, then the world itself appears to alive from top to bottom. There are many on both sides of this issue who want to treat all things according to their preference for dialectics or analytical thought. Dialectic tends toward an image of natural growth while analysis tends towards the concept of a machine with removable parts.

The analytic language of causal relationship is found at the extreme referential end of the spectrum of metaphorical language whose other end is the iconic image -- a symbol that stands for itself. Referential language must necessarily continually point beyond itself to a meaning found in the context of conventional language.

*Note: Mysticism
It is common to hear the statement: "not this, not that" as a sort of mystical shorthand for the notion that all language is dualistic & creates illusion. This is a "pointing" language -- & points to something "beyond" this & that. In general, mysticism's critique of "language" is aimed at this sort of rational causality & not at creative language. It tends to privilege the iconic over the arbitrary often ignoring the fact that the iconic image in the mind is a "representation" & by no means the "real" world.

The Formless Void & Creativity

I'd like to do just a little bit of a summation to the examination of the mystic ideology from the point of view of experiential metaphor. It is worthwhile noting once more, that the formless, selfless world, the timeless world of oneness is in reality simply privileging one side of the metaphoric equation – that is to say, a particular aspect of experience. The aspect that is privileged is the flow of perception itself, the flow of perception un-modulated by conventional understandings. In the model given above, this is one part of the creative process. In that model, one reverses the process of control so that perception itself is allowed to control convention rather than the other way around (which occurs in the everyday world). Stated baldly, one stops the flow of conventional thought & perception in which everything is instantly recognized for what it is, and by doing so one is immersed in the flow of fresh perceptions in which things are not known, not conventional & the world appears as a sort of mysterious limitless wonderland. This is the privileged world of the mystic journey, a world, touted as beyond language, beyond all form & thought. In a way it is, but it can only be experienced in its more or less "pure" form for short periods. For the most part the flow of perception is simply part of the process by which meaning is made. For the creative person, this step, although necessary, simply precedes using the new insights, this new experience to create new metaphors, new art, new medicine, new technology, new programs of all sorts, and this is at least as interesting as the entrance into the wonder of the world, this emerging with some real goods, something fresh & new, although not innocent.

It should be noted that one does not "stop the flow" so easily. There are a great many personal as well as institutional ways of aiming at this goal. The primary one, perhaps, in the mystic ideology, is meditation, along with chanting, repetitive mantras or prayers, fasting, dancing, exhaustion &, of course, drugs. Others engage in different sorts of contemplation, the immersion of oneself in nature, different sexual practices, & so on. Coming close to death & the process of dying may also tend to shut down the general control patterns that serve to limit & objectify the flow of perception.

Another difference twixt the spiritual & the creative process is that the former is essentially passive while the latter is active. But in both cases, there needs to be some sort of discipline or else, of course, one goes mad. The formless world, if it has no meaning, is terrifying: things are all mixed up, one cannot tell the difference between oneself & others, or objects for that matter. If trapped in that domain for any time, without the necessary tools, symbolism, or discipline, one becomes confused, paranoid, and full of fear or rage. Although touted as the formless realm, in fact this special spiritual realm, accessible only to the enlightened, is understood very much in terms of the highly valued symbolism of the all & everything, the supreme being or state of being, the good, selflessness, generosity, love and so forth. The creative person, on the other hand, in many ways is in love with that wonderful world of fresh insight, the world of the muse, intuition, & creativity. To "dry up" is no fun at all.

George Bataille, Sacrifice & the Sacred Domain

For Bataille also, the world of "nature" is the world of continuous undivided flow; it is a world outside & beyond the world of convention where convention, language, naming, and repression all block and shape the flow of energy & perception in various ways. He is interested in how religious or spiritual ideology conceives of the relationship between the two domains. He is interested particularly in religious sacrifice. He argues that "sacrifice," specifically sacrificial killing within the context of "the sacred," operates principally to demonstrate this world of flow, the world we will all enter upon our death. We witness this entrance into the cosmic flow & the leaving of our world of separation when we witness the sacrificial death. As witness to this passage, we are horrified & in awe. We are also refreshed & renewed. Of course, we are also made very aware of exactly where the boundary lies that divides our civilized world from the sacred dimension.

Presumably, we all ultimately desire to enter into our state of oneness with the universe, our commingling with the whole, but on the other hand, for the most part, we don't want it to happen just yet. We don't want to die just yet.

In addition, the world of the sacred is very often closer than we'd like to the world of the profane, for while death on the one hand brings us to an awareness of the sacred dimension, it is also the punishment for excessive or criminal behaviour. In both cases, we witness the exit from the individuated world, the world of multiplicity & separation into the world of unified & selfless flow. Thus, we contain our selfish passions – we are "good" so that we may remain a while in the world of sin, the world of individuation, of corruption & separation from the sacred.

It also occurs to me that precisely because the sacred world is outside & beyond the world of language & separation, it is naturally associated with the wilderness, the wildness that is also beyond the conventional civilized world. The sacred, then, is in a strong sense, exactly the wilderness. It is the wilderness that we enter when we die. Many of us, I suppose just wander off into this wilderness.

The Two Worlds of George Bataille

Always in Dialectics there are
the two worlds,
although they may be called
by different names

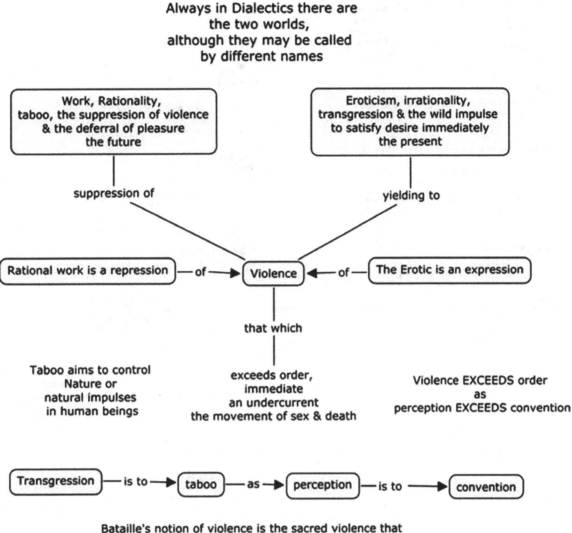

Bataille's notion of violence is the sacred violence that
disrupts the rational order of things -- of work & the
deferral of pleasure. But, in that case, violence may be only
the quiet erasure of boundaries, the impulse to enter the
flow which is in a sense pleasure but also more than that.

Sacred violence is "excessive" -- something that exceeds
boundary, something that cannot be contained. This is
not the development of the soul but the ascension of the
spirit.

Erotism
George Bataille

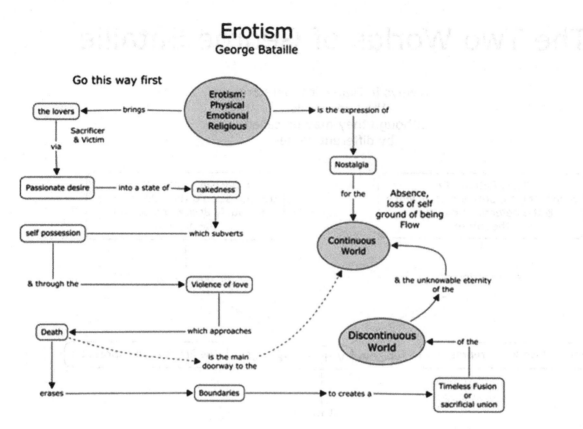

Go this way first

Individual Isolated Self
Habits
Subjects & objects
Social Organization
Boundaries

A Note on Ambiguity & the Distinction between Scientific & Creative Language

At the outset, it should be noted that "ambiguity" in our understanding of the nature of things is exactly that which creates anxiety and ruins our calmness & peace of mind. In the service of clarity, ambiguity must be banished. This is never so clear as in the context of science, where unambiguous definitions, laws, & rules are sought. One might say, that the main task of science is to disambiguate our experience. We want to know exactly why things happen the way they do. We want "fact" not opinions, random thoughts, or even poetry.

In order to have facts, we must have completely clear boundaries in our definitions. In this domain, we are to have no repression & no ambiguity. We are, of course, to have no mythology or anything that smacks of it, but unfortunately, this is not quite the way it is. It has been shown over & over again that although science might aspire towards such a state it is nowhere near it. Science as a discipline is quite enmeshed in the greater social realm & as such, its theories take on mythic proportions & its facts continually seem to change.

Creative language, on the other hand, is understood to be rich & have depth precisely because it is ambiguous & multi-faceted. This is to say, that is has un-repressed some, but certainly not all, of the similarities between its categories. As such, creative endeavor would seem to lie somewhere between the ordinary conventional world & the world of ambiguous, non-boundaried flow. In some ways, this connection between the two worlds may be thought of as similar to the mystic connection, the path to enlightenment. In the creative world, with its connection to the natural world of flowing perception, one can at least be better or worse. Perhaps to be a lousy artist or writer is to be unable to break out of the conventional way of expressing things, or perhaps to be a lousy artist is not to even be able to accomplish the conventional. Maybe it is only the "great" artist that can break away from convention in order to create new forms. The "conventional" artist would then be just that person who maintains & manages the conventional signs in a goodly & competent way, not something to be scoffed at.

To make a bald distinction, then: scientific language aims at clear unambiguous boundaries between its categories while creative language aims at un-repressing clear boundaries & ambiguity in the service of creating multi-faceted meaning. As such, scientific language is as far away as one can get from the actual energetic flow of the perceptual world while creative language attempts in one way or another to embrace & encode the ambiguous & flowing nature of the perceptual world.

Evil & Taboo

The two terms good and evil are perhaps the quintessential items to demonstrate the nature of how meaning is constructed in the network of language. Before moving on to that discussion, however, I will speak of evil and taboo

Evil is the forbidden & the repressed & this is exactly something that occurs at the edge of categories, so evil is a category, or perhaps more correctly a meta-category, that refers to exactly the repressed elements between categories, especially those categories surrounding sexuality, killing, giving birth, etc. that are charged with emotion. Evil, in pre-modern tribal societies, is surrounded by taboos. In earlier pre-modern small-scale societies, activity was controlled in all the important emotionally charged areas by way of taboo. When categories are mixed, or one category is contaminated with another, the taboo is violated and one must engage in some sort of "purification." This purification pertains to purifying the categories once more, setting things in their proper relations, cleaning up the ambiguity.

Dirt - matter out of place. (Douglas, 1966)
Girl- woman - evil at the boundary, menstruation
The constellation of terms from anthropology: dirt, ritual, ritual reversal, taboo, purification.

A note on dirt, purity & taboo: All intense human relationships especially those involved with sexuality & violence have multiple "strands" as it were that connect one to another – there are many ways of having sex with many sorts of beings & there are many ways to kill. Thus, each culture conspires to designate the "proper" way for them. Such intense relationships must be managed in just the right way or big problems will occur, the Gods will be angry & tragedy will befall the people. Thus, there are "taboos" on certain behaviour – all intense relationships are hedged around with taboos, that is, designated ways "not" to do things. These are all in the negative: don't have sex when you're not married, don't have sex with the wrong type of people, from a different class, a different race; don't have the wrong type of sex, etc. There is always the interdict. The "pure" or "proper" way of doing things is just such & such & no other way. And, of course, when a taboo is broken, as they must often be, then the one who is "polluted" or "dirtied" by the wrongful relationship must be "purified" once more & brought back into the realm of "proper" people with proper attitudes & proper behaviour – in other words, their desires (id inspired or not) which were improperly expressed must be banished, controlled & managed – disappeared if possible.

A Little Note on Good & Evil

These two terms are constructed as polar opposites and there is a very definite repression at the boundary between them. They are also very highly charged, emotionally. This repression of similarities between the two is very often, in the service of clarity, thought to be best left unexpressed. To express the similarities between good & evil would, of course, make the difference between them somewhat ambiguous. In terms of the peaceful & well-ordered arrangements of society, this is exactly what is not wanted. It is desired that there be an un-ambiguous boundary between good behaviour & bad behaviour, between good & evil.

Of course, these days, in our modern & post-modern multiplicity, the distinction cannot be maintained by some simple taboo or even some simple set of laws. In fact, the boundary between the two is very ambiguous indeed. This, of course, is what is so discouraging to conservatives of all sorts, and liberals too. The liberal mentality doesn't desire to return to some other pristine age when the lines were clearly drawn, as does the conservative mind, but it does want to deal with social inequity especially as it has become institutionalized in capitalist society & the institution of war.

What then are the repressed similarities between good & evil? Almost an evil question, that. I mean that even to entertain the thought that good & evil might be similar in some respects seems somehow "wrong."

Right off the bat, one might name "energy." Both good & evil seem to have some energy, although it seems that evil might have more energy than good because after all evil actually has to break conventional boundaries whereas good has only to act within the confines of convention. The next thing that pops to mind concerns the activity of a criminal (an evil one) & the activity of the artist. They both are involved in breaking conventional boundaries. In this sense also, of course, the criminal & the artist are related to the political activist & the revolutionary.

What should be clear is that I am talking about good & evil as social categories, categories that certainly vary from culture to culture & from time to time.

Let's talk about sex for a moment, a subject also highly emotionally charged & a subject central to the construction of a "good" or "bad" person. Certain kinds of sexual behaviour are labeled evil while others are labeled good. We also have rules concerning who can engage in the good behaviors & who cannot. It is easy enough to see that in most cases, certainly of consensual sexual behaviour, there is a great deal of similarity between "good" & "bad" sexual practices. The similarity between the two is that they both are pleasurable. Various practices such as oral sex or anal sex are at various times thought to be bad or even evil, as are sexual relations between same-sex partners.

It should be understood that the establishment of the categories of good & evil in domains such as the sexual has very much to do with social control, very much to do with the establishment & maintenance of power. Likewise, the establishment of the boundaries has very much to do with the deep-seated fears & desires of everyone, of all of us. Such fears & desires cause a great deal of anxiety. To have desires such as these controlled & limited calms that anxiety.

The fear is that, if we loosen the definitions of good & bad and acknowledge that in fact what we choose to call evil is very often quite similar to that which we call good, everything "will go to hell." People will do anything they want. There will be no social control. Everyone will go wild. All this, I suppose, is precisely because these arenas of good & evil & sexuality are so highly charged

& they have so much to do with powerful biological realities: sex, territoriality, aggression.) The appeal of fundamentalism is that it provides "clarity" in the moral domain. However, in doing this it also characterizes the "desire" of individuals as essentially evil & prone to go out of control if not rigidly limited by rules of conduct. In general, we have a great fear of disorder, chaos, & anarchy, & fear & mistrust of oneself is promoted by fundamentalism. In order to control the unruly desires, fundamentalism creates very hard & fast categories of good & evil.

Social Change: Power & Authority: the Dual World — Form & Formless

In the first place, I should say that when I speak of "social change" I am speaking primarily about social discourse & its change. In order to make "real" social change, of course, one must be able to change society in "real" ways, change its laws, its actual on-the-ground institutions, & so forth. This can happen in peaceful or violent ways. I have nothing much to say about how this is done.

In terms of our discourse about metaphor & the dual world, it should also be clear that here I am speaking primarily about the "social" world, the world of convention & everyday secular profane reality. My argument, however, is that in the process of social change, the ordinary conventional world must be "opened up" & exposed, as it were, to the existential flow of the sacred or perceptual world in order to accomplish change. Social change is a creative process. From this point of view, it can be said that social change is accomplished by changing the social discourse, changing the metaphors we use & the ways that we use them.

In the simplest possible way, social change occurs when we open up & then re-create the boundaries of the categories that we use to communicate with each other. Change the way we talk & we change the way we are. There is no question of "Oh, that's only words," or "That's just semantics." The way we are considering words & metaphors means that there can be no real separation between language & reality, or between words & the way things really are, or between metaphors and real experience. Language & real experience are combined in every instance in a myriad of ways. They are inextricable related in the same way that a biological entity & its environment are. In the biological case, the entity & the environment mutually influence each other & evolve together. In the case of ordinary experience, language & the body of the speaker in its real-life context mutually influence each other & evolve together.

It is important to remember that the conventional world doesn't just appear, it is created &, insomuch as it is the world of social relations, it encodes the power relations that exist between the people in that society. This social creation occurs over a great deal of time & it continues to change over time due to various pressures: social, economic, political, religious, etc. At any given time, certain power groups control the definitions of things, or, as William Burroughs has it: certain groups have got control of "the reality concession."

The domain I am especially concerned with here is the moral domain. I am thinking of how good & evil are defined in various different contexts. Such definitions apply in the general understanding of a good person or a good project (& this might be controlled by religious groups) but also in terms of the law (controlled by the legal profession, political groups etc.) – certain things are "bad" or "evil" & if one engages in them, one is punished as a criminal. Of course, it isn't as simple as this, Michael Foucault argues that the rules of society evolve & change in the context of a great number of different discourses produced by the legal profession, educationists, the media, political parties, medicine & so on.

The domain of morality is concerned primarily with establishing control over deeply rooted biological instincts, primarily those of sex & aggression. Freud argued that it was necessary to repress the free expression of both of these urges in order to have a civilization at all. More recently, others have challenged this assumption. They believe that people are in fact more able to self-regulate than previously thought and that there really is no need for such repressive measures in order to keep our animal wildness in check. The very image of these desires continues to change in many different ways. For us, now, however, it is enough to note that we are dealing with deep-rooted emotional issues highly charged with desire & fear.

In general, then, any given set of conventions at any given time, actually satisfies the wishes & desires of a certain segment of society, while it leaves other segments more or less unsatisfied. Depending upon the political, historical, and environmental situation, this dissatisfied portion of society may manifest a pressure for change.

Thus, at the root of social change are certain pressures from within society & perhaps from without: aggression by others, an influx of people with a different culture, etc. There are historical & general environmental forces that press towards this or that way of doing things, which press towards social change. Then there is the question of leadership.

A leader, it is presumed has some sort of deeply rooted desire for social change. This may be a very selfless desire to better the community in some way and bring satisfaction to the dissatisfied segment of society, or it may involve a more selfish personal desire for power. In either case, the leader must be able to mobilize the energies of the dissatisfied population & in some way overcome the satisfied segment of the population who are, by definition, conservative & wish to preserve the way things are. Of course, the situation may be reversed: those of a liberal sensibility may have established various new institutions & programs in society, & some group, essentially conservative, may attempt to overthrow this liberal regime & replace it with what used to be.

It should be noted that the leader & the dissatisfied segment of society are bound to share at least some of the same reasons for dissatisfaction. These "reasons" may be the result of social conventions or they may be the result of early experiences in one's family and elsewhere. The actual nature of the program that one & one's group are going to institute is formed by a combination of the influence of one's early family life & a particular cultural context & is conditioned by the group's ideals, fears, needs, ethics & so on.

At the root of all programs, however, is the concept of "desire." The manifestation of this desire, in a more or less organized way, then, initiates social change, but how, then, is this community desire, initiated by dissatisfaction, organized in such a way that it accomplishes social change?

Why, it opens up the definitions (conventions) in the social discourse that it has problems with & works to establish new definitions (conventions). It seeks to establish new sorts of boundaries in social discourse.

Mysticism & Ordinary Reality

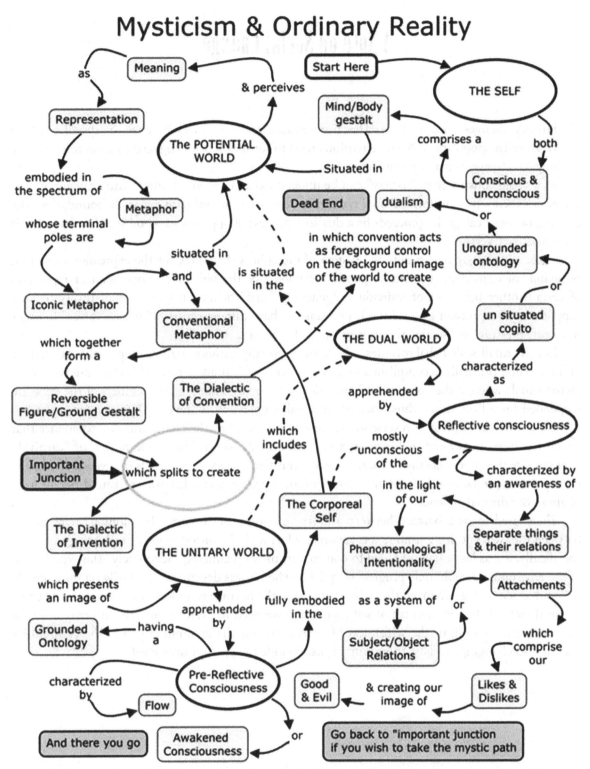

Mysticism has nothing to do with changing the way the world is, it only is interested in changed one's way of being in the world.

A Note on Social Change

History changes, society changes because tensions arise in society because the systems fails to satisfy all of the population, & these tensions tend to form polarities engaged in a contest, the one pushing for change, the other resisting it.

As a social construction, "society" can be understood as a system of interlocking categories. The categories themselves are formed by a systematic repression of ambiguity at their boundaries. The creation of social categories proceeds by a dualistic process of oppositions: good is defined as what is not evil & vice versa.

Thus, one can say that society is a system of metaphors that allow for the expression of certain behaviour of individuals (generally "good" behaviour) & the blocking, suppression or repression of certain other behaviors of individuals (generally "bad" behaviour.) Because of the systematic suppression & repression in society it is necessary to have different sorts of "release valves" in order to let off "pressure" or "steam" that is pent up in the system.

In early small-scale tribal societies, which are essentially authoritarian (Groupthink), this letting off of pressure is usually accomplished by different sorts of "rituals of reversal." These are very often sacred rituals wherein the conventional attitudes & behaviors expected of members of the tribe are suspended for a brief time. Thus, the conventional suppression is "reversed" & pressure is let off. Rituals of reversal suspend or reverse social conventions & allow the community to experience that which has been suppressed, wildness, the unconscious, & so on. The whole notion of "carnival" operates like this, but generally in contemporary stratified society these rituals of reversal are for the most part not present, so the pent up energies in society are expressed in war, racism, different sorts of abuse & criminal violence.

There used to be a balance between society & nature, or at least a harmonious relationship between the two, but this harmony was apparently lost with the introduction of technology, or more specifically, it was lost when we failed to control our use of technology adequately. The exploitation of the environment could only progress so quickly when it was dependent primarily on pure muscle power, but technology changed the balance. Because the balance is no longer enforced by the brute physical facts of the case and is not self-regulating, we need to exercise our ethical prerogative. In essence, we need to limit the selfishness of individuals for the communal good. The community itself is also changing. Today's community must include the environment itself.

A Note on William Burroughs & Language as Virus

Burroughs develops through his work the extended metaphor of language as virus. By this, I take it that he points towards the way that language attacks a person & establishes a set of conventional meanings that are harmful to the individual & probably the community. It jumps from one person to another like a viral disease, infecting one after another, & taking away their freedom. This is a particularly graphic way of describing what I have simply termed the "conventional world" or what the spiritual disciplines call the world of form, Maya, & so on.

A Note on Wilhelm Reich & the Bodily Unconscious

From the point of view taken in these brief essays one may say that Reich treated the human body as a text & that the meaning of this text was set up in the same way as in any other text, by a systematic set of repressions. These repressions in order to create the categories of expression, however, are not comprised of words, rather they are made up of a set of chronic tensions in the body such as a bent back, (the metaphor of "world weariness"), a "stiff neck," a constricted throat producing a high pitched whiny voice & so on.

This is, however, as I said, an unconscious text, so the meanings are not set up to create an intentional message but rather communicate an unconscious one. One is "given away" by one's body.

In order to attain some portion of freedom, to re-gain some flexibility & to re-gain access to the energies locked up in such chronic tensions, one can go through some sort of program of exercise (perhaps both psychic & physical). In the process, of course, one will re-define oneself & at least for some time while this process of change is occurring, create a certain ambiguity in one's posture in the world.

In an extreme instance one could, at least theoretically, gain so much access to both physical & mental energy in this process of the suspension of the repressions of body & mind that one could enter an ecstatic state, escaping the conventional world entirely. One could move from the world of form, conventional ideas, & the repressed conventional body, to the world of the formless. Practices such as exhausting the body very often in rhythmic practice makes perfect sense for regaining access to energy locked up in chronic tension.

A Note on the Erotic & the Formless Domain of Mysticism

The erotic is excessive. Excess breaks the boundaries. Bataille & Freud agree that the erotic & sexuality must be controlled if we are to have a civilized world.

The parallels between erotic & spiritual ecstasy are easily seen & often commented upon. The question at one time or another has been which is the more fundamental, the spiritual or the sexual? Jung chose the spiritual, Freud the sexual. Certainly evolutionary theory points clearly to the sexual. I see no reason not to believe that the energy of the ecstatic trance comes directly from the un-repressed sexual body.

From this point of view then, there is a fundamental similarity between the disappearance of the self in the "other" in the ecstatic convulsion of body & mind whether spiritual or orgasmic. This disappearance testifies to the fragility & instability of "the self" in both experiences. Given this, it certainly seems somewhat perverse to insist on their utter separation – that the one is "high" while the other is "low" & polluted. Although many regard the ecstatic trance as a "purification" of the process, I for one am not at all sure that it is an "advance" to be able to have a "virtual" orgasm with an invisible other without touching oneself in a sexual way.

METAPHOR OF EROTICISM

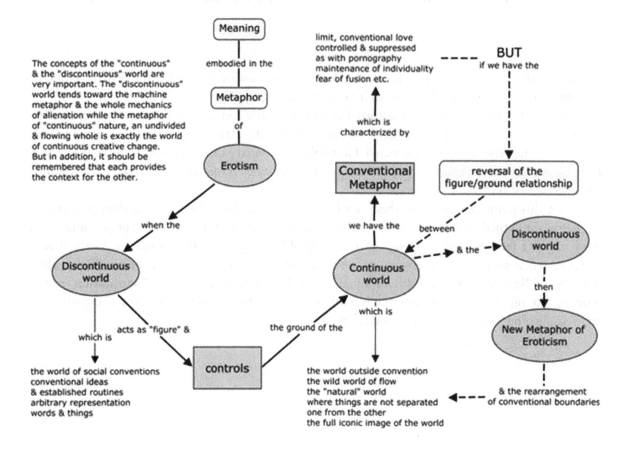

The concepts of the "continuous" & the "discontinuous" world are very important. The "discontinuous" world tends toward the machine metaphor & the whole mechanics of alienation while the metaphor of "continuous" nature, an undivided & flowing whole is exactly the world of continuous creative change. But in addition, it should be remembered that each provides the context for the other.

Meaning

embodied in the

Metaphor

of

Erotism

when the

Discontinuous world

which is

the world of social conventions
conventional ideas
& established routines
arbitrary representation
words & things

acts as "figure" &

controls

the ground of the

Continuous world

which is

the world outside convention
the wild world of flow
the "natural" world
where things are not separated
one from the other
the full iconic image of the world

we have the

Conventional Metaphor

which is
characterized by

limit, conventional love
controlled & suppressed
as with pornography
maintenance of individuality
fear of fusion etc.

BUT
if we have the

reversal of the
figure/ground relationship

between

& the

Discontinuous world

then

New Metaphor of Eroticism

& the rearrangement
of conventional boundaries

The economy of desire or The ecology of Transference & desire.

Throughout our lives, images, interpretations, emotions, ideas, desires, the objects of our desires, etc. are transferred from one part to another "inside" the psyche & transferred or projected "outside" into our system of relationships. We are embodied beings historically situated in nature & in culture & the boundaries between inside & outside, the social & the individual are always changing. Our desire, initiated by lack, motivates the movement of energy in the system. The internal structure of the psyche conditions the nature of our social relationships & vise versa. At various times the flow of energy & information throughout the system is blocked or impeded. At these times, some sort of therapy is an option.

We come to understand ourselves through a complex process of expression, interpretation & re-construction. In the context of Art Therapy, the psyche (parts of the psyche, transference etc.) are embodied in the art. Through this expression, our contemplation & interpretation of this art we come to know ourselves, our difficulties & desires. What we do with this knowledge & this art is up to us.

A Note on the "Fetish"

Marx took note of the fetishization of money. Originally the "fetish" was a sexual object considered to have a spirit in it. It was a thing imbued with power. Where did the power come from? It came from the people who designated it as such. It embodied the metaphorical conjunction of a "thing" with a "power". The thing's home was "nature" while the "power" came from mind – social mind. It was thus a "magical" object which could accomplish things in the real world like ensuring that the game animal it represented was killed in the hunt, or that one's wishes were carried out over a great distance (the magic of money), or that sexual energy was available when desired. In the case of the sexual fetish, the "power" comes from a more or less "unconscious" association of the "thing" with infantile sexual pleasure.

A Note on the Order of Creation

We are concerned here with "myths" of origin. I contrast the mystic (or generally religious) view with the materialistic view concerning which came first – spirit (life) or matter. There is actually no way in which to "prove" either case & so they both must remain in the mythic zone. (Actually, this last statement assumes or creates a hierarchy between the "facts" of science & mythology or metaphor. From the point of view taken in these short essays, this distinction is not accurate. From the point of view of metaphor theory, the "facts" of science are simply a different sort of metaphor than those of "myth." They are two different sorts of stories. This desire to have scientific "proof" is a very deeply seated desire. Both mystics & scientists are very concerned with it. For science it is simply the way science is, but for the mystics, to be able to "prove" their theories - is to gain legitimacy in the "real" world.) Anyway, such "proof" is as elusive as the ability to "prove" the cause of any given action on my part: do I do it myself, or does the world call my action into being?

From the religious or spiritual point of view, thought or spirit comes first. This involves the pre-existence of some sort of "God" or some all-encompassing force, & it is this thought or spirit that creates or crystallizes into matter & the material world. According to The Bible: "In the beginning was the word.".Spirit creates matter & then, if it is allowed, matter may evolve, but, in any event, ordinary human thought is always below or less than the original god-force; it is "fallen," in some sense, & must always attempt to re-discover what it used to know or perhaps already knows, the knowledge of spirit. It is this re-discovery or discovery of spirit that puts us in touch with a "higher" self & in some way or other pertains to the moral sphere of thought.

From the "scientific" or materialistic point of view, matter evolves (let's just say we don't know how it all began) and part of this evolution is the development of beings who can think (humans) & who thus become the thinking & moral element of nature. The brain & thinking, which may involve more of the body than just the brain, evolve & in doing so "create" new social forms as well as change the environment.

In this materialistic view I'm leaving out, simply because it seems "wrong-headed," the notion that seems to have developed along with this contemporary mode of thought, that we humans are actually separate & morally superior to the natural world. We are very much a part of nature & I myself like the view that we are the moral & ethical "part" of nature. (Bookchin, Leopold) Other members of the animal world do not seem to have developed much of a concept of compassion or social justice. We are the animals that have. As such, we have a certain obligation towards the environment, in essence our mother.

Evolution, itself, involves the interaction between organism & environment over time & "natural" selection sometimes via sexuality. The interaction between organism & environment goes both ways, the organism "adapts" to the environment (the environment changes the organism) but also the organism "changes" the environment. In the mainstream understanding of "natural selection", it appears that a part of the process whereby the organism "adapts" to the environment, involves the wilderness world of "random selection". This chaotic world of the random certainly has some symbolic similarities to the "enlightened" world of the mystic. "Things" remain un-labeled in the random world of natural selection as well as the formless world of the mystic journey. There is a "wildness" about both "moments."

The distinction between the "wilderness" & "civilization," the wild & the tame, is very interesting in a number of ways. We learn from Van Gennep that rituals concerned with identity change follow a general pattern: individuals move from their given position in society into a liminal stage outside of the social norms before being re-introduced back into society in their new role. Individuals move out of the world of tame civilization (the world of form & convention) & into the world of the wild (where ambiguity reigns, where things are mixed up), the world of "flow." They move from the world of controlled flow to the world of uncontrolled flow, & thus they move from a conventional state of mind into an altered state. In this "wild" or altered state of consciousness, the individual is subjected to various experiences, many of which illustrate in very strong terms the benefits of social life & the pertinent elements of the new role.

A Note on the distinction between religion & spirituality

Let's pause for a moment & look at the distinction between "religion" & "spirituality" that I come across so often these days. In most instances, the person I am speaking to acknowledges the historical & bureaucratic wrongness of "organized" religion while saying at the same time that they themselves are involved in "spirituality" which is understood to be the more or less pure form or essence of religion. Religion, per se, as the social form of spirituality, merely distorts the true message of spirit.

But, what exactly is this essential spirituality? On the one hand, it would seem to involve a personal communion with deity, or with some larger being, understood to simply be above, control, or look after this world. Very often, it seems that "spirit" & "nature" are essentially the same thing. Very often in addition to the idea of a simple communion with a spiritual entity or entities, it has as its aim the development of oneself as a better person. That is, it has a more or less pure moral aim. Rather than joining in a particular community adhering to an older established religion, those involved with the "spiritual" tend to either engage in some sort of practice with a small group of like-minded people or on their own. These "practices," such as spiritual dance, meditation, yoga & so on, are "magical" rather than "religious" in the sense that magic has always had as its aim the enhancement or empowerment of the self. Religion, in this context, then, is seen as essentially concerned with social control while these more individualistic practices that use religious symbolism are understood to enhance human freedom. In this distinction between religion & spirituality, we have the distinction between the community & the individual.

I have found, to my own surprise, that I am more comfortable with "religion" or "ethical religion" than I am with these other "magical" or "spiritual" practices. I have come to see religion as having, by & large, a good moral social program & in spite of continually making horrible historical mistakes & supporting really bad power arrangements, nonetheless the aim is essentially good. On the other hand, the magical or spiritual practices involve the creation of altered states of consciousness in conjunction with a sometimes dubious value system & cult or charismatic figures.

Belief

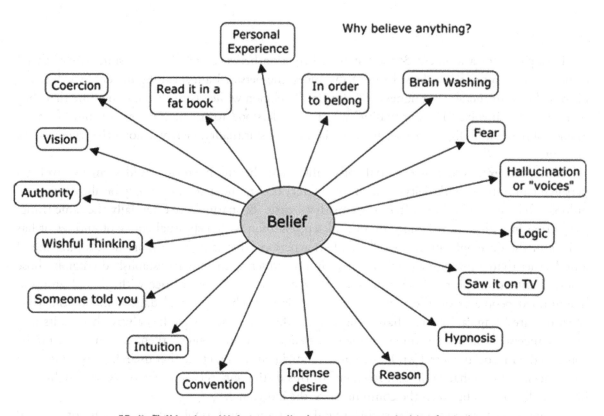

"Belief" (Merriam Webster on line) 1 : a state or habit of mind
in which trust or confidence is placed in some person or thing
2 : something believed; especially : a tenet or body of tenets
held by a group 3 : conviction of the truth of some statement
or the reality of some being or phenomenon especially when
based on examination of evidence

The Positive & Negative Aspects of Spirituality

The general distinction being used here is made between religion as a social and ideological form & spirituality as the private domain wherein one communes personally with the divine. But this private domain of spirituality needs to be subdivided into a) those practices which are primarily religious but simply private like prayer, a communion with nature, etc., and b) magical practices like astrology, meditation, shamanism, yoga, etc. which also include "spiritualism" the "occult" & so forth.

Positive Aspects

1) <u>Purpose:</u> Spirituality is positive & evolutionary insomuch as it desires the growth of knowledge & consciousness & that this consciousness involves connecting or tuning into some larger shape of reality, (a more truthful image of reality) in particular the whole of the natural world ("Nature.") Spirituality promotes goodness, compassion: do unto others as you would have them do unto you, etc. It involves some notion of "contributing" to the growth of knowledge, consciousness & to the betterment of all of nature including human kind.

2) <u>Techniques & Practices:</u> It has techniques & practices for acquiring knowledge, increasing consciousness & healing. Meditation, ritual, etc. Calming the mind in the midst of the hubbub of modern life is OK as long as it's not seen as the highest state to be achieved.

3) <u>Image of the Spiritual Community:</u> It provides the comfort & safety of community without closing off dialogue with others. The boundary is porous. It is non-unified, open-minded towards other's beliefs etc.

4) <u>Social Justice:</u> It promotes action with regards to social justice & the betterment of all aspects of society & the natural world.

5) <u>Image of the Self:</u> Its notion of increasing consciousness involves the integration of the psyche, that is the dark & the light, good & evil, etc. rather than merely repressing one side of the value-dualism. The locus of knowledge & action is with the individual.

6) <u>Language & Reality:</u> Positive spirituality has a good understanding of the richness, power, & place of language (metaphor) in the development of knowledge & consciousness. It does not mistake metaphor for reality, i.e., chakras are metaphoric not "real."

7) <u>Creativity:</u> Positive spirituality highly values human creativity & may even equate it to spirituality.

8) <u>Authority:</u> Values lived experiences as opposed to historic authority or the arbitrary authority of current leaders.

9) <u>Personal freedom:</u> Understands that the individual is free to have his or her own spiritual relationship & doesn't need any priestly mediation.

10) <u>The Nature of Nature:</u> We live in a world where ambiguity, complexity, & diversity are ubiquitous but spirituality doesn't try to impose a single "unified" image on the world (or on the self). Nature is sacred. Natural not super-natural.

11) <u>Model of the Mind:</u> In its dealing with the "mind" positive spirituality differentiates between the chaotic jumble of mind chatter, instrumental reason & the larger philosophical reason – this latter probably involves the differences between analytical & dialectical thought. Place of intuition? Creativity?

12) <u>Relationship between Spirit & Nature:</u> Spirit & Nature are the same. The spiritual is the natural. Usually found in non-monotheistic spiritual practice & pre modern communities. There's non-dualistic integration of mind & body. May see non-human entities, insects, mountains, etc. as "spiritual" entities (not invisible people-like things). May tend to be animistic, rather than theistic.

13) <u>Relation of human to non-human:</u> That human kind is very much a part & not separate from or master of the natural world. My preference is to think of humankind as the conscious aspect of nature. With this consciousness come rights & responsibilities. "Spirits" etc. are recognized as human thoughts & emotions.

14) <u>Attitude towards Technology:</u> Positive spirituality may criticize our contemporary technological society & so on but also understands that technology is here to stay & that it is a question of its place in the scheme of things. Technology is also a part of nature.

15) <u>Image of Good & Evil:</u> Acknowledges the need to integrate both sides of the equation & thus does not project "evil" onto the other.

Negative Aspects

1) <u>Purpose:</u> Spirituality is regressive insomuch as it is driven (usually unconsciously) by fear (especially of death) & the desire for security. That is to say, it is comfortable & because it is so, it blocks the difficult job of acquiring knowledge & consciousness. It probably promotes some idea of good behaviour but has a limited understanding of it & may perhaps tend towards the repression or suppression of "badness" or "evil" so that it remains unacknowledged as one's own & is projected onto others. Because it splits the self & divides up "us" & "them," it promotes good only for the in-group & not for all. Selfishness.

2) <u>Techniques & Practices:</u> Its techniques & practices are primarily aimed at the consolidation of the community, the closing down of individual thought & the promotion of obedience, etc. Its practices promote conformity rather than growth.

3) <u>Image of the spiritual community:</u> Splitting, dissociation, & dualism: it tends to use a particular belief to denigrate other beliefs & believers. Tends to promote "projection" of evil onto others of different belief.

4) <u>Social Justice:</u> It promotes passivity with regard to injustice in the world. Promotes passivity with regard to some overwhelming idea of deity. Selfishness. The model of religion masks power & legitimizes inequalities as the "natural" order, or necessities for learning. For example: women "naturally" should be subservient to men, animals to humans etc.

5) <u>Image of the Self:</u> It has a concept of the self that places agency & the creative imagination outside of the embodied human being. Or it involves the idea that "we are all one" – which is to say that we are all God or some such. This sort of notion tends to severely limit the ability to use the critical intelligence. It promotes splitting & repression twixt good & evil etc. It is non-integrative. The self is passive & deity is active.

6) <u>Language & Reality:</u> It has some idea that "spirit" is first in the world rather than the last & highest ideal of humankind. This usually goes along with idea that certain aspects of the world are "naturally" spiritual or sacred. Tends to denigrate "language" as a lie, inadequate & a distortion of the truth rather than understanding its relationship & place within lived experience. Thus it is essentially anti-intellectual – that is to say that it often looks at the mind as mainly an interference in the process of acquiring spiritual knowledge & often promotes the idea that the "heart" & intuition knows better the correct path.

7) <u>Creativity:</u> Human creativity is considered different & lower than divine creativity thus creating a dualistic image.

8) <u>Authority:</u> It tends to depend upon the authority of past leaders rather than actual experience. It tends to promote the idea that only the guru or spiritual teacher knows the proper way & that one cannot understand properly without this teacher. Fundamentalism.

9) <u>Personal Freedom:</u> The individual is bound by the authority of the community & needs continual help in the interpretation of the sacred. Deviation from the rules of the community is very much frowned upon.

10) <u>The Nature of Nature:</u> The natural world hides the real truth of the divine, a veil over the sacred etc.

11) <u>Model of the Mind:</u> Doesn't distinguish between mind-chatter, instrumental & broader reason. Intuition is promoted as knowledge or fact.

12) <u>Relationship between Spirit & Nature:</u> It can promote a dissociative split (dualism) between Spirit (which tends upwards) & Nature (which tends downward.) This split is also between spirit & body and it has some idea of God or deity that is larger, more real, & better than the whole of the natural world. That is to say that the physical world is some sort of illusory veil over the real spiritual world. Spirit is above Nature & humankind is separate & above the natural world. It engages in a value dualism whereby one side of the equation dominates the other and tends to promote the idea that there is only one clear & right way of looking at the world, only one interpretation of events: fundamentalism.

13) <u>Relation of human to non-human:</u> It promotes the separation of the self from the natural world. This usually involves some notion of mastery & self above nature. It often sees the material world as merely a "veil" which obscures the real "objective" spiritual world. It has some notion of "spirits" ethereal entities etc. that it does not recognize as comprised of human thoughts & emotions.

14) <u>Attitude towards Technology:</u> It either sees technology as what God has given to the good, ignores it entirely, or promotes its destruction or avoidance.

15) <u>Image of Good & Evil:</u> It promotes some idea of the good & tends to repress & project the image of evil as demonic, the devil etc. Often there is an idea of evil as some autonomous force. In the Eastern idea of evil as illusion - of separation from the whole there can be difficulty with the model of the whole or unity itself, the proper or correct relationship which evil then deviates from (ignorance etc.).

SOUL

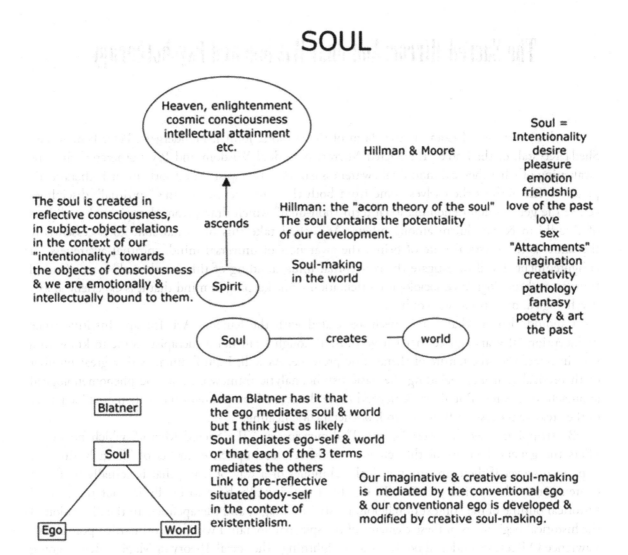

Heaven, enlightenment
cosmic consciousness
intellectual attainment
etc.

The soul is created in
reflective consciousness,
in subject-object relations
in the context of our
"intentionality" towards
the objects of consciousness
& we are emotionally &
intellectually bound to them.

ascends

Spirit

Hillman & Moore

Hillman: the "acorn theory of the soul"
The soul contains the potentiality
of our development.

Soul-making
in the world

Soul   creates   world

Soul =
Intentionality
desire
pleasure
emotion
friendship
love of the past
love
sex
"Attachments"
imagination
creativity
pathology
fantasy
poetry & art
the past

Blatner

Soul

Ego   World

Adam Blatner has it that
the ego mediates soul & world
but I think just as likely
Soul mediates ego-self & world
or that each of the 3 terms
mediates the others
Link to pre-reflective
situated body-self
in the context of
existentialism.

Our imaginative & creative soul-making
is mediated by the conventional ego
& our conventional ego is developed &
modified by creative soul-making.

79

The Sacred Mirror: Non-dual Wisdom and Psychotherapy

In this short essay I examine the claim of the authors, John J. Prendergast, Peter Fenner, and Sheila Krystal, of the book "The Sacred Mirror: Non-dual Wisdom and Psychotherapy" that the awakening of what they call non-dual awareness can help therapists of all sorts in their therapeutic practice. The authors themselves come from both the "therapeutic" & the "spiritual" disciplines & use the general non-denominational term "non-dual" which draws from the spiritual traditions of Buddhism & Hinduism among others. As such, I take this non-dual state to be essentially the same as the mystical state of being, the awareness of universal mind, spiritual awareness, or enlightenment. I will investigate the conceptual understanding of this "awakened" state of mind from an anthropological & sociological orientation while keeping in mind that it is experienced as a psychological or spiritual state of being.

I should also say that I have been associated with the Kutenai Art Therapy Institute since its inception 10 years ago & that I have thus, although I am not a therapist, come to know in a very intimate way, the nature of therapeutic presence. As well, I am familiar with a great number of theoretical elements including the basic psychoanalytic framework and the phenomenological approach to research. But above & beyond these elements, I am aware of the truly incredible power of the creative process itself in the work of therapeutic healing.

By stripping away the overt "spiritual" dimension of "The Sacred Mirror" which no doubt offers the general benefits of the religious worldview & implicit elements of "faith healing," I hope to discover if there are any practical techniques or a way of being that is actually useful to contemporary therapeutic practice. To do this I will initially have to briefly lay out the general historical outline of the context of religion, mysticism, magic, and therapeutics. In the discussion of the historical beginnings of these elements of the spiritual domain I will draw primarily upon Daniel Lawrence O'Keefe's wonderful book: "Stolen Lightning: The social Theory of Magic." Before going into that discussion another very important distinction must be made: that between ideology & the experience itself. Thus, there is a distinction to be maintained between the ideology and social reality of mysticism or "non-dual" awareness on one hand & the inner experience, whether it is purely psychological or essentially "spiritual," on the other.

I admit at the outset that I have no real way of knowing the difference between "psychological" & "spiritual" but I am aware that those involved in the spiritual disciplines may be able to see a distinction where I cannot. I suppose that the distinction is likely to be similar to that made between the "social" & "spiritual" itself. As far as I know, the only possible kind of judgment regarding the dichotomy is an intuitive one.

In any event, I use the occasion of commenting upon this book to explore a host of subjects that simply "come up" in the course of thinking about the issues. If the reader is not up to a brief ramble into the foundations of sociological & historical critique, or willing to detour into discussions regarding therapy & mysticism in general, he or she can skip ahead to the "End Note" & get my last thoughts on the subject, which is, I think "The book." Or not. Check it out.

Mysticism

As I stated earlier, "non dual awareness" appears to be a sort of generic term for the awakened spiritual, mystical, or enlightened state of being. Of course, mysticism in general seems to partake of elements from both religion & magic. I won't go into any detail at this point but simply give a list of general characteristics taken from the book "Mysticism: A study and an Anthology" by F.C. Happold.

1) A mystic state is "ineffable," that is it defies expression in ordinary logical terms. It thus resembles a state of feeling rather than a state of intellect. In fact, all sacred states in their early manifestations are couched in extremely vague language.
2) But a mystic state is also a state of knowledge, or gnosis. It conveys a great sense of certainty & possesses a "noetic" quality.
3) In general, mystic states can't be sustained for long. They seem transient except in exceptional cases when an individual mystic is understood to dwell in the illumined state indefinitely.
4) Mystic states have a passive quality, a sense that they are "given" not seized or attained by the strength of will
5) There is a consciousness of the Oneness of everything. There is a unity between the one & the many, the perceiver & the perceived, subject & object. All dualities are resolved in the unified state.
6) There is a sense of timelessness, a sense that one dwells in eternity, or in the eternal "now" rather than in the fleeting historical dimension.

From the above characteristics, the ordinary "dualistic world" can easily be recognized as the world of conceptual thought, characterized by uncertainty & ambiguity rather than by clarity. It is the world of multiplicity, the dualistic categories of language, the world of activity & action, time & history. It is the world of subjects & objects, the world of reflective consciousness. But perhaps above all, with regard to awakening to the mystical state of being or "non-dual awareness," it is the world of the separate self or ego. Certainly, this world, in the Buddhist view at least, is characterized by pain & suffering. In general, with the awakening of the mystic state of being, the ego or separate self somehow disappears or is annihilated & merged with the oneness of all things, with the ontological ground of being, with the "void," with the cosmos, God or spirit. It appears that the mystic journey, as a social form, actually recapitulates the magician's initiation, the main element of which is the sacrifice of the individual self in order to gain the sacred self.

A Little History: Religion & Magic

As the authors note, the term "non-dualism" is an odd term that few are familiar with and thus they briefly define it in their introduction. Because of the ineffability of the non-dual state, they define it in terms of what it is not. Unfortunately most people in the therapeutic professions as well as many who are engaged in the vast upsurge of spiritual practices today remain unaware of the long tradition of scholarly investigation, from the position of believers as well as non-believers, of the fascinating topics of religion, mysticism and magic. Thus, unfortunately again, in order to make any real sort of critical examination of this material I will have to define some basic terms. Let me say right at the outset that these terms will sometimes be quite different than what we ordinarily expect from our "everyday" understanding of the world. Just as the philosophers of the sacred need to somehow get underneath or beyond the ordinary frame of conceptual mind, if we hope to begin from the phenomenological substrate, as I do, we must somehow set aside our ordinary understandings & the way things seem to simply appear before us, immediately understandable, as if by magic. I suppose I also should say that this phenomenological understanding & historical (sociological) point of view would tend to be somewhat different than the religious or mystical point of view. It is not, however, a question of arriving at a "scientific" understanding as opposed to a "spiritual" one. Rather I aim to get at an "experiential" understanding rooted in historical, psychological, & social reality.

Let me begin with the general context, then. I take my general orientation toward the different aspects of this cluster of subjects (religion, mysticism, magic) from the long tradition of French sociology whose central figures are Emil Durkheim & Marcel Mauss. From this school I take religion to be essentially the "projection" of the social. The realm of the sacred is thus a symbolic image of the structure of the society we are examining. It is the symbolism of the collective. In contemporary times, we have pretty much forgotten the origin of our imagery of the sacred, but, if we go back to the very beginning for a moment, I hope this concept will become clear. It should also be clear from the beginning that the "experience" of the sacred is not at issue; this powerful experience has apparently been present from the very beginning of history & continues to be present in consciousness to the present day. It will no doubt continue far into the future. So, while the "experience" is not at issue, its origins & interpretation are. Thus, we will be involved with the phenomenology as well as the hermeneutics of the situation.

Concerning the beginnings of religion, there are as many theories as there are writers. Luckily for us, I hope, we don't really have to accept any one theory to understand the notion of religion as the symbolism of the collective. I myself like the theory that religion began with the concept of "mana" -- a sort of inkling of primitive man's own personal power, something like charisma. Wherever such a sense of personal power ultimately came from, (the sky, the mountains, the sea, the beating of one's own heart, the breath, light,) it manifested itself as the social individual's awareness of some sort of "transcendental power." Whatever the beginnings though, we do have record of the historical development of society from the individual in a very small group to the development of clans characterized by various animal & other totems and with different initiation & sacrificial rites. The "mana" theory sees this development as the "generalization" of mana. In the beginning, we have the simple symbolization of mana in sacred "objects." Later we have the development of a symbolic vocabulary & what will become the central elements of religion: initiation & sacrifice.

In any event, in the eventual historical amalgamation of these totemic clans and the blending of their different elements we have the development of a generalized "religion." This religion, then, codified the general relations of the various social groups, their separate magical institutions, their sacrifices, their identities, ideas, gods & demons, their myths of origin, & so on. In this sense, then, we can say that religion is the symbolic projection of the social. The developing complexity of the social symbolic of the sacred leads to the formalized practices of religion proper. No matter exactly what these symbols refer to in the consciousness of different peoples over time, they are socially developed & codified. Over hundreds of years, these social symbols come more & more to be reified, and in their ideological or theological form come to appear as "naturally" sacred elements such as gods or "God," the "Void," various deities as in the Buddhist & Hindu religions, Christ in Christianity & so forth. To say that they appear "natural" is to say that we have forgotten the diverse social & cultural contexts as well as the individual experiences that precipitated them.

Magic

But let's move on now to a rough definition of "magic" as the context in which various yoga and meditation practices began. I don't think it really matters which came first, religion or magic, but it does matter that we have at least a general sense of their historical & practical relationship. Again, we need to go back to early beginnings in small scale pre-literate societies. Magicians, for example, the Magi in Christianity, shamans in a great number of countries, magicians or sorcerers in Africa, medicine men in America & so on, practiced magic in those societies. Witches, warlocks & alchemists also practiced various types of magic. I will characterize magic here in the way Daniel Lawrence O'Keefe does. I should perhaps say here that the nature of "magic" & its relationship to religion, the mystical, spiritual experience in general & so on has been & continues to be disputed. One, perhaps trivial, aspect of this is that "magic" continues to be a very loaded term today, & very often those involved in more or less secular practice of yoga or meditation object to their practice as "magical." All I can say to this is that we attempt to get as objective an understanding as possible & recognize that at least initially we are dealing with the "historical" development of these practices. On the surface, it would seem that there is a contradiction between "truth" which we all seem to want & "magic" which has to do with "illusion." In the sense I wish to speak of it, however, magic is a concrete social practice with concrete psychological & perhaps spiritual effects. This social notion of "magic" concerns "power" and the individual.

If religion is the projection of the social, then magic is a protest against its conventions, conventions that tend to keep the individual in a subservient place. Magic, in this sense, is social action & aims to accomplish something for its myriad of clients. While empowering the individual & protecting him or her from magical attacks & the sometimes overpowering messages of conventional religion, it ultimately aims at some sort of social change. That is to say, it aims at some change in official religion, given that religion, in those early days, was the main arbiter of social & political reality. Initially however, magical practice appropriates sacred imagery such as gods, demons, spells, initiation rites, etc. from religion & uses the power of these symbols for its own purposes. Magicians mounted magical attacks on other magicians and used spells & rites to protect the individuals who hired them. They also engaged in divination and magical healing while also utilizing yoga & meditation magic for various psychological and social purposes.

O'Keefe gives us seven types of magic. Obviously, the field could be divided up in a great many different ways but these seem useful enough. They are:

1) Religious magic (exorcisms etc.),
2) The occult sciences & the Theosophies (I Ching, astrology, kabala)
3) Medical Magic,
4) Magic Cults & Sects (charismatic protest cults etc.)
5) Ceremonial Magic, (Magic for the collectivity, hunting magic)
6) Black Magic, (witchcraft, sorcery & so on)
7) The Paranormal (ESP, altered states of consciousness, UFOs, etc).

These various more or less "official" magical groups are overlapping and sometimes quite ambiguous, but they all aim to harness "power" in some sense & use it for specific practical ends like the banishment of ghosts, healing, enhancing the self, & so forth. But there is also a weaker sense of magic that we use in everyday speech. Things happen "like magic." Children at a very young age engage in "magical thinking." Money appears to operate in some ways like magic – secretly & from a distance. Freud understood neurotic symptoms as magical modes of defense against "id" urges and against overpowering super-ego messages coming from parents and/or from such institutions such as religion. But our definition will stand simply as: a) that sort of social action that utilizes the sacred imagery of religion in order to accomplish its own purposes, & b) the central purpose of magic is to protect or enhance the ego or the "self" of the client or person utilizing the magical method. We need to keep in mind that in these long ago times, the ego or self of primitive peoples was considered a weak and vague sort of entity. Only in small ways did the early ego rise up out of the collective.

Of course, our central concern here is with medical magic or therapeutic magic. As such, we are interested in the "presence" of the magician or therapist & "meditation magic" as well as the process of "awakening" which characterizes the symbolism of the "non-dual state" of being. The authors of "The Sacred Mirror" argue that this process of "awakening" can serve to aid individuals in their struggle against personal pain & the problems in their lives. Our understanding of "magic" continues to be useful insomuch as therapeutic magic continues to be involved with the healing & enhancement of the individual self, however that self might be historically developed.

Before going on to look at the application of non-dual wisdom to psychotherapy, we need one more sociological concept. This is the concept of "social construction." This basic concept posits that the social world & indeed our whole idea of the nature of the world is socially constructed of metaphors or symbols. These symbolic constructions organize & guide behaviour. As such, all aspects of the social world, including the self, all social institutions, including those of religion & therapy only appear to be fixed or "natural." In fact, they are malleable & very changeable as can easily be seen in any cross-cultural study of social institutions. With regard to the social construction of the self we need only say here that our development takes place over a great number of years in the context of social forms & other people. In order to become a person in society we must learn the language, learn how to behave in different situations, learn how to be a "good" person (or not), learn how to work & to play, take on our identity (with regard to gender, ethnicity, sexual preference etc.) & take on a role or actually many roles. There are a great many developmental theories regarding exactly how this social construction takes place (& how problems come up) but for now all we need to be aware of is the general idea that our inner "psychological" life, including our sense of self, is as socially constructed as outer social life. The general spiritual or mystical understanding of this idea is that our ordinary life is "illusory." This concept, at least, is shared by sociology & mysticism alike.

But to get back to our discussion of "social magic," let's briefly look at the way in which O'Keefe believes that it works. According to him, there are four parts to the process:

1) The loosening of the conventional frame of symbolic consciousness,
2) The creation of a light trance occasioned by this loosening,
3) The patterning of this light trance by a number of "magical" suggestions, setting up an expectation for certain things to occur,
4) And that this patterning by way of suggestion involves an essential agreement between practitioners & clients, an agreement to agree.

Let's be clear about one thing from the beginning. The conventional mind-set or frame of consensual awareness that is our ordinary consciousness is an extremely fragile thing. This goes for our self-concept as well. The way the world appears & our investment in a particular kind of self change often as we apparently go into & out of light trances on a non-stop basis. Lack of sleep, repetitive music, the seductions of advertising, & so on, continually change our state of being. With even quite brief stints of sensory deprivation, our sense of reality deteriorates dramatically. And without pretty constant reality maintenance or upkeep, mostly through conversation with other humans, we slip off into altered states. Most of these changes in our fragile sense of world & self are random & un-programmed, but, with the processes of magical healing, we are dealing with a controlled social & psychological system. And to control the situation, symbols, as always, are central.

We also need to remember that this definition comes out of a historical context. When magic "works" in small pre-literate societies, it works precisely because of the expectations set up with the individuals involved. These individuals & their expectations are deeply embedded in a social context that is organized by a belief system, including institutions and religious & magical symbolism so that at all levels these expectations "make sense" and are believed to be "true." In short, these expectations are understood to be an intrinsic part of "reality" & the way reality is known to work. In this sort of context, there is a sense that magic is "automatic." Certain incantations are made, certain recipes are followed, & the individuals as well as the community have a common understanding of the causal relationship between symbols & physical reality. There have been several studies that demonstrate that people can be killed by spells. It is their expectation of death that kills them.

"Social" magic in the sense that we have been speaking of is obviously both "psychological" & "social." Individual psychology is deeply embedded in a particular social reality; society is "inside" the person in a clear & powerful way. At the risk of being overly repetitive, we also note that this "society" that is "inside" the person is "symbolic." It is a symbolic structure or a system of interlocking structures. It is obvious that our contemporary social life & identity are quite different than that found in the distant past. Today we have a complex mixture of many different beliefs & institutions. The central position of religion as arbiter of reality has been pretty much taken over by science. This social complexity is still "inside" us but just because it is "complex," our contemporary "self" is forced to choose between beliefs & behaviours & indeed have its own interior moral sense. In earlier identity in the context of simple small-scale society, this moral faculty could remain essentially "outside" the person as a set of religious or magical moral principles. One was guided by external "rules," stories or mythology whereas today one is exhorted to look inside oneself for guidance. In short, there has been an historical social development from the time in which the "person" was embedded in the context & mythology of small-scale pre-literate society to the so-called "rational individual" in contemporary society. This historical development means that there is a great deal of difference between the "interior life" or psychology of earlier persons & us. We should expect that this difference in interior life will mean there is a difference in the way "therapeutic magic" actually works insomuch as it is concerned with "healing" "psychological" or "interior" wounds.

Therapeutic Magic

Thinking of O'Keefe's notion of the process by which social magic operates, we can recognize that the loosening of the client's conventional frame of beliefs about the world & self begins the moment he or she enters into the realm of therapy. It is generally understood that in therapy one will, with the aid of the therapist, work towards changing one's self, or at least solving a few problems. Going further, a very common understanding in the therapeutic community is that this work of change involves the "undoing" or untangling of one's old beliefs & the creation of new beliefs. This is perhaps most obvious in the context of the therapeutic enhancement of self-esteem. The first very strong expectation of the client with regards to the therapy focuses on positive personal change & the enhancement of the self. This idea of psychological change is perhaps the primary metaphor of "therapeutic healing." It is only a short step from the notion of general "psychological change" to the notion that this change essentially concerns the symbolism of consciousness. What is to be changed are my "symbolic" ideas about myself, my place in the world, the nature of reality & so forth. Consciousness is a symbolic structure, & such belief in the ability to transform oneself through changing of the symbolism of self pre-supposes the general notion of the social construction of self.

The initial loosening of the conventional frame of symbolic consciousness occasioned by the act of stepping from the ordinary world into the world of therapy with its expectation of change begins, almost automatically, to create that light trance which is the second step of the magical process. In therapy, one enters into a special relationship with a powerful person. The therapist is contracted to help the client change him or herself, and to protect & enhance the self of the client. The therapeutic "situation" is thus imbued with the "aura" of medical science combined with the still lingering aura of the "spiritual" or "magical" origins of psychology. To say, as we have, that the early self was formed in the context of society, primarily organized by religious symbology, means that the very symbolism of the interior life was that of religion, the movement of spirits, demons & other magical entities into & out of the body & the mind.) Our contemporary therapeutics, then, partake of both of these worlds – the "magical" world of religious imagery & the "scientific" world of rational medicine. To step, then, from the ordinary world into this "special" therapeutic place is to enter into a space that is doubly blessed, a world at once magical & scientific. One is, in a sense, instantly disoriented.

What exactly is a "light trance?" I type these magic symbols: www.google.ca "Click" & I type in "dictionary," click on dictionary.com & type in "trance." I first find the following concerning this "altered state" from general dictionaries:
1) A hypnotic, cataleptic, or ecstatic state.
2) Detachment from one's physical surroundings, as in contemplation or daydreaming.

3) A semiconscious state, as between sleeping and waking; a daze

Then from *The American Heritage® Stedman's Medical Dictionary*
1) A state of partly suspended animation or inability to function
2) A somnolent state (as of deep hypnosis) characterized by limited sensory and motor contact with one's surroundings and subsequent lack of recall

& from *Merriam-Webster's Medical Dictionary*
1) Psychological state induced by (or as if induced by) a magical incantation [syn: enchantment, spell]
2) a state of mind in which consciousness is fragile and voluntary action is poor or missing; a state resembling deep sleep
3) as a verb: attract; cause to be enamored; "She captured all the men's hearts"

& from *WordNet ® 2.0*

(Gr. ekstasis, from which the word "ecstasy" is derived) denotes the state of one who is "out of himself." Such were the trances of Peter and Paul, Acts 10:10; 11:5; 22:17, ecstasies, "a preternatural, absorbed state of mind preparing for the reception of the vision," (comp. 2 Cor. 12:1-4).

It's certainly easy enough to see that a "light trance" is just the thing for the therapeutic situation & its expectation of psychological change. In this altered state of consciousness, one is "detached" from one's physical surroundings and the hold of one's ordinary beliefs. The very structure of one's mind & sense of self is loosened; one is suspended as it were between one reality & another, between waking & sleeping, between one's old self & one's new self. To add the idea of hypnosis & then ecstasy is again very interesting in terms of our therapeutic context. Hypnosis is, of course, often used in the therapeutic situation today & we won't really deal with that most obvious way of creating the therapeutic trance. And we should not expect, at least in the beginning, that therapeutic clients would enter into ecstasy, (& thus be "out" of themselves) although later on one might expect some euphoric moments. All this is interesting enough but then to hear that "trance" is a state induced by or "as if" induced by "a magical incantation" is quite wonderful.

We might ask as to exactly what the therapist's magical incantation is or we might, as I do, argue that this light trance is almost automatically induced by the crossing of the threshold into the magical-scientific world of therapy & the entering into the special relationship with an authority on inner change. In this context, one is disoriented & then re-oriented towards change. The verbal form of the noun trance -- "to entrance" is also very interesting in the therapeutic context. There are certainly a great number of charismatic healers around.

The next step in the process of therapeutic magic is to proceed with the "patterning" of this trance with certain "magical" expectations of change. These new patterns or symbolic structures or metaphors may be "discovered" or "created" in any number of ways. The early history of the client & an "understanding" of the causes for different problems are given different weights in different therapeutic orientations. In some, there is almost no "depth" work at all; in others, there is almost nothing but. For our purposes here, it doesn't really matter how it is arrived at but only that some new pattern is arrived at. When we think of "magic" we think of a certain "automatic" functioning, but in this case the magic of therapy may just as well involve a rational understanding of our personal psychology, but it may not. There are certainly a great number of therapists & clients who don't really care how or why change occurs; they only care that it does occur. One's psyche may be "fixed" in the same way one's car is.

The fourth essential ingredient of the magical process outlined by O'Keefe – the agreement to agree – is, one might say, the therapeutic contract: the agreement that client & therapist will work together for the good of the client. In this process, there will be a certain suspension of contradictory beliefs. This agreement might be simply that the client agrees to accept the work & authority of the therapist or the agreement might be that the client himself will dictate directions taken or any other sort of agreement.

I suppose that this "magical" expectation for change is essentially the same for the client of therapy as for the student who begins to study some spiritual discipline with a guru. We enter both under the sign of "transformation." There is a sense of "initiation" in all of this; the client or student is initiated into a different way of understanding the world, into new knowledge & a new way of being. There is also an element of sacrifice. The individual self will be sacrificed for a unitary vision of health & clarity. The implicit understanding of sacrifice is that something one loves will have to be given up. One will have to, at the very least, forgo some pleasure.

Back to the Book

It is my experience that any kind of useful conversation can go on only if one has a clear understanding of the words one is using. It would have perhaps been good if the authors of the book "The Sacred Mirror" had taken the time to give more precise definitions or at least imparted a little more of their own general understanding of the various aspects of non-dualism. I expect they will be somewhat different than mine. As it is, I am afraid they do what many authors of the do-it-yourself variety do: assume that somehow, in some magical way, everybody will know just what it is they are talking about. In fact, they seem to simply accept the symbolic language of the taken-for-granted world. Given that the authors are going to have much to say about the nature of thought & the trap of mental constructions it would have been useful if they had attempted to go a little beyond the ordinary assumptions of "spiritual symbolism."

In fact, it would seem that the authors of "The Sacred Mirror" are for the most part talking to the converted, those people who will readily accept general "spiritual" language as "natural," that is, readily understood to refer to natural entities or known spiritual states. Beyond this reification of "sacred" symbols & because the mystic state of awareness that they generalize as "non-dualistic" is essentially ineffable, they only give us an image of what it is not, as opposed to what it is. Thomas Merton in his essay on Zen tells us that this tactic is quite common with explanations of the Zen experience. The tactic is also linked to a teaching technique that aims at truth only in the negative because any positive understanding will be "wrong" insomuch as the enlightened or "non-dual" state consciousness is "beyond" the reflective mind & its conceptual understandings.

Where to start? Well, let's look more specifically at what John J. Prendergast has to say in his introduction.

> Non-duality is a rather curious and uncommon word that so far has been used by a relatively small number of scholars and teachers. It derives from the Sanskrit word advaita, which means "not-two." Non-dual wisdom refers to the understanding and direct experience of a fundamental consciousness that underlies the apparent distinction between

perceiver and perceived. From the non-dual perspective, the split between self and other is a purely mental construct. This understanding, rooted in the direct experience of countless sages through millennia, is at the heart of Hindu Vedanta, most schools of Buddhism, and Taoism, and mystical Christianity, Judaism, and Islam. Non-duality is a particularly elegant and clear formulation, since it describes reality in terms of what it is not (unsplit, undivided) rather than what it is.

Although hardly complete this gives us several ideas that accord well with the general model of mysticism: the notion that the dualisms or mental constructs of ordinary mind are not split but are unified in non-dual awareness & also the notion of the necessity of "direct experience." For the rest, he gives us the historical authority for the use of the term. This notion of the distinction between self & other & that between the perceiver & perceived as merely "mental constructs" falls under this heading of "non-dual" but for anyone not familiar with this sort of apparently non-rational idea, it is apt to be confusing. At various times, it certainly has been for me. For myself, I do have to say that I continue to find the use of the word "merely" to characterize the process of thought & the creation of "mental constructs" as somewhat irritating. If taken literally, it seems to denigrate the finest attribute of the evolutionary process, the ability to think, while at the same time valuing a state of mind that is apparently incapable of making simple distinctions such as that between the self & other. Even animals seem to be able to make this distinction. What can be meant by it then? Well, I'll try to leave my irritability aside for the moment & consider the meaning of another term for non-dual awareness used by the authors, the term "unconditioned mind."

I have a sort of confession to make. I'm not sure that this is the right place but I have to make it somewhere. Between the first writing of this essay & the present re-write, I read an essay on Zen by Thomas Merton which was very useful in deciphering the apparently irrational language used in the description of Zen awareness. In my first version of this essay, I concentrated on attempting to understand this non-dual state of awareness as a "psychological" state, one that, to my mind, had a number of problems with it. The first part of the essay up until this point has remained substantially the same but in the earlier version I'm afraid my irritability got the better of me here & there, especially in the later parts of the essay. With my greater understanding after reading the Merton essay, I hope that this irritability has less a grip on me & I am able to better concentrate on the illumination of the subject. I believe that the more or less mystical/magical ideas put forth by the authors do have some problems but the book is no longer in my hands so I can't quite be sure that the problems are not with my own interpretation.

In any event, I do have a lingering irritation with what I perceive to be the grandiosity of the language & symbolism often used by those "of the mystical persuasion" although I find that I have no trouble at all with Merton's characterization of the Zen state of awareness "satori" as an "ontological intuition." Although this intuition is of a very grand state of affairs, the apprehension of the "void" itself, I do not find the usage to be too "full of itself." In his essay, Merton discussed the distinction between two schools of Zen, the primary one to his mind being the one I have mentioned, the other being the "mirror wiping" school which is characterized as a sort of covert aggrandizement of the self because the practitioner (& that entire school) has made the mistake of thinking that the image of enlightenment & all that it means can be "held" in the mind. The mistake is in thinking that the mirror of consciousness can be wiped clean (the mind can be "purified") & be thus able to perceive the true nature of the world.

Those engaged in this type of Zen understand "enlightenment" as a "psychological" rather than "spiritual" state & have been fooled by their engagement with the aesthetic elements of meditation

& the ascetic life style in general. As I said earlier, there is, from my own orientation, no real way to tell the difference between a psychological & a spiritual state of being, but I can catch a glimpse of what Merton is talking about when he makes the distinction between the self which sees itself as purified & thus able to hold the consciousness of the enlightened world, & the self which is dissolved in the enlightened world which is everywhere around one. It has to do with the location of "power" (under whatever name – all-encompassing love, void or divinity) either "inside" the self or "outside" the self. The image from inside is a "calm" aesthetic & psychological state while that consciousness which subsumes the smaller self inside its own self is the true unity of enlightenment.

I had thought we would look at the notion of "unconditioned mind." Again, at first look, it would appear that such a thing as an unconditioned mind is impossible, at minimum a magical thing. How could there be a mode of consciousness that is unconditioned by any mere "mental construct" one that does not distinguish between the self & other, subject & object? Perhaps at the very beginning of life, a child may possess such a thing, but if this is a state to be sought after by the adult, & a therapist at that, the authors cannot mean this sort of psychological regression. How can a mature adult mind be unconditioned, or, as characterized elsewhere, "empty," or "formless"? One of the important things I got from Merton regarding this language usage is that it is important to keep in mind that we are not in the same domain as "science" or even "philosophy." More often than not, we are in the domain of poetry. This, of course, does not mean we cannot speak of "truth," but simply that we are speaking of a different sort of truth than either science or philosophy. We may also, of course, refer such language to a phenomenological understanding of the contents of consciousness.

Anyway, looking no further than the net to which my computer is attached I find that the unconditioned mind, at least from the Zen orientation, is the mind when it awakens & opens, when it "questions." As Zen master Soeng Hyang has it:

> This moment of questioning, however fleeting it is, is a manifestation of a pure and unconditioned mind. In this moment all filters of pre-conception and pre-judgment are taken away and only pure questioning remains." (Net: A Kong-An is Nothing Other than the present Moment).

The mind is not "literally" unconditioned, by anything at all, but metaphorically unconditioned by "pre-conceptions" & pre-judgments. The "unconditioned mind, then, is simply the "open" mind, the mind that leaves the question of "what is going on" open. This is essentially the state of mind aimed at by phenomenological research, the mind open to the world & to wonder.

Or again, we have Sandra Hammond (2002) tell us that:

> When the mind is quiet, something amazing happens: we can experience with clarity the spontaneous arising and passing of body/mind activity. Once we experience this spontaneity of mental and physical activity there is no doubt about the truth of Dharma: we know it for ourselves.... To maintain resistance to the truth we keep ourselves distracted, mentally over- stimulated and emotionally agitated by life and by what is arising as we practice.

She goes on to say:

Without stillness, it is hard to perceive the spontaneity of experiences and so we are tricked into thinking we are in charge, making it all happen. But as we cultivate and strengthen stillness, we develop a mind that does not move around all the time, that does not follow each object as if we were bloodhounds hard at work. A trained mind can sit back, so to speak, and open with relaxation and ease to its own basic nature of unafflicted, unobscured spaciousness.

For this teacher, the unconditioned mind is the trained mind that has attained to a certain "stillness" and is not always agitated or "at work." In addition, this "training" is not so much to create a certain sort of mind space but rather to discover or re-discover its own "basic nature" of "unafflicted, unobscured spaciousness." Without going into it too deeply, we can assume that the untrained mind is "afflicted" with its need to make judgments, its agitation, its business, its need to reflect upon its "objects" & so forth.

In general, the authors of "The Sacred Mirror" assert the importance for therapist & client of "awakening" to "unconditioned mind." They refer to being in contact with unconditioned mind as "presence." Prendergast tells us of the primary & secondary impacts of awakening. Presence is the primary impact & is expressed by an ease of being, unpretentiousness, lucidity, & joy. In addition, the therapist is no longer restricted to the role of therapist or even to the role of being a person. Problems & problem solvers apparently magically disappear & one has the enhanced capacity for acceptance, & unconditional love. Allowing the clients to come close to Presence facilitates their transformation. I'm not quite sure where the notion of "unconditional love" comes in but I take it as characterizing the state of awakeness itself – this "is" the void, the all, the foundation.

I am not at all sure how the therapist is to gain this "ease of being, unpretentiousness, lucidity & joy." This seems to go far beyond the simple notion of the mind being unconditioned by pre-conceptions or the "stillness" to be gained by calming the mind in meditation practice.

These attributes are quite obviously "magical" in the weak sense of the term as, without intervention, they apparently accrue, according to the authors, in a natural process as one awakens into non dual awareness.

Although this state of consciousness supposedly underlies ordinary consciousness & is more "fundamental" than ordinary consciousness, it is easy to imagine these spontaneously appearing attributes as "suggestions" that pattern a light trance occasioned by the loosening of the conventional cultural frame. There can be no doubt that the clarity of a trained mind, no longer driven by compulsion or under the illusion that "reality" is a fixed thing, will have an easier time of it than the continually anxious mind continually seeking answers to the myriad of problems that beset us. The possessor of such a mind will certainly find it easier to be happy, accept the way things are, and so on. But to say that the light trance or slightly altered state of consciousness that is occasioned by the loosening of the conventional ties on the mind will "automatically" lead to these things would seem to be an overvaluing of the altered state of consciousness itself. From this orientation, it is not so much the state of consciousness itself but the suggestibility of this state that is important.

When one is in an altered state of consciousness with the ties to conventional reality loosened & with the expectation of change for the better, nothing is quite so clear as that there will be a tendency for change to happen in this direction, especially if we are in the presence of an "authority" whom we have come to trust. This is, you will recognize, precisely the general context of "magical healing" practice as described earlier.

But perhaps we have gone forward too quickly or with not enough thought. In particular, does this notion of the "patterning" of a light trance do justice to the very ancient notion of enlightenment or awakened consciousness that lies on the other side of all duality? Perhaps, perhaps not! Or do we have that sort of "mirror wiping" Zen that is practiced by those who do not understand the true path of Zen. Merton argues that when the enlightened state of mind is itself held in the mind & capable of being reflected upon, then we are not practicing Zen properly, because this is simply a subterfuge of the self, a way of aggrandizing the self with the holding of this notion of the perfected self in mind.

Chapter two of "The Sacred Mirror" is by Peter Fenner &, not surprisingly, we have some playfulness with the paradoxical nature of the mystic program. Thus Fenner tells us that what makes non-dual therapy unique is that it doesn't exist! Soon enough, however, he goes on to outline the structure of this nonexistent therapy.

Non-dual therapy begins with the introduction of the concept of the unconditioned mind and is discussed in the context of psychotherapy. This mental state of supreme awareness is understood to be the "ultimate medicine" because it is beyond suffering. Soon we learn that we have a natural instinct toward this mental state that reconditions thought patterns and emotions & brings us into the here and now. This awareness or spiritual force works in us towards bringing us into this state. This idea is one that is common to a number of spiritual paths; certainly, it is present in Christianity. In addition, Jungian psychology has a similar idea that the archetypes (spiritual entities themselves) guide us towards the recognition of our true selves. Fenner goes on to tell us that this mind state is comprised of the union of love and wisdom, love being exactly the capacity to identify while the capacity to undo this identification is wisdom. Both are understood to arise simultaneously and without conflict.

It should be clear by this point that the book has very little to do with "therapy" per se. Rather it argues that this mystical state of being termed non-dual awareness is "therapeutic" on its own. From the anthropology of religion, we learn that this idea is a very common one in the domain of the sacred. The sacred is by definition "wholeness" & to bring our "partial" or "injured" being into contact with cosmic wholeness is to make ourselves "whole" again, unified & beyond separation from god or the void.

Nonetheless, we have a number of interesting ideas here. To follow the notion of "patterned trance," a purely psychological idea, we can see that therapy involves the setting up of expectations of a magical transformation to a state of mind & being that is beyond suffering. Who doesn't want this! This is an enhancement of the self indeed! And what's more, it seems lucky that we already have some sort of inborn instinct to move towards this natural healthy state. I don't believe that this means we need to do nothing to advance towards this state. There is still need for discipline but it is not the discipline that will accomplish all. But let us back up for a moment: this notion that the client has all the knowledge needed for his or her own healing & that, in fact, we do instinctively move towards health is a fairly common notion in the contemporary therapeutic profession generally. It is certainly an idea at the centre of the human potential moment. But, in order to help us on our way, there is also a very strong patterning of our expectations replete with the symbolism of the unconditioned mind. We also have a piece of real practical understanding: the notion of love & wisdom conjoined as the process of identification & dis-identification. I personally was very happy to read of this simply because I tend to get very uneasy when the enlightened mind appears to be nothing so much as a calm, non-impassioned "impersonal" mind. This may be my own bias, but the prospect of a generalized impersonal love doesn't really grab me. This conjunction of love & wisdom points towards the flexibility & spontaneity of the healthy self that can attach & detach with equal ease. The image of the dual world as something only to be defended against or escaped from seems to miss the mark.

Also interesting is the notion that certain attributes of non-dual awareness work like "clockwork." They are automatic. We learn that one "creates space around a problem" & it just naturally dissipates. This effect certainly seems magic. If one does not "feed" a problem (or a thought-spirit), after a while it just starves. Or alternatively, if not paid attention to the vegetation of one's mind just withers away. The interesting notion here is that there is no need to understand the nature of any given problem just as there is no need to understand why it arises. The only important fact is that it is there & you don't want it there. Something, or someone, is getting in the way of wants.

I am uncomfortably aware that I am erecting alternate explanations for the nature of "enlightenment." I like very much the ontological intuition proposed by Merton. I am uncomfortable with this simple psychological notion. I need to be clear that there is a difference between the one & the other. The mirror wiping – the cleansing of the mind – the emptying of the mind – learning to control it but the subterfuge of continuing to hang onto the subject-object distinction. Why do I need the notion of "patterning?" This is already a fine notion – the notion of "cleansing" & ordering the mind – the focus upon charity or love. What is the relationship of this notion of the social construction & social construction via "patterning" – or are they both psychological "patterning" – cleansing – controlling, reflecting upon etc. Yes. I like this. This is the process of patterning, training the mind. But it is not the spiritual intuition. This is spiritual ambition. This must make the assumption that "god" is everywhere & not a development of individual minds. That is to say, it is a spiritual intuition. This assumes as a first principle that the "power" is located out there in the world & that the individual mind is but a small reflection of it. The mind must be subsumed in the larger cosmic mind. But, of course, this also can be a patterning.

This process of simply not bringing awareness to an issue has certain similarities to classic Freudian repression. One hopes that if one just doesn't think about a thing it will simply go away. And as noted, in many cases it does just go away. But, I wonder, if there actually is an underlying cause for the symbolic structure in the first place, what is to stop it from re-occurring? Actually, nothing. And it will return. This is exactly the "repetition compulsion" except, of course, if one can stay loosened from fixed concepts and persist in non-dual awareness –which is to say "openness" of mind. Most of the time, one presumably just continues this attitude of not paying any attention. The acquisition of this state of mind (the ultimate medicine) means in essence that one practices continual healing. In general, this means for most people, an ongoing meditation practice. Also I assume it means for many if not most, an ongoing conferring with one's guru or therapist. One's knowledge about the nature of human problems or the nature of one's own problems does not advance in any way; the knowledge that does advance is knowledge of the defensive pattern of non-dual awareness. In fact, the acquisition of this state of awareness is precisely an ego defense posture that keeps unwanted "id" desires, nasty super-ego messages, etc. out of consciousness. One goes beyond the conceptual mind by ignoring it.

I am well aware that the scenario that I have proposed is probably a misunderstanding of the "true" nature of the non-dual state & I have omitted the "spiritual" niceties concerning eternal love, the development of peace & serenity, openness, & so forth. I have done so because it is by no means easy to see exactly how one avoids such mistakes. The stakes appear to be very high indeed, & who does not want to enhance the self by attaining all of the suggested "powers" that seem so available? Again I am aware that the attributes of this kind of awareness are not usually these days designated as such but that is in fact how they function. A person becomes more serene, more able to calmly order their life, avoid suffering, make good judgments and so on, all by engaging in a magical something which is actually nothing & in fact one hasn't really got to do anything anyway because it all happens automatically. That is if you associate with the right people.

The fact is that this type of magical healing was born in the context of small cultural groupings with strong religious symbolism & generally fairly weak egos. I mean the clients have the weak egos. The medical magicians & others who have died to themselves & awoken to new being have very strong egos indeed. This is true whether or not they call them egos or some other designation and whether they consider themselves selfless & acting in the name of a superior power which is some sort of symbolism of the collective. In this context, healing for the most part is understood as healing the social fabric as well as healing the individual. While in one sense the healing is aimed at strengthening the individual against the social messages that tell him or her that he is not good enough, is weak & unable to look after him or herself, it actually crystallizes the new identity in the context of the new smaller social group & the continuing practice of the magical healing. Once one is healed, one, in effect, joins the healing cult. This is an age-old occurrence & continues to take place all over the world. The anthropological literature is full of such cases.

Along the path to awakening or in the process of awakening, one meets obstacles of course. Foremost among these are our "attachment" to conceptual ideas & thus to our suffering, our habitual need to "figure things out," the need for "meaning" & all sorts of fearful projections about the unconditioned mind itself. Will I really lose everything? What if the powers don't come my way & I'm left disappointed. For me, it seems really difficult to see the eternal "quest for meaning" as an obstacle to knowledge. Knowledge *is* meaning. And perception of anything is the perception *of* meaning. Certainly, the state of non-dual awareness is pitched as a highly meaningful state, perhaps the most meaningful thing that can be attained. How, then, is meaning an obstacle? Well, immediately we become aware of the tricky language games that go on: it's not really "meaning" that is meant but our attachment to certain meanings, to "correct" meanings and our continual neurotic searching for meaning where not much meaning is to be found. As usual, we find that what is merely called "mind" or "ordinary mind" is actually "neurotic" or "ineffectual" mind. It's a mind that doesn't really work right, that is full of obsessions, unhappy desires, uncontrolled emotions, & so on. So, we really need say no more about this particular aspect of blocks to power.

But, of course, we do need to say something of that perennial bugaboo "attachment." Or do we? When we look at it, it turns out that non-attachment is simply a characteristic of a more or less healthy mind. Thoughts occur, emotions flow through, ideas come & go. If we are to be able to think clearly or get beyond the conventional way of thinking about anything at all, we can't be "attached" to any given scenario, even our own stories about ourselves. Perhaps this is not simply characteristic of a "healthy" mind, but it certainly is a necessary attribute for the "creative" mind. There does seem to be a fairly high awareness that we shouldn't become "attached" to ideas of our own "spiritual" progress any more than we should be attached to our suffering.

How do we begin our awakening? In the more or less usual ways, by observation of ourselves, by trying to remain in the moment, opening ourselves to what's actually going on inside ourselves, engaging in practices that lead to calmness & serenity, never mind resting in healing-bliss. And of course, we can also use a general deconstructing of fixations, use of paradoxical koans, illustrative stories. There is much about the "purity" of listening & speaking. Rituals of purification are age-old, of course, and here we find them again. When does one need to be purified? When one has broken a taboo or contravened some rule, that is to say when one has contaminated sacred space in some way. Well the ordinary mind is a whole junk heap of contaminations. Just to think is a contravention of the sacred rule.

For the most part, this approach to therapy seems primarily to do with the "presence" of the therapist rather than any real consideration of therapeutic skills per se or any real investigation of the nature of the self. In general, the thing of central importance regarding therapeutic skills is that the therapist have a high degree of non-dual awareness. The ordinary self is simply seen as a general grab bag of thoughts, feelings, and sensations characteristic of the dualistic world. The "problems" of a client are seen as illusory and generally are caused by the fact that the client is "attached" to these ideas & thoughts. The image of the "true self" is the image of the mind unconditioned and essentially empty.

The mirror, of course, has a very long history in mystic thought characterized by the hermetic notion: as above, so below. There is no doubt that the image is ancient, but the notion of mirroring is also a very common psychotherapeutic metaphor, as for instance, in the object relations theory of D.W. Winnicott. Winnicott understands the identity of the child to be created in the process of being mirrored in the eyes of the mother. Such an idea is also central to the notion of identity formation found in existential philosophy. Thus, in a very general way, the psychotherapist can be understood as a sort of stand-in for the mother in the therapeutic situation. Difficulties in the development of identity can be revisited & reconstructed or re-symbolized.

In general, in my admittedly somewhat limited experience, there are two types of mystical literature. One type is quite interested in the nature & structure of the dualistic world; the other has very little interest in it & is mostly concerned with escaping from it. The authors of this book seem to be primarily of the latter type.

As should be clear from the above, my sympathies lie with that literature interested in the workings of the dual world & the nature of the self, even though it is a self & a world that, from the mystic orientation, must be left behind in the pursuit of illumination.

It is clear that much mystical thought understands the socially constructed nature of social reality. But it also seems that this light on our social understanding is quickly darkened by its lack of interest in the nature of exactly how language patterns the dual world. In addition, it seems that there is a more or less complete denial of how language & symbolism pattern the world of the sacred itself, which, from the anthropological orientation, is social from top to bottom.

The authors propose that one can have the direct experience of a fundamental consciousness that underlies the apparent distinction between the perceiver & perceived. This notion of an underlying unity is certainly one of the primary elements of the mystical worldview. In a general sense it seems to mean that rather than the "separation" of the individual ego from the rest of nature, we can experience a sense of "belonging," a sense of our interdependence & continuity with the rest of the world. Again, as with the notion of the "unconditioned mind," the use of language is quite imprecise: we are not really talking about being unable to tell the difference between the perceiver & the perceived. If this was true in the ordinary sense we would have a complete lack of ego boundaries, a complete lack of separate identity. This sort of problem is quite clearly evident in paranoid schizophrenia & other illnesses. But, there is, admittedly a state of being that can be achieved alone in which one seems to melt into & become one with the universe. This state is naturally quite short & completely inappropriate for interacting with other people.

There is, however, another sense that we can speak of the underlying unity of the perceiver & the object of perception. From the phenomenological orientation, it is true that in the making of a signal such as a wave of the hand to a friend, one can't tell if one "intended" to wave or if the environment has elicited the wave. In addition, we must add that perception is always the perception "of" something. It is the perception of a meaningful something. In short, it is the perception of meaning. We can thus change the statement to read as follows: we can experience a fundamental consciousness beneath the apparent distinction between the perceiver of meaning & the meaning of something. If we can't tell the difference between these two, it is apparent that meaning is all pervasive and everywhere. Everything in our perceptual awareness if meaningful including ourselves; we are "swimming" in meaning, as it were.

It is important to remember that magic, & certainly medical magic, is aimed primarily at strengthening the ego. I don't want to get caught up in all of the various "parts" of the self & whether or not the "ego" is only a part of the dualistic self. Perhaps it would be safer to say then, that magic is aimed at the strengthening of the self, even the "true" self, although the assumption of a "true self" is merely to privilege a certain sort of self; the one we are talking about is termed the non-dual self. But then we get caught up in the "witness" part of the self & so on. Let's simply say that meditation magic is aimed at strengthening the self. Yoga also aims at this. There is no doubt that the acquisition of consciousness by way of the mystical journey gives the mystic great "spiritual" power. "Spiritual" power, of course, is the same as any other sort of psychological power, often called charisma. Beyond charisma, the ability to think clearly & logically about the world & the people in it is power. Of course, the mystic, who "comes back" from unity as it were, usually becomes some sort of teacher, often within one tradition or another, & either takes an authoritative role in a preexistent power structure or establishes a new one.

The mystic path imitates the initiation of the magician that is characterized by death & re-birth (the ultimate sacrifice of the self only to be born again in the unified vision) & the journey to heaven to get power. There are, of course, many different types & degrees of mystic awareness. Some are very dramatic indeed while others focus upon the calm lucidity of the state. The authors of The Sacred Mirror prefer the latter. They like the idea of calm clarity & promote a particular image of "presence" for the therapist. This is a state of flexibility & fluidity, a state not wedded to any particular way of working, any particular interpretation, any particular goal outside of helping the client to understand where he or she has come from & where he or she is going. Although the way the authors speak of attaining this state of awareness or presence is somewhat simplistic & laden with "spiritual" talk, the state of being advocated is straightforward enough.

If one were merely to change the charged term "non-dual awareness," weighted with all of its wonderful spiritual characteristics, to some other term like "big new idea," one would think those advocating it had a very puffed up understanding of the idea & themselves indeed. Speak of egoism! Prendergast in his introduction wonders if we have "a new school of psychotherapy" here. In fact, the authors have very little to say about psychotherapy per se. They do have something to say about the presence of the therapist & this is essentially for the good, but, in my experience, it is hardly anything new.

Prendergast in the introduction gives us an image of a horizontal & a vertical axis on which he maps all the therapies on the horizontal axis & non-dual formlessness on the vertical axis. Thus, at every moment, the non-dual can inform & deepen whatever kind of psychotherapy is being practiced. The grid brings to mind the basic structuralist grid used in the analysis of the sentence. In this second grid, the horizontal axis is given the dimension of the syntactic arrangement of a sentence (or a therapy as given by Prendergast) but the vertical dimension is given to the timeless substitutions that are available with the use of metaphor. Syntactical development gives us a basic cause & effect relationship, very much in time, but there is no doubt that the metaphoric grid whose lines intersect the horizontal axis at each word, tends towards the timeless. Every given word or element in the syntactic construction can be replaced by other words that are then in a metaphoric relationship. The sentence "He has a red ball" can become, "She has a red ball," or the ball may become many different colours, or sizes. In this case, the "he" & the "she" are in a timeless metaphoric relationship as are the different substitutions for "red." Metaphor in its grasp

& embodiment of meaningful symbolic entities in the world is timeless until it is linked with the horizontal construction of the sentence that gives us the meaningful "story."

Superimposing the two grids, what we have in this metaphorical grid is a demonstration about how the creative use of metaphor, on the axis of non-dualism, deepens the syntactic story of therapy. This makes perfect sense. All language partakes of both dimensions, the timeless & the time-bound, the unconditioned & the conditioned. The structure of meaning found in structuralism (although it certainly has its limits & is surpassed in post-structuralist deconstruction & metaphor theory) demonstrates quite clearly the dualistic element in symbolic construction noticed by mystical thought. What is apparently missed by the spiritual orientation is how the perceptual dimension -- the un-named "flow" of perception or, to use the jargon, the "unconditioned" -- is always present in every interchange. I am aware that this may perhaps be what is being pointed to when it is claimed that with the flowering of non-dual awareness "nothing changes" or that we are all already enlightened. But I don't really see any reason to play paradoxical mind-games around this fact. It is straightforward enough.

Awareness of the metaphorical dimension is absolutely necessary for the good therapist. Metaphor is absolutely necessary in order to grasp the past, the present, & the future, & in order to re-construct the self that, even if illusory, remains absolutely necessary. The thing is not *to not have a self* but to have a fluid, unfixed, spontaneous, creative self, a self that can make decisions in calmness, that is, be objective, but that can also act passionately when the time calls for it. The "no-self" of the mystic involves a paradoxical loosening of the old self & the old frame of reference & the re-introduction of a "new self," one aligned with the common good, that is to say, with the symbolism of the collectivity. One gives up one's individual self in order to gain a public self; one gives up oneself in order to gain the community.

Society & the Self

Our society is organized via the division of labour & if we are interested in freedom we need to pay attention to both the social-legal "individual" self as well as the psychological "self." The non-dual teaching apparently pays attention just to the psychological self. It assumes there is some sort of real or true self underneath or beyond the dual self & that this true self will somehow be released or "realized" after it is discovered. Whatever it actually does, awakening to non-dual awareness is aimed at the strengthening or renewal of the self, allowing the person more confidence, a better ability to organize activities, & so on. We awaken from the dream of the objectified "me" & our identification with roles & attributes, with being "good" or "not good enough" & start to sense joy or simply pleasure, ease of being & so forth. This "awakening" then is an awakening to some understanding of the fluidity & also the fragility of the socially constructed self. It is an awakening to the possibility of a certain clarity of mental operation with a sense of "belonging" in the greater context of life, nature, the cosmos.

Unfortunately for the construction of non-dual reality, it creates in its ideological wake a new dualism, that between ordinary mind & illuminated mind. If, for a moment, we take away the whole notion of the illuminated mind as "sacred" & very special, what we have is an ordinary or conventional state of being & a nonconventional or altered state of mind or being. Within the ordinary state the self is unconsciously attached to ideas about itself, its desires, its failures & so on. These "attachments" are "personal" in the sense that they arise in the context of ordinary developmental processes, & they are "social" in the sense that the ideas & emotions that we are attached to arise in the broader context of the society we grow up and live in. We are attached to "conventional arrangements" as well as to our own personal characteristics which are nonetheless always in relationship to conventions in society. The content of ordinary mind, so described, is basically a rather sickly self, an inflexible neurotic self, deeply involved with its own pain, anxiety about being alone & death, & so on. On the other side, the illuminated mind is really simply the mind loosened from its social constructions, loosened from the super-ego messages from parents & other authorities, loosened from the unpleasant uprising of unconscious desires, pervasive anxiety & so on.

When I say the mind is "loosened" I simply mean that the person is no longer identified with these thoughts & feelings that arise in the mind. By not identifying with these thoughts, of course, we set up another dualism: that between the self that is "watching" & the mental constructs that arise. Due to this "loosening" of the grip of conventional symbolism & conventional understanding, we alter our conventional state of being & gain a certain clarity. But it should be noted this clarity is achieved by the creation of a dualism: me & not me. Beyond this, we have all sorts of "sacred" symbology that it is proposed that we do identify with: calmness, a feeling of being merged with the universe, joy or bliss, & so on.

Mystical social construction

It's as if we've got some kids playing in a sandbox. One kid makes a huge industrial fortress. The other kid makes an "alternative community." Then we got to tell them both that the world they've made is illusory. It's not the real world. They look up at us & say: so, we're playing a game.

It doesn't really matter how you put together the elements of a life, its always going to be an illusion. It's always going to be a game simply because we recognize the illusory elements. But all these "games" & all these "illusions" have real consequences: people live & die by them, good things happen & bad things happen, & they all happen because people are playing games with illusion.

It's all very well for somebody to come along to the kids with some ancient wisdom about the illusory nature & the game playing & the horror & sorrow of it all. It's quite something else to really help people get on with the business of leading good & meaningful lives, lives that take into account in the largest sense one's neighbors and the context one lives in (the environment), lives that do what one can for the huge amount of social injustice there is in the world, and so on. Waking people up to the nature of life on the planet is a damned good thing, but then to mystify the situation by failing to understand & communicate the real nature of mystic presence or awareness as thoroughly social & symbolic & instead giving the "seekers" a whole song & dance of illusion concerning the attainment of godhead or void and claiming that their problems will just naturally wither away, that they can discover the "true" self & so on – well, it's just a pity & a shame. There is some real possibility concerning body & mind techniques for cleansing awareness, as it were, but the whole thing collapses under the weight of traditional religious symbolism.

In a very simple sense, repression of an unpleasant aspect of consciousness, thought, or worry, etc. works by "not thinking about it." This is essentially what mediation teaches: how to withdraw attention from thoughts. It is true that when one withdraws attention, the thoughts seem to just magically disappear. But, of course, one better keep meditating or guess what, they'll come back. Meditation is, in this sense, (& it is also other things) simply another defense mechanism, a method of avoidance.

So, by all means meditate in order to gain some control of your thoughts & increase your self-esteem & protect yourself both from the eruption of id desires as well as overbearing moral super-ego messages. Just don't buy into the cult. Get your added awareness, & then use you head as well as your heart & figure out things for yourself because nobody knows very much about you or about what's going on in the world right now. We've never been here before, &, never mind the cyclic nature of history, things change. This is the first time we've been right here, right now.

To be fully human we must certainly face the emptiness & the illusory nature of the symbolic constructions of self & world. We also need to defend ourselves against the attack of super-ego (religious) messages as well as from our own strange & wondrous desires. I know, I know, the term "attack" just ain't politically correct & neither is "defense." It doesn't really matter though what fancy words are used or how seductive the powers that are held out. We simply have to live our lives the best way we can and not give away our power.

Such an individualistic approach is fine in one sense. It's sort of just taking the process one step further. Magic expropriates religious imagery for its own purposes; now individuals can expropriate various magic elements for their own purposes without actually joining the community of the magicians. But in another sense, it isn't fine at all. We don't really want to perpetuate this system of cultic revolutions of magic, that loosen the consensual frame of reality in order to pattern it with whatever the magicians want to pattern it with. It locks us into a system whereby knowledge & power are in the hands of an elite. Does this lead to freedom of the client? It does not. What does the client need? The client needs real knowledge about how the structuring of self & world came about, techniques for loosening the grip of the conventions, and skill & practice being a creative person. This does not come from the highly trained passivity of the mystic with his little bag of ancient wisdom. This comes with laying your cards on the table & sharing knowledge that is not esoteric knowledge but simply the real knowledge about how symbolic meaning is created & maintained & also how power is exerted over these symbolic creations.

Identity & the therapeutic process

In the context of the mystic journey, one withdraws one's identity & love from "objects." In the context of ordinary life it is common to find that one does exactly this, withdraws one's attachment & love (**?) before the "objects" do. By "object," here I mean objects in the mind that may well be other people. The good thing is that by withdrawing your love & attachment, you become less dependent. But then, very often (in meditation), one is enjoined to place that love & acceptance of attachment back onto the self. Returning one's consciousness, for instance, to the heart chakra or to one's own breath does this. This is fundamentally a narcissistic move whereby one takes love away from the world (things external to the self) & brings it back to the self. As stated earlier, there needs to be a certain amount of self-love for healthy functioning, but ultimately this is a selfish vision if it goes too far. The end point of withdrawing all love from the world (thoughts etc.) & placing back on the self is a sort of narcissistic autism.

We hear a lot about the absolute: absolute truth, the absolute now, the real self, the unbounded, all-encompassing space of pure being, absolute liberation, perfect love, transcendence, nirvana, trans-human liberation, unconditioned mind, non-dual awareness, god, the infinite, deep inner peace, bliss, the void, emptiness. The language is very seductive, especially for a person who might be quite desperate & in the midst of life problems. I am very aware of the grandiosity of the language.

In 'The Sacred Mirror' there are a number of attempts to describe & explain various states of being, the process of "awakening" & so forth, but they are for the most part very simplistic. Certainly the therapeutic understanding appears simplistic. There is very little interest in the structures of consciousness, for instance, and everything is just thrown into a single pot of the "ordinary self" or dual consciousness. This is simply comprised of thoughts, worries, neuroses, emotions, & what have you. "Mind" as such is not really "mind" so much as the malfunctioning mind, the weak ego, the neurotic self. Then to go "beyond mind" is actually simply to approach a healthy relationship with mind. I do not really know enough about it to say whether this sort of simplistic thought is a problem with the early practitioners or with the contemporary translators.

The primary mechanism of liberation involves the awakening to non-dual awareness, a non-compulsive and non-driven mind that is functioning fairly well that has a general awareness of the experience of being alive. There is a general existential awareness of simply "being" along with an awareness of the presence of "emptiness" or simply "death." With the coming of this basic functioning, one's "problems" simply wither away. So much for psychology.

What we have with the general notion of non-dual awareness is a certain approach to the "presence" or simply the "being" of the therapist, who in this case is really undistinguishable from the student of non-dual thought, or someone on the mystic path. The psychology, as such, consists primarily of "suggestions." A number of the practitioners are involved with EMDR (Eye Movement Desensitization Reprogramming), a practice that is replete with hypnotic suggestion. Others are involved with the basically spiritual psychology of Jung.

What we have, then, is a basically "spiritual" approach to healing. It is involved with healing into the community in some sense. It has a great deal of "faith" healing that has precisely to do with establishing a system of strong beliefs. In this case, it is the symbolic structure of mysticism. This "spiritual" approach to healing also involves the practice of initiation in which the separate self is sacrificed in order to gain the non-dual self & the spiritual powers that go along with it.

I have found myself irritated from time to time by the paradoxical & circuitous attempts at describing or explaining aspects of the mystic process, the state of mind & so forth. I can readily understand, as can most people I think, that it is very difficult to describe an experience that is in great part an emotional experience without having experienced it. Try explaining the feeling of being in love or having an orgasm to someone who has never had them, for instance. On the other hand, one can approach the understanding of the nature of a giant jump of 10,000 feet by extrapolating from the experience of jumping say 10 feet.

In addition, metaphors were invented for just this purpose of grasping the nature of something vague by bringing it into contact with something known. Thus, we have metaphors of romantic love that stand in for cosmic love & so on. But the real reason there is so much run around with explanations & descriptions is that there really is nothing to describe, nothing to explain – all there is, is the process of describing & explaining. This is exactly the system of post-hypnotic suggestion that is the mystical experience itself. One loosens the conceptual frame, initiates a light trance, & then patterns this trance with a lot of ambiguous, highly paradoxical language. This is then joined with a practice of calm contemplation, aimed at further loosening the conceptual & conventional framework (the social construction of reality) while systematically building up a new conceptual symbolism comprised of a) the defensive posture of controlling the attention & b) attributing bliss & serenity to the new construction.

I am well aware that believers in this kind of magic will disagree strongly with most of what I have said. For them, there is a true self waiting to be discovered and a real zone of sacred understanding; bliss is a natural attribute of non-dual awareness, & so forth. To attribute all this wonderful material including ecstatic trances, ESP, magical divination, feelings of cosmic bliss, & so on to the "mere" conjunction of social symbolism & biology, as I am proposing, seems beyond comprehension. It seems, in fact, more difficult to believe than magic.

On the other hand, I do hope that there are some students of therapy who will heed my words of caution &, even though they may be swayed by the very seductive come-on of the mystical path to knowledge, they will not swallow the whole pill. It certainly seems that various kinds of magical practice, primarily meditation magic, but also yoga & various other ways of loosening the physical as well as the mental unconscious, can be very helpful in developing a strong therapeutic presence. As all therapists know, the deconstruction & reconstruction of life narratives goes forward by way of illustration & suggestion. It is not for no reason that Zen masters & other practitioners of magic (think of NLP, for instance) prefer to tell stories rather than give advice. There are also other aspects of magical practice, notably types of initiation as well as the symbolism of sacrifice, which can be useful in the service of therapy. But it is well to be cautious with all use of magic in medicine because it is far & away the largest aspect of medicine that causes iatrogenic illness. Very often, it invents the illness that it cures.

End Note

After writing the above, I had several realizations, one of which had to do with how extremely fortunate I have been to be associated with Monica Carpendale & her practice of art therapy. I have long been disappointed in the "therapy business" in general, seeing that most therapists don't really know what they're doing. I mean this in the sense that while most therapists are actively engaged in trying to "do good," they don't really understand how the nature of their own beliefs effects their clients. Thus, we have all sorts of quasi-hypnotic methods whereby the therapists present all sorts of "suggestions" to their clients while insisting they are "discovering" new diseases & new cures. Medical therapy in general is very prone to iatrogenesis; it creates diseases in the wake of its practice. If we accept the distinction between "disease" as biological & "illness" as including the psychological aspect of all disease then we can say it creates "illness."

This is not the case with KATI (Kutenai Art Therapy Institute.) I am very conscious of the incredible attention paid to "therapeutic presence" & the great emphasis placed upon adequate "supervision" which may be lacking for most therapists & counselors. The best thing of all is that the art therapy practice has at its centre the creative process itself; that is the very process involved in the taking apart of symbolic life & putting it back together in new ways. Whether one is making a garden, a painting, or a new self, the process is fundamentally the same. Beyond this, the art therapy I have been in touch with is informed by a phenomenological approach which has as its essence a contemplative practice that aims to discover exactly what is really happening rather than what we "think" is happening, what other people say is happening, what our theories tell us is happening. All that. I am aware & value the aspect of the non-dual program that also has a strong phenomenological practice and makes a real attempt to find out what is happening, "beyond" conventions & the conditioned mind. But I see no reason why this non-dual approach should aggrandize itself & believe that it stands upon some "sacred" ground. I myself am much more satisfied with the distinction between "illusion" & "truth," even though both terms are relative, than the distinction between "secular" & "sacred" or any of the other religiously tinged symbolism. For one thing, the term "sacred" seems to lead right back into a world of illusion very quickly, given all of the wonderful "powers" that are supposed to adhere to it.

I also realized the other day while thinking about these things that the problem with mystic ideology is the same problem any other foundational discourse such as psychoanalysis or Marxism has. Each of these discourses claimed that its interpretive method was the one that provided a real place to stand and purported to have a corner on the ultimate critique. Every foundational discourse proposes that it can provide the leverage of ultimate truth. Only thus can it critique all other discourses & not have to turn its critical eye upon itself. I can remember quite well how disappointed I was when I realized how the sociological discipline was averse to critiquing its own practice. Such is my disappointment with the mystic practice; the discourse on non-dualism is pretty much the same as the mystic discourse in general. It has the insight to see that the social world is illusion & nothing but a symbolic construction, but when it comes time to see its own discourse as also a symbolic construction, it shies away, as well, it must, if it desires to spread & gain students.

I am not only speaking of the discourse, the linguistic practice. I am speaking of the actual mystic domain, the state of non-dual awareness. This also is a symbolic construction & so in no way does it go "beyond" mind or beyond symbolic construction. All it goes "beyond" is the conventional symbolic construction of mind, self, and the world. It goes "beyond" in order to create an altered state of reality. This is simply what happens when the bonds of conventional reality are "loosened," but this altered state itself is certain patterned via symbolism. The non-dual state is a particular symbolic construction & can have no more claim on "ultimate truth," "perfection," the "ultimate medicine" & so forth than any other discipline. Its claims are based upon "tradition" & the charismatic authority of its "masters."

Why is this particular discourse so attractive at this time? It's obvious that at least part of the attraction comes out of disappointment in the political process & also the recognition that a therapeutic discourse such as psychoanalysis is culture bound in many ways. Both of these discourses have always proposed a great deal of really hard work. I don't think that most people are up to it any more. Many are extremely tired of the pap being fed us in our consumer society, the deadening effect of TV & other media, the incredible rising whine & noise of technology itself, as well as the recognition of the worsening state of the environment. In many ways, things on the planet appear hopeless. Certainly the proposal of simple hard work doesn't do much for people. They can see quite easily that the ethic of "hard work," which is supposed to gain one a real place in society, no longer does so. It's all about "luck," winning the lottery, attaining one's moment of glamour by making just the right purchase.

Science has in many ways replaced religion, which has been on the wane for quite some time, if not exactly dead. Touted as our savior, science has utterly failed to provide any moral bearings whatsoever but it has provided the tools to various elites to control vast populations & vast wealth. The time for magic is when people feel generally powerless. And we are having a magic revival. Before long, hopefully, it will become clear that the hopeful magic of meditation, non-dual awareness, yoga, shamanism, & all the rest will not provide the cure either. It will allow for a sort of marginal elite that will not be penniless by any means and will actually control quite a lot of "good" or "green" business, but it won't really threaten the status quo. It won't do much besides actually re-vivify traditional religions and make them more charismatic, more willing to dispense magic solutions to the populace, more ready to spread their own particular types of illusion. Already we have talk about how to handle our spiritual "money" & how we can remain blissfully calm in the midst of our ordinary business dealings.

Another end note

I just realized that one of the reasons that the symbolism & practice of meditation magic moves so easily in contemporary Western society is that it basically has a cognitive-behavioral approach to change. Cognitive behaviorism is, of course, the primary mode of therapy in the USA. The way has been paved, as it were, for meditation magic. Of course, behaviorism has moved a long way from its early days of Pavlovian psychology. The manipulation of the cognitive function via metaphor & symbolism in order to change the lives of clients has been in effect for years. So has hypnotism for the same purpose. It is commonplace to note at this point that our ideas about who we are, our ideas about our illness, our ideas about how we "should" be, are all highly influential in the way we "actually" are.

For example, a person who is depressed may be prompted to greet people differently than in the usual grumpy disheartened way. The usual response to a grumpy greeting is to return the greeting in a somewhat similar way. When, however, the person, despite how they really feel, greets people with a smile & a happy hello, he is surprised when the other person returns the greeting in a happy & genial way. Thus instead of the self-fulfilling prophesy of "nobody likes me" the client comes away with the feeling that people like him, people are happy to see him. By changing one's behaviour, one changes one's experience.

In general, the various "suggestions" about an ideal mind state (non-dual awareness, or simply enlightenment) are conducive to good in the world. As such, the current set of magical & mystic practices outside of the confines of the major religions, gives us a fairly standard list of moral goodness: helping others to become enlightened, compassion for the sick & the ordinary, engagement in charitable activities & so on. By greeting the world in a joyful way, there is a tendency for the world to respond in a like manner. Like magic!

Sociological & Anthropological Notes on Interpretative Practice

Introduction

I draw together the various elements of my interpretive practice that come primarily from language theory (structuralism, semiotics, metaphor theory) & anthropology (primarily social or cultural anthropology). My practice is essentially eclectic & I attempt to record the salient aspects of the different disciplines I draw from in as simple a form as I can. As with all subjects, there are murky areas of theory, contradictions, & elements that draw one away from one's central theme. I have tried as much as possible to circumvent these and keep to the main track.

The Social World

As Roy Wagner points out every culture has to work out the two movements or forces: the collectivizing movement & the individuating movement.

People's everyday actions reinforce and reproduce a set of expectations - and it is this set of other people's expectations that make up the 'social forces' and 'social structures' that sociologists talk about. As Giddens puts it, 'Society only has form, and that form only has effects on people, in so far as structure is produced and reproduced in what people do' (Giddens & Pierson, 1998: 77).

The Two Worlds

Our perception in the ordinary world is conditioned by dualism (polar opposites, darkness & light etc.) There are the two worlds. One is the world of unity & the one. The other is the world of multiplicity, the world of the many, constituted as a system of polar opposites. One returns to the world of the one by undoing the oppositions, by erasing the boundaries. When one does this, then the self is undone, even eradicated, & merges with the one.

The "world of forms" is the world of individuation, & individuals have experience, even the experience of the underlying unity of the cosmos.

Mystical experience of unity, whether Hindu Oneness or Buddhist Void, entails the transcendental sense of something beyond material phenomena, beyond the world of contradictions. When one enters this world, one is illuminated & the experience is often one of "conversion." One is converted to the mystic worldview.

The mystic experience is ineffable. It appears to be more similar to a feeling state than an intellectual state, and thus the nature of the experience is difficult to express in somewhat the same way as it is difficult to tell someone who has never fallen in love what it's like or explain the nature of colour to the blind. Dualistic categories appear on the side of ordinary consciousness. This is the dual world. The mystic world is devoid of dualism, but because mystic ideology is perforce expressed in the dual world, these dualisms appear as the split between mystic consciousness & ordinary consciousness. This is why it is said that the mystic experience cannot be expressed & when it is expressed, it is a lie.

In the mystic experience we have the reconciliation of the polar opposites. But, in fact, this unitary world that is supposed to include all good as well as all evil, all darkness as well as all light, love as well as whatever the opposite of love is, is actually weighted towards the side of the good, the light & love.

A short meditation on the Dualisms

Whole, part
Love, hatred (anger)
Joy, sadness
The contemplative, the actor
Divine, prosaic
Eternal, transient
Soul, body
Spiritual, carnal
Knowing, unknowing
Knowledge, ignorance

A note on gestalt (figure / ground)

Let us take the classical anthropological set of polarities: nature & culture. In the "natural" order, culture is figure & nature is ground. We can describe or refer to the large world (the ground) using our conventional symbols. With the reversal, we have the cultural world of forms and categories (the world of multiplicity) as ground, & nature becomes just one more category or concept in the cultural world, the world of language, the world of symbol & ideology.

In the "natural world," the undifferentiated non-dual world, the dual world is somehow (along with the self) annihilated, hidden, or absorbed in the flow.

In the cultural world, the multiple dualistic world of ordinary consciousness, the undifferentiated world is hidden inside & beneath, but it is always present. This at least in some sense is why the mystic teacher can assert that the student already knows everything he or she needs to know. The enlightened world is actually no different than the non-enlightened world, it is just a matter of seeing or being.

Also, it seems obvious enough that the notion of "non-attachment" functions here also. If one is not attached to the fruits of one's actions or indeed to the very definitions of the world, then one is always aware of the underlying flow of energy that permeates every aspect of our perceptual world, which is, to my way of thinking, the only world we have.

Dialectics & the Gestalt

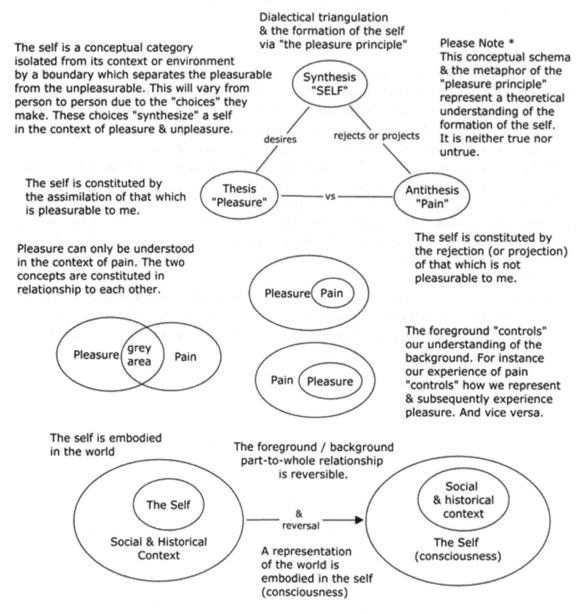

Dialectical triangulation
& the formation of the self
via "the pleasure principle"

The self is a conceptual category
isolated from its context or environment
by a boundary which separates the pleasurable
from the unpleasurable. This will vary from
person to person due to the "choices" they
make. These choices "synthesize" a self
in the context of pleasure & unpleasure.

Please Note *
This conceptual schema
& the metaphor of the
"pleasure principle"
represent a theoretical
understanding of the
formation of the self.
It is neither true nor
untrue.

Synthesis "SELF"

desires   rejects or projects

The self is constituted by
the assimilation of that which
is pleasurable to me.

Thesis "Pleasure"   vs   Antithesis "Pain"

The self is constituted by
the rejection (or projection)
of that which is not
pleasurable to me.

Pleasure can only be understood
in the context of pain. The two
concepts are constituted in
relationship to each other.

Pleasure (Pain)

The foreground "controls"
our understanding of the
background. For instance
our experience of pain
"controls" how we represent
& subsequently experience
pleasure. And vice versa.

Pleasure grey area Pain

Pain (Pleasure)

The self is embodied
in the world

The foreground / background
part-to-whole relationship
is reversible.

The Self

Social & Historical
Context

&
reversal

A representation
of the world is
embodied in the self
(consciousness)

Social
& historical
context

The Self
(consciousness)

We "perceive" meaning & this meaning has been socially constructed over time. This social
construction, however, is not "free" but occurs within the constraints of historical context.
The meaning of my individual life must be seen understood in social & historical context.
Alternately, how this context has influenced my development must be seen in the context
of the meaning of my life.

Various authors have held that Dialectical thought is appropriate for dealing with human social
& psychological life while analysis is appropriate for understanding the workings of the material
world. Why?   * Note: See CMap "Analysis & Causal Relationship"

Religious Paradox

At the heart of all religious experience, there is a paradox. God is in us unknown by intellect & unknowable, but with some sort of "higher faculty," achieved by the cleansing of perception & the purification of our desire, we can be united with the God unknown & unknowable. Thus by knowing nothing, we know that which is beyond knowledge.

Thus our "knowing" is of a different sort. It is intuitive & occurs by our "participation" in the Godhead, the universal energy, the void or whatever it is called. The observed & the observer, the subject & object become one.

By unbinding "knowing" of forms, one comes to "know" the unknowable (that which cannot be named) that is simply the flow of perception the undifferentiated phenomenal world. This participatory knowing of the undifferentiated phenomenal world is particularly intense if the "unbinding" of the categories of the dualistic world occurs in the body as well as in the mind. Wilhelm Reich investigated the encoding of the bodily unconscious in the body, and we may consider the body itself as conditioned by the polarities of relaxation & tension. The body's chronic tensions, such as a particular texture to the voice or one's "posture" in the world, may in fact be understood as the personality. The unbinding of the intellectual system of categories releases energy and the unbinding of the body releases energy.

This unbinding occurs as one goes along the path, on one's journey, follows the way, goes from one stage to another, and ascends the ladder or stairs. As one goes along the way, one engages in various rituals of purgation or purifying.

One thing to keep in mind is that the mystic state or mystic way of being in the world does not usually occur on its own. It is a state to be reached by a great deal of training.

A note on Ambiguity

If one can imagine a scale going from complete clarity of categorical knowledge to the undifferentiated flow of perception, unboundaried, then one has an image of the symbolic path from the dual world to the undifferentiated world. Such a scale, entirely on the cultural side of our equation, would go from the one end where we have the clearly delineated categories of science to the other end where we have the mixed categories of the mad, or perhaps the concrete poet. At one end we have clarity, at the other ambiguity.

We can look at "ambiguity" from two points of view. From the scientific point of view, ambiguity is a negative quality that one must try to do away with. From the point of view of the artist, ambiguity is simply one of the qualities of symbolic language that can be utilized to convey meaning. Metaphor itself tends to create multiple meanings & thus ambiguity. This quality creates the illusion of "depth" in writing or speech.

One would think that the world of undifferentiated flow is nothing if not ambiguous, and yet it only sometimes seems to be so. Perhaps this has something to do with the discipline of the practitioner & also something to do with the identification of the self with the other, the subject with object, observer with the observed. Perhaps it is exactly the distance between these polarities in the dual world that creates both the reality & the illusion of clarity & ambiguity.

We might be able to say, though, that as the multiplicity & ambiguity increase, one is coming closer to the world of undifferentiated perceptual flow, closer to the creative world, closer to confusion & madness, closer to illumination. There are loose links, then, between the spiritual, madness, & creativity.

A note on Identification & Mimicry

The metaphoric world is conditioned by similarity. Thus, imitation brings together the imitator & the thing imitated in a single embodied entity. By imitating the behaviour of a certain animal (granted, in a special way) one actually becomes that animal. In general, one might say that we become human beings by imitating the human beings in our proximity, initially the members of our family, then later all the other people we come in contact with.

Paul Shepard (1978) argues that in the beginning we imitate animals & that this practice gives us a solid metaphorical ground to build identity upon simply because animals have their own agenda. They aren't us. Thus, he argues against the establishment of identity by the imitation or interiorization of the image of machine & mechanism.

A Note on the Mask

I began thinking here of the notion of the self as wearing masks or adopting social personae, as somewhat new, a manifestation of the modern self as a social phenomenon that hides the true self and allows for a social mobility that was impossible in earlier times. Of course, the mask itself has been around for a long, long time. Its beginnings are probably rooted in ritual & the ritual transformation of the self into other beings, primarily animals. Collapsed in the image of the mask are the whole idea of "mimicry" & the production of identity via imitation. Also in the image of the mask as transformative agent is the notion that if one changes the "outside" then one will accomplish a similar transformation "inside." We are obviously in the domain of "magic" & the "sympathetic" power of similarity. By wearing the mask of a lion, I take on the identity of the lion – that is I acquire certain powers, which are manifest in the lion's behaviour. The magical sympathetic power of course is nothing so much as the power of metaphor. The person "metaphorically" changes into the lion & there remains the distinction between the "real" lion & the man. Nonetheless a power is transferred & it goes without saying that this transferal is not simply "automatic" but is dependent upon a deep lived culturally determined knowledge of how lions behave & how things are to be done.

To make the leap then over to the case of mysticism, which is in many ways the cultural development of earlier forms of magic, we see that the mystic is also engaged in the acquisition of certain "powers" or a certain identity – that of the godhead itself. But in this case, we have the appearance of a reversal; the mystic does not obviously put on a mask but takes off the illusory mask of ordinary humankind. The notion of de-masking is supposed to lead to the true "fundamental" spiritual nature of the self. This notion, however, goes counter to the understanding of evolution whereby the mental (read spiritual) functions have evolved from lower or less developed forms. So, we must ask: what kind of mask is it, this nakedness, this unmasking? The answer is not at once obvious. For one thing, it seems clear that if a mask (the un-mask) is actually donned it is certainly not a material or "visual" mask. The common religious prohibition against the making of images of god, or self for that matter, comes easily to mind. But it is also just as clear that there is a pretty well developed "verbal" or textual creation of a mask. This mask is the one we are familiar with & it elaborates a way of being as well as a number of attributes, powers, & emotions.

I also realize upon brief reflection that there are in fact many images of the mystic mask – we have to look no further than the calm contemplative mask of the Buddha, the anguished visage of the Christ, the image of the transported St. Theresa, and so on.

A Note on the Great Historical Divide

Here I want to speak of the historical division between the pre-modern & the modern. I really don't want to go into any detail on this one. There is a great deal of literature on the supposed boundary marked by what we call "the Enlightenment." Before this, things were a certain way & after it, they were another way. But what can we say is the essential difference? Or can we say?

The differences of interest to me here are played out in a number of different spheres. I will simply list them for starters:
- The place & meaning of religion & magic
- Social Organization in general
- The growth & nature of knowledge
- The changing image of the self.

In a great many ways this great transition can be summed up as the reversal of the relation between what was right & proper to express & what was bad or improper. Another way of saying this is that there was a reversal in the dialectic between the collectivizing impulse & the individuating one. In the early situation, the collective was the important thing, and the individual was absorbed in the needs of the collective. In the modern situation, the individual has come to dominate the idea of the collective. In fact, the collective itself is seen as an expression of the individuals within it, whereas in the earlier case the individual was an expression of the collective reality.

The pre-modern gestalt has the image of the collective as figurative control of the background image of the human psyche. In the modern situation, this gestalt is reversed so that we have the image of the individual as the figure in control of the meanings of the background collective.

Thus in the modern, we have almost continual social change as the collective organization shifts & changes in order to accommodate the changing needs of the individuals within it. All kinds of different groups advocate one change or another: feminism, gay rights, aboriginal rights, & so forth.

I have said elsewhere that the collectivizing & the individuating impulses work themselves out in different ways in the pre-modern & the modern. Now, let's look at the reversible dialectic that occurs between the two historical ages themselves.

A Note on the Imagination

Here I want to look at several aspects of the imagination. In the first place, I want to look at its supposed location. Where is it? Is it out there somewhere with God or gods or other invisible forms, or is it inside oneself? Or perhaps it is both places.

Again, I want to refer to the pre-modern tribal situation & the modern one. In the pre-modern situation, imagination is given to God & thus is outside & beyond the self. In the modern, the imagination is given to the self.

A Note on the image of the self over time (Levi Brule)

In the literature we find essentially two different sorts of self, the one existing in small tribal pre-literate societies & the modern (& postmodern) sort of self. In the former case, we have the image of the self as primarily a social role, in a system of social roles. Individuality was not promoted & if found it was viewed with distrust & fear. It was sometimes accorded certain positions of power, but in general individual desires were frowned upon & the dwelling upon one's own desires & oneself in general was seen as selfish & evil.

This self has been called a "participatory" self, because the boundaries between the self & the world of spirits were considered quite porous. One "participated" in the landscape in a different way than we do today. Spirits & different magical entities could come & go in the individual self, sometimes taking up residence, so that one needed to resort to exorcism of one sort or another to get rid of them. Thus, one might easily say that some demon got into one & made one do some bad thing like steal from some member of the group (selfishness again.) Obviously with such an explanation for wrong-doing, the thing to do was get rid of the evil demon that caused the problem so that the poor individual could get back to being a good person.

This notion & evil & the porous nature of the participatory self led to what are essentially community healing efforts. The evil entity is banished within the context of the collectivity so that one may assume one's proper role in the social network. It can easily be seen, from our own perspective, that any given individual may be occupied by this demon & then healed any number of times.

In terms of our overarching concept of the two worlds, the world of convention & the world of undifferentiated flow, it would appear that the earlier version of the self was closer to the cosmic sphere than our version of the self. In this context, the two different worlds can very easily be called nomos & cosmos.

The Dialectical structure of culture in general

Culture can be understood to be the product of the dialectic between the collectivizing & the individuating impulses.

One of the primary distinguishing characteristics between small tribal cultures & modern cultures is that the earlier cultures were essentially religious, whereas modern culture is essential secular. In the first instance, this means that all of the institutions of the earlier culture had aspects of what we understand today to be religion. In our modern culture, there is certainly still the religious institution, but it is not accorded the power or place it once held. We go to great lengths to ensure that religion & government, for instance, stay strictly separated. Thus, the dialectic between the collectivizing impulse & the individuating impulse that is present in all cultures tends to work itself out in early culture in terms of the dialectic between the religious & secular domains. In modern culture, this same dialectic is worked out in terms of the class structure. In more than one sense, the ruling elites have taken the place of the religious institutions in contemporary culture. Some of our contemporary gods & goddesses are created by Hollywood & our mythology has become in many ways the mythology of advertising.

A note on Selfishness & Evil

In general & in most cultures selfishness is the overarching image of evil. This is certainly true in pre-modern tribal society, but in many ways it remains the same today, although the term "evil" is not usually used.

For myself, I have found that what is considered madness or neurosis in our own society can most often be seen to be rooted in a self-centered way of being in the world, in a word, a selfish attitude. This is true of depression, so-called personality disorders, schizophrenia, & so on. I am very well aware that this line is not politically correct, but I am also aware that the boundary between the moral domain & the clinical medical/scientific domains is a socially established one. We "choose" to see a certain behaviour as the manifestation of a moral failing, possession by a "spirit" or a clinical "disease." By "choosing" to see an aberration (socially designated) as the manifestation of an objective phenomenon (disease,) we - by & large release the victim from personal responsibility. There seem to be many cases where this is the correct way to proceed, for example when the biological breakdown of the body far outweighs any psychological factors at work. On the other hand, there are a great number of aberrations where the psychological & moral factors have at least as much to do with things as any biological causation. This is not to say that there aren't objective "chemical" causes that manifest as psychological abnormalities.

All I wish to point out is that the movement of causation from the moral sphere to the scientific one is not quite the "objective" process it purports to be. We do indeed continue to discover "scientific" causes such as viruses, chemistry and so forth, but at this point we certainly do not fully understand the interface between the mind & matter. If we are going to say that the mind has a great deal of influence on bodily functioning, we must mean something like that the mind is able to influence chemical & other processes in the body. To simply "discover" these chemical changes & then claim that the situation is wholly "chemical," "objective," or whatever is simply to miss the point.

A Note on Experience & Language

It is a commonplace when speaking of the visual arts or any kind of art other than writing to note that words cannot encompass the meaning of the work. This is certainly true; otherwise, everyone would simply write & not bother with the other art. Not as common but just as true is the fact that language can never capture all of the meaning of our perceptions in general. One look out the window tells us that it would take a little longer than forever to write down all that we can see. At best, the written word can only sketch out in the briefest way what we see out the window: a car, even a red Buick, even a red 1987 Buick with a dent in the right front bumper, but we will never ever get to the experience of what is actually seen, the experience of seeing. If we think of language as trying to "capture" reality, we are inevitably disappointed.

Very often there is a differentiation in the context of discussions of mystical understanding between language & experience. Of course, language always comes off second best and is sometimes characterized as downright misleading or only able to communicate lies about our true experience.

I want to note that this polarization between experience & language is itself somewhat misleading. There is obviously a difference between our perceptual capacity & our ability to communicate in language. The question we need to ask is this: is there really something called "experience," that is beyond or before or utterly different than language, that a mature language-using homo sapiens can experience? Or is this differentiation & polarization, in fact, a false dichotomy?

I would like to bring in the notion of "meaning" at this point because what we are really talking about is the "meaning" of our experience. We are talking about the fact that language can never communicate the full meaning of our experience. As I've said, this is true enough. But how does "experience" mean anything without language? Granted there are some "universal" core experiences that seem to have meaning beyond & before language, among them perhaps the image of the mother's breast, an infant's tears, & so on, but these universal meanings hardly begin to help us in describing what is out the window. My suggestion is that "experience" cannot be really differentiated from language in any meaningful way because experience is always "meaningful" experience & meaning comes with language. For the most part, of course, when looking out the window, we are not aware of language, per se. In fact, we are simply instantly aware of the fact that there is a car, a tree, the blue sky, whatever. In fact, the landscape outside the window is immediately "given" to us as immediately understandable, immediately meaningful. To try to then reduce this meaningful experience which is a combination of sensory & linguistic experience to language only is a failure. It is just as much a failure to try to reduce it to simply visual elements that have no immediate meaning. That is to say, if one sees something like a car, it very much tends to be understood as a car, not merely light striking "something" we don't know what. This "givenness" of the world in its immediacy is exactly the world of everyday reality that must be set aside in the context of phenomenological enquiry in order to get to the essence of experience. In this way, we are not looking for something "beyond" language, but rather a clarification of language in context.

So far, we have only spoken of the elements that make up experience as if we passively receive information. In fact, our "experience" is not "passive" but very active in the sense that we do give language to the mix. This is, actually, the creative element in our experience. Our experience very much depends upon & is modulated by the language that we give to our experience, not simply the language we give "after" experience, but the language that is intrinsic to the experience itself. For instance, a forester gives different language to his experience of the forest than an ecologist does. A depressed or paranoid person has a much different experience of the world than someone who is happy-go-lucky. This "mood" as an "emotion" can only be understood in terms of language & an unconscious interpretation of biological activity in the body & this is then introduced to experience in general. There is a whole general understanding in psychology that we "filter" our sense experience so that we only receive a very small portion of "what is going on." This is certainly true, but this psychological filtering is very certainly to be understood in the context of our linguistic understanding of the "meaning" of things.

We have a creative & active part in our experience & can do much to change it. This is the essence of the social constructivist view. I am aware, however, that this explanation goes some way to rectifying confusion about "experience" & "language." It certainly does not go far enough with regard to mysticism, all of the various ways mysticism goes about using language to try to capture the experience of the "escape" from language & apparently from meaning itself, & the entrance into the unifying mystic experience of being at one with god or the void.

But just as an initial note, I can say that, from the social constructivist point of view, the recognition that we continually influence the nature of the world as it appears to us (& is thus "subjective") is not a bad or negative thing. The point is to recognize our creative input into our experience & not to try by way of disciplining the mind & body to find some "objective" reality or absolute "truth" beyond this creative interaction with other people & elements of the world. I should note that although the world that appears to us individually it is "subjective" to a degree, the fact that we can "get along" & understand each other, is predicated upon the assumption of a more or less similar state of consciousness in each of us.

It makes a very large difference, in our thinking about such things, where we "place" our understanding of the life force or spirit. The two major "placements" of the life force energy are a) within "the biological entity" or even the self, & b) within the whole cosmos. In this latter case, we as individuals possess (if we can say we possess anything) only a flickering spark of this divine essence. The "great divide" or the so-called historical "enlightenment" in the Western world can, in some sense, be understood as the shift from the "placement" of the imagination from "god" to the interior of the individual which involved a shift from religious to secular life in general. One can also note that there is a certain ambiguity concerning "intentionality" in the context of phenomenological studies. There really is no way of knowing whether "intention" resides in myself or in the world outside myself, whether I "intend" to act or the world calls to me.

The world appears to us in the light of our own intention toward it. It is the work of the reduction or the process of "bracketing" to give us insight into the world without this intention. That is to say, what we bracket out is our own intentions toward the world. This gives us a glimpse of "essence" beyond ourselves. I find that in my own thought, I very much like or am even "attached to" the notion of my own intentionality & the way that it creates my world. At the same time, my feelings are ambivalent regarding the idea of once again separating subject & object from each other. While there is this sense of "objectivity," it is not the objectivity of science; we are still speaking of the way in which the world appears "in consciousness" cleaned, shall we say, of individual passion or bias, (shades of the mystical mirror) but the consciousness of the subject nonetheless & the world shall appear as an "object" in consciousness. There is the appearance of a conflict or contradiction between the dictates of the creative life & the philosophical (or mystical) one.

A Note on "Mystics & Zen Masters" by Thomas Merton

Merton's question in his first chapter concerns whether Zen is by its very nature committed to a search for "rest in the inmost essence" of one's individual self: Is Zen meditation aimed at a purification of the self by rejection of the material world and of external concerns in order to seek fulfillment impure interiority? (1967, p.6)
He goes on to say:

> What I intend to question is simply the idea that Zen mediation is simply a rest in individual "essence" which abolishes all need for and interest in external and historical reality, or the destiny of man (1967, p. 7).

Further:

> Buddhism is generally described in the West as "selfish" even though the professed aim of the discipline from the very start is to attack and overcome that attachment to individual self-affirmation and survival, which is the source of every woe. The truth is that the deep paradoxes and ambiguities of Buddhism have led most Westerners to treat it as a mixture of incomprehensive myths, superstitions, and self-hypnotic rites, all of it without serious importance (1967, p. 8)

Zen is "aggressively opposed to all forms of logical analysis" (1967, p. 9) but, he goes on to say, "The tea ceremony, properly understood, is a celebration of oneness and convergence, a question of multiplicity and of atomization…" (1967, p. 10).

Thus, we get the outline of Merton's argument. He sees the tea ceremony as a contemplative exercise "which does not manifest a spirit of individualism, withdrawal, and separation, but rather of communality and "convergence" at least in a primitive and schematic sense" (1967, p. 10).

These are the two sides, as it were, of the argument: individualism vs. communality, separation vs. convergence. We don't have to wonder very much which is the "good" side, the proper understanding.

He then broaches the loaded question: what exactly is Zen? The question is loaded because "the Zen tradition absolutely refuses to tolerate any abstract or theoretical answer to it." He goes on to say that "Zen simply does not lend itself to logical analysis" (1967, p. 12). We are instantly into the "strangeness" of the mystical quest.

We are into the game of "what it is not." What Zen is not seems to be easier than what it is. It is not "a method of meditation." It is not a kind of spirituality. It is a "way and an "experience," a "life," but the way is paradoxically "not a way." It is not "a religion, not a philosophy, not a system of thought, not a doctrine, not an ascesis "(1967, p. 12). It is also not, supposedly, mysticism either. Merton tells us "Zen insight cannot be communicated in any kind of doctrinal formula or even *in any precise phenomenological description*" (italics in original) (1967, p. 13).

In general, "Zen illumination" is not an "experience" which a subject is capable of having. In short, there can be no subject-object relationship precisely because this is what Zen is not. It evidently is not "individualistic" or "subjective purity." It is not a "spiritual self-gratification," nor is it a "withdrawal from the outer world of matter to the inner world of spirit" (1967, p. 13).

Zen evidently abhors this dualistic division twixt matter & spirit. Of course.

Let's set up our linguistic system so far:

- Individualism vs. communality,
- Separation vs. convergence.
- Separation of spirit & matter vs. unity of spirit & matter.
- Purification of individual self vs. experience of unity
- Withdrawal from the world vs. emersion in life of the world

Mostly this has to do with the main dichotomy twixt individual & the communal.

Merton tells us "Like all forms of Buddhism, Zen seeks an "enlightenment" which results from the resolution of all subject-object relationships and oppositions in a pure void." But this "void" is not pure negation & one cannot attain 'satori' (enlightenment) by the suppression of thought, in fact "it is not an experience or activity of a thinking and self-conscious subject" (1967, p. 13). It neither affirms nor denies, it simply *is* (1967, p. 13). Because it is "beyond" the "thinking" subject or any sort of "self-consciousness" or any sort of "reflective" consciousness, Merton sees it as being "purely spiritual (1967, p. 14).

That gives us the starting place, that it's beyond subject-object relations. Right at this point I think it must be clear that the life force itself cannot be understood to be situated "inside" the conscious individual, at least not in the enlightened state of being. If it were, how could this state of subject-object relations not exist? It is clear that consciousness, again, at least in the enlightened state must be "everywhere," and if it is "everywhere" it probably didn't originate in the individual. It probably pre-existed the individual. Only by setting up this a priori "belief" can the argument go on. But once it is set up, there is an inevitability regarding its unfolding. But, of course, I am getting ahead of myself.

In point of historical fact, Zen was not suddenly "introduced" to China by any one person. It is a product of the combination of Mahayana Buddhism with Chinese Taoism. Zen was later transported to Japan and further refined there. Though Bodhidarma is regarded as the first in a line of Zen patriarchs who have "directly transmitted" the enlightenment experience of the Buddha without written media or verbal formulas, the way for Zen was certainly prepared before him. The four-line verse (*gatha*) attributed to Bodhidharma and purporting to contain a summary of his "doctrine," was actually composed later, during the T'ang Dynasty, when Zen reached its highest perfection in China. The verse reads:

> *A special tradition outside the scriptures (i.e., sutras),*
> *No dependence upon words and letters,*
> *Direct pointing at the soul of man,*
> *Seeing into one's own nature and the attainment of buddhahood* (p. 15).

It is clear that there is a preference for "concrete practice" as opposed to intellectual meditation or any other way of attaining enlightenment. There is a preference for "direct pointing" rather than the use of "language."

Merton notes that the use of the term "soul" in translation is unfortunate because what is indicated is nothing that the conscious person could "have" or possess. Alternately, it is sometimes translated as "mind." In the Zen context, we are not speaking of "mind" as a psychological concept but rather as the "ultimate reality" which is the ground for our being. It is enlightened & aware, being in contact with god or the void. It could be roughly equated with "spirit" in the Christian context. Its ontological value is close to that of "nature."

The list of terms is strange indeed: the soul, the mind, nature, ontological ground, ultimate reality, and enlightened awareness. With this sort of list, which is comprised of approximate metaphorical equivalents, it is clear that we have a blurring of the boundary between self & other, or self & world, or individual & community. Let us take it for the time being that what is being pointed to is "ultimate" reality which perhaps in the enlightened state our mind partakes of, or is immersed in, or is at least aware of. But, of course, this is an a priori assumption & in no sense is being argued. It is ultimately a matter of faith.

The Zen insight, as Bodhidharma indicates, consists in a direct grasp of "mind" or one's "original face." This direct grasp implies rejection of all conceptual media or methods, so that one arrives at mind by "having no mind" (*wu h'sin*): in fact, by "being" mind instead of "having" it. Zen enlightenment is an insight into being in all its existential reality and actualization. It is a fully alert and superconscious act of being that transcends time and space (p. 17).

Time & space, of course, are the foundations of reflective life & encompass the theatre of operations for "evolution." We can note that the "beyond" of language assumes a certain definition of language & of course a certain definition of "time & space." With regard to language, the concept of "phenomenological metaphor" that I have used in these essays already is "beyond" the ordinary concept of language that one can "possess" in mind & which refers to things in the outer world. The notion of experience as always already containing language & the notion that language always already contains sensual experience is "beyond" the ordinary conceptions of either language or experience. We may see, then, that these concepts may in some ways be similar to the understanding that Zen arrives at. Perhaps, perhaps not. But something to look for.

Merton tells us that:

> The Zen insight is the awareness of full spiritual reality, and therefore the realization of the emptiness of all limited or particularized realities. Hence, it is not accurate to say that the Zen insight is a realization of our own individual spiritual nature. Zen insight is at once a liberation from the limitations of the individual ego, and a discovery of one's "original nature" and "true face" in "mind" which is no longer restricted to the empirical self but is in all and above all. Zen insight is not our awareness, but being's awareness of itself in us. (1967, p. 17)

Yes, indeed! The notion of the life force or god as all & everywhere plays itself out. When we understand that this is an a priori assumption, the discovery of it is in no way very mysterious. It is inevitable. And Zen is the way. Thus, "identity" is not to be found in the separate ego or in "separation" at all but in oneness. In addition, Merton tells us, this new identity is not to be discovered via a negation or denial of one's own personal reality but "its highest affirmation" (1967, p. 18).

Merton goes on to describe the differences between the northern and southern schools of Chinese Zen. The primary distinction is encapsulated in two verses, the first from a senior & learned man in the community.

The body is the Bodhi-tree (under which Buddha was enlightened),
The mind is like a clear mirror standing.
Take care to wipe it all the time,
Allow no grain of dust to cling to it. (1967, p. 18-19)

The second is a response from an untrained peasant.

The Bodhi is not like a tree,
The clear mirror is nowhere standing.
Fundamentally, not one thing exists:
Where then is a grain of dust to cling? (1967, p. 19)

Merton explains that the first (from the Northern school) is readily understood by Westerners & is often taken to be the "real" Zen." However, real Zen masters reject it with "impassioned scorn" (1967, p. 19). To explain the strange 3rd line which denies the existence of everything, Merton cites Suzuki, perhaps the foremost scholar of Zen, at least in the West, as saying "When the Sutras declare all things to be empty, unborn and beyond causation, the declaration is not the result of metaphysical reasoning; it is a most penetrating Buddhist experience (1967, p. 20.)" Merton tells us at this point that "statements about the "nothingness" of beings and of "oneness" in Buddhism are to be interpreted just like the figurative terms of Western mystics describing their experience of God: the language is *not metaphysical* but poetic and phenomenological (1967, p. 20)"

This is, of course, no argument but brings us to that notion common in mystical thought that in order to understand something one must have personal experience. This is, I suppose, an instance of that "direct pointing" that we heard of earlier. While the notion that the only road to understanding is personal experience is true in a general sort of way, it is not to be considered as a metaphysical or scientific explanation, but rather it should be interpreted in a poetical & metaphoric way. This is the sense of things that one has in the mystic state of consciousness. It is a description of a state of consciousness. I have a thought that one could link this idea to the notion of intentionality in the context of phenomenology & the distinction between noesis & noemata in the formulation of the experience of essence, transcendent with respect to ordinary reality.

Anyway, Merton goes on to speak of the central Zen metaphor of the mirror & that "mirror-wiping Zen" is not the real Zen, not the real way. This shows, Merton tells us, that Zen is not a technique of introversion by which one seeks to exclude matter and the external world, to eliminate distracting thoughts, to sit in silence emptying the mind of images, and to concentrate on the purity of one's own spiritual essence, whether or not this essence is regarded as a mirror of the divinity. Zen is not a mysticism of introversion and withdrawal (1967, p. 20-21).

Merton tells us that this does not mean that Hui Neng (the proponent of this type of no-mirror-wiping Zen) thought that there was no need for formal preparation via meditation. Rather he refused to separate meditation as a means (*dhana*) from enlightenment as an end (*prajna*). For him, the two were really inseparable, and the Zen discipline consisted in seeking to realize this wholeness and unity of prajna and dhyana in all one's acts, however external, however commonplace, however trivial.

Hui Neng thought there was a common wrong attitude towards meditation in the mirror-wiping school and had three objections:

- This mirror-cleaning metaphor gives primacy to ego-consciousness, the empirical self that sets out to achieve "illumination" or "enlightenment." No matter if one rejects thoughts & achieves an "inner silence," it is still "ego."
- The empirical self-conscious self views its own thought as a sort of possession situated in this "mind" which must be polished like a mirror.
- When the mirror of the mind is cleared then one will be illumined and will then experience "emptiness" & "suchness."

This notion that the lower self will be dissolved in the universal transcendental ideal is actually a crafty trick by empirical ego-consciousness. The "spiritual" is regarded as an attainment & an object possessed by the mind. It is ultimately narcissistic. Evidently, deep spirituality cannot operate "according to the imagery which is adequate for ordinary, everyday life" & so it must be discarded. Thus, it must be described in other terms. Here the terms are according to Merton's understanding of Hui Neng.

For Hui Neng the central reality in meditation, or indeed in life itself, is not the empirical ego but that ultimate reality which is at once pure being and pure awareness that we referred to above as "mind" (*h'sin*). Because he contrasts it with the "conscious" empirical self, Hui Neng calls this "ultimate mind" the "Unconscious" (*wu nien*). This is equivalent to the Sanskrit prajna, or wisdom. Merton notes that this "unconscious" is totally different from the psychoanalytic unconscious. The "unconscious" (*prajna*) is a principle of being and light secretly at work in our conscious mind making it aware of transcendent reality. But this true awareness is not a matter of the empirical ego standing back and "having ideas," "possessing knowledge," or even "attaining to insight" (*satori*). That might be all right in the Cartesian realm of scientific abstraction, but here we are dealing with the vastly different realm of prajna-wisdom. Hence, what matters now is for the conscious to realize itself as identified with and illuminated by the Unconscious, in such a way that there is no longer any division or separation between the two. (1967, p. 24)

The words that stick out here are that the true mind is "secretly at work in our conscious mind making it aware of transcendent reality" and also that the small self should be "identified with and illuminated by" the true awareness of the "unconscious mind."

In the usual way, nothing much is explained but rather much is asserted. What is this "principle" which is secretly at work? I'm afraid it sounds much like an angel; certainly it can have nothing to do with the conscious will or the self in any way. It does sound like some sort of spiritual guide that manifests itself in us, a something that we are told to "identify with" and be "illuminated by." It leaves one wondering, among a number of other things, how one is to "identify" with something without using the conscious will.

Merton goes on:

> Indeed, it is not the empirical self which "possesses" prajna-wisdom, or owns "an unconscious" as one might have a cellar in one's house. In reality, the conscious belongs to the transcendental unconscious, is possessed by it, and carries out its work, or it should do so. (1967, p. 24-25).

What we have it seems is a reversal: the small self cannot "have" enlightenment, but rather "enlightenment" can "have" the small self. As I pointed out earlier this was an assumption that was made early on – with the very definition of "mind" we have the foundation of truth located everywhere all around us. It is but a small step to work out some way that we should become aware of this truth without it being a conscious decision on our own part because then it would be "ours." Just so it can't be ours, we must perforce assume that it will make itself be known. This is, of course, the essence of the spiritual view – that we have no control of god but rather that god must have us. Nothing new is discovered. Except, of course, another argument for "faith" – we should no doubt have faith that this awareness will grow in us if only we don't actively desire it or in our "identifying" with it, we somehow don't do it with our own self. Thus, the way is not the way, the mind is not the mind, and attainment is not attainment, etc. ad infinitum.

Thus, Mirror wiping is useless because "there is no mirror to be wiped. What we call "our" mind is only a flickering and transient manifestation of *prajna* – the formless and limitless light (1967, p. 25). Surprise! True enlightenment cannot be through the purification of the empirical Cartesian mind. This is pure illusion.

Oh My! We must be illuminated by true mind & in fact "become" that light & see the light in everything. External objects and concepts are irrelevant – they are real enough but irrelevant for our illumination, in god or the void."

The void (or the Unconscious) may be said to have two aspects. First, it simply is what it is. Second, it is realized, it is aware of itself, and to speak improperly, this awareness (*prajna*) is "in us," or, better, we are "in it." (1967, p. 27-28)

I must admit that this is very hard for me to take seriously. I can quite accept that I cannot attain nirvana by personal struggle; this has always seemed to be a somewhat impossible goal. Alternatively, if attained it would be a complete illusion – no more an illusion than everyday reality – but similarly illusory, it would be a self-constructed state of being. So, to learn that this is not the true enlightenment is not so hard to take. What is hard to take is that God or spirit is going to illuminate the mind such that the subject-object distinctions disappear. And what do I have to do with this? Nothing much.

All opposites are resolved in the void and self-awareness is overcome not in the purification of the mind (mirror wiping) not by the acquisition of an empty mind or absolute purity of the mind cleansed of all objects but by an attaining that is not-attaining, because

> the "purity" of *sunyata* is not purity and void considered as an object of contemplation, but a non-seeing, a non-contemplation, in which precisely it is realized that the "mirror" or the original mind (of *prajna* and emptiness) is actually a non-mirror, and "no-mind." (1967, p. 31)

There are two types of Zen. In the mirror wiping kind the mind is purified & can stand upon something "beyond" the confusion of the "everyday mind." This primordial reality is sought as an objective basis for contemplation. The other way is the non-way. It is simply "pure seeing," beyond subject and object, and therefore "no-seeing." This distinction, which at first seems absurd, is actually quite simple. In the first case, we have "illumination" as an "object" in the reflective mind, something that is attained & then possessed by the self. In the second case, we have this same sense of the purity mind but we are seized by the world and by the Unconscious mind. This means nothing other than that we should be in the world in an unattached way. In the first case, we have purification, but attachment to purification, in the second, we have the case of the unattached mind. It is not a question of cleaning out all the objects and concepts but rather to simply recognize them, and be unattached. This cannot mean having no intentions towards them at all, for from the phenomenological perspective this would seem to be impossible precisely because the world is given to us in the light of our intentionality. Rather then, we might say that with illumination, one becomes "flexible" with regard to intention rather than fixed in the ways in which the world appears. Thus we have the notion of the illusory world, created in our subjectivity, & the notion of attaining a flexible unfixed view of this world but not in the sense of an individual attainment but rather that we are "in" the world and our "attachment" to it approaches its attachment to us – which it is supposed is hardly any at all. (But what do we do with the notion that God loves us?)

The idea is to liberate the mind from its objects, even its very special objects such as imagined spiritual states. One finds this liberation in the midst of "everyday" mind.

I realize at this point that Merton is really laying out the differences between two conceptual schools of thought in Zen & we do not have to accept or even be very interested in his notion of which is right & which is wrong. The really important distinction between the two, that is the distinction which is relevant to us, is that one is involved in cleaning the mirror of consciousness of thought & concept while the other occurs in the context of the thought & concept in use in everyday life. But this is not quite it either. Let me try again. The real distinction is that the one maintains that "illumination" is an object of consciousness while the other is taken up, as it were, in an all-abiding consciousness. Both, it would seem are interested in that old theme of "non-attachment" but the one (mirror wiping) retains a covert attachment while the other avoids this pit-fall by its non-possession of "illumination" itself. Instead in this latter case there is the notion that a sort of "world consciousness" that illuminates small consciousness & brings it to itself. Again, we might say that in the first formulation consciousness begins & ends in the individual, while in the latter formulation it begins & ends in the communal or in the cosmic as opposed to nomos. I suppose the criticism is essentially that the first school maintains, albeit in a covert manner, the subject object relations while in the southern school subject/object relationship is really dissolved in the identification of the small self with the vast cosmic self or consciousness.

Within phenomenology, there is no strict subject-object distinction in everyday reality because all objects are intentional. By bracketing "intention" with regard to objects, we supposedly come to "essence" & "truth." This issue revolves around the relationship to "intentionality." Can one truly have no intentions towards an object? Or perhaps we could re-phrase it in terms of the mystic dichotomy we have been discussing: can one truly have no intentions while maintaining an individual reflective consciousness? Is the only way around this to actually posit that our individual consciousness is always already a small piece of primordial consciousness? Does this get around the problem? I don't think so. We still, then, "intend" this. It doesn't really matter if we say we simply intuit that this is the true nature of reality & it has nothing to do with our own desire. The fact is one has to maintain an openness about this issue entirely. It may be one way or the other. Intention may spring from the individual self or from the world at large. No way of knowing. The way of un-knowing.

The differences between the two schools focuses on the difference between the location of "cosmic consciousness," if we can use the term, as either "inside" as "object" or "outside." In this last case I can't help but think that the individual mind becomes "its" object, but never mind. Let us go on.

On the one side then we have the notion of meditation as a calm retreat from & rejection of "the world." This is the escape from "passion" familiar in the context of Christian mysticism & in the context of the ascetic contemplative life in general. Thus, "Together with the bodily discipline of 'sitting,' there is also a necessary interior discipline of detachment, of passionlessness, and of inner peace (1967, p. 35)." This "detachment" is founded upon a contemplation of the transient nature of life on earth. Especially also it is important not to desire to be enlightened. One must not, from Hui Neng's position, look for enlightenment as "a special psychological state (1967, p. 35)." In this (mirror wiping) type of practice we find a certain sort of "faith" & a sense of the "automatic" getting of illumination.

The Rinzai School following the teaching of Hui Neng does not promote "quiet sitting" but "seeks to plunge the Zen disciple into *satori*, or a metaphysical intuition of being by non-seeing and emptiness, through struggle with the *koan* (1967, p. 36)." The mind that is emptiness, void, and *sunyata* is the *prajna* mind, the metaphysical ground of being. Where Hui Neng prescribes a detachment from meditation and from inner psychological states in order to favor this ontological intuition of the ground of being, Dogen, a follower of the mirror-polishing school, follows a way of quiet and tranquil meditation which renounces seeing and intuition in order to dwell in an affective silence of the passions. (1967, p. 36)

Interesting: we have this privileging of an "ontological intuition" as opposed to the acquisition of a "psychological state." From Hui Neng's point of view, meditation, when it is used as a sort of resting place, serves as an obstruction to illumination understood as this "ontological intuition" into the emptiness of the void.

Here once again we must be quite clear that when Hui Neng speaks of "non-seeing" and "no-mind" he is, first of all, not describing a psychological state but a metaphysical intuition of the ground of being. Secondly, we must remember that his "non-seeing" is in fact "seeing." Thus, what we have is a breakthrough in which subjective and psychological consciousness is transcended; there is an awareness that does not look at being (or the void) as an object but enters into the self-awareness of the being-void, which is the *prajna-mind*.

I'm not exactly sure how this "entering into the self-awareness of the being-void" is not a psychological state but it is clear that we are dealing with this distinction between the location of "awareness" either "inside" or "outside." I am also not sure exactly how this "metaphysical intuition" conspires to avoid being a psychological state. The closest I can come to understanding this idea comes from phenomenology & the state of being achieved by the reduction & the bracketing of "intention." (I am not at all sure but it seems that we might have a somewhat similar distinction here between Husserl's notion of the "transcendental self" capable of viewing the world with objective clarity, as opposed to what could be considered the ontological intuition envisioned by the existentialist phenomenologists.) I am still left to wonder at the state of mind accompanying this ontological intuition. I also realize I am quite comfortable with the idea just as I like the notion of the non-rejection of the world. It is not as if "intuition" is in any way "automatic;" rather it requires a great deal of work in order to "set it up" as it were.

Merton insists on the distinction between the idea of "emptiness" as a "psychological state" & as a "metaphysical concept." With this we have

> a breakthrough which does not simply produce an enlightened state of consciousness or super consciousness in the experience of the individual – which for Buddhism would be a fundamental error and evidence of "ignorance" (*avidya*) – but which allows being itself to reveal its light, which is no-light and void. (1967, p. 39)

Merton sees this as the "light of pure ontological contemplation" (1967, p. 39) with, ultimately, "Being, Seeing, and Acting" being interchangeable. The "ground of being" is the "pure void which is light and act because it is fullness and totality" (1967, p. 39) And ultimately we are told "This means inevitably a fulfillment in love" (1967, p. 39). This supposedly comes from the Trinitarian structure of being. I can really follow Merton's reasoning on this, but it is not difficult to understand the primordial ground of being as "love." In fact, this is probably the most common way of looking at the nature of god or void. Over & over again we have heard of the submergence of self in an overwhelming love.

We only need to link this notion up with the "affections" & with the notion of "emotion" or desire as "intentionality" to know that we are back in the world again, if we ever left it. It is not hard to think that this overwhelming fulfillment of ontological love is different than those desires that originate in ourselves, but it also seems that we cannot ignore the similarity. But, of course, it is always a question of the inner psychological state as opposed to "the world."

Merton goes on to tell us

> It is evident that when we understand the true originality of Hui Neng we see that his Zen is not a "liberation" from matter in order to "bind" us to interior purity, *dhyana*, illumination, and so on. It is a liberation from all forms of bondage to techniques, to exercises, to systems of thought and of spirituality, to specific forms of individual spiritual achievement, to limited and dogmatic social programs. Hui Neng's aim was the direct awareness in which is formed the "truth that makes us free" – not the truth as an object of knowledge only, but the truth lived and experienced in concrete and existential awareness. (1967, p. 41)

A Note on Science, Phenomenology, mysticism & spirituality

In this note I wish to make the distinction between the methodology of empirical science & phenomenology, & then from this distinction show where the fruitful pursuit of mysticism & spirituality lies. First are some broad & general definitions.

This gleaned from Wikipedia on the Net: Scientific investigation should adhere to the "Scientific method" a process for evaluating empirical knowledge which explains observable events in Nature as a result of natural causes, rejecting Supernatural notions. In addition, a proposition or theory cannot be scientific if it does not admit the possibility of being shown false. It must be falsifiable. Fields of science are commonly classified along two major lines: the Natural sciences, the study of the natural phenomena including biology & the Social sciences, the systematic study of human behavior and society.

I am interested here in the beginnings of Phenomenology, the works of Edmund Husserl and the development of his and other's thoughts by the existential phenomenologists. I could simply outline Merleau-Ponty's methodological principles, but I have done that elsewhere & I think it would be useful to have just a taste of the development of the ideas.

Again from Wikipedia: For Husserl, phenomenology is an approach to philosophy that takes the intuitive experience of phenomena (what presents itself to us in conscious experience) as its starting point and tries to extract from it the essential features of experiences and the essence of what we experience.

Husserl borrowed the notion of intentionality from Brentano, the notion that the main characteristic of consciousness is that it is always *intentional*. Intentionality, which could be summarized as "aboutness", describes the basic structure of consciousness. Every mental phenomenon or psychological act is directed at an object — the *intentional object*. This is the key feature which distinguishes mental/psychical phenomena from physical phenomena (objects), because physical phenomena lack intentionality altogether. Intentionality is the key concept by means of which phenomenological philosophy attempts to overcome the subject/object dichotomy prevalent in modern philosophy.

Husserl made the distinction between the act of consciousness (*noesis*) and the phenomena at which it is directed (the *noemata*). "Noetic" refers to the intentional act of consciousness (for example, believing, willing, hating and loving, etc.) while "noematic" refers to the object or content (noema) which appears in the noetic acts (the believed, wanted, hated and loved).

What we observe is not the object as it is in itself, but how and inasmuch it is given in the intentional acts. Knowledge of essences would only be possible by "bracketing" all assumptions about the existence of an external world and the inessential (subjective) aspects of how the object is concretely given to us. This procedure Husserl called *epoché*.

Husserl later developed his notion of the pure transcendental ego, (what was left after the "bracketing" or reduction) as opposed to the concrete empirical ego. Existential phenomenology differs from transcendental phenomenology by its rejection of the transcendental ego. Transcendence is maintained in existential phenomenology to the extent that the method of phenomenology must take a presuppositionless starting point without presuppositions, transcending claims about the world arising from, for example, natural or scientific attitudes or theories of the ontological nature of the world.

The central ideas then are:

> "Intentionality" illustrated in the differentiation between the act of consciousness (noesis) and the phenomena at which it is directed (the noemata). The idea that we are searching for "truth" as the "essence" of phenomena & that we can only do this by "bracketing" all our assumptions & the intentionality of the everyday givenness of the world. It means setting aside the meanings instantly attributed to phenomena in our ordinary consciousness to reach the essence, the presuppositionless transcendental starting point for existential phenomenology. Beyond these four main ideas, (intentionality, bracketing, ordinary world-context & essence) in Merleau-Ponty's scheme, we have only the fundamental process of "description. Because phenomenology is primarily a descriptive practice rather than a scientific one, we have descriptions of what occurs in consciousness rather than explanations.

The question then is: what relationship does mystical thought bear to science & to phenomenological thought?

Mystical thought does not pretend to be "objective" in the sense of science but I myself often forget this because the language is often so similar. Where mystical thought holds itself to go" beyond" empirical mind, beyond logic & science, what can it mean? It means for a start that it holds its "spiritual" position to be a priori "beyond" the everyday reality. It takes "science" to be the epitome of this everyday reality in the sense that it is only concerned with the "material" world, a world by definition (from the supernatural viewpoint) lesser than the "spiritual" world. In this sense, this "beyond" doesn't mean anything but that those of the spiritual persuasion hold it so. That is, not much. There cannot possibly be any "proof" because "proof" is of the lower material order anyway. The "spiritual" ultimately is concerned with the phenomenological; that is to say, it can deal with nothing but a description of the nature of consciousness. When it points to "truth," it does not point to the objective truth of science but rather to ontological truth, the truth of being, the truth of the conscious subject. Thus to be "beyond" science doesn't really mean that its truth is simply a greater truth on the same continuum. It is a truth of another order: it is a philosophical truth or a phenomenological truth. As such, it needs to make an "argument." It needs to present its case. Its truth is based upon an argument & some sort of demonstration of how this truth was arrived at. It is necessarily a "meaningful" truth even if it does purport to be beyond subjective consciousness & its need for "meaning." In a sense, the "world" or world consciousness (God, the void etc.) has no need for "meaning," & in a poetic or metaphorical sense we can know this & thus simply "be" without the need for meaning. But as soon as we are aware of being aware of this sort of "knowing," that knowing changes into the ordinary sort of knowing, that is a knowing that "cares" about knowing, about meaning, about the world and about the self in the world. To live in the "ordinary" world of intention & struggle is no easy thing.

Metaphysics (From the Greek "beyond nature") is a branch of speculative philosophy concerned with explaining the world. **Ontology** (also from the Greek "the study of being") is the most fundamental branch of metaphysics. It studies being or existence and their basic categories and relationships, to determine what entities and what types of entities exist. Ontology thus has strong implications for conceptions of reality.

An Anecdote regarding Freedom

I was speaking today to a friend & he expressed the notion that we are not free except as we are free of "concept." This notion that our freedom is to be found on the other side of language & in non-attachment is all too common. He described a state of mind wherein he had the feeling that he did not "prefer" one thing over the other; he was suspended in a kind of calm & peaceful state. He felt it healthy. He tried to preserve it, which, he laughingly explained, is where he made his mistake. I wondered what he had liked about it & why he preferred that state to his previous state of anxiety. In a sense, my friend had reduced his "intentions" toward the world not to none, but to very few: he preferred to be calm rather than anxious. Thus, the world appeared to him as his intention showed it to him – his preferred state of being could be accomplished if only he didn't care or didn't care passionately about what he did or what happened to him. Such a state can only be maintained for a short while. It is, in my opinion, essentially boring.

The reflective process & the mystic thought of Swedenborg

I am reading a book by a clinical psychologist about the work of Emmanuel Swedenborg, the Swedish mystic of several hundred years ago entitled 'The Presence of Other Worlds' by Wilson Von Dusen (1968).

Swedenborg notes somewhere that love (affection) is at "the root & source" of all other aspects of mind & action. What one desires effects all else. Our desire is at the root of our "intention," & it is this desire that guides our mind & our action in the world. The world does not appear to us except by way of our intention, our desire for it. This desire, of course, includes all negative emotions as well: we see by the light of our love, our distaste, our boredom, our interest, or excitement.

Swedenborg lays out the reflective process in the following way. There is a linkage between: a) the end, b) the cause, & c) the effect. The end is the ultimate interior end that is ultimate love; this causes the affections & perceptions in the mind & these in turn cause actions in the world. In religious terms, "charity" is the effect of love. Thus, Swedenborg's internal "witness" is "interior thought" which is spirit, & this interior thought/spirit watches the "exterior" thought, sees whether it is good or evil & corrects it. The process goes from interior thought to exterior thought to act.

It should be clear that therapy works to enhance this "interior thought" whether or not it is flagged as "spirit." It must be admitted, however, that it is at a "higher" level of abstraction; that is to say, it is "positioned" so that it can "see" or have access to the "lower" mind. In psychoanalytic terms, we are thinking about the "super-ego" & the refinement of the super-ego messages that begin with parental authority & religious messages concerning what it is to be a "good" person.

However, as soon as I say that, upon reflection, I realize that there is something in me that in turn is at a "higher" level still & which can "observe" & reflect upon this interior/spirit, or super-ego thought. This higher reflective aspect of mind may simply be termed sociological or anthropological reflection. Presumably, this process could go on ad infinitum, as one ascends higher & higher in the reflective process. I suppose, though, that this "ascending" of levels in fact is the process of spiritual or simply reflective refinement, the end product of which is, in mystical terms, an ultimate uniting with god in a universal love. This is, of course, if one accepts the mystic program, specifically its hierarchy whereby "emotion" is "higher" than "thought" in the sense that "desire" (emotion) brings thought into action and that in fact all thought goes on in the "environment" or atmosphere of desire/emotion.

Upon reflection, then, it would appear that perhaps it is not right to speak of emotion as being "higher" than "thought," but rather, in terms of a figure/ground gestalt, "emotion" (desire) is, in the beginning, the foreground focus (in consciousness) with the background being the potentiality of thought (all the sentences in the world.) The reversal of the gestalt has the particular thought, so inspired, rising to the forefront of conscious to become the foreground focus or control of the background emotion. There is also the sense that because the foreground aspect (whether thought or emotion in this case) which rises to the surface of awareness in general resides in the background context, this foreground "control" is always already suffused with the whole of the context within which it usually resides.

But what if we do not accept the mystic hierarchy or "privilege" of emotion/desire over thought? Certainly one could privilege thought in the sense that the refinement of the reflective process appears to go foreword via the process of thought. On the other hand, the argument could certainly be made that this thought is always already suffused with desire. The argument is perhaps fruitless, but another issue comes to mind & it also has to do with hierarchy. The question arises concerning the topography of consciousness with regard to the higher & the lower or the interior & the exterior & also the foreground & background.

Is there some sort of fixed system of levels or layers wherein the process of intellectual or spiritual refinement takes place? Off the top of my head I would say that no, there is no fixed system but rather an ongoing process whereby an observing aspect of mind separates itself from the rest of consciousness in order to observe. This aspect then sinks back down into the general context of mind & only appears again when there is a particular "theme" of thought which is being pursued. In this case, there is a sense of continuity between the original observing aspect & the aspect of mind that again surfaces to reflect upon the same theme or issue. From this point of view, the "observer" that arises is actually any number of "observers" that only have continuity with themselves insofar as they pursue the same subjects.

Upon reflection, I am not at all sure if this is an accurate representation because it certainly seems that one could categorize the "themes" one contemplates in terms of "highness" or "lowness." In addition, one could argue that the reflective process itself (the separation of some aspect of mind to observe other aspects) is already thematically tied together. In this case, any individual contemplation of "themes" would take place within this larger context of the "theme of reflection."

The categorization of themes in terms of higher or lower "levels" is, of course, replete in such mystical models as that of the "chakras" or the different levels of heaven & hell. I suppose this reflective aspect of mind, whether a single entity in itself, or retrospectively assigned this role, is the figure of the "guide" (as noun: the tourist guide, the escort, exemplar, guru, inspiration, mentor, paradigm, conductor, chaperone, counselor, exemplar, genie or genius, guiding spirit, scout, superintendent, usher, guiding light, lodestar, sign, shepherd, or as verb, to guide is to conduct, guard, lead, advise, admonish, advocate, caution, encourage recommend.) All of these, then, can be seen to pertain to this role of the reflective interior (other) this leader in consciousness, this guide, conductor, and advisor.

Without much thought I have given this "guide" the title here of "other," when, of course, many think of this aspect of consciousness as the "true self," the interior self or "spirit." But, for me, there is an otherness about it simply because its purpose is to utilize "unclouded rationality" (Swedenborg's term); its function is to objectively analyze the contents of "exterior thought" (the contents of consciousness) and judge & advise. In some sense the "true" me is the wayward me – the wayward self – wandering in the wilderness, & this interior & judging self is some social authority other than myself, a fragment of consciousness working for society, even a secret society. This is, of course, Freud's view: the super-ego is in the service of the moral agents of society.

With regard to my own personal creative work, I like the terms "guide," "usher," & "escort." But I haven't really hit on the right term yet for someone who leads you around, advising here, commenting there, showing you the sights, warning you about certain problems or "neighbourhoods." This person obviously is in "the know" about the territory he is guiding one around. Previously I had the character of the "security man" & more lately the "tourist guide." One goes on the "tour," visits the famous places, the historical neighbourhoods, and places of historical or cultural interest. One gets on a bus. The tour guide wears a grey uniform. Therefore, in a real sense, the "guide" is not "higher" than those he guides but rather is in the service of those he guides. He simply knows a certain territory that is of interest to these "tourists" who have their "real" lives elsewhere. In addition, while a "guide" may be in some sense "wise" beyond his somewhat superficial role, he is neither the one that has made history or nor the one that has created cultural art. He has a map of the territory & can give brief synoptic talks on things. This is the exterior garb of the tourist guide.

But, & it is a large "but," the particular "guide" I am thinking of is "really" a sort of imposter because he really is "in the know." He is not "just" a tourist guide. He knows the deeper workings of the system that you, the tourist have entered. He knows who "pulls the strings" & how things get done. He knows the "secrets" of the social order, the way pleasure & money work. He is, in fact, a higher being & is quite capable of "judging" situations & people.

De Chardin & Swedenborg: Religion, magic, ethics & love

I am reading "The Phenomenon of Man" by Teilhard de Chardin (1955) as well as "The Presence of Other Worlds" by Wilson Van Dusen (1968), a book about Swedenborg the mystic who lived a couple hundred of years ago. First of all, I should say that I am rather bemused with the sense that I am making my peace with religion before magic. This is just to say that I feel more comfortable with ethical philosophy, essentially an intellectual pursuit, than I do with mysticism, which is essentially an emotional one. If "religion" is understood to be essentially interested in the promotion of ethical action – do unto others & the bringing of love into the hearts of people --then I'm all for it. Insomuch as it is an ideological institution that continually seems to mistake its own program for that of "God's" I really do hate it. Insomuch as we humans appear to have the job of shouldering moral responsibility in the context of the rest of nature, we are also free to make mistakes. We make mistakes over & over again, but mistakes are not what we aim at. I assume the same goes for religion. Magic, on the other hand, has a more ambiguous relationship with ethics.

Teilhard de Chardin argues, if I take his meaning correctly, that there is a "centralizing" force as well as a "diversifying" force in the evolution of humankind. He sees cultural evolution as coextensive with biological evolution, and consciousness or "spirit" arising precisely because of increasing complexity of matter. Increasing complexity is obviously occurring in our intellectual life, primarily in science, but the centralizing or essentializing force is also at work. This force is nothing less than the desire to create a just & ethical world inclusive of humankind & the whole of "nature." This is our "usefulness" & usefulness is the object of all thought.

Swedenborg speaks of the "atmosphere" of thought & the idea that "affection" or "love" is at the root of & colours all thought. And love is, of course, the "highest" emotion. Thus, Swedenborg & De Chardin both argue that love is at the root of the spiritual adventure, which is the human adventure. What we have here is a constellation of thoughts: love, emotion, desire, & intentionality. Love is a particular orientation toward the world & all the things in the world. The world appears to us in the light of our "desire" that is to say its "usefulness" to us.

Magic & the "desire" implicit in its usage are in a rather ambiguous relationship with religion given that they use the imagery of "spirituality" for more or less personal rather than collective purposes. I am using the term "magic" precisely to designate those activities that use religious symbolism, ritual, & practice to accomplish things in the world for individuals. As such, "magic" can generally be assumed to be at the historical root of the emergence of the individual from the collective. The desire for the enhancement of the self is hardly a "spiritual" thing in its fundamentals. But, of course, with regard to the mystic journey, this self enhancement (via yoga, meditation, astrology & so forth) does have as its ultimate goal the abolishment of the individual self in favour of the "emotional" conjoining of self & the divine, under the banner of an overwhelming & cosmic "love." However, very few seem to actually reach this ultimate goal & so "the self" itself remains somewhat ambiguous & in an ambiguous relation with the rest of the world.

The notion that desire & intentionality colour all thought & that love is the essence of desire, is at the root of De Chardin's evolutionary ethics as well as Swedenborg's mysticism. I am fine with this formulation. So, what exactly is my remaining discomfort with the magical arts? I think it simply has to do with the hocus-pocus & the big deal made of ancient secrets & so forth. The main thing that one has to do with the mystical program is dig through & get rid of all the excess baggage. What is really at the root of the process seems to be the advocacy of love as a way of being & that this way of being, self united with godhead, clarifies thought. It is not hard to imagine that the "purification" of one's intention to the degree that one's psyche is full of "love" utterly changes one's relationship to the world & its inhabitants. This is a fairly clear statement if not at all easy to accomplish.

In addition, the mystic & magical arts tend to lodge the creative ability in its leaders & teachers rather than being clear about the centrality of the creative element in human life in general. Further, these social forms of the "spiritual" impulse seem to actually stop short of a real formulation of the creative process in culture. Instead, they settle for a notion of the "discovery" of some pre-existent ideal self that is waiting for us if we would just follow the correct path. Again, rather than this somewhat convoluted notion which involves the insertion of the end product at the beginning, it is rather more logical to think that the development of altered states of consciousness displace the conventional construction of self so that it can be then "creatively" formed in a different & better mold. For my money, the process is essentially "creative;" it creates a certain sort of self deemed "spiritual." This new pattern is, of course, replete with a set of moral injunctions. Again, the psychological implantation of moral ideas is simple enough to state but somewhat more difficult to implement. It would seem that much of the aforementioned "baggage" has to do with the establishment of an arcane & ancient "authority" to provide authenticity & support the drive towards perfection.

In essence, then, the mystic path is emotional, ethical & psychological. Its aim is ultimately the transformation of self in the service of "ethical action." The action I am most interested in is "creative action." Thus, there really is no need to resort to the various sorts of "magic" in order to know how to make decisions, think about how one should relate to the world, come to understand oneself better and so forth. At root, the human journey appears to involve the development of awareness of the ways in which desire & all our intentions "create our world." We need to work with the idea that our "loving intention" & our rigorous reflection upon ourselves & the world we live in is ultimately in the service of the ongoing evolutionary unfolding of the world. It's something we just need to get on with, never mind the various spheres of angels, arcane alchemical symbolism, authoritarian gurus, divination & all the rest.

A note on sado-masochism power & pleasure

Reading a short passage in Teilhard de Chardin's opus, I had the intuition that the subject of sado-masochism was not off to the side as it were, but actually central or at least potentially so to the consideration of mysticism & perhaps religion in general. I realized that within the context of the sado-masochistic situation I could explore "power" in the spiritual context as well as aspects of "sacrifice" as well as even perhaps "initiation."

I spoke with a friend today over lunch & he was interested to know if there was a method or reflective practice that was very good or especially good for the investigation of one's self. He brought up a "problem" which he had chewed over for a good long time & wondered if this would be a good "example" with which to demonstrate such a method. At the time I wasn't really sure exactly what he was asking about or exactly why. On the one hand there was the idea expressed above but at the same time it was clear that he had some sort of special or personal interest in knowing about this particular problem. Two things then: we are speaking to the method & knowledge "about" the "object" of enquiry.

I briefly told him about the practice of phenomenology & Merleau Ponty's 5 key concepts to a methodological program which was nothing so much as an analytical breakdown of "what we already do" when we are thinking about something with the idea of discovering meaning. In the abstract I don't think the points meant all that much to him. I reiterated that the starting point of an exploration of such a subject as he wished to explore was to have as clear & as detailed a "description" of the issue as possible. But let's see what can be done with the little story that he gave me.

It seems he fell in love at first sight with a woman quite a long time ago. She was married. A number of years later he heard that this couple were breaking up or separating. They had moved closer to where he lived. It seemed that this relationship was quite abusive. He wondered why this woman (& women in general) often return again & again to these sorts of abusive relationships. He had the opinion that women were "hard-wired" for this behaviour.

There certainly is something mysterious, something enigmatic about this. Why does somebody return over & over to a situation that is so obviously not good. Why? Why do we, as humans, return over & over again to our pain, to our suffering? The return to our suffering is one aspect of the problem, but there is more than this. Why this particular sort of suffering, this particular sort of relationship? What is nature of the sado-masochistic situation? What is its hold over us, never mind, our suffering? These are, I think, two different questions. These two questions emerge from a simple laying out of the facts of the matter, the briefest & most general of descriptions, but where do we go from this? What next?

Well, let's deal with the first question to the best of our ability. To begin, again, we need to lay out the geography of the return to suffering. Why? We obviously are involved in some way with the play of pleasure & pain. We need to first of all acknowledge that there must be some "intention," some "desire" or some "need" for this behaviour. In a general way, then, & without dealing headon with the idea of sado-masochism, which will come later, we have to account for the need or the desire to return to our suffering, to our pain. Is this desire to suffer a conscious or unconscious desire? Because there is something mysterious & not at all obvious about this, we are led to think that there is something of the unconscious at work. There is something that operates in us, at an unconscious level, that takes us again & again back to our suffering, back to bad relationships and bad behaviour, that leads us to make the same mistake over & over again. If this behaviour is not actually consciously desired we must assume that we made some sort of mistake so that we believe that our behaviour, our return to pain, will "this time" get us what we really want? This time it will work!

Having thus set out a little the general contours of an exploration, the next thing that comes to mind is the question of exactly what must be initially set aside, bracketed, in order to get any real sense of the subject. Going back to the original few words above, we will need to set aside our ordinary understanding of what gives pleasure. This is exactly one of those instantly "givens" in ordinary life: what is pleasurable & thus also what is not pleasurable. This is no small thing because we will have to give up one of our leading guides as it were in understanding the world. If we can't say that we are attracted to the pleasurable & repulsed by unpleasure, (suffering or pain) what can we say about our movements in the world? We undoubtedly will have to find some other organizing principle, some other principle of attraction that guides us in the world. At this same time I want to make another correlation which has just occurred to me, the correlation between "the return to suffering" & the "abdication of our own personal power." The first we see as essentially neurotic, but will have to put this thought aside, while the second we see as essentially "spiritual" in the sense of giving ourselves over to a higher power. Naturally enough there is the political dimension of giving over our power whether in our daily life or in the context of education or spirituality. There is certainly the sense that ethical action must have its limit with regard to the impingement of self on others. This is different than the actual willful abdication of one's power to some other, where one could be expected to act on one's own, in the context of living & even in the return to our suffering. In this latter case, there is the sense that we have given up our power to the one who perpetrates our suffering. Why?

Already we have a clue with the notion of "impingement" because certainly this return to a situation which is outwardly "abusive" has this aspect of the one who causes suffering impinging upon the life & being of the one abused. As a passing note, we must realize, of course, the need to set aside our ordinary understanding of "abuse" first of all in the sense of it being some "universal" concept with regard to other universal standards pertaining to "proper relationships," the understanding of "universal human rights" or the "rights of the individual." Secondly we need to set aside our own personal feelings regarding this emotionally charged term "abuse" & its connotations of harmful sexuality, the wrongful exercise of power over children, & so forth. Perhaps these are simply slightly different aspects of the same thing.

To return, then, to the term "impingement" we turn to the concept as it appears in the context of Winnicott's object relations theory. This theory holds that when the needs of the mother "impinge" upon the needs of the infant, the normal developmental progress of the infant is distorted. This is so because normal developmental progress necessitates the mother's initial catering to the global power & self-centeredness of the infant, his or her omnipotence. This is the ground zero of the developing personality, the ground of confidence in one's own reality. Only slowly should this sense of personal omnipotence give way to the needs of others in the development of an individual self in the context of the society of other selves, each with its own needs. If, however, the infant grows into a child without his or her needs being adequately met but rather has had to learn "to look after" the mother (or main caregiver), then an inauthentic or "false self" comes into being, a self that is not centered in one's own reality, but in the reality & needs of the other. In simple terms, one grows up to be always looking after other people & lacking an essential self-regard.

In one sense, at least, this understanding would go some way towards explaining why a person, a woman, would return to an abusive relationship: she was not looking after herself but looking after the needs of the abusive man. In the same sense, one could say that this fact could be an influence in all cases whereby one gives up one's own power to the power of another. This notion of a "false self" & a lack of self rooted in one's own personal needs & desires hardly seems enough, however. Although it certainly pertains to our early recognition that the unconscious figures in the picture for this catering to others, this is what might be said to be a "moral masochism." (I remember reading I think, Theodore Reik's book regarding masochism in general & a chapter entitled "moral masochism." & no doubt my thoughts at this time are coloured by that reading although I have lost all detail.) In the case at hand all I am referring to is the situation in which one "gets pleasure" from satisfying the needs of others to the detriment of oneself.

Although I was thinking about the woman in her abusive relationship, as soon as I'd written the above sentence I realized that it sounded exactly like the general situation whereby one gives charitable service in a secular or spiritual context. One of the major tenets of religion & mysticism is precisely that we refrain from "feeding" our "small self" & indeed escape from it. The major ways of doing this are by denying ourselves pleasure and in general adopting an ascetic life-style & serving others. There is no doubt, however, that this rightly applies to the person with a "healthy ego" & should not arise out of a neurotic need. That being said, it is extremely difficult to tell the difference between a behaviour that serves a "neurotic need" & one which is "socially sanctioned." One might say that many of our socially sanctioned "good" behaviours started out as "neurotic needs." An easy example is the accumulation of material goods in our lives. We virtually sanctify the rich while the need that drives one to acquire riches is very often neurotic at its root.

What do I mean by "neurotic?" I mean behaviour that has the person in its grip as opposed to behaviour that the person is in control of. Thus neurosis is exactly that which blocks human freedom. Having said this, however, I am instantly aware that there is a certain difficulty with this definition as soon as we refer back to the notion that there is an undecideability with regard to whether the locus of control is outside or inside ourselves. It is clear that enlightened humanism places the locus of control "inside" while the religious or spiritual sensibility places it "outside" even though one with a spiritual outlook may say that God is found "inside." There still remains a difference because the God "inside" is still quite different than the ordinary empirical ego "inside." This leads us into the problem of the "small self" & the "large self" – the individual self & the cosmic self & their right relations if such are discoverable. Thus, it becomes clear that my statement re neurosis comes from the position of enlightened humanism & an ideal of individual freedom not found, in the same way, in the religious outlook. To exhibit my bias even further it should be obvious to see that it is easy enough to extend the metaphor of neurosis to actually "include" the spiritual outlook itself. From this point of view, the spiritual outlook is the social transformation of a neurotic need. We have been speaking of this particular "neurotic need" as the need to serve others but we could easily enlarge the need to include the "need for meaning." It's of course, much more difficult to argue that the need for meaning is "neurotic."

So many concepts: "impingement," the false self, the true self (in this case the "true" empirical self, having no spiritual connotations whatsoever), neurosis, pleasure, suffering & "the return," the return to suffering. We have, then, one notion, that of a distorted early development, which can be understood to lead us to look after the needs of others to our own detriment. However, in this case, the "suffering" we do is merely a by-product that we essentially ignore for the benefit of the other. This is less than satisfying because of course we wish to understand exactly the "pleasure of suffering" whereas we have only discovered the "pleasure which is worth the suffering." Again, this statement very much points to "spiritual" for we do not normally think that the saint or the mystic undergoes suffering at all for the pleasure of it the suffering is undergone in order to reach a greater goal. We are still searching then.

Several concepts come to mind & instantly the notion that they must, of course, be set aside. But first what are they? They are the concepts of "fetish" & the over-riding notion of the early developmental need for "relationship" in the development of a self as opposed to the "pleasure principle." Let me set aside the notion of "fetish" for a moment & deal with the second notion which in many ways is akin to the notion of "impingement" discussed earlier. My understanding is that this notion of the importance of the "relationship" comes from another proponent of object relations theory, W.R.D. Fairbairn, in the context of the development of psychoanalytic thought. (The notion of paternalistic society also springs to mind - itself as an explanatory idea re the precisely "female" return to the abusive relationship. Again, I must get back to this later. I only mention it now because I am interested in demonstrating how the mind works, how it jumps about in the pursuit of its object. With these words "the pursuit of its object" immediately also comes to mind the notion that I am concerned with the reflective capacity of the mind & wonder instantly if "reflectivity" itself can hold some key to the notion of the return to suffering – obviously an inability to reflect upon an object – it's unconsciousness would hinder one but...) To get back, then, to Fairbairn's idea that a young child is more interested in establishing a relationship of whatever sort, even if a very abusive or bad one, with its parents than having none at all. Fairbairn saw the significance of the libido as having adhesive qualities. This concept regarding the object-seeking behaviour goes directly against Freud's notion of pleasure-seeking behaviour in the development of the self. In the Freudian scenario, "bad" relations, "bad" feelings of aggression & sexuality would be repressed & later projected onto others while one would internalize "as self" only those "good" feelings, thoughts, etc. But this notion does not exactly address the question of "the return" which is at the very core of clinical work in psychoanalysis: the return to our suffering, the return to neurotic behaviour, the constant chewing over of the same old things, a return, I should say, that is only sometimes alleviated by conscious knowledge. Even when we know the roots of our neurosis in our childhood traumas this does not necessarily mean that our neurosis goes away. Far from it.

I immediately think of sexual aberrations of all sorts. While there are certainly arguments that certain behaviours are "natural" & only our society's attitudes are "un-natural" & deviant & suppressive, there can be no doubt that many of such behaviours or aspects of such behaviours are rooted in shall we say "less than perfect" early development. Whether it is in early development or later attitudes, "society" has its hand as it were in the problem. In addition I think of the work of Wilhelm Reich who also addressed this notion of "the return" with his concept of the "bodily unconscious." Conscious knowledge of the roots & development of our neurotic behaviour does not free us precisely because the neurosis is locked into our body in chronic muscle tensions. But I want to jump outside the bracket at this point realizing that perhaps this is not a "wandering off" or "aside" but still on the point. This notion of the bodily unconscious can also go a certain way towards explaining the return to an abusive relationship. The only question then would be the exact nature of early development that would lead one to either "enjoy" suffering or be willing to "put up with it" for some greater good.

As I have said, the "putting up with it" explanation seems easy enough. So far we have the notion of "impingement," the over-riding need for relationship of whatever sort" & now also the notion of a bodily unconscious that would encode our very need in our bodies, out of reach of the reflective capacity. But I realize that I didn't finish my thought with regard to the second idea "the over-riding need" because I got caught up in the idea that this was "different" than Freud's notion of the operation of the pleasure principle. The idea is, then, that the child's need for relationship at all costs over-rides the pleasure principle. Thus the child makes the "attachment" in whatever way is possible, never-mind the abusive, self-centered or neurotic behaviour of the care-giver. Never mind the distancing, the pushing away, the denial of love, the child "needs" the relationship above all else. Thus, for instance, in my own case, my attachment to my father has a general "melancholic" cast. This is precisely because of my own father's anguish, his emotional distance, his inability to express love (except under the influence of alcohol & in his painting). The first was detrimental to his well-being, the second, painting, his salvation. My experience of what is most "authentic" has been coloured by this sadness, the sadness rooted in the emotional distance between myself & my father in my early years. Thus I have come to feel that the "truth" of the world is essentially melancholic, & this experience colours my creative life, my most authentic expression. I do believe I "understand" this to a great extent, although perhaps not "all," but this understanding has changed my sense of melancholic authenticity not at all. Perhaps this is not quite true because my awareness that this is not "really" the nature of "all" truth but rather the nature of "my truth" means that I am more flexible in my understanding, more able to take the position of the "other" in my understanding of the world & its situations.

This notion of "being able to take the position of the other" stands at the centre of human "empathy" & thus compassion. It also is the essential notion of the "engine" that powers "moral development" & also I suppose intellectual or cognitive development in general. This understanding comes out of my discussions with Jeremy Carpendale & neo-Piagetian thought with its emphasis upon human inter-action. "Development" in general, then, concerns the ability to take more & more different "positions" into account when making a decision with regard to anything at all. This notion of "development" very much concerns the reflective capacity & the conscious "holding" of "objects" in mind in order to "reflect" upon them. From the "spiritual" point of view this notion of "development" has very precise limits insomuch as it is ultimately concerned with the strategic relations between subjects & objects in consciousness.

It hardly needs to be said that the possession of empathy & compassion is another social or "moral" reason for undergoing suffering, but it is clearly that sort of suffering undergone for the sake of a higher goal. Although it may be somewhat difficult to see the "higher goal" in the suffering undergone in an abusive relationship, it really takes no great leap to the realization that a woman who returns to such a situation sees herself as the "salvation" of the abusive partner. This notion of women believing they can "change" men is very much a cliché in contemporary life and the current social psychological thought. It seems to be quite common in the context of alcoholism & has led to the notion of the non-alcoholic's complicity in upholding the alcoholic's "world." It should be clear enough that this willingness to undergo suffering in order to "change" a man is very much in the domain of "moral masochism" mentioned earlier. There is no pleasure in the suffering or, at least at the level of our current understanding, pleasure in the suffering is not the main point.

So, let's look at it for a moment "head on." What can it mean to find pleasure in suffering? But for that matter, what can "head on" mean? I could mean, I suppose, "defining" our terms. What is the nature of "pleasure" for instance. All this while I have been discussing it, I have never "set aside" or bracketed my common understanding of "pleasure." What is it? Something is pleasurable if it give pleasure. Yes, indeed! If it "feels good." OK. There is almost an element of "sensuality" or sensual perception as an aura around the notion of pleasure. There is something "bodily" about it. Although, of course, one might have intellectual pleasure, one feels that this is an extension of bodily pleasure & that the body is at the root. Some things "feel" good, while other things feel "bad" or are at least "uncomfortable." Comfort & uncomfort, then. It would seem that we are back at the "pleasure

141

principle" simply stated as "pleasure" is that which we are attracted to while "unpleasure" is that which we are repulsed by. Pleasure, then, is in direct relationship to our "desire," our "wants" & our "needs." Pleasure is that which "satisfies" a desire or a need. Unpleasure is that which fails to satisfy. I have the sense that we are closing in on something but we aren't there yet. Although we have this idea of "satisfaction" we still don't know what a desire or a need is or why we have certain desires & how is a need different from a desire?

Without being able to answer our questions re desire or need, we can go back to re-state our initial question or to make a statement about it. The problem is, then, how to understand "suffering" as satisfying a desire or a need. What sort of desire or need is satisfied by suffering? But before we can even think of that we realize that although we have a little insight into "pleasure" we have almost none into unpleasure, i.e. suffering. Let us look a little more closely at "suffering" & thus at the bodily root of it that is "pain." What is pain? It is that which "hurts." It is a "sensation" which is unpleasant & that we instinctively wish to avoid. Can we apply these two terms, "sensation" & "instinct," to both "pleasure" & "pain"? Is there an "instinctual" attraction towards one & a repulsion by the other? The simple answer seems to be "yes." Yippee, our problem is solved by the idea of "instinct." But, of course, we don't yet know what "instinct" is, or at least we don't know anything more than what we "instantly" know: that is, instinct is some force in the body that is outside or by-passes our cognitive abilities & makes us do things or desire things. The essential instincts are: hunger & sexual desire &, of course, aggression, in the defense of our self or territory.

But how does this sensory spectrum with pleasure at one end & pain at the other fit into the "instincts?" Pleasure & pain certainly seem to have a "natural" place in our understanding of how the body works. We also, of course, have begun, in a general "scientific" sense, that there is a great deal of cognition in the mix; in fact what we feel as pleasure or pain actually involves a lot of "interpretation" not necessarily at the level of conscious thought. Perhaps we might have to think of these terms as only partly instinctual or "biological" with some other part that is interpretive or social. Just as with emotion in general, there is an interpretive aspect, not conscious, but nonetheless present.

There is surely a "biological" component to both pleasure & pain, but at this time I really don't know how to talk about it much. There is a notion, I think, that "pain" has something to do with the "intensity" of a sensation, the notion that beyond a certain "threshold" a sensation which may have begun as pleasurable becomes "painful." This seems to be true as a phenomenological reality; a light blow or stroking of the arm may be pleasurable or certainly not painful, but when the intensity of the sensation is increased, the hardness of the blow or even of the stroking becomes painful. Without going deeply into it, we could say I think, with not too much chance of disagreement that with pleasure there is a physical as well as psychological component. We could also say that there is physicality to pain & also a psychological aspect. Certain physical sensations may easily appear to be more "painful" than otherwise warranted simply because they are not desired or signal displeasure, for instance.

Where does this get us? Well, one could say that we now have a slightly different situation, a slightly different problem. Now, we question how does one come to "interpret" (whether consciously or unconsciously) a sensation that in ordinary circumstances would be painful, as pleasurable? With this re-phrasing of the question, we are right in the middle of the sado-masochistic dilemma. We also have to recognize that while this may be an element in the abusive situation under consideration, there is also a psychological or social factor, large or small, that may have nothing whatsoever to do with the sado-masochistic transformation, if such it is, of pain into pleasure. Clearly there are a number of factors at work. Perhaps this is the place to enumerate them and stand back for a moment & take a look at the situation. We have a) a social factor (patriarchal society with attitudes concerning the "place" of women, their relationship to men & so on) b) a psychological aspect (that concerns developmental issues concerning "sacrifice" of self for other due to early "impingement" & the need for relationship – in this instance, a non-sexual aspect, & c) a sado-masochistic element, (which may or may not be present, but which also concerns the psychological domain & probably developmental issues.)

Our explanations so far, as partial as they are, go towards explaining how the behaviour of returning to an abusive situation "functions" to satisfy certain needs or desires. We have elaborated these needs & desires in terms of the patriarchy & the satisfaction of role expectations concerning women, developmental psychology & the satisfaction of the "need" to look after others & the "need" to have any relationship rather than no relationship. We have also spoken briefly of the notion that one is "needed" for the salvation of the other & also the satisfaction of the need to be a "good" person by being charitable.

Let's look particularly at the sado-masochistic element with the notion that this may function in the sexual domain as well as in the moral & indeed the "everyday" realm of our activity. Head on, the question is something like: why do I desire to be abused perhaps in painful ways, both physical & psychological? It pops into my mind that a simple answer might be: because I believe that I'm the sort of person that deserves to be abused & punished. What can this mean? How would I come to such a conclusion? The easy answer is that from my very early years I was treated in this way. My mistakes were over & over again pointed out to me, & I was punished over & over again for even the smallest infractions of rules. rules that were no doubt inadequately understood or kept changing so that I never knew exactly how to satisfy my parents. Easy – I grew up thinking I was a stupid person who didn't deserve pleasure or success. What is more, given the general psychological need for relationship in order to be any sort of "real" person at all, in my adult life I continue to reach out for exactly the same kind of relationship I grew up with. I loved my father, abusive or not, & subsequently I love my partner, whether abusive or not. In this case the painful psychological & physical abuses are exactly the known terms of my "love."

I realize, having jumped to this "easy" answer that I have avoided the head-on question of sexuality, or perhaps I have just realized that the sexual dimension is not really that pertinent. Perhaps it is in reality, a sort of red herring that merely deflects us from the proper consideration of the question. Perhaps. Perhaps not. In any event, the situation is a little different than the one in which I merely put up with suffering in order to achieve a higher goal. In this case, the suffering has been directly substituted for the goal – a slap, shall we say, for a loving stroke of the neck. The notion is that I can come to love the slap because I "interpret" it to mean that "I am loved. After all, if I was not loved, my partner wouldn't even bother with me at all. Never mind that he says that he hates the sight of me. That is simply because the poor thing doesn't properly understand his own mind."

Here, a whole new can of worms has been opened up: the can of worms that is the other partner in the abusive situation. So far we have dealt with the situation only in terms of the one side of the equation, the woman's part, (or rather we should say the passive partner because it is sometimes the man,) & her return to the abusive situation. Perhaps we really have gone as far as we can go without actually looking at the "relationship" between the two. Perhaps, perhaps not!

So far we have only dealt with the notion of "power" in a sort of tangential way: the "power" of the parents to "impinge" upon the needs of the young child is implicit in the situation as well as the overwhelming "need" for the parent-child relationship of whatever sort. But now, with the consideration of the abusive "relationship" itself we come up against the clear exercise of power in the adult situation. Power! It is a fascinating and enigmatic idea. What is its simple meaning? Some old political definition comes to mind: power is the ability to get other people to do what you want them to do. This idea still seems pretty good, so let's start there. The question is, then, why do I let this other person who abuses me exert power over me? Or why do I abdicate my own power in this situation?

Putting things together with each other, just letting ideas rub up against each other without understanding their relationship is sometimes a useful thing to do. Power & pleasure. What is their relationship? What is the relationship between power & sexuality, power & the moral good? Just beginning to think about the relationship of these ideas, it jumps into my mind, at this moment, that we have not yet discussed the notion of "transference" in the context of psychoanalytic thought. Transference is the notion that we bring over unconscious aspects of our early relationships to our later mature relationships. Thus I am apt to bring over to various different sorts of authority my own early relationship with authority, and I do this in an unconscious way. I "project" this way of being or "attitude" upon other people or situations. This understanding, then, is intrinsic to our earlier discussion of "impingement" & the need for relationship as well as the feeling that I am undeserving of anything but abuse. I "transfer" these feelings & understanding of others in their relationship to me from my early experience to my present life.

This notion of transference goes some way towards explaining the "repetition" compulsion, the notion that I return again & again to the same problematic situations & behaviour because I am unconscious of the dynamics of the early relationship & have "repressed" them or simply "forgotten" them or perhaps because I never really knew them at all, I transfer these feelings & ways of behaving onto others in the present. In such a way I carry my past with me at all times; in fact, I am a sort of slave to this past & cannot help myself. This is the "power" of the past, the "power" of the unconscious. Of course, as soon as we open up this, even very brief discussion of psychoanalysis, we also must mention the idea that what we "forget" or repress is exactly that which we don't like (unpleasure), i.e. murderous thoughts towards our parents or "dirty" sexual ideas or desires of all sorts that don't fit into either the concept of a "good" person or a "good" society. In this case, the general case, perhaps the pleasure principle seems to retain explanatory power. Precisely because these desires have gone "underground" so to speak, they are nonetheless "locked into" our behaviour & our bodies in such a way that they are active in our behaviour & being. We are unaware of this activity & its influence on our being. Others, of course, are often very aware of these aspects of ourselves that we are unconscious of. It is not at all easy to bring them to our awareness when very often these unconscious elements are deeply woven into our very conception of the nature of "reality" & "truth" not to mention just "the way we are." Thus, there is need for the therapeutic disciplines.

This is the notion of "power" then in the relationship, both the "power" that is brought over from the past for both parties of the abusive relationship & the "power" that is exercised by one over the other. I suppose that we could go into the dynamics of the powerful one, the development of the abusive personality, & the nature of sadism in its psychological & sexual aspects but I prefer to let that wait, I think, & let it unravel with our continued focus on the masochistic return. I haven't used this term "masochistic return" before, nor, for that matter, have I come up with any definition of masochism or sadism. I suppose it's another spectrum. In the sexual domain we have the simple understanding of the sadist as one who gets sexual pleasure by inflicting pain on others while the masochist is one who gets sexual pleasure from having this pain inflicted. An easy observation is that these two need each other. For some reason it seems funny, the fact of this mysterious mutual need that seems to elude our ordinary logical understanding. The humour no doubt comes from the anxiety surrounding this enigmatic relationship that seems to be so much at the root of our own psychology, although we have a great deal of difficulty speaking of it or understanding it. As I say, even with cognitive understanding, we still need to come to grips with the reality of the situation: the relationship of power, pleasure & sexuality.

I take this, then, the relationship between "power, pleasure & sexuality" to be at the root of the moral "social" situation. For me, the social situation is the extrapolation & expansion of the bodily relationship between these three or to say it another way, the relationship of power, pain & pleasure in the domain of sexuality. Perhaps I need to say a word about this priority in my thought. This is the general priority, I believe, for enlightened humanism whereas those with a spiritual orientation tend to reverse these priorities so that the "spiritual" comes first & the physicality & mentality come later & more often than not act as a distortion of the spiritual. As I've noted elsewhere, this seems to be a main difference between the scientific orientation of Freud & the spiritual orientation of Jung. For Freud, & for Reich after him, sexuality is at the root & models our experience & understanding of the sacred. For Jung, spirituality comes first & sexuality is a distortion or a "lower" manifestation of this energy. The basic denigration of the body in relationship to the mind or spirit comes from the essentially spiritual orientation, at least in the West, & its emphasis upon the distinction between the purity of the "higher" & the impurity of the "lower" bodily aspects of reality. Shit is the lowest.

Obviously enough, I follow Freud in believing that sexuality came first. This is, of course, also the position of evolutionary thought in general. Certainly in the context of evolution we were sexual beings before thinking beings. We are carried into the future on the wings of the past, or we drag the past into the present with us. We are firmly in "time." Memory is how we get wherever it is we get to as well as what we bring along. What are the roots of the sado-masochistic sexual relationship then? Or first, sexuality, what of its general dynamics? What of the genitals, the penis, the vulva, the anus, the breasts, the buttocks? What of 'fucking' & 'being fucked'? What of penetration & being penetrated? What of mouths & tongues & hands? What of the feet, the eyes, the hair? What of being underneath or on top? What of tying up or being tied? What of vaginal or anal intercourse? What of heterosexuality & homosexuality? What of pornography & eroticism? What of kissing & sucking, 'blowjobs' &... but wait a minute. How are we supposed to tell the difference between "natural" sex & un-natural or "perverted" sex? That is to say how are we to tell the difference say, between the general dynamics of sex & sado-masochism?

The fact is, it's a mess. Talking about it is not at all easy, not as easy as talking about mysticism, for instance. The body & sexuality as objects of reflection are deeply disturbing, & perhaps most disturbing of all is the topic of S & M. Years ago I read a book that I thought was really quite good. It was a combination of psychological insight & practical suggestion and was entitled, I believe: S & M, the last Taboo, although I'm not sure. I don't remember very much in detail from that book except that it gave a lot of permission to explore different sexual desires & ways of behaving. I thought it was a really good idea at the time and still do. The idea that S & M was essentially a "theatrical" arena was, I thought, a really great insight. It brought sexuality into the domain of the story: one could act out in rudimentary outline various stories that intrigued one. These stories inevitably turned out to be quite simple & they revolved, simply enough, around "power," particularly the extremes of power – absolute power & abject slavery. I don't think there's much need to go into this theatrical aspect in any detail except to note that putting it into that domain placed what was going on firmly in the ranks of conscious activity. Thus it brought the twin notions of pain & pleasure into the domain of "play acting" & thus, of course, emphasized the psychological aspects of pain & pleasure, power & subjugation. The dynamics of power had to do with the subduing of "natural" wildness, the bringing into play of early psychological attitudes & traumas including humiliations of different sorts, embarrassment concerning the genitals, bodily excretion, etc.

In the clearly conscious domain the one subjugated, bound, forced (in the context of a rape fantasy, for instance) is offered a clear way of getting around any & all aspects of engaging in "bad" behaviour, behaviour that one shouldn't by any stretch of the imagination actually "enjoy." Because one is "forced" then it's not one's own fault that one does all those "naughty" things that are so much fun. The concept of "dirt" & "dirtiness" is, of course, central here. [See the note on Mary Douglas & "Dirt."] The "dirty" & "impure" are exactly where conceptual categories are "mixed up" & this is precisely where "energy" lies. The "breaking of the rules" releases energy [see Bataille].

Identity & creativity: a short note on the self

I recently met someone who was a clinical hypnotist & as far as I can tell he had no way to speak about the nature of the self, its development or its place in thought, except of course he could assert that "I am." He thought that a discussion I was having with another person about the social construction of the self & so on was "just words" & that the way you could tell you had an authentic self was you just looked at yourself & your thoughts & then you could tell. When asked, "Who looks" he just replied, "I look." "Who are you," I asked. "I am me. I just am," he answered. He went on to assert that the self is not "constructed" or "maintained" but existed right from the beginning when a person was born. He was willing to admit that some change did occur over time but didn't really know how to articulate this. I was aware that this person operated with a series of unexamined assumptions concerning the self. In phenomenological terms, he articulated his understanding of the "everyday world" of meanings that are transparent & immediately obvious. Beneath that, at least in conversation, we could not go.

Such an attitude is common. Most people do not examine their felt sense of being an individual, having a self that is unique & belongs to them. However, it is disturbing that the concept was so unexamined by someone who was a clinical hypnotherapist as well as holding other therapeutic roles. Having said this, the question I ask myself now concerns whether this is really a lack of awareness, as it appears, or whether a radically different conception of the self is in play & that in the context of our "western" & "intellectual" discussion, the very terms of the discussion meant that this person could not participate. In more general terms, I suppose, the question concerns "indigenous psychology" & what could be called the "pre-modern" sense of self in relationship to the "modern self." In a general way, the self that we all just "have" as a natural birthright is thoroughly embedded in a set of cultural beliefs. It is in the context of this set of cultural beliefs that this "ordinary" or "natural" self is created or simply "appears."

Let us look first at the notion of "indigenous psychology." This will clearly involve a discussion of different psychological ideas from around the world embedded within the context of larger belief systems. With regard to earlier psychological systems, this larger context will be primarily "mythological." I realize that I have not anywhere really discussed the nature & meaning of mythology. Such a discussion will obviously be useful in many different contexts for it will necessarily deal with the place of mythology in the contemporary world and the relationship between mythology & science or rational discourse. Of course, "mythology" has not "disappeared" from the contemporary scene, neither has it changed its essential nature. But perhaps it has assumed a different position & status in the discourses of power at work in the industrial & post-industrial world.

A Note on Mythology

Before getting into the discussion proper, I would like to make a few initial general remarks about the nature of mythology. First off I would like to note that often today we have the notion of "mythology" as something not true, something that is illusion, purely "mythical." This places the truth of mythology in direct opposition to the truth of science & factuality & finds it wanting. There is certainly some truth to this assertion, but it surely misses the mark concerning the real nature & meaning of mythology. It is something like saying that a statement is "purely poetic" and therefore not really "true." Just as obviously, "mythology" & "poetry" do not aim at the same sort of "truth" as do science and rational discourse. Today, "mythology" to a great extent has entered into the domain of popular entertainment & advertising.

But what is mythology? The most succinct definition I can think of right now is that myths are stories that are meant to guide behaviour. Many today feel that we have no mythology, or that we need the wisdom of the world's lost mythologies or at least their wisdom, perhaps embodied in new stories. In a general way, I suppose this feeling that we need the old myths is that we need new moral & ethical guides for behaviour & especially religious or spiritual ones. Of course, one of the more obvious facts about the old mythologies is that they are embedded in the context of cultural beliefs dominated by religious symbology. Mythology & ritual comprise, in fact, the main components of pre-modern religious life.

There has been a feeling for a very long time now that, with the collapse of the traditional authority of religion & its capitulation to science, we have lost our way with regards to moral behaviour. The fact is that the burden of moral decision-making that has fallen on the individual, in the wake of the collapse of religious guidance, seems too heavy a burden for the individual to bear. There is, in a general way, nostalgia for community & the unity of that community brought about by a common religious bond. Certainly, this felt need is one very good reason why religion seems to have survived long after it was prophesied to be dead. The "old" myths are understood as embodiments of spiritual wisdom that has been lost in the West, forgotten in the pursuit of materialistic values.

This is certainly true to a certain extent, but it is also important to remember that these old stories, while they embodied spiritual knowledge, also embodied a whole way of life that included political power. The stories were then, as they still are today, concerned with showing the "right" & the "wrong" ways of behaving, the "proper" & the "improper" ways of being. They encoded cultural history & philosophy & power. Today, we tend to lose track of this relationship to political structure because, for the most part, the myths are taken out of their context & generally "read" for their "universal" spiritual content. It hardly needs to be said that this approach is very likely to arrive at meanings quite different than the original meanings intended. On the other hand, we tend to read our own mythology concerning the relationship of men, for instance, to their cars, or the relationship of cars to women. These relationships are encoded in small "stories" about the purchase of certain items & the "spiritual" or "emotional" elements that one will somehow magically acquire with this purchase. Because the religious has been usurped by the scientific in a materialist consumer culture, our "spiritual" values have tended to be replaced by "monetary" ones. This does not, however, stop some of the new age prophets from attempting to link older "spiritual" values & the acquisition of money.

Another important element that differs in the older & the newer mythology is the widespread substitution of technology for animals. The older myths were created in the context of totemic culture, a world in which animal life was incredibly important. The implicit context of "nature" inhabited by animate forces & animal ancestors may be contrasted directly with our own focus upon city life &, of course, our romantic conception of nature as a place to get away to in order to experience the freshness & innocence of our own early days.

Roland Barthes has a very good essay entitled I believe "Myth today" in which he outlines the mythology of bourgeois culture in advertising. In that essay, he defines mythology, at least today, as that kind of story that is "parasitic" on history. Myths of all sorts reduce historical personages to "types" even "archetypes" by eliminating historical detail & leaving only essence. For Barthes these essences were parasitic on historic reality. Now, in terms of wisdom, "essence" is a very good thing but when we reduce contemporary Industrial era Bourgeois culture (with all of the distortions in human relationships occasioned by capitalism) to a set of "essential" characters who appear as heroic archetypes, all we do is perpetrate a lie. Unfortunately, we must assume that such a process was also going on in the earlier mythology; that is to say, power was embodied in "mythic" stories in such a way that it looked "natural." Power & the structures of power in society (whether to do with gender, status, money, heritage) always wish to appear natural because then everybody simply accepts the way things are because, well, that's just the way things are. The fact that we are no longer interested in the actual historical context of the old myths means that we miss this disjunction between mythology & actuality "back then" & are left with only the heroic "universal" figures. We certainly do need to continue to keep our eyes peeled for the presentation of the "natural." Myths, as stories about the right & the wrong, good & evil, always present themselves as universal truth.

Existentialism & the Self

I have just gotten a philosophy magazine dedicated to Sartre on the occasion of his hundredth birthday. In the first article, the author states that Sartre's philosophy that of existentialism is predicated upon a single statement: existence precedes essence. From this come a number of other statements, among them: doing precedes being. This statement is, of course, in opposition to the spiritual understanding of the world as created by a Supreme Being or power. For those who are religious the reverse statement is true: essence precedes existence. In addition, Sartre's existential statement precludes such quasi-spiritual notions as the archetypes & idealism in the sense of there being pre-existent ideals of a moral life which we are meant to fulfill. No, from the point of view of existentialism, which is a practical common-sense view, first we exist having come into being in the process of evolution. We are free, free to create our ideals, our notions of essence. God didn't make us; we made God.

With regard to the question of freedom & the continual need to choose between courses of action in order to accomplish our projects to change ourselves & the world, Sartre has said, "we are what we make of what others have made of us." The two sides of the human equation are in this statement: 1) we are made by others in the context of history & 2) we are free & this freedom is expressed in our creative role in the world. In terms of our consideration of the self, this means we must take account of how the self is made or constructed in the image of others & how the self gains its freedom, its ability to create or re-create itself & the world.

Question: Is this self constituted as self-consciousness & consciousness "of" something and involved in projects as it is, in contradiction to the "pure consciousness" which has no self, no object & has no project which appears to be the case with Zen as put forth by Merton? With Zen, we discover over & over again that it is not "really" emptiness of consciousness that is aimed at. If there really is no project, what are these Zen masters doing teaching people, even in their obscure way? What we find, in fact, is that we are speaking of escaping from the ego that "craving" its objects & whose only sense of pleasure is the completion of its projects. It is not consciousness itself which is seen as different from the two points of view, rather it is the concept of "desire" that is at issue. Whereas Sartre emphasizes the necessity of human freedom and choice, in balance with responsibility to the community, as expressions of desire, Zen emphasizes doing away with the desirous condition itself. It's not that to be human we have projects, but to be an enlightened human we attain to having no desire, no projects. This lack of the desire of ego & its projects is aimed at precisely because it is seen in the context of the briefness of life & the apparent meaninglessness of our desires & projects in the context of eternity.

But, what exactly does this state of mind, if it is a state of mind, achieve? Most obviously perhaps this "equanimity" is understood to bring a deeper & more abiding satisfaction. That is to say that it avoids much suffering although it does not, together with all other philosophies, avoid death itself. The problem, & this is the cause of many of the simple but contradictory <u>language games</u> played by Zen, is that one cannot "aim" at this state of mind because then one would just be having one more desire, the desire for enlightenment. Thus for Zen, this acquisition which is not an acquisition, of a self which is not a self, of consciousness which is a void & a void which is consciousness, is a tricky business.

What is aimed at is an "indifference" to personal attainment & the death "of that ego-identity or self-consciousness which is constituted by a calculating and desiring ego." (Merton, 1968, p. 242).

The term "language game" can refer to Wittgenstein's usage "to designate simple forms of language, 'consisting of language and the actions into which it is woven', and unified by family resemblance. The concept was intended 'to bring into prominence the fact that the speaking of language is part of an activity, or a form of life' (Wikipedia). Meaning is created in language somewhat like a move in a game: there are a set of rules, a context, & certain moves may be made, while others may not.

Zen language usage with regard to the Koan is a sort of game to be played, the aim of which is to bring about sudden awareness beyond the ordinary solving of a puzzle. It is not a rational game.

The puzzle always always always concerns "desire." This is the force that is problematical. For desire constitutes the self. The self is created in relation to that which it desires, and everything that appears in consciousness is defined by, if not created by, our "intention" towards it which is our desire. Our relations with others & the world are defined by our desire. Our happiness is attained through the attainment of our desires. Desire may run the whole gamut from sensual desire to spiritual desire. Love, of course, in all of its different manifestations, is the expression of desire. Hatred & anger & all of the negative emotions have their origin in the frustration of desire. Thus all of our happiness as well as all of our unhappiness have its origin in desire.

From this it is easy to see that a different state of consciousness could be achieved if one were freed from desire. One would have a different sort of self, a different sort of relationship with the world, a different sort of being. This is not so easy to accomplish, even if one strongly wished to accomplish it, for one cannot aim at this accomplishment. One cannot desire the lack of desire. One cannot desire the death of the self without losing one's lack of desire.

Merton gives us St John of the Cross's "dark night of the soul" as the complete frustration of all attainment: memory & understanding are gone and there is complete darkness. Indeed his description of the state sounds like nothing so much as a profound depression. It is in this place where nothing is seen, nothing is attained, nothing is desired, and nothing is thought or imagined, that the soul is safest for it is not drawn to one thing or another, one desire or another.

A brief Note on the Western Contemplative Tradition

When trying to contemplate the notion of "pure consciousness," consciousness with no concept of self & of one's relations to the world, the tendency to resort to analogy with animal consciousness is very strong. Even "instinct" if it is present is silent & not in the mind but in the body, certainly not in reflective consciousness.

For myself the notion of the "pure" is suspect in the context of consciousness just as it is suspect in all other aspects of life. Purity is seen as the distilling of a substance to its "purest essence." Everything extraneous is taken away, and of course all "ambiguity" must go. All "dirt" must vanish, for dirt is simply that matter which is "out of place." For purity to be achieved there must be nothing out of place. I can't help but thinking that what "goes" when one "purifies" anything at all, is its relationship to other things, other states, other beings, to anything other than itself.

Think of the purity of something that is constituted as a single element, something like "water" for instance; water is constituted as something in itself with a particular molecular structure. Extraneous elements or dirt may be filtered out. But what happens when we attempt to "purify" something that is more complex & involves "relationship" or even many relationships – that is to say, for instance, something like a "sexual relationship" or "marriage" or "building a house" or "running a race." Then, presumably one would engage in trying to find the essential nature of the sexual relation or running the race. But always there would be a relationship; there would be very little sense in trying to define the "pure" sexual relationship or the "pure" race by describing only the being of one of the lovers or only the interior state & activity of the runner. No, if there is to be purity, the relationship must remain. No matter what difficulties, & there are many, the relationship remains of the essence. One might even say that an approach to the essence of a sexual relationship is to note that there are at least two people involved in sex or that the essence of a race is that it involves the activity of at least two entities who try to better each other.

How do we, then, approach purifying consciousness which is in its "natural" state apparently something that involves a relationship, the relationship between the subject & an object? Consciousness is always consciousness "of" something. How do we arrive at the state of pure consciousness which does not involve a relationship, has no subject or object. In the light of our above brief discussion, the notion of purifying consciousness in this way makes no sense. But given that the proponents of Zen must mean "something," what do they mean?

I propose that they mean nothing so much as that essence precedes existence, that the ground of being, that is, large consciousness, precedes the emergence of individual consciousness in it. Once this is established, then the relationship between individual consciousness & its objects becomes trivial & ephemeral, just like a passing shadow, in the context of the larger consciousness which engulfs the little flame of individual consciousness. One becomes an "object" in the eye of God, whose vastness cannot be reflected upon simply because it is so vast. To hold such an idea is very difficult in the first place because it so goes against common sense. I mean there is very little support for the notion that there is a God, or that there is an enveloping consciousness that includes everything, or that our meaning is pre-made for us. While on the other hand, there is every evidence that existence precedes consciousness: that consciousness is the result of evolutionary activity & individual development, and that consciousness is constituted as a relationship, & that we make our own meaning. To reverse the common sense understanding in this way is to bring the concept of "faith" into play.

Thus we have "faith" in play & "pure consciousness" which involves the identification of the small self with the larger self which is the all & everything. In order to achieve this identification we have various practices which aim to kill desire & eradicate the small self, for it is by killing our own desires that we fall in line with the desire of the cosmos.

Thus we see that much of the confusion involved in trying to understand Zen & mysticism in general (no matter if Zen is mystical or not), is caused by the fact that while the surface appears to change (object, no object, self, no self, desire, no desire) in fact what has changed is the underlying "ground" rules of the game. It is so difficult to understand how these changes can come about in consciousness & the self when consciousness & the self are constituted in the way they are, as intentional relationships. This is precisely because these changes cannot occur in the context of existence when the individual self is seen as the center of consciousness, that is, when existence precedes essence. Only by re-locating the center of consciousness in the "everywhere" can we re-conceive of the individual self in different terms. This new self is predicated upon essence (God or Void) preceding individual consciousness. That is to say, the mystical self inhabits a certain sort of world, one understood to be "spiritual" in nature. The central problem it seems to me, then, is the problem of human freedom. If essence precedes existence, where is human freedom? We are doomed to the continual rediscovery of what already is. That is the scientific task devoid of creativity, because of course; creativity is re-allocated to the all & taken away from the individual. This is a reversal of the humanist revolution.

There can really be no doubt at this point that far from disappearing, religion is going through a vast renovation or transformation, & is very powerful in the world. We cannot simply say that this is a retrograde development, although in many regards it is. No, we must acknowledge that we are entering a new age in which "faith" will re-assert itself in some new form.

I made a statement above that I would like to comment upon: "For it is by killing our own desires that we fall in line with the desire of the cosmos." For many, to bring one's consciousness into harmony with the consciousness of God or even with "nature" is a good & a wonderful thing. The morality of such a position has been spelled out in more or less clear ways in the context of religious belief worldwide. For me, however, believing as I do that existence precedes essence, this "moral harmony" gained by identification with godhead is actually a covert projection of one's own values. It seems to constitute in Sartre's terms "bad faith" insomuch as it denies one's human freedom. However, this may not be so for one may argue that one can choose this harmony or choose to go one's own way as it were. In any event, the situation appears to me much like that of the masochist who, in order to achieve pleasure, pretends that he or she is being forced to participate & is in fact punished for exactly taking that pleasure, and all through no will of one's own. Don't get me wrong, the masochistic position in sexual play or anywhere else is as legitimate a position as any other; it is the question of "fooling oneself" that is the difficulty.

For some time now I have said, with regard to what I have called the "Ancient Wisdom Scams" & the enhancement of consciousness in the context of New Age beliefs, that the worst sort of scammer is that one who has actually scammed himself. There is the crook & then there is the crook that has persuaded himself that he is a good man. The case of Hitler comes to mind. I came across a statement on the bottom of someone's e-mail to the effect that religion is a terrible thing: without it good people would do good things, bad people would do bad things, but it takes religion to have good people do bad things. I suppose this is a little obscure. At the start I do not really believe that there are many "scam artists" out there who are really cynically running a number on people. This means that in fact what I have called "scams" are not really scams in the ordinary sense. They are scams in the sense that all "spiritual" enhancement & magical practices which are organized so that individuals give up their freedom to some sort of authority are scams. People are "taken in" by the dangling of the succulent carrot of enlightenment, no more worries, eternal life & so forth. Pretty much all of the perpetrators of these projects, the gurus, teachers, and leaders, have been themselves previously "taken in" by the enticements & by their ability to advance up the ladder of spiritual attainment. They have continually hidden from themselves the fact that the program they are advancing is not really true insomuch as it keeps its practioners dependent upon themselves as the leaders & thus does not promote human freedom but human bondage.

The Ancient Wisdom Scam, then, is just another way of pointing to the bad faith of those gurus & teachers who purport to have an inside track on "ancient wisdom" & are selling it in the market place.

Universality, context & truth

I have become aware of a peculiar type of argument in the last while. I'm sure it's always been around but I've just become more aware of it. I think the last time I came across it was with regard to a discussion about "mythology," that is the old type of mythology which is assumed to embody ancient wisdom. I think I was questioning this "wisdom" in one way or another & expressed the opinion that we should perhaps stop depending on these old ways of looking at things which were embedded in a very different context with a very different sort of self-concept & indeed a very different concept of the nature of the world. Someone then asked that didn't the fact that these old myths appeared over & over again in different contexts around the world mean that there was truth in them? I think I made some flippant remark that it's just as likely that the same mistake was made over & over again & that mere repetition had nothing to do with whether something was true or not. I stand by this, in a general way, but I would like to say a few more words about "universality" because this very concept of universality does seem to underwrite a notion of "truth."

The idea is that if we have the same sort of construct appearing over & over again, in the context of culture, it expresses a universal "truth." I admit that there may actually be something in this, but there are a number of difficulties. If we may take, for instance, the often repeated idea that men are superior to women (in the sense say that women are "traded" in early culture), as "true" in a very wide social context, are we to accept that this is "wise?" I don't think so. This does point up the fact that we really do have to always consider the context of a particular idea. It seems to me that we simply tend to feel that certain oft repeated ideas are true because we approve of them. The fact that we do approve of them demonstrates in some measure that these ideas are "universal," that is, relevant beyond their particular earlier contexts.

The idea that repetition makes something true doesn't really hold water. There is another side to this thing which bears thinking about and that is ritual. Ritual is some sort of human activity that is taken to represent an "essence," & it does so by the activity being stripped of extraneous details & then repeated "in exactly the same way." This exact repetition seems to lift an activity out of the historical domain of everyday activity & into the spiritual domain of eternity. That is to say, this sort of repetition also seems to underwrite the equality of "universality" with "essence" & eternal truth. The notion of "universality" seems to have an affinity with the notion of "essence" in the sense that only those things stripped down to their essence could possibly be "universally true." Individual particulars are always going to vary while essence will endure in a universal way.

Thus, the repetition of myth seems to imply "essence" because only essence is repeated. Essence is itself by definition "universal" insomuch as all humankind is "essentially" the same.

What I am asserting then, by insisting on the wisdom of mythology being context dependent, is that what appears as "essence" (the myth) is actually variable detail which has been repeated simply because the context although varying is "essentially" the same. What is important to take note of, then, is "duration" & also why exactly we "approve" of something & not other things.

A note on asceticism & aesthetic appreciation

There is a common notion in our culture, originating perhaps in our Judeo Christian heritage, but I'm not sure, that "spirit" is good & higher than the not so good (even evil) body which is "low." Of course, the pleasures of the body, that is, sensual pleasures are also low. In fact, pleasure itself is something that needs to be severely regulated. In our brief exploration above, the Zen ideal seems to have close affinity to the ascetic lifestyle & an aesthetic that leans towards the "clean & uncluttered." Its opposition to the self & ordinary mind with its desirous intentions towards objects & projects is essentially an opposition to any sort of desire &, naturally enough, its satisfaction. Does this mean it is anti-pleasure or anti-body? It certainly seems so, but I'm not quite sure. Perhaps there is a sort of disinterested pleasure that is permitted, a sensuous enjoyment that needs no object. Perhaps. But you know what, I think most of this is simply "reaching," reaching for the beyond, simply to be reaching for the beyond – not that there is something there – or the no-thing. The work of reaching, with its outwitting of the cosmos which just might be the self, is what satisfies some people, although they wouldn't admit.

One other observation that I picked up from somewhere is: the notion that the "cluttered" look in one's home & environs is essentially schizophrenic like the schizophrenic drawings with their shattered atomism & detail, detail, detail. It is the very look of madness. On the other hand, we have the clean, clear look, & this is perhaps related to the depressive point of view. The whole quest for the killing of desire in oneself seems to be essentially depressive, except of course for the aesthetic appreciation of "just the right thing." I suppose it is a love of essences, a love of ritual & the gesture paired down to its essentials. I confess to a love of the schizophrenic outlook: I like to have the elements of my world to hand, ready to be incorporated in yet another pattern. I can appreciate the "cleared space" but find no comfort there. I suppose it is a matter of taste.

Centering Prayer

I am reading two books: Centering Prayer and inner Awakening by Cynthia Bourgeault Cowley, (2004) & Descartes' Error: Emotion, Reason, and the Human Brain by Antonio R. Damasio. (1994). The first was loaned to me by a friend while the latter we've had around for a while. It is simply fortuitous that I picked them both up at about the same time. As it has transpired, I completed the book on prayer, about a one-day read, although my reading of the second half was somewhat cursory. Only after this did I pick up the book on the brain & the relation twixt emotion & reason. In any case, I must say reading this second book is something of a relief after reading the first. When reading the prayer book I made hand written notes as I went along &, in general, I found the book to be quite informative with regard to meditation practice in general & the historical "re-discovery" of meditation practice in the Christian tradition of "contemplation." For instance, I hadn't realized before reading this that Thomas Merton had been so instrumental in this "recovery." Thomas Keating, the "inventor" or "re-inventor" of centering prayer writes the introduction to the book.

First, I must do a little analysis of my intense irritation that arose when beginning to read the book. From Bourgeault's point of view this irritation no doubt stems from the resistance of "ordinary mind" to "letting go" into "deeper consciousness of god" but from my own point of view my irritation is understood in a somewhat different way. First of all, it stems from experiencing what can only be called the author's great scorn for those "ordinary" mortals with a poor "small" self formed in the light of ordinary consciousness' subject-object relations. As far as we can tell this sort of self is wandering, full of craving, can't concentrate, full of anxiety & schemes to satisfy itself. In fact all this has nothing much to do with subject-object relations. It is as if having any sort of relationship other than that between the purified consciousness & God is, if not wrong, at least trivial & worthy of any spiritual technocrat's utmost scorn.

But, let's back up for a moment. I have been struck before how so called "ordinary" consciousness has been characterized in these ways & have always wondered at what seemed to be obviously a damaged self (a neurotic self) is characterized as the norm. One of the things that has really bothered me about this is how quickly & easily this "ordinary" self-reflexive or self-reflective consciousness is brushed away without as far as I can tell very much understanding of how it works. The notion of subject-object distinctions is of course quite accurate; consciousness understood in the common-sense way of existentialism is always consciousness "of" something. Thus, consciousness is always a "relational" thing. It connects one to the world & to other people. For me this is a great insight. Also from the existential viewpoint, everything we are aware of in consciousness we see in the light of our own intentionality, that is our own intentions towards it, our "desire." Thus, the mystical viewpoint in general & the one expressed by Bourgeault are fundamentally similar. To take the next step, we may also understand that our ordinary "self" is constituted in the context of these subject-object relations & our intentions (characterized as "attachments" & so forth). Thus, we have "ordinary consciousness" characterized by subject-object relations & a "self" whose relationship to the objects is "has" in consciousness is "intentional" with regard to our emotions & thoughts concerning them. This is the ordinary consciousness that is brushed aside in favour of the "deeper self" or the "large self" which is aligned with or identified with God.

157

I guess what I was meaning to say was that the problem is initially not so much with subject-object relations as with "desire" & the fact that we see the objects in consciousness in the light of their usefulness to us, our likes & dislikes. But, as we have seen there is a "whole ball of wax" that comes with this "desire" including the subject-object characterization & the self that participates in this activity. I characterize the author as a "spiritual technocrat" because she along with others with the same "spiritual" attitudes seem to have them precisely because they possess what they feel to be a superior "spiritual technology" comprised of specific practices which enable them to move from small mind to big mind. (I suppose I should state that my own interest is in these practices insomuch as they can be stripped of the excess baggage of "spirituality.")

Anyway, I do want to make clear that I think it is misrecognition to characterize the nature of a damaged or neurotic self as "ordinary self." But after reading the book I think it is quite clear that what has happened here is that the author (in company with a great many like-minded thinkers) has simply misrecognized her own sense of self as the general condition. This makes complete sense in that those with the strong yearning for the spiritual life & the satisfaction of this yearning should have a somewhat similar experience of self – certainly a sense of self that is characterized by "lack." For them, something is missing. They characterize this something as "God" or higher consciousness. I would tend to characterize it much more simply and with less grandiosity as the lack of satisfying social relations or even more simply as the lack of a satisfying relationship with their mother. For this I simply follow psychoanalysis & see the mother-child relationship as the first model of relationship with the child first being completely incorporated in the mother's body & having to go through a complex process of individuation. Thus, the first sense of "lack" at the origin of yearning of all sorts is separation from the mother. Even if this separation & consequent individuation proceeds in a healthy way, this is still the first instance & essential origin of yearning. Thus, we have "ordinary mind" as "craving" & jumping around like a monkey. This is rather than "ordinary" the image of mind as a mixture of childishness & neurosis.

As I have said, I believe there is a misrecognition of neurotic childish self as "ordinary self" or "ordinary mind" but that being said, it is also clear that ordinary consciousness does operate with the subject-object distinctions made & the objects of consciousness do appear in consciousness in the light of our intentions towards them. The point I wish to make I suppose is that the nexus of the misrecognition concerns this intention or "desire." To my own mind, ordinary consciousness certainly is characterized by intentionality but that through a process of "contemplation" (not the Christian practice) these intentions can be "bracketed" & set aside to reveal the essence of situations & the relationship of self to them. That is to say I believe that consciousness can be "purified" in a completely rational way & this involves the disciplining of the mind & practice with the hermeneutic process. Thus, the nature of ordinary mind is preserved while at the same time there is the ability to apprehend the world, as it exists beyond our intentions towards it. I would also hasten to add that this purified rationality is only useful insofar as it can clarify & bring our ethical consciousness into play with regard to our intentions, in particular our "creative" intentions.

The word "creative" reminds me that this is another aspect of self that has been missed or ignored by Bourgeault – creativity. What she has described is not only child-like & neurotic; it is also only the self as others have made it in the matrix of society. It is the self-created by others. She has ignored the self – although it is not "ordinary" that is self-created. I suppose she just lumps the two together, the created & the creative because they are both in the matrix of subject-object & they both have "feelings" & "intentions" towards the objects in consciousness. She makes no distinction between what are subject-object relations, as they are constituted in "language," & the re-creation of self in world by the innovative re-arrangement of language. I'm not quite sure why but Bourgeault doesn't go on about language being inadequate to express big-mind, because it is so mixed up in the subject-object dichotomy, as so many religious & spiritual thinkers do. Small mercies. (In fact, later on in the book, the author does seem to be interested in the "purification" of ordinary mind, as the difficulties in achieving large mind accrue. But, I really should get back to my notes.)

But, to get back to my notes is to get back to my irritation. Bourgeault tells us that by finding the "on/off" switch for the noise of ordinary mind we experience the silence that is beneath it. Again, her initial supposition is both simplicity itself & accurate. What is my irritation, then? It is that she immediately appropriates this silence as "a compass bearing to God." My initial reaction was Oh my God, (just kidding) the God people have high jacked even silence. How incredibly selfish. If you have ever had the intuition that all forms of neurosis & even psychosis seem to have something to do with selfishness, it will come to you as no surprise that we find it here once again. I admit that I probably over-reacted; it is to be expected that a writer will write from his or her own point of view & obviously this writer's mind is god-filled so she might be excused from noticing that there are some "good" things in the world that don't come from God. Although in this case I can't help but think she is caught up in the horrible situation where she has an actual subject-object relationship with this God-thing. In any event, as the book goes on, I became more accustomed to the God idea being fundamental in all aspects of thought. She began the book with the good intention of not "preaching to the choir" but very quickly lost sight of this goal & went for it. Merely sitting still for a bit & emptying one's mind gives us God's silence. I suppose if I were a little more possessive, I might have thought silence was actually mine & then I would have been really pissed.

When I say that the whole book & the way of thinking & being explored is saturated with the notion of God, what I mean in a more abstract sense is that this author along with religious consciousness in general has before them the formula: essence precedes existence. That is there is God or "something" that is the primary & fundamental creative force that precedes our being in the world & that then must necessarily be taken account of. You might have noticed that this formula is the exact opposite of the existentialist formula: existence precedes essence. From this point of view which is the point of view of both science & common sense, human consciousness evolved in the context of the world & that it is human consciousness that has created the notion of essences in order to get at the true nature of things. The sequential order these two elements are seen to be in (essence & existence) give us the two major orientations towards reality: the god-filled universe & the universe that is only itself. From this formula come all the arguments & ways of looking at things especially with regard to "meaning." For the Godly, meaning is pre-given & must be discovered. For the humanist, meaning must be created in the context of living.

A little aside about science & religion. It can be noted that the religious or at least the mystical project has certain similarities to the scientific project, or at least the scientific project as understood by mystics. Both the notions concerning mystics & scientists are no doubt prejudiced but I give you them anyway, simply because these notions do exist as "social facts" in the world. Science & mysticism both believe there is some sort of objective & knowable world "out there." Science & mysticism both believe that you need to "purify" one's thought processes (get rid of subjectivity) in order to properly access the "truth." that they both look down upon the "emotions" & the "body." They are both concerned to create a technology that can accurately "read" the truth. Both also, of course, have a rather grand idea about themselves but for the most part I find the mystics to be far more grandiose certainly than what I could call "real" scientists, that is, scientists that have emotions, understand the place of creative thinking in the creation of models & paradigms. For the most part, this sort of scientist, Damasio for instance, the author I mentioned earlier, is far more ready to call his understanding provisional, far more humble in his relationship to knowledge than

I find Bourgeault, whose main man apparently knows everything & is everything there is to be known & the technology she describes is as close to a "sure-fire" way of getting the big picture & making direct contact with God. It's as if a scientist were always able to say, well I don't really know what's going on very much but way back we had the original scientist & he figured everything out & all we have to do is follow in his tracks & then we'll know everything too. I am only being partly facetious. But, which part? I suppose the analogy doesn't really fit, given the existence precedes essence formula. The analogous situation would be the scientist who asserts that he doesn't know "yet" but science in the future will eventually know. A main difference between the two projects then – for those who believe in the precedence of essence, knowledge & being are already given, for those who give precedence to existence, as I do, knowledge & being are to be both discovered & created. Another difference: for the essence-people...

I am aware of creating a certain sort of tangle as I move back & forth with these ideas & at this moment I want to return again to the notion of self. As I pointed out earlier, "ordinary consciousness" was simply if accurately described in terms of the subject-object distinction & the self itself was understood to be based upon this distinction. This, of course, does not go very far in the understanding of the self before dismissing it for better things. In fact, the author does give us a somewhat more complex picture of the "ordinary self" which particularly deals with the notion of "divine therapy" & speaking specifically about the "neurotic self." In that context the author mentioned the "super-ego," defensive practices, & of course the "ego" itself. In fact, ordinary consciousness is termed "egoic consciousness." This shows that the author has some concept of depth psychology but for the most part she is satisfied with the behavioral cognitive approach & mentions several new-age approaches to psychotherapy, including the Transpersonal approach which I would like to look into a little more deeply later. What she never mentions at all is the Freudian notion of the "id." But, in fact, & this is the point I wish to make, the "ordinary consciousness" she describes is consciousness ruled by the id drive for pleasure. Certainly early childhood is ruled by this principle & neurosis of one sort or another usually involves repressive techniques of getting rid of id urges, techniques that ultimately don't work, or socially "odd" ways of accommodating id impulses.

As a brief aside, then, I will give the psychoanalytic view of "ordinary consciousness" & the self. The self, as ego, mediates between two forces – the id desire for pleasure & the expression of aggression & the super-ego forces for the suppression of sexual & aggressive urges. The id, then, desires immediate satisfaction while the super- ego, coming primarily from parents & other authorities, tries to institute a "moral" value system that quashes these id desires. The ego is constituted as that entity which tries to arrange for the expression of as many urges as possible while remaining in the good graces of society. Beyond this, of course, there is the division between the conscious & the unconscious aspects of mind. Things that have been repressed disappear in the unconscious, & much of the ego itself remains unconscious. Various defensive postures are assumed, by the ego, in order to protect it from being overwhelmed either from without or within. Beyond the notion of "repression," we also have the notion of "dissociation" or "splitting." In this case, we have a horizontal differentiation of the self rather than the vertical split involved in repression. In the case of dissociation, the split is neurotic insomuch as one aspect of self doesn't know what the other aspect is doing.

All I want to accomplish here with this very simply description of the dynamics at work in "ordinary consciousness" is to show how the spiritual project of "centering prayer" & indeed, meditation techniques in general, fit into this dynamic. Specifically, given what we now understand about "the unconscious" as metaphor & the way in which knowledge of ourselves can be "ignored" or be "out of sight," it is easy enough to see what will very often occur when we meditate: our "desires," intentions, schemes & so forth, our "cravings" as the mediators have it, will simply "disappear," & consciousness will be "purified." In fact, what we have is a very efficacious way of suppression or repressing our "thoughts" (which include, pains, emotions, in fact anything that enters into consciousness.) It can be argued that the technique of simply "letting go" of thoughts when they arise & not paying them any attention is not repressive but this is sonly to be ignorant of the very complex ways the mind works. If one doesn't give a thought our attention, it is not "energized" & after a while, it just goes away. Yes indeed. The same thing will happen to a child: if you don't pay any attention to it no matter what the child does, it will eventually go away. But, the child goes "somewhere" & it seems likely enough that a very deep human desire, of whatever sort, will not just go away, it will go "somewhere." In addition, it is very easy to give all the wonderful images of God, by whatever name, to the super-ego. What does the super-ego want: it wants to suppress & get rid of id desires. What does the "spiritual" yearning part of consciousness want: why it wants to get rid of desires, wherever they might come from. Seems like two different names for the same thing.

Let's look for a moment at this element that leads us toward direct contact with spirit. On the one hand, we have the notion that as soon as one can shut off the noise of ordinary consciousness, one experiences a silence that gives us orientation towards God.

Bourgeault at first insists that we need have no "witness" or observer aspect of consciousness because we just "let go" of thoughts as they arise & there doesn't need to be any continuity of consciousness for this "observer" part. Later on, she acknowledges that practitioners do need this observer or witness part for reasons I can't quite remember at the moment. But for now, all I want to do is point out there needs to be some aspect of self that desires to take part in this practice to get close to God & get rid of ordinary consciousness. What is this part? In the context of psychoanalysis, it is the super-ego that seeks to repress desire, or it is some part of ego that wishes to protect itself. The notion of the protection of the ego by magical means, of course, harks back to our discussion of "social magic."

What is highlighted in this discussion is that various aspects of consciousness & its dynamics with regard to the self can be named different ways & fit into different schemas of "development." These schemas may be boldly split into two: psychological ones & spiritual ones. The question: how does one tell the difference between psychology & spirituality? The answer from the side of "existence" is that there is no need: spirituality is an aspect of psychology. The answer from the side of "essence" is that we can tell by way of authority or by way of intuition. From this side, something is spiritual because we are told it is spiritual, or because we simply "feel" or "intuit" that it is. These intuitions & feelings, of course, are highly conditioned by what we have heard from authority – the feeling of a certain sense of generalized love, for instance, is said to be spiritual because this is a common feeling in the spiritual discourse. One feels a love of this sort & it comes on as "overwhelming" & the very fact that it is overwhelming is pointed to as "proof" that it is of spirit. There is no "proof," however, and emotions by their nature exist of a spectrum from absolutely overwhelming to hardly discernible.

The upshot is, one orients oneself to "existence" or to "essence" & there seems like there is very little likelihood of intelligent discussion between those who hold these two different orientations. This has been my experience, but I am saddened somewhat by it because I suppose I am something of an idealist in the sense that I would hope for some ideal community in which "all" ideas could intelligently be discussed. I think I could go so far as to hold in abeyance the notion of god (the agnostic position) in order to have a conversation, but wouldn't be entirely honest because it seems quite clear that the atheistic position & the primacy of existence constitute a true apprehension of reality. I feel this in an intuitive sense & more straightforwardly; the counter arguments are very weak indeed.

I am forced to ask the question, then, why do I continue to read these books about religion & the mystic path? I read them because I am interested in them as social problems or social institutions. Yes, I do see "religion" as a sort of social problem. In the simplest possible way, they are organized around a misapprehension of the facts. A common one, but a mistaken one, nonetheless. As soon as I say this, however, I need to quality the statement because as I have mentioned elsewhere I have been surprised to discover that it is not "religion" per se that I am so suspicious of but rather that magical or mystical element of "spirituality." The religious aim of becoming a better person, more moral & more ethical in one's relations with the world & other people is a laudatory one. This is a very human project. God, in this project, remains far enough away to not pose any real threat. But when we leave the arena of human & "natural" projects & get into the "super-natural" & contact with the inhuman – God or Void or whatever, that's when I have a problem. What is my problem? My problem is that this seems like a dangerous mistake, dangerous to the individual & dangerous to society. The danger to the individual is obvious – mental institutions are full of those with religious delusions – one might almost say that delusions are always "religious" or "spiritual" delusions. The danger to society is not quite so obvious – but where there is strong belief in one's own "rightness" & a specific God, given that beliefs are formulated in the context of their oppositions, there is a strong belief in "wrongness" & the evil of non-believers. In addition, the creation of the split between the "enlightened" & the "non-enlightened" the "awakened" & those who carry on with "ordinary mind," creates a hierarchy that threatens fascism. In particular, I suppose, I am suspicious of any discipline that asks that one gives away one's authority & will.

A big difference between followers of existence & those of essence concerns concepts of "time" – the former are primarily concerned with historical time while the latter are primarily concerned with the apprehension of eternal time.

I turn back to my notes & find the question: what is at the root of this scorn for the "ordinary" & subject-object relations? The tentative answer is: it is a scorn for the body, in particular its ability to "do" things, particularly with other people. This "doing" has two poles: love expressed in sexuality & hatred & anger expressed in violence. (These, you will notice are the expression of the id.) It seems that the whole scornful position is rooted in a deep suspicion of "desire" in all of its forms. Its whole focus is on the movement from "low" desires & attachments to "high" desires & non-attachment. As previously discussed "desire" characterizes subject-object relations of all sorts although the notion of "intentionality" seems less emotionally charged. The fact that the self is constituted as a "relational" entity rather than in its separate aloneness seems highly interesting & significant to me. However, for those persuaded by "essence" "ordinary consciousness" is seen as precisely that which is cut off & separate & alone. The scorn, then, extends itself to humankind in general & well as, I suppose, "the world." Other people & the world itself are not fit to have relationships with – it's got to be God or nothing.

OK. We have this scorn & the desire to escape the neurotic entanglements of ego in the world & in order to do this we have practices aimed at Mind-cleaning or emptying out – purification. This is, it seems to me of special concern to a certain sort of person, or shall we say a type of person formed by experience & nature in certain ways. As I pointed out, this person is subject to a neurotic distortion regarding what are called "attachment" issues, but this kind of person also seems very set on elevating themselves above other people in their identification with God. This latter must be accomplished covertly of course: the whole problem of spiritual materialism as laid out by Trungpa is very well known at this point. Harking back for a moment to our earlier discussion regarding social magic & the notion that "magic" & magical practices are periodically purged from religion per se & then mount their own counter-attack on religion but end up by re-vivifying it, we can see that something like this very thing is at work in Christianity.

As described by Bourgeault, Thomas Keating was frustrated in the early 60s to realize that young people wanted a "path" to enlightenment & that they were finding this in alternative religions like Buddhism. As earlier stated, such elements as meditation & also Yoga, & various other ritualized activities may be understood in the historical context of "magic" & the function of magic to enhance the individual self as opposed to the function of religion which is to bring together community & communal worship. We have, then, a clear case, of a magical/mystical revival in Christianity with the incorporation of mediation & contemplative prayer in its practice. This move was expressly meant to re-vitalize Christianity & take contemplation to "the people" & out of the Monasteries.

I read a passage in Merton the other day where he compared the image of the dark night of the soul as given by St. John of the Cross with the state of mind aimed at by a certain sort of Zen practice. The "illumination" ultimately occasioned by this dark night of the soul was that in this deep & endless "darkness" the journey of the soul was "safe" precisely because it had no inclination towards anything at all. The described state was perhaps one of the best I've come across for a deep clinical depression. The wonderful thing about this depression was that there was a complete lack of desire & thus the soul was not distracted & safe for God. I found this almost stupefying in its wrong-headedness. This was the same state, Merton felt, aimed at by the Zen meditation practice – a state that ensured the safety of Zen consciousness & its contact with the Void. From these descriptions one can glimpse the "empty mind" as the depressed mind – not that there are no emotions, in fact the mind is suffused with a global sorrow but that one is able to maintain a detachment from all objects of consciousness.

Now, this is rather a horrible state of being so we must ask exactly what is to be gained by the willingness to undergo it? The answer comes back – direct contact with God, or the Void – cosmic consciousness, large mind & so forth. From an admittedly psychological point of view, one must assume that one gets a great deal from this state – wonderful feelings of love & being loved, a wonderful sense of expansiveness & "space" – a sense of the very large self – not one's "own" self admittedly but one is so identified with God & the largeness of consciousness, it might as well be. But these are "personal" reasons for in a sense "torturing" oneself in order to reach higher consciousness even given that one cannot do this in a direct way – one must do it selflessly with no hope of attainment. Bourgeault makes this very clear when she says that Christ was not "setting up" the resurrection by being crucified, although one might be forgiven for seeing it in this light from this distance. Even beyond that, when one thinks that the tradition of the crucified God comes out or a very large mythic context whereby the sun god was killed every year. How could one suppose that the King wouldn't know that he was a dead man come the new year. And certainly in the contemporary context it is very difficult to know how one could hide one's ambition from oneself when engaged in perhaps the most ambitious human project there is – to become one with god in unified consciousness. (When I say this is perhaps the largest project, I mean in its ambition; the project is itself, essentially imaginary. Again, imaginary projects are quite wonderful – fiction & myth, fantastic realities – the problem is that it is not understood correctly. It is not understood as the functioning of the imagination. In that sense, it is wrong headed & dangerous.)

I turn back to my notes & find a reference to the Buddhist characterization of "ordinary mind" as "monkey-mind" & then wonder what is the mind of the realized mediator. Even given that it is supposed to be in direct contact with God, it sounds like nothing so much as milk-cow rumination. Certainly the "monkey-mind" is a mind ruled by id desires – almost completely so -- & perhaps we should take it like that. What is to be "tamed" is the id. In psychoanalysis, the name of the tamer is super-ego. But who is super-ego in Buddhist thought? I'm not quite sure. In "centering prayer," it would appear to be "God." It certainly has become abundantly clear that the path of meditation or contemplative prayer is a path of "discipline" & high training in a technical sense. Why shy away from it, then, the task is essentially "domestication" –the domestication & training of the mind in the service of the Lord by whatever name. The wild-neurotic id-driven ego is to be tamed & trained to carry out the will of the bigger & the biggest.

It turns out that a profound scorn for desire & internationality is actually scorn for the emotions in particular the "wild" emotions. What are to be tamed are the animal emotions. In fact, to "purify" the links between self & world is to sever them & "cut off the self" & this severing of self from consciousness & body is what allows the huge illusion of God to enter & "take over" the individual mind.

In centering prayer as in most types of mediation practice the ordinary mind or "dual-consciousness" with its subject-object relations is ALL ruled to be wrong relationships. In this sense, all relations must be purified & this purification involves the training of the mind to hold no "attachment:" to this or that relationship. One must not "like this" & "dislike that." No. One must exist in equanimity & only thus can one make contact with the highest of the high. The purification, then, is total & the only "mediation" that "should" occur (although we are warned that this "should" signals the presence of super-ego) are those relations mediated by God. God very much wants us to be trained to a sort of calm detached equanimity. Alternatively, somebody does. Or something.

For my part I very much am put on the alert when I hear the notion of "purification" or purity or "purifying" because this puts me in mind of "dirt" & that "relationships" of all sorts always have this possibility of getting "dirty." The process of communication itself is very difficult & the use of language is always getting "dirty" with the use of imprecise terminology, the inability to tell the difference between a "fact" & a "metaphor" or "being" & "doing." Thus, when I hear the word "purify" or purification I am aware that there are going to be certain ideas about what is pure & what is dirty & that these ideas will vary from person to person & from culture to culture & time to time. Thus, the term "purity" is right up there with the notion of "nature" as terms to be highly suspicious of. And lo & behold very often we have these two terms used together – a certain purification is held to be "natural." When this happens, time to beware. Because you know, absolutely know, that you are about to be sold a bill of goods." That is to say, look sharp to see what's in the whole package that you're being asked to buy. Because the definition of what is "natural" has this nasty habit of being in the hands of those who hold some sort of power. When you buy the package, you become part of a certain community who upholds that version of reality – a community of those who buy the package. Do you like them? What else do they do besides the things designated in the package of beliefs about the nature of things. How do these beliefs play out in the real world? And so on.

The Symbolic vs. the Literal

In the first place, I want to insist on the distinction between facts & metaphors, the literal & the symbolic, reason & the imagination.

a) "Facts" concern the "objective" world – causal relations, the repeatability of experiments & falsifiability. They are verifiable by the community.

b) The "symbolic" is comprised of the reality created by metaphor – that is meaning created by correspondences, similarities & substitutions. These are essentially subjective & created by the imagination. They may be corroborated by the community or they may not be. In any event, a certain sort of world is conjured up by the play of the symbolic imagination, a world that is metaphoric & illusory.

c) "Language" partakes of both "facts" & their causal relations, & also metaphor & substitutions on the basis of similarity. Two different sorts of language emphasize the one or the other. In general, both aspects are present. This is represented on the structuralist grid with the two axes of syntactic (causal arrangement) & the metaphoric (axis of substitutions). The causal relationships set up a system of "differences" & separate one thing from another – the metaphoric relationships set up a system of similarities & joins one thing to another.

The image of the "little self" or the "ordinary self"

There are a number of terms used to designate the self. The most common are the "person," "identity" & "personality" & also "character." There are various different typologies of personality including such notions as extrovert & introvert, phlegmatic & so forth. The Myers-Briggs typology. The name of a person is very important for a person's identity & is often thought to participate in the intrinsic nature of the self. The notion of the "person" comes from the "persona" which is a mask. The self, then, in its most general sense is the social mask one wears in society & with which one participates in the various social dramas that constitute daily living. It almost goes without saying that the mask is worn on the body of the actor. One plays the part of this or that "character" in the play that is daily life or history. Gender is perhaps the most essential distinction that identity is built up around. Certainly, one's place in society or "class" is important. One's ancestors figure in one way or another, as does wealth. Knowledge of the self & the healing of the self when it becomes sick are to be found in the study of "indigenous psychology." There are a number of contemporary "developmental" theories that try to account for how the self develops & the various problems & distortions that occur. In addition, there are the notions of the "soul" & the "spirit" which are sometimes used interchangeably with the "person." At other times, they are used as quasi-technical terms designating specifically spiritual attributes. I myself, at this time, am not quite sure of the usage of these terms in different contexts. Very often different attributes of the self are given to different organs in the body & sometimes the self or aspects of the self are thought to be able to exist on their own outside of the body. Sometimes the self or some aspect of the self is understood to survive the death of the body while at other times, it is thought to die with the body.

a) According to mysticism: this ordinary consciousness is "monkey-mind." The self is constituted in the light of the myriad of subject-object relations -- the likes & dislikes of the self that are characterized as "attachments." The mind acts essentially like a machine that thinks thoughts, jumps around in a random way & is generally noisy with its projects, anxiety & justifications for behaviour & desire. The self is seen as a more or less "fixed" illusory entity that is difficult to change. This is essentially a primitive image of the self, drawn from pre-modern religious understanding of the self. It is often called the egoic self with the understanding that "ego" is essentially selfish & small. It can be understood to be the exact opposite of the "large" self or mystical awareness or "enlightened mind." It is time-bound as opposed to eternal, separate as opposed to unitive, tugged this way & that by emotions & thoughts as opposed to being filled with love.

b) According to anthropology: There are essentially 2 different kinds of self, one constituted in the context of pre-modern, pre-industrial, small scale culture – the "participatory" self, the other constituted as the modern "rational" or "individual" self. The former self "participates" in the world – that is it is integrated into the natural world & is quite porous in the sense that demons & spirits can enter into & leave it. It is essential a social self based around a particular "role" in the community. Early society is for the most part dominated by religion & its attendant mythology & so this self may also be understood as the "religious self" in the sense that it is understood to be under the control of higher powers & the creative

166

imagination is lodged somewhere outside of the individual body & its identity. In pre-modern times, ancestors figured very importantly in the constitution of the self & very often new selves were understood to be the re-born selves of ancestors. On the other hand, the modern individual is understood to be a free moral agent, with an internalized moral sense. The creative imagination is located in the self of the individual & the self is generally believed to be located in the head.

c) According to social constructivism: The self is socially constructed in the eye of the other. That is to say, the self is constructed in relationship to what others in society think of us. It is thus, at least originally, constructed as a social entity in reaction to other social entities. There is a further dimension, that of creativity. At a certain point, one may begin to change oneself & aspects of one's personality that one doesn't like & so forth. The self is constructed essentially of language in conversation with others & must be continually maintained. The self is seen as socially constructed & in need of constant maintenance or else it will collapse. It shares the notion of the unconscious with psychoanalysis and has a healthy respect for the power of metaphor as it functions in society.

d) According to phenomenology/existentialism: Consciousness is always consciousness "of" something. Thus, consciousness is essentially relational & the self is constituted in the light of our "intentionality" towards the objects of the world that enter into consciousness. There is also the ability to "bracket" one's intentions & thus gain a more objective view of the world. The self is constructed in the eye of the other. In the first historical instance, the self is "given" & there is no freedom. In the second instance, one works towards individual freedom & discovers in that process one's responsibility for the community & the freedom of others. There are a number of basic tenets concerning our human identity including: we are each of us essentially alone in the world, we all must die, & we all must discover our own meaning in the world. (A later note added after reading Kruk's on "situation" – there is a way to contact the pre-reflective world via contemplation of the embodied self in situation.)

e) According to metaphor Theory: This model takes from phenomenology & the theory of the metaphor. The self & all other institutions in society are created by a process of metaphoric unfolding whereby small metaphors pertinent to individual consciousness unfold to create large frame metaphors that govern large social forms. In the first instance, the self is constructed as a "conventional" self (in the eye of the other as in existentialism) & in the second instance one may exert the capacity for "invention" & change the self. Thus, we may speak of the dialectic of convention & the dialectic of invention, the dialectic in each case involving the relationship between a conventional aspect of language & a perceptual bodily aspect of experience. We have a reversible gestalt. In the conventional case, the conventional meaning of language, in the foreground, controls the iconic perceptual image of the world. In the case of invention, the bodily perceptual capacity & its iconic & full image of the world controls the meaning of language that has become the background.

f) According to psychoanalysis: The self is a dynamic entity with a number of parts that engage in a sort of drama based upon the function of body parts & roles in the family. It is comprised of a mixture of social aspects & biological or instinctual aspects. The "id" or "it" is essentially instinctual & comprised of instinctual animal urges primarily for sex & aggression. On the other side & attempting to control the "wild" impulses of the id, we have the super-ego, the introjected image of the moral parents. As such, it may ordinarily be understood as the conscience. Ultimately, this image of the super-ego is a unitary image

– an image of the primal scene, the mother & father together as one in coitus. The image of the unitary whole, however, is multiple & is modeled on the unitary body of the child inside the mother. Thus, we have with the "id" specific drives that aim at individual satisfaction, separation & aggression, while the super-ego is essentially an image of the whole -- social & of the community -- an image of Eros & Thanatos combined: the sexual union is also the sexual struggle. The "ego" which is often used as the short form for "self" actually is only a part of the self that attempts to mediate between the id & the super-ego – allowing the self to be satisfied while remaining in the good graces of the community. Beyond this trinity of parts, there is a split between conscious & unconscious aspects of the self. Various urges generally from the id may be repressed & thus disappear into the unconscious. A large part of the ego as well as the super-ego may also be unconscious. There are a number of "defense mechanisms" that may be used to control the id & protect the ego, among them, introjection, projection, repression, intellectualization and reaction formation. The image of the self is complex & there is great emphasis placed upon symbolism & the control symbolism can have on the body & its behaviour. In a general way, the self is understood to constitute itself by "introjecting" things it likes (good things) & "projecting" onto others the things it doesn't like (bad things.) The self is governed by several "principles" including the Pleasure principle & the Reality principle. A great deal of theory is concentrated on the "neurotic" distortion of the self which primarily is occasioned by the inability to gain enough "satisfaction" of primary desires in order to have a useful or meaningful place in society. The self is difficult to change primarily because it is difficult to get at the unconscious.

Note: Perhaps a little further along I will be able to fill out this picture of the self in terms of evolutionary theory & new meme theory & also include the early self psychology of the Americans, the mirror-self or the looking glass self of Cooley & Mead, ego psychology, transpersonal psych, eco-psychology & Reichian self as character structure. Eco-psychology adds the notion of nature as mother & advocated a "way back" to our connection to nature through a simple engagement with it & a recognition of the spiritual dimension in nature. Eco-psychology does not so much have a different image of self as say, psychoanalysis, but rather it is concerned with the healing of the sense of separation & the juvenile developmental disruption that leads to a need to "dominate" nature. An ecological orientation views humanity & human consciousness as the moral dimension of nature with the responsibility towards the "cradle" of our development – the environment itself.

I would like to look at some of the similarities & differences between these notions. First off, it is quite clear that the self is generally seen as socially constructed, changeable & able to take on different roles that are enacted in the context of participation in society. There is general agreement that ordinary consciousness & thus the ordinary self is constituted in the context of subject-object relations & that the self has "intentions" or "attitudes" or "likes & dislikes" with regards to the objects in consciousness. The ordinary self is embedded in a context of positive & negatively characterized relations. Personal "desire" for pleasure or satisfaction is generally understood to be a prime motivation for the self. "Instinct" is understood to have a greater or lesser hand to play.

On the other hand, there are a number of differences. The mystical understanding of self is, I think, primarily drawn from the pre-modern or "participatory" self. On the one hand, it has "roles" while on the other, different "desires" seem to randomly surface in consciousness. Consciousness would be a general chaos if it wasn't "held together" by the sense of continuity given by a sense of self. Most of the more modern conceptions of self & consciousness have more concern for freedom & most have some place for the creative imagination. From the point of view of psychoanalysis, the characterization of the ordinary self approximates the neurotic, childish id-driven self. That is to say that the ordinary self as understood by mysticism in the Self Centering Prayer book in particular appears to have had developmental problems, have what appears to be a rather weak ego in the sense that the ordinary self is thought to be quite unhappy & plagued with unsatisfied cravings & so forth. In addition, "id" is understood to have rather free play & there are obvious "attachment" difficulties. With regard to psychoanalysis again, there is no aspect in the "ordinary" self that appears to have the function of the super-ego. That is, there is no internalized unity, short of the meditation idea or prayer, which acts as a check on instinctual or randomly generated desires.

What actually emerges, however, when contemplating the mystical concept of "ordinary" consciousness in relation especially to the model created by Freud & later thinkers, is that a more complete model of mind & self emerge once we include the image of the transformed or "larger" self. All at once, things come into focus. "Ordinary" consciousness is developmentally immature; apparently it has the expression of instinctual desires & a weak ego unable to keep them in check. As soon as we hear about the nature of the God self or direct contact with the void, we realize we have something that is very close to the notion of the Super-ego. In the transformation we have to suppression or repression or even "killing" of the early self, we have strong id & weak ego, precisely the function that Freud gave to the super-ego. We also have a mediator, but not exactly an image of the healthy ego, in the "witness" that merely "observes" the relations between the "ordinary self" & the "new large self." We have, without looking too deeply, the situation whereby the superego has essentially taken over the identity, completely quashed desires or "attachments" so that they no longer sway the self in any way. In terms of conventional & inventional modes of consciousness described above under the head of Metaphor theory, we have the collapse of the dialectic of the foreground/background perceptual gestalt. Nothing much comes to the foreground & thus the background context remains in awareness as a sort of calm & even awareness of the whole field. Neither "conventional" thoughts (language) nor bodily perceptions are allowed to grasp or control awareness & thus the self so constituted is neither "conventional" (i.e. socially created) nor creative (engaged in the re-making of self or world.) It is in a sort of in-between place, a kind of vague state of being which is neither this nor that. It is also understood to be infused with a cosmic love, a sense of the eternal, a felt-sense of a unity with the whole cosmos & so on. I should perhaps quality the earlier statement re the collapsed gestalt, Bourgeault in her book tells us that the witness keeps an eye on both the objects in consciousness as well as the whole field, but there is no special attraction to one or another of the objects in consciousness (foreground.)

Thus only in the transformation do we have a complete sense of the parts, at least as theorized in the context of psychoanalysis. This large self, this type of awareness or enlightened consciousness & the self to go with it are of a particular type. It is not the ideal of the free but responsible self of existentialism. Neither is it the healthy ego or self of psychoanalysis. It is not the phenomenological self organized around the two dialectics of convention & invention. It is a particular form of identity created in a particular way. (We might go as far as to say that this formation of unity is at once a discovery & a creation.) Let's look now at a central concept that actually appears in a number of different attitudes towards the self – namely, the notion of "purification" which might also be termed "development" because the purification of consciousness is always aimed at the development of a "better" state of being.

I must next address the notion of mystical Purification as well as the ideas of sacrifice, the killing of the small self & initiation, not necessarily in that order, and also, the image of mystic Unity.

Untangling Metaphor

Metaphor's We Live By by George Lakoff & Mark Johnson U of Chicago Press, Chicago, 1980.

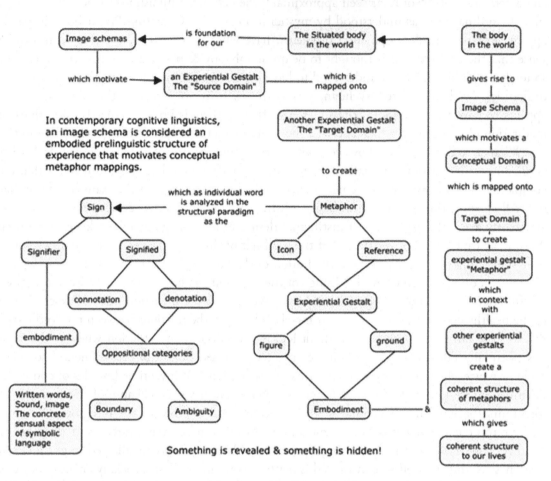

In contemporary cognitive linguistics, an image schema is considered an embodied prelinguistic structure of experience that motivates conceptual metaphor mappings.

Something is revealed & something is hidden!

Cognitive Frame or conceptual domain = a map of conceptual profiles of all of the things that make up the domain i.e. a restaurant. All of these frames are linked to base domains which are image schemas.

An Image schema is a recurring structure of cognitive processes, which establishes patterns of understanding and reasoning. Image schemas emerge from our bodily interactions, linguistic experience and historical context.

Analogy is either the cognitive process of transferring information from a particular subject (the analogue or source) to another particular subject (the target), or a linguistic expression corresponding to such a process. Understanding arises with the analysis of the structure of human experience along the natural dimensions of experience, part/whole structure, the nature of our bodies & our culture.

Recurrent experience, interaction between organism & the world leads to the construction of categories -- experiential gestalts -- metaphorical frames. This gives coherence to our lives.

Phenomenology attempts to reveal the meaning of a complex human situation -- a complex of more or less integrated metaphors. Interpretation (Hermeneutics) like phenomenology, hermeneutics desires to reveal the meaning of complex human situations but in contrast to phenomenology it is focussed on unpacking the way in which situations are historically embedded in the cultural milieu.

Metaphor
(Icon to Reference)

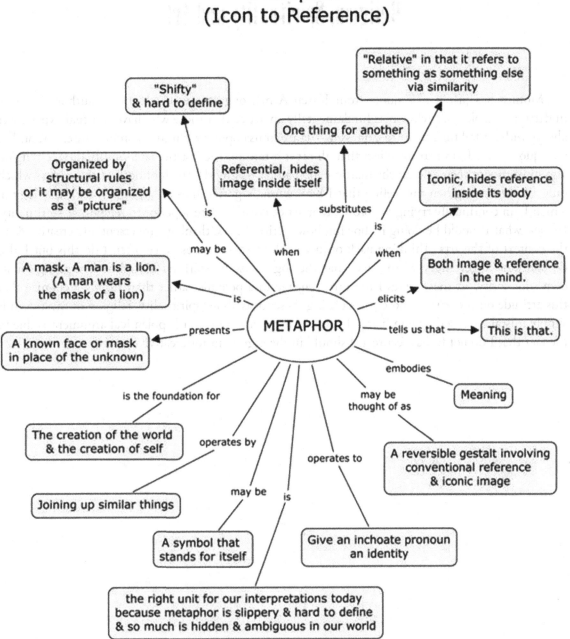

Religion, Spirituality and Art

Monica has just read a quote from Karen Armstrong to me in which the author comes to understand theology & religion as fundamentally an art & that those who have spiritual experiences always without fail turn to art to express it – dance, music, poetry, painting, architecture. The author also quotes T.S. Elliott to the effect that all art is a raid on the inarticulate. Spirituality & religion also must mount their raid on the inarticulate. I am struck by the truth of both of these ideas which only serve to strengthen my feeling that I have wrongly gotten into an argument with theology in which I am continually trying to "prove" that art & creativity are superior to religion & spirituality. In fact, what I should be doing is showing how spirituality & theology are essentially creative & in the context of the arts. Thinking back on my work in these "notes" very often I do this but I also do continually get angry when I feel that theology or some spiritual discipline is arguing for its own superiority. At these times I too often engage in a polemic rather than simply recognize that this attitude on the part of those perpetrating these ideas about spirituality, religion or mysticism is simply mistaken & self-aggrandizing. I suppose my own pull towards polemical argument is due to the fact that I do not feel as secure as I should in the argument for creativity & art.

Mystic Unity, Purification, Identification and Phenomenology

Let's return for a moment to the idea of mystic unity. This is characterized in general as union with godhead or with the Buddhist void. There are a great many ways of working towards this goal but in general the goal itself has to do with the getting rid of the small self via various methods of "purification" whose aim is to gain a state of equanimity wherein one has defeated or erased all one's "attachments. Beyond this disinterested non-attachment, there is the identification with or merging with the "all" however that is named. With regard to this there is the particular problem that one cannot merge with or identify with an image of this unity or totality "within" consciousness, or as an object of consciousness because this would merely be a covert operation by the small self to aggrandize itself & ultimately preen itself in the light of its spiritual/material accomplishment of enlightened being. This merging with unified being must be accomplished by a sort of "trick" whereby the small self is "dissolved" in the larger self; one must have an apprehension of the unity & one's own disappearance in it. The "trick" to this as I have pointed out elsewhere probably is no trick at all but simply the logical outcome of the establishment of the preliminary "ground" of being as this unitary totality. It is simply too large to hold in consciousness – rather the self & subject-object distinctions must be dissolved in it. And this without any expectation of gain. This trick that is not a trick involves in some sense "forgetting" what one is about while still staying unwaveringly on track. In the context of psychoanalytic thought, this "trick" obviously involves the moment into & out of the unconscious. And it is this "trick that is not a trick" that is obviated & understood to be an outmoded concept necessary to maintain the illusion of re-birth but not necessary for the mythology of renovation. In fact, this sort of forgetting that is aimed at & not aimed at (whose ultimate purpose appears to be as a frustration to the logical operations of consciousness) is exactly that which must be continually "re-membered" in the context of renovation with its emphasis upon the wisdom of "experience" as opposed to the benefits of a return to innocence.

But what must be re-membered (put back together again after being forgotten or "dis-membered" is that the whole system of imagery is exactly that it is a system of imagery or symbolism, socially created & deployed in such a way as to create a particular sort of consciousness & a particular sort of social action or activity. It is "factual" & "true" in the sense that it creates real effects in the world but these real effects are accomplished through the manipulation of symbolic reality – thus it is in the domain of creativity & art. Having said that, it is also necessary to re-member the original reality upon which this symbolism has been modeled: the imagery of evolution, sexuality & the birth process. With regard to evolution, I mean that developments in reflective consciousness, after its biological development advance the evolutionary project in the realm of social reality. In addition, one must keep in mind the general process of evolution whereby the organism evolves in a particular environment & in the changing adaptation of the organism, it, in turn, adapts the environment to itself so that both organism & environment change together over time. This organism/environment is a "reversible" gestalt whereby at one moment the organism "controls" the meaning of the environment & at the next, the environment "controls" the meaning of the organism. By "meaning" in this context, I mean the actual "functional" relationship of organism to environment. When the organism is "in control" then it changes the environment to its own benefit, whereas in the reverse situation, the organism must adapt to the environment for its overall development. The fact that we do not know where evolution is leading does not negate our seeing it as "development." It is certainly developing towards "something" & leaving out the idea that it is developing towards a horrible catastrophe, it seems clear enough that it is developing towards increasing complexity & also, following Chardin, it is developing towards a certain centrality. The fact that reflective consciousness developed in the context of evolution seems to bear this out. It also seems clear that the notion of unifying the whole of humanity in a peaceful, more just, & more conscious form is a strong force in the development of morality & ethics in general.

Having re-membered that we are dealing with a creative social symbolism & that the very ability to create symbols has come about in the process of evolution we must also re-member that our own individual being is as the result of the sexual behaviour of our parents. Sexuality is, of course, the activity through which evolution operates. In the context of the evolutionary process, we have a more personal image of what psychoanalysis calls the "primal scene" – the image of father & mother in coitus – one body, one unified whole. Primal unity. Also our own experience of being at one with & "inside" the mother: mother/child unity. The image of mystic unity then, as with any other notion of a unified whole is based upon our own visceral flesh & blood experience of it. Our image of parental coitus & later of course the substituted image of ourselves & our memory of unity with the mother while "inside" & also when "outside" at the mother's breast. An incredible power & truth shine through these very simple yet utterly mysterious processes & ways of being. That having been said, it can also be acknowledged that Freud & a number of subsequent writers in the psychoanalytic tradition, including Normal O. Brown in their delight in this profound simplicity & the real joy in finding such an incredible & visceral "reality" at the root of human thought & behaviour, do perhaps take their talk of the penis & the vagina to greater lengths than they need to in order to make their point. On the other hand, to assert that sexual desire is a misrecognition of "spiritual yearning" as, for instance, Jung does, appears as nothing so much as an over-reaction. We certainly have intimations or intuitions regarding a lost intimacy or identity with unity, & certainly we experience yearnings for this unity whether considered as lost or not. But to think that these are as if born on their own & not part of our own very real very early experience is somewhat obtuse to say the least. One can only place such rejections of our early experience in that general category called the "rejection of the body" which is so often referred to with regard to Western sensibility.

I do not want to be too long distracted by this, but by acknowledging that spirituality & theology actually belong in the realm of creative art, it appears that we might in fact be saying that existence precedes essence & that the notion of the precedence of essence is simply "wrong" but this is not actually the case. There is a cyclic development that produces the image of the spiral. Of course, this image of the cyclic return is itself an image of unity: & thus we return again & again to the primal scene & the 2 in 1 but each time in a different way.

The image of mystic unity then collapses the imagery of "nature" (organism/environment,) the primal scene, (father & mother in coitus) & the merged reality of the mother & child (child in the womb & at mother's breast.) The process or at least part of the process by which one is to achieve mystic unity is that of "purification." It is obvious that the very image of mystic unity has been "purified" of its sexual & visceral aspects so that it appears as nothing so much as a "high" state of total disinterested awareness imbued with a generalized intense feeling of love, but not certainly sexual love. Perhaps the "oceanic feeling" referred to by Freud. Exactly how we get non-attachment & the killing of desire from the image of coitus is a little hard to figure out. Quite a lot of "forgetting" going on there. But, of course, the very large, ubiquitous image of "re-birth" very obviously refers back to our first birth. Thus, the mystic image of unity certainly involves a symbolic return to the womb & a symbolic separation of mother & child & the child's assuming a new role. On the other hand, it seems in a sense that the self is "re-born" into the eternal unity of mother & child. The re-birth in a sense is reversed so that the child/self goes back inside the mother & stays there. It's hard not to see the image of the child as phallus because in actuality it is the phallus that goes back into the womb & it is as if it finds the child in there.

But in general the notion of "purification" actually concerns the process of "letting go" watching a thought surface in consciousness during meditation & then just letting it go & returning to some simple bodily process like breathing or just "watching." This practice requires a more or less continuously "real" entity or part of consciousness to be split off as the "witness" or "observer," or a single word (sacred because chosen) is used to banish the thought. After a while this word operates from the unconscious so that thoughts can be banished without "thinking about it." In this way, or through the repetition of a mantra or sacred phrase or counting one's breaths one purifies one's consciousness so that ultimately one is not swayed or attracted or repelled by any thought that emerges. One attains to a state of disinterest.

Let's look for a moment at the notion of "purification" in the context of early religious practice. I believe I have gone over this elsewhere but I will go over it once again. For the most part oneself or one's consciousness needs to be purified when the self or consciousness has been contaminated or dirtied by the breaking of cultural rules or taboos. When one breaks a taboo, one opens oneself to attack by negative forces, because this improper behaviour in some way weakens the self – the self has stepped outside of the normative reality established by the taboos surrounding intense & "dangerous" activities such as sex, killing, dying, childbirth & by doing so one loses the protection of the culture itself. This sort of early "participatory" self can thus be seen as almost completely dependent upon its place in the cultural milieu. By purification, then, is meant the practice of bringing the self back into a right relation with the community & the world. We notice that the "dangerous" situations all involve crucial "relationships" between subjects & objects (the subject-object relationships within which self is formed) but with this sort of purification it is not a question of getting rid of or letting go of "attachments" but rather to the management of these relationships & ensuring that they are proper or "pure." Purification, then, usually involves some sort of ritual involving the imagery of washing or cleaning, perhaps including vomiting (to clean out the insides). This ritual of purification, then, is aimed at banishing any ill forces that have gotten inside the permeable self (demons, or objects inserted via witchcraft) – the return to the "clean" or "innocent" state & some process of "re-birth" into one's proper role again. By breaking the taboo & with the pollution of the self, one is separated from the community, one moves outside culture into the dangerous "wild." Purification if the purification of the self in its relationship to the community & its system of beliefs.

Purification in the context of phenomenology can be understood as the phenomenological reduction or bracketing – a process by which all assumptions & attitudes towards the object or objects in consciousness are "bracketed" or set aside in order to see the objects & indeed the "situation" in its own "being" outside & beyond our own concerns. By way of this reduction & bracketing, we aim to discover the essence of the situation – that is to say, its true nature – the "objective" reality nonetheless "in" consciousness. These assumptions & attitudes are generally termed our intentions, & by a descriptive process, we aim to discover our "intentionality." It is easily enough to see this intentionality as "desire" or "un-desire" & this relationship as our "attachment" to the objects in consciousness. Thus purification in the context of phenomenology & mysticism is in both cases aimed at the subject-object relations but in the case of phenomenology it is not the withdrawal of our attention from these objects, for we do not wish them to go away, but only the withdrawal of our "intentions" towards them. The aim, however, is probably ultimately the same for only in the initial instances is awareness continually withdrawn in meditation practice. In later stages, it seems that awareness of the world & its relations is maintained but now with equanimity & lack of attachment. Objects & situations are still present in consciousness. After enlightenment, mountains are mountains & men are men.

One may also think of "purification" of relations in language. In this case, we would be primarily concerned with establishing the truth relations, with linguistic denotations as opposed to connotations. In cleaning out connotations, we are purging language of subjectivity and the imaginative. As such, we are primarily focused upon the syntagmatic dimension – the sequential relationships & the logic of the relations set up. Or we are dealing with precision of definition – making very clear what is "inside" our definition & what is "outside" or being excluded. Inclusion & exclusion. With regard to the metaphoric dimension, it is not the range of substitutions that are possible that is important, but rather the "right" metaphor. The precise one must be chosen. It is interesting to notice the affinity of the terms "purification" & "precision." In the latter case, the imaginative is kept "in."

Thus, we have the process of purification aimed at limitation & reduction of the emotional & conceptual relationship between self & other in order that we may be re-born but this re-birth appears as the symbolic reversal of our natural birth. In fact, we can look upon the whole process as a reversal. In the normal course of events, we are born of coitus, grow in the womb & then are born & establish our myriad of relations in the world. The process of mystic rebirth means a regression or going backwards in which we sever our relationships in the world, re-enter the womb in our innocence characterized as non-attachment & stay there in the unified relation with the mother understood as the "all" which she was in the beginning. Because this is in no way a literal return but a symbolic one, the cycle does not end up where it began but at a "similar place" on the gyre or spiral, a higher or more developed place.

But setting aside this more fleshy or visceral account of the symbolism, we can quite easily superimpose the notion of super-ego on whatever it is that is the motivation for engaging in the process of meditation in order to achieve a higher level of awareness. It seems that this element is partly "inside" consciousness as the "witness" (a split off part of consciousness that is essentially a passive observer), partly some aspect of the ego, weak as it is, that desires to gain better control of the id. This, in a sense amounts to splitting the ego into a part that wants to align itself with the larger self & one part that in its weakness will be banished or killed. The super-ego function, however, is understood to not reside in consciousness but rather in the world, or rather it "is" the world, the unity of all. The unity of the world is glimpsed in the "silence" beneath the noise of the primitive small self & in the world perceived without attachment to it. This image of the world, then, the fullness of the iconic image, the perceptual image, not the concept of it, is understood at the "guide" the ground of being itself. This "ground" of course is also glimpsed in the "teachings" as well as in theology, discussions with other practitioners in the community involved in the same process.

The interesting insight that occurs here is that this reversal & the notion of the fullness of the iconic image of the world, devoid of attachments – that is, devoid of anything that comes into the foreground to "capture" or hypnotize awareness – is exactly the image of the dialectic of invention we briefly discussed earlier. In this reversal, the fullness of the perceptual image "controlled" conventional understanding. In this case also we find the background perceptual image of the world (as a unity) "controls" the "meaning" of our conventional "thoughts" & this meaning, precisely because the background is conceived of as a unity & that this awareness must never be lost sights of, is that this meaning should always be interpreted "as if" it had nothing to do with us. This "as if" tips us off that whatever else is going on, a role is being taken on – there is an actor & the presence of an actor, whether large or small, always presumes an audience. The mystic, engaged with the process of creative transformation, is still in the world & performing a certain role. This role is necessarily an evolutionary one & I assume pertains to the bringing together of people & the raising of consciousness in the world community – the salvation of humankind.

We have discussed various different notions of the self, the image of unity, purification & the mystic process of re-birth in the light of psychoanalytic thought. It remains that we deal with "sacrifice" & I suppose "initiation." Perhaps we need not say much about these at this time. Certainly, the sacrifice as it stands is the small self that is killed in order that it shall rise again, & initiation always involves a re-birth, a purification & the establishment of a new identity.

Let's turn our attention for a moment to the notion of "altered" states of consciousness. What we mean by an "altered state of consciousness" is generally a state of consciousness that is not governed by our usual or conventional understandings & aware nesses. For one reason or another our perceptions of the world & our relation to it has changed. One of the most common ways of altering one's consciousness is by the taking of drugs. One may also alter one's consciousness by any number of other ways such as fasting, remaining awake for long periods, engaging in great exertions, repetitive drumming, music or dance & so on. One may also do this by breaking very strong cultural rules such as the interdict against killing, robbery & so on. Nothing is so clear as that consciousness is quite malleable & quite easily changed at least for a short period of time. It is, however, difficult to maintain this change over time. This requires work.

At the centre of the mystic process is the sacrificial death. A killing in fact. Once more, we have the image of unity but this time in the sadist/masochist pair. This is actually a rather good image of unity for the mystical journey precisely because of the apparent contradictions at its core – pleasure from pain, either administered or received. In addition, of course, perhaps the foremost character of the actual enactment in the context of sexuality is its theatrical orientation. What is being enacted is the theatre of domination, humiliation & punishment. In addition, the sadist is identified in the most dramatic instance with the highest form of impersonal authority. The bonds that tie the masochist are exactly the bonds of the self – the punishment is exactly the punishment for the pursuit of pleasure. It is the theatre of good & evil & exists at the very core of the sexual experience. I do not wish to really argue this case. For those who have not yet intuited this I can only say keep an eye out. There is a violence & drama to "good" sex that can easily be missed when the romantic or gentler aspects of the act are emphasized.

I would like to look briefly at the idea of "identification." What exactly is this idea & what are the surrounding ideas? The notion of identification is central to individuation & the development of the self. It is similar to other ideas such as "incorporation" or introjection – both of them pointing towards the process of taking the other inside oneself so that ultimately we are "like" that other & act like they do. Given that we can't actually "eat" the other, how do we take the other inside ourselves? The simple answer is that we "imitate" them; we incorporate or introject the other by imitating them. The notion is simplicity itself: by acting like the other, we become the other. Identification = imitation. In the more theatrical sense, we don the "persona" or mask of the other as an actor & proceed to execute the appropriate role. With the added notion that we "imitate" that which we admire & reject what we don't admire, this is precisely how we gain a self. It is not necessary but very often, because we actually have various traits that we don't admire but don't wish to admit it, we repress these so that we are no longer aware of them & then because we will not admit to these we actually project them upon other people. I am not like this – they are! Thus, we have the two processes introjection (or identification/imitation) & projection at the foundation of the self. This is exactly the situation how mysticism as well as psychoanalysis sees the situation: the self is formed in the matrix of subject-object relations with which we have attachments, the term "attachments" designating both desire & rejection. It is this same type of theatre & its process of identification by which we attain the second & larger self. It is simply a question of exactly what we imitate & identify with. In early tribal cultures, various magical transformations are made in the context of theatrical ritual & the wearing of masks. I hardly need add that we are still aware of the notion of eating the other in order to gain specific characteristics of the other; the eating of the heart of the lion in order to gain courage remains in our current mythology.

I would like to briefly look at the phenomenological way of "looking at" the psychoanalytic idea of "repression." As I think I have mentioned earlier, the notion of "repression" is metaphorical; there is no specific "place" that repressed ideas & emotions go to. It is the idea that there are specific psychic processes that keep certain knowledge out of awareness. We noticed that one way of doing this, of course, is the common meditation practice of "letting go" of thoughts as soon as they come up. Alternately we may think that the refusal to give a thought attention means that we withdraw "energy" from them & that they eventually disappear. Again, they do not go anywhere special – they are simply out of consciousness. They disappear. In the context of psychoanalysis repression is generally understood to be a more active process than this but then again it is not all thoughts that are meant to disappear just particularly unacceptable ones like the desire to kill one's parents or make love to one's mother. The child's repression of the overwhelming rage & desire to murder the parents is in a sense a practical necessity. One cannot go on living, dependent as one is on them, with this thought in mind. The thought must go. In a sense, I suppose one simply says to oneself I will not think this thought – this is a bad thought (that's the super-ego talking) & lo & behold after a while the thought is just mysteriously gone. The difference between the psychoanalytic & the mystic situation however is that from the psychoanalytic point of view, even while out of consciousness, the idea still has motivational power. It may still operate from the unconscious & emerge years later as a "memory" & even years later overwhelm the ego with this murderous desire. It seems likely enough that in the context of mysticism there is a distinction between neurotic thoughts (which need therapy) & more ordinary thoughts that may be controlled via meditation practice.

What, then, of the phenomenological view? If the notion of an unconscious is one of those interpretive concepts that must be bracketed & set aside, how does phenomenology deal with the fact that various ideas & emotions seem to disappear from consciousness? In general, phenomenology does not believe that certain drive energies that are unpleasant & subsequently disappear are "repressed, rather they assume that the consciousness of the person in question is formulated in the first place as just that kind of person who doesn't have those unpleasant thoughts. That is to say, the very development of personality excludes them from the very beginning. And then if as an adult such thoughts emerge, they don't emerge from the unconscious, the being of the person & his consciousness change for one reason or another so that he or she is now the kind of person who can hate their mother or how their father treated them. Thus, the emotions or ideas don't return, but rather they are later felt or thought for the first time. In this formulation, there is nothing to "believe." One simply observes that what didn't used to be part of the person now is. This idea, although moving away from Freud's conception of the unconscious, is actually closer to that of Wilhelm Reich, who theorized the bodily unconscious & that emotions & thoughts were actually locked in the body via systematic chronic tensions. For Reich, the character structure was the muscular structure of the body. He called it armor, body armor. In order to get at the bodily unconscious one goes about releasing the chronic tensions in the body. Thus we have huge boost to therapeutic massage of many different kinds, the bio-energetic therapy, therapeutic dance & so on. (**what do you want here?)

In the transformational act we have a sort of depressive behaviour (I am thinking of St. John of the Cross) & the safety of the soul when the mind is shrouded in the cloud of unknowing & does not incline to one thing or another, i.e. is not distracted from God. There is also an obsession with purity & the purification of the self. Very often, there is an abstention from sexuality & eating. Purification has always to do with "dirt" & pollution & the return to proper behaviour, so we must assume that the subject-object relations & subsequent attachments all concern a "fall" from grace, or at least a development that must be reversed or transcended. All this is at the service of a murder. It is a sado-masochistic murder in which one plays both parts in order to identify with, or re-identify with & also re-cover, the conceptual reality of "unity" which, as we have seen, is the image of parental coitus and/or the image of mother & child united in the one body.

I have used the term "transcend" in the above paragraph & perhaps it is the time to say a little about this idea for it actually encapsulates or embodies the whole process of transformation. This mystical transformation is understood to be a transcendence of the ordinary self. What does the term mean, then? I will begin with my own understanding. Where else could I start? Transcendence is just like consciousness always transcendence "of" something. We have said that the mystical transcendence is of the small self but we have characterized the small self as that self-created in the matrix of subject-object relations. Thus, transcendence is transcendence of exactly this dualism. Transcendence in a more general sense is the third term in a dialectic between polarities or dualities: thesis, antithesis & transcendence. In the simplest way possible we can take any concept, see that it is formulated in terms of its opposite (black & white, for instance) & then see that the third term somehow supersedes these two via some "mixture" of the two to create a third "transcendent" entity. Grey is the obvious transcendent third & supersedes while taking elements from both black & white. The "compromise" is also a form of transcendence in that it is a developmental 3rd which partakes of both sides of a dispute. In the context of spiritual thought, however, transcendence is thought of in a somewhat different way. It does not aim at compromise but the rising up to an entirely different level beyond whatever dualism it supersedes. It aims to completely collapse the dualism inside itself to create a perfect unity. To transcend means essentially to "go beyond." As a symbolic concept that is unity & beyond all duality, the concept of the "all" must be identified with, imitated, donned as the ultimate mask of consciousness. Never mind that it is too large to "hold" in consciousness, that it is not a mask but a "direct" confrontation with god or the void, never mind that it is a "pure" image of the transcendent "all" – never mind all of this hyperbole & this insistence on what it is not – it IS a symbolic concept & the only way to "disappear into it" is to "become" it. As we have seen in order to become or be transformed into something, we must identify with it.

Let's put aside this insistence for a moment & return to the notion of "altered consciousness" & add to the ideas we have already mentioned the idea of phantasies & hallucinations. Phantasies come from the unconscious – they are stories or scenarios that, although distorted, express unconscious wishes in a way similar to dreams. Hallucinations also seem to come from or at least be modulated by or articulated in the light of unconscious desire & aggression. With hallucination, we actually come to see what we fear or desire. It appears to us as real. We have auditory hallucinations & visual hallucinations. They are closely associated with schizophrenia, which remains a somewhat obscure but terrifying disease. Certainly, hallucinations have something to do with chemical changes in the brain. This is born out by anybody who has taken acid or any of the other hallucinogenic drugs. Altered states of consciousness & hallucinations may also be produced by the various other methods already mentioned. The body in extremis produces hallucinations.

All I am really trying to do here is to tease out just a little the relationship between altered states, identification (with unity), & hallucinations. Also I should perhaps bring in the concept of hypnotism here because hypnotism is quite a simple way to create both altered states in consciousness & hallucinations or at least messages that appear to be hidden in the unconscious which later are able to "trigger" certain behaviour. I recently came across in my reading somewhere that hypnotism occurred when awareness was taken over by one sense to the exclusion of the others. For example, hypnotism occurs when awareness is taken over by the visual sense only. I think this probably came up in the context of communications theory & a discussion of McLuhan & television but I can't really remember. The term "hypnotism" is close to the term "fascination" in the sense that one may become "fixed" on a certain thing to the exclusion of all others. In a general sense, our ordinary selves have been characterized from time to time as "robotic" & "fascinated" by the play of things in consciousness. The contemporary advertising world is sometimes blamed for this society of the Spectacle & our subsequent hypnotized fascination with the shiny things of this world. A magazine like "People" (**how to cite) seems to exemplify this with its emphasis upon the "stars" & their fashions.

Return to Centering Prayer

The self fostered by spiritual awareness perceives through an "intuitive grasp of the whole and an innate sense of belonging." p. 13. The author characterizes our ordinary state of consciousness as "the tyranny of mind" & the sense of selfhood that goes with it. Tyranny. This sounds very much like the dominance of "instinct" which is seen as more or less fixed & concerned with overwhelming needs. Nowhere does the author really deal with any sort of distinction between ordinary mind & instinct or how instinct functions in mind so we may be excused from seeing them as fundamentally the same thing. The other way to look at it, I suppose, is that she is talking about the sort of mind that has pretty "fixed" ideas. The image is of a very conventional sort of person, someone of the fundamentalist bent, perhaps, or certainly one who cannot be persuaded by reason. Although this doesn't really seem to be so because she characterizes her own thought, before meditation practice, as being of this sort – although she was well educated, held a PhD in fact & had authored several books. The main concept seems to be the lack of ability to concentrate on one thing for any length of time. I can only imagine that she didn't really think it very worthwhile to bother to give a good description of the "ordinary mind" & settled for a more or less "traditional" one drawn from Eastern religion.

I found it useful that she gives us a brief typology of meditation practice.

1) Concentrative. This utilizes a meditation practice focused on a mantra of some sort.
2) Awareness Methods. This involves aligning the self with an inner observer & simply watching the play of mind.
3) Surrender Method. This is the method of Centering Prayer, the central idea being that as soon as a thought comes up one just lets it go, sometimes reminding oneself to do so with a single "sacred" word. After letting it go, one comes back to one's "intention." The author asserts that this method does not need to create a "witness" or "observer" because there is no need for any continuous entity of this sort in consciousness because one is continually just "letting go" & returning to "intention." One still must question where exactly this "intention" is lodged in consciousness. It comes from somewhere & then disappears to somewhere. On the other hand, we may understand that the "silence," which is itself a magnetic orientation to God, is the guide. One continually "surrenders" to this understanding.

In a general sense, all of these methods depend upon "identification" – in the first case one identifies with the mantra, in the second with the passive observer, in the third with the image of the all. The image of "surrender" of course conjures the notion of surrender in battle, in this case surrender to a far superior force. It also conjures up the image of the lover's surrender to the object of adoration.

The author also makes the distinction between two fundamentally different types of prayer:

1) Cataphatic prayer, which uses ordinary faculties of reason, memory, imagination, feelings, & will. It takes place in the context of ordinary awareness & egoic selfhood.

2) Apophatic prayer, which bypasses the "faculties" (reason, imagination, visualization, emotion, memory). It is "formless" & the way of negation, but it is not really empty or formless; it just uses more subtle faculties of perception or the "spiritual senses." It uses ecstatic & mystic prayers to transcend egoic perception. To go beyond, one simply shuts down all normal consciousness & makes contact. We yield to it & make contact -- a sort of direct God awareness, unmediated.

It would be really great to hear much more about these more subtle faculties of perception, the spiritual senses, but it is exactly here, where the actual experience lies, that description breaks down & we are left with only the assertion that something wonderful happens. In fact, accepting for a moment the split in mind between conscious & unconscious, the shutting down of the conscious portion of mind is very likely to leave us in contact with the unconscious mind. Certainly, this is more or less what happens when we go to sleep. The rational "story-making" aspects of mind seem to shut down & the various elements of our consciousness are strung together in altogether different ways – ways apparently more motivated by unconscious than conscious desire. On second thought, this doesn't seem that likely. Rather both ordinary conscious as well as more or less unconscious ideas & so forth would tend to surface in the ordinary sitting practice so that when one has pretty much "let everything go" for long enough, there is simply nothing left, nothing, of course, but a quite altered state of consciousness, one which seems to have abandoned its essential relational nature. But given that this really is an impossibility & what we are really talking about is the manifestation of desire or intention, what we are reduced to is a single desire, a single intention – the desire & intention to merge with godhead – the fact that the image of godhead has systematically been obliterated in consciousness doesn't really mean that much because we already know what this unity is modeled upon – & know in our bodies especially perhaps, the feelings that are engendered.

All at once in the very midst of the most frustrating aspects of our struggle, we discover a clear way, a way out of the labyrinth, a way that clarifies every relationship, a way that is at once miraculous & completely ordinary. Our struggle to make contact with God is our struggle to make contact with god & the struggle itself is suddenly & all at once recognized as exactly contact with god. This is it! Or that was it! What next?

Boundary

Let us speak of separation & boundary. Separation in egoic self, in language. Boundary as referred to by Norman O. Brown. Boundary in definition & in "dirt" & taboo. Boundary in the theatrical sense, boundary in myth. Boundary between above ground & underground, here & there.

In anthropology, perhaps the most classic boundary is that between nature & culture, the boundary that divides the civilized from the wild. A similar boundary in psychology is that between nature & nurture or instinct & learned behaviour. In different theories & in different cultures the line is drawn in different places. The establishment of this boundary concerns what is "inside" & what is "outside." In language, boundary is forever in play as that which establishes the categories of thought – what is inside & what is outside the notion of "time" or "the person" or "yellow." As such, the concept is absolutely crucial in all aspects of thought & conceptualization; for instance, in order to transcend anything, one must establish the categories that are to be transcended. Sometimes the boundary is vague & ill defined, other times it is very precise. Very often the boundary is argued over endlessly. What "should" be in a particular definition & what should be excluded? What is "democracy" or what is the true nature of "man?" As we have seen, there are a great many different ideas concerning the nature of the "ordinary self" & the "transcendent self."

I have spoken of the suppression of ambiguity at the boundary of overlapping categories earlier. The idea is central to thinking about taboo & purification. Where two categories overlap, for instance the categories of "man" & "animal," we can see as their "similarity" to each other. The two categories obviously have a number of elements that are different & a number that are similar. Now, the relationship between a man & an animal is a very important one precisely because animals are so useful to man. In addition, even in very primitive people, it seems there has always been the intuition if not actual knowledge that the animals are our ancestors. There is, in fact, a great deal of affinity between humankind & animals. This relationship then is one of those very important subject-object relations for ordinary consciousness. Learning how to negate or have no attachment to such a relationship is in a sense learning how to negate one's essential humanity. One must get over one's desire for a good or proper relationship & one's distaste & desire to avoid an improper or tabooed way of being & acting.

We have, then, two overlapping important categories. We have similarities like the fact that both animals & humans hunt – they "trick" each other in order to get food. Other more psychological attributes seem similar. Some animals & some humans are courageous or sneaky. Both have eyes, some have legs, & so forth.

Because of the importance of this category "animals" the relationship between humankind & animals is also very important. This relationship may have a number of different orientations or features – of these orientations may have to do with veneration of animals as ancestors, another might have to do with killing as food, another might have to do with getting knowledge as in the shamanic trance, another might concern domestication. Each one of these relationships must be carried out in a correct way &, because of the importance of the relationship, all wrong or incorrect ways of relationship are tabooed.

We have, then, a constellation of ideas that concern the important relationship between different entities. The entities themselves are "nominal;" they are nouns & have names. The relationship, however, is "verbal" & pertains to action.

Two categories: "self" & some important "other," (subject-object.)
1) Categories overlap: There is a "grey area" due to similarities between the two.
2) Establishment of the boundary between the two by suppression of some of the similarities in order to establish the essential differences.
3) Establishment of the right relationship between self & other predicated upon difference.
4) Incorrect relationship or mixing in the grey area is established as "dirt."
5) Restriction & Taboo regarding the "dirty" or wrong relationship between self & other.
6) Breaking of the Taboo by forgetfulness or selfishness.
7) Pollution & dirtying of the self because of the broken taboo.
8) The impure person is now dangerous to others.
9) Purification of the polluted self & the re-establishment of proper self & proper relationship.

We can see how important the establishment of boundary is & that when the boundary of the relationship is breached, the boundary of the self is also breached & dirtied. The process of purification re-establishes correct boundaries rather than abolishing them as in the mystical theatre.

Originally, there was the one body, a wholeness, & the ego was merged with this wholeness. The separation of the self from the world is a conventional separation, not "natural." This is perhaps the original boundary. There were indeed natural distinctions between things (before they were individual things) but one thing flowed into another so that any boundary was always indistinct. Perhaps "flow" is the operational principle & the opposite, if there can be one, of the boundaried world of individual things, of separation, of private property. It is distinction & the establishment of boundaries & therefore "categories" that "creates" the world as it is found in our everyday engagement with it.

In a sense, the unified world of flow was metaphorical & its relationships were essentially vertical with regard to the structural grid. Certainly, the early world was structured via myths whose distinctions were much more symbolic & metaphorical than our world today whose relationships are essentially horizontal with regard to the structuralist grid, & these relationships are essentially causal & sequential ones. The world of flow tends towards the eternal whereas our everyday world today, the world of boundary & separation, tends towards the temporal & the historical.

Boundaries & polarity. Self & non-self, inside & outside, love & hate. A part of the external world is given up as "object" in consciousness & taken inside via the process of "identification" & designated as "mine." This is an illusory process & creates the illusion of separation where in fact there is none. It is all very well to understand that the world of flow is previous to ourselves & to reflective consciousness, but quite another to live our daily lives in which we must severely limit our consciousness in the ways I have outlined above by suppressing, repressing, forgetting & ignoring "similarities" between things (before they were things) that were part of the flow. Similarity is simply the intermediate zone where one thing flows into another – a boundary zone as it were, but with no distinct boundary line. In the world of flow, it is impossible to distinguish where one thing begins & another ends. With our creation of boundary & category, we "arbitrarily" establish the "edges" of things & by doing so actually create the "thing" as a separate object, able to be named & referred to. The closest we can get to the perception of "flow" is to "bracket" all that we know of our conventional separations, established primarily in language, & "gaze" at the world. (I remember some time ago coming across an author who made the distinction between the "gaze" & the "look" – the gaze taking in the fullness of the perceptual field while the look focused on some foreground aspect.)

In our conventional way of being in the world, meaning is produced by the composite gestalt of convention & perception (convention pointing to our boundaried world of category & classification, perception pointing to the fullness of the iconic image.) The term "icon" is here used more or less as it is in semiotics to designate an image characterized by similarity – an iconic image of a mountain "looks like" a mountain. The conventional word "mountain" looks nothing at all like a mountain but nonetheless points to it. Or rather, asks us to re-member when we were in the presence of a mountain or some more iconic representation of it. Convention conjures up the iconic image just as the iconic image of a mountain conjures up the word for it. Language conjures up experience just as experience conjures up words with which to describe it.

The closest we can get to the world of flow is, we are told, by way of the process of meditation or contemplation. As I have said, this is a symbolic formulation & as such attempts its symbolic raid upon the inarticulate.

To have or to be. That is the question. I am to "have" something that is mine, possess it or actually be it, become the thing that I desire, identify with it. Or are having and being the same thing? Up to a point? In order to "have" something I introject it, bring it inside, & in order to "be" something I identify with it, I imitate it. In the former case, I change the external object in order to take it inside; in the latter case, I change myself in order to become the other. Both processes, however, appear to use the process of "identification." These actually seem to mimic Piaget's notion of assimilation & accommodation in the process of learning.

The outer split is the inner split within the ego. The outer establishment of boundary involves an internal repression; the split in the ego is twixt conscious & unconscious.

The reality principle is the overvaluing of external reality, & its overthrow means that we come again to value the imaginary on an equal footing with the real. The real & the imaginary. Thoughts are as real as things. Animism, magic, & omnipotent thought are recognized and the distinction between the wish & the deed can be seen to be false. This is darkness.

Norman O. Brown

In the evening, I picked up Love's Body by Normal O Brown (1966). I read this book in part a number of years ago when I was writing my thesis on the image of the body in Wilhelm Reich's work. It's just one of those fortuitous things for I just re-read it at exactly the right time. When I say I re-read it, I certainly didn't do this in detail but read a great deal of it, jumping around in the various chapters on Person, Unity, the Trinity, Boundary & so on. I highly recommend you look at it. It is episodic in high degree, advancing as it does by way of quotations. For me, it reminded me of the centrality of the symbolic world & gave every permission to "read" mysticism as drama & the mystical journey as a theatrical presentation. His version of psychoanalysis is mythic, romantic & excessive. A real pleasure to watch the movement of his mind & imagination. I also realized that my own current work – Notes on this & that – proceeds in a very similar way, but without the reliance on quotation.

My general feeling is that I have been drawn into a debate (certainly I have initiated this) with the general argument for mystical consciousness & Centering Prayer in particular in a way that does not entirely suit me. What I mean is that I have resorted to a too "literal" exposition precisely because this is the general "mistake" that I find in the literature itself. My own argument in reaction to this overly literal exposition has become overly literal itself. I have, in a sense, lost faith in the power of the imagination & the symbolic world. I have felt that I had to backtrack & go back to simple & very clear arguments that engage with the problem at all points & point by point. I have felt that because of the intense distrust of subjectivity & the imagination & indeed language itself, I could not make any real convincing argument in this fashion because I would be ruled out of court to begin with. And this simply because I wanted to try to actually speak to those who held these overly "literal" beliefs & who could not, in my estimation, properly tell the difference between a fact & a metaphor. I believe that Brown's sheer joie de vivre & willingness to engage with both the body & imagination has in some measure released me from these strictures. That is my hope, in any event. What this means, I suppose, or hope, is that this will bring my more academic project closer to my creative one. I also hope that my sense of humor will be allowed to expand & that I will not resort so much to my own scorn in response to what I feel is the scornful attitude I have found in "Centering Prayer."

Anyway, I return to my notes on Centering Prayer but am worried that they may seem already outdated, not really what I want to say. However, I suppose I must work through them in some way. They begin: "For the essentialists, everything that "develops" develops towards God whereas for those believing in existence 1st all development is development towards the more "human" ideals – full knowledge, objectivity & so forth. For the God driven as for the scientist the world is to be discovered & both also abhor "subjectivity" the "Imagination" the body & the emotions for these "distract" one from the one thing that is important the god-self or objectivity.

I really do need to align myself with a third group, identified with neither the mystics nor the scientists. I suppose it is clear enough that I am not a mystic (perhaps a little later this will come into question) so it is a question of differentiating my position from the strictly "scientific." I suppose to align myself with phenomenology & existential philosophy more or less does the trick. I should also mention social constructionism & a general sociological/anthropological outlook. At times, all of these disciplines align themselves with science in general & I do also, but mostly in the sense that I firmly believe in the functioning of reason & the processes of logic. I understand the limits of logic & the sense that poetry can in certain ways surpass these but in the present context I very much want to produce a strong argument & this means both a logical & a reasonable one. This will not suffice for "believers" but then nothing really will except that which serves to fortify belief & the functioning of "faith."

I should also say that I lean quite heavily on language theory & how "metaphor" functions in the individual & society. What I want to say about this common distrust of emotions, the body, the imagination & symbolic language in general is that relationships, especially human relationships, are always "dirty" in some sense. The point I am making has nothing to do with pornography or any particular tabooed subject but rather that when we have relationships between entities (each with its own essence) there is always dirt or noise in the system. Relationship by its nature must dirty the essences because it involves a mixing together of the essences & this "mixing" is the essence of the relationship. Of course, one may move on to the establishing of the essence of relationship – that is the establishment of the "proper" relationship. The establishing of the proper way will involve "purification" & the denial of "improper" (so designated by society) ways of relating. The improper are "taboo." Social authority establishes this taboo & in the context of the individual self this social authority is exactly the super-ego.

Fear is the primary motivation for the setting up of the "proper relations" & the surrounding of intense human relationships by taboos. In some sense, one can say that a world defined by fear is an inauthentic world & a life hedged in by fear is also inauthentic. All we are saying really, however, is that the social world, as constituted in the outside domain as well as "inside" the individual is illusory from top to bottom. It is a social creation, in need of constant maintenance & always subject to change.

Discovery & objectivity are revered & the emotions, subjectivity & the life of the body are rejected. Further to my brief list of "hopes" above I also hope that my own argument will move away from the attempt to refute & show where the mistakes in mystical thought occur & rather concentrate on a correct interpretation of mystical thought in the light of psychoanalysis & other interpretive practices. With this, it should become evident that my interest in mystical thought is intense & personal when it is understood in its true nature – imaginative & symbolic. When it is stripped of its "sacred" trappings & can be shown to be a practical & realistic project for increasing consciousness for ordinary people in the midst of ordinary life, it becomes very interesting indeed. To be stripped of sacred trappings means we won't be needing the term "God" or anything like it & we will need to lose the notion of any sort of literal reincarnation or re-birth of the body. Stripped of this we can see that mysticism is essentially the practice of practical magic whose driving force is the human imagination & which takes place in the symbolic domain.

The creation of self & society are social constructions or shall we say "theatrical displays" both on the outside & in the inside & the mystic journey is itself a theatrical display replete with the creation of witnessing audience, the putting on & off of various masks including the mask of God or gods. Thus, the exposition of the "drama" will naturally look to the types of actors created & the types of episodes that strung together make the story. All this is not to say that the symbolic display of self & society have no real ramifications in the world. On the contrary, it is this illusory display invested with power that is the totality of what we call human life on planet earth. With regard to "what happens" historically, it is always a question of who controls the "reality concession" or which version of reality wins out in the conflict of the reality wars.

Always the return. Desire & the emotions in general may be thought of as "elements" in the natural world – winds, hunger, a shiny thing – all that lifts something or other into the foreground of attention. Our attention is "caught" or "snagged" by something or other & it is this foreground entity that then "controls" our interpretation of the background. Given this functioning of "ordinary mind" it is easy to see that mystic consciousness involves the collapse of the figure/ground gestalt & everything becomes slow moving & background – nothing comes to the foreground as an "attachment" to distract us from the general field of awareness. In order to accomplish this process of being caught by a thought that naturally comes to the foreground, it is necessary to mount an attack upon "desire." Or "desire" & its opposite. Our likes & dislikes. In a little while, perhaps we will discuss the construction of the self as a system of likes & dislikes, of the introjection of what we like & the projection of what we don't.

It is clear that mystical thought, at least what's found here in Centering Prayer, is obsessed with cleanliness & purity. As we saw with the writing of St. John of the Cross, it is also depressive & concerned with "context" or "background" which is re-named GOD (silence) but which cannot be possessed (introjected) as a foreground object, into the self. No foreground object, no relationship (subject-object) should distract from God. On the surface of the thing, it would seem that this pursuit severs all relationship & separates the self from the world. Of course, I will be accused of misunderstanding because I have understood this in an intellectual way only & in my turn, I accuse them of misunderstanding their own project. Oh my.

It seems that the God driven want to reduce the situation of desire to its essence & suffer by cutting all bonds with the world & its denizens – this is suffering in order to exist in bliss that is occasioned by uniting one's essential aloneness & separateness that one has suffered to achieve with a purified vision of the all.

The All from the point of view of psychoanalysis is the unified, the 2 in one – the father & the mother in coitus on the one hand, the child & the mother unified in the other. The image of the single unified entity is based upon the first flesh & blood occurrence in life.

I really wish to simplify. Super-ego is the introjected parents (conscience) & it is this aspect of self which desires re-birth & the re-creation of the All, the symbolic unity of mother/father & mother/child. This is to replace the small self which is predicated upon separation from this unity, individuation & subject-object relations which are not illusory themselves but which become illusory if "believed" that is if these relations are not understood to be socially created & thus mutable. The self is thus a socially created entity that is mutable & engaged in a drama; identity is created through the donning of persona, the mask. It is created through identification & mimicry (imitating.)

Mysticism aims at a sort of ruthless discipline that rids the mind of desire. To do this it aims to kill the self. This murderous impulse turned inward against the self is thus suicidal & comes into being due to a vast disappointment with the world. This cosmic ambition sees in the death of self, this assassination & suicide of the self the hope of a re-birth on a higher plane.

This "play" involves the sado-masochist play twixt the sadistic super-ego & the masochistic ego. Subject & object collapse in this play. The Self has super-ego, id & ego. Ego tries to mediate between super-ego & id but id is repressed & returns to the unconscious & the ego is then killed. The super-ego itself is comprised of an ideal unity comprised of the image of the primal couple in coitus & the mother-child unity. With the death of the "self" – primarily the ego, the super-ego takes over the self – it is the "large self."

What I wish to do, I suppose, is actually show how the mystical project may be re-interpreted in the light of the sociological interpretive practice (with a strong leaning on psychoanalysis). In this re-interpretation there are a number of notions that need to be defined & re-defined.

I am lost in Norman O. Brown. He appears to be advocating a regressive mysticism, but I also glimpse a symbolic way of understanding the whole thing. I glimpse the state of mind whereby we understand what we have done to create ourselves (introjection/eating & projection) – the illusion of it – but we also know that this is illusion. We know the true state of things before we did this, before we created ourselves – the unity of all – of ourselves as integral part of the world. This is before the advent of reflective consciousness, when we were in fact one with desire & solely driven by instinct, before we divided ourselves from the world & divided our interior selves, before the unconscious provided the vague & unknown zone that connects us to the world. This is our zone of flow, the zone where there is no distinct boundary, but where we make a boundary between the conscious & the unconscious, & between ourselves & the world. So we see the reality of both: that we have gone beyond unity into our separate reality and that this is both necessary & illusory. It is necessary & evil in itself, this separation, this repression, this ignoring, the paring things down to separate things & entities, and the reduction of the flow. But we are here & must live & we must live in this way. This is the birth of ethics: to know that we are founded on illusion & evil & that we cannot go back, but must go forward taking our whole history with us.

"Boundary," "Separation" & the Mystic Experience of "Oneness"

I have put forth the concept that we are socially constructed in a system of meanings that is essentially linguistic. Language, then, is at the center of our conventional everyday understanding of the world. I have briefly given a model of metaphor from the phenomenological (experiential) viewpoint. Now, I would like to look a little deeper at the actual network of meanings produced in language. Right off the bat, I'd like to say that "meanings" are created in the broader context of language by creating boundaries between one definition & another. Nothing, as a meaningful entity, exists alone, but always in relationship to other meaningful entities. Thus meaning-making, at least with language is essentially dualistic. It continually contrasts one thing with another thing & makes the distinction between those aspects that "are" a thing & those that "are not" a thing. Thus, a ball is round & can be many colours and sizes. A ball is a 3-dimensional sphere. It can also have the capacity to roll. A ball, however, cannot be a cube, nor can it be a table or a house.

Meanings are made via an extensive set of similarities & differences by reference to other items in language. In language, as such, the attempt to define a thing is an endless task, because each definition refers to some other item that must then be defined ad infinitum. As I stated earlier, however, meanings are actually made in real life situations, in embodied situations by embodied beings. Thus, although there is no one-to-one relationship between a word and a thing, words & their meanings occur in real situations and so there is always a phenomenological, experiential component to meaning. At some point, I am in a field with a cow. Language is present & so is the boundaried world.

The system of meanings as constituted in language may be conceptualized as a system of overlapping circles (or other enclosed shapes) with each enclosing circle or shape understood to contain the elements that a thing is, while all the elements outside of that particular shape are not what the thing is. Inside the circle called "Blake" there are a great number of attributes, including the ability to type, think, have a back-ache, etc., while outside my definitional circle, are all the things I am not. I am not the computer I work at. I am not the chair I sit in. I am not pain itself, but I do have a little bit of it. I may also say that in one sense I am my body whereas in another sense I am not my body, or not "only" my body. The point I am making is that the various definitions sometimes overlap each other & partake of each other's qualities.

I will now look at a special case of language & how meanings are made. This is the fact that any given definition is always created in specific contact with its opposite. (This is, I suppose, the most extreme expression of dualism.) Thus, the colour "black" is precisely related to its opposite, "white." Man is juxtaposed to woman, adult to child & so forth. We have then a sort of system of essences defined precisely by their opposites. Of course, categories overlap, as I have already stated. It appears, then, that what seem to be "pure" isolated definitions are not at all pure but are contaminated by that which lies between them. The most interesting cases are for us those that can vary from culture to culture and from time to time – those that are most obviously "socially constructed." An obvious pair, then, is "man" & "woman." As gender identities, these are constructed quite differently in different contexts.

The point I want to make, however, is that the so-called "purity" of either side of the polar equation is established primarily by a "repression" of certain attributes that they both have. What we have, then, is a set of "differences" set up by a repression of certain "similarities" between the definitions. Thus, "man" is given many so-called "manly" qualities & woman credited with a natural possession of many "womanly" ones. Men are intellectual, women are emotional, men are strong, women are weak, etc. It is obvious that I am creating stereotypes here, but that is just the point: stereotypical definitions are created by a systematic repression of similarities. This is most interesting to us, as I said earlier, in the domain of a culturally created moral system – the creation of things that are "good" & things that are "bad."

The system of definitions, then, is created by a system of stops or blocks on the flow of perception. This creates the world of boundaries, separation, & difference. Conventional metaphor embodies meaning in such a way that it includes certain similarities & excludes others. The "system" of metaphors includes certain knowledge & excludes or represses other knowledge.

These places of repressed similarity between metaphors (repressed similarities between men & women for instance) are tabooed areas. For instance we have the taboo against a man wearing woman's clothing, or the taboo against women baring their breasts, the taboo against men crying, the taboo against women intellectuals, etc. In fact, a great deal of energy is repressed and controlled in this way. A system of control is encoded in a systematic set of repressions in language. Thus, we have the same system in the mind. If we look at the body as a language system (the expressive body) then we can see that we also have a set of systematic repressions encoded in the body. Reich called this bodily armor, in essence a set of chronic tensions in the body.

Imagine for a moment then, if we un-repressed the systematic set of definitions that created our more or less "pure" categories. That is to say, imagine what would happen if we removed the boundaries between the meanings of things. Then things would flow together, as it were. One would not really be able to tell where one thing ended and another began and, as I have stated, there would be a great release of repressed energy. Suddenly released energy would rush through the perceptual system. With personal identity, there would be the experience of a dramatic flowing of self into the world of all things, without boundary & free. This essentially, then, is the experience of "oneness." There is the sense of entering into an eternal domain away from the separate & dual temporal world, a sense of identification with the vastness of the domain, a lack of fear because, after all, one is not separate & thus one is not, essentially, alone. In this unitary state which has released one from all boundary, one will also very often experience feelings that one has left behind all one's petty concerns with the self and self-centeredness, etc., and that one is god or part of god.

The Distinction between Ideology & Experience

This difference is essentially between a set of concepts or principles, in this case, the ideology that is mystic as opposed to the mystic experience, an experience characterized by that fact that it cannot be captured in language. One must experience it. In fact this distinction between that which can be captured in language & that which cannot is the basic distinction between the two sides of experiential metaphor: on the one side we have convention, on the other perception. The fullness of experience & all experience can never be fully captured – it is truly endless. One looks out the window & even if one could describe in words every single item, one would not truly capture the experience of simply looking out the window. Neither would one capture it by taking a picture of it, or painting one. Language of any sort can never capture the whole of experience; it always captures some aspect of experience. It only "captures" (discovers) part of the perceptual experience, the rest it creates.

But, as we have seen, it doesn't really make sense to separate out the world of formless perception from the world of forms. Meaning is always a combination of the two. We can "experience" this feeling of "oneness" but as soon as we step back from that experience we see that we are simply participating in a dualistic ideology that separates the formless world from the world of form and does this very often by trivializing the world of form. There is nothing trivial about the world of form.

In addition, we cannot really have the experience of mystic union outside of the world of form, because then the experience would be essentially meaningless. In fact, as I have stated, a great many meanings are attributed to this experience & it is placed on high as the sacred realm. Whenever we have any experience, it always must mean something. We can only say an experience is meaningless if it has no meaning for our current intentions.

The notion of god (whether existing everywhere, in oneself, or in particular entities) in the conceptual sphere of language and human communication is our most abstract concept. This is not at all to say that a person's "experience" of God, the void, oneness, is abstract. It is imbued with a myriad of feelings, insights, thoughts, and perceptions. As stated earlier the experience itself does tend towards certain feelings of love, the merging of self with the cosmos, timelessness, lack of fear and so forth. Where the problems of authority come up are not so much in the realm of experience itself as the social organization of that experience. Evidently the experience of non-ordinary states, transcendence, and ecstasy itself can be had by anyone & should be considered as one of many bodily capacities, including the ability to think.

Short versions

1) Creation: In the beginning – unity = evolution -- later, we have the creation of the Ordinary World = evolution in the realm of consciousness. The dialectic of invention.
2) Ordinary world = subject-object & "things" = duality & conventional gestalt
3) Ordinary Self = the subjection = introjection & projection = ordinary consciousness & separate self or ego self, conscious & unconscious (id, ego, super-ego)
4) Ordinary consciousness = conscious "of" = relational consciousness & duality, intentionality
5) Duality = ordinary subject-object world which must be transcended in order to attain unity = transcendence of dualism
6) Transcendence = going beyond & the resolution of duality in unity
7) Unity = the all & everything = God = Void = coitus of the parental pair = mother & child = the 2 in 1 = the flow of the world
8) The non-ordinary self = the Large Self = the awakened self = enlightenment = contact with divinity etc. It is reached through an ascending dialectic & resolution of duality
9) Dialectic = developmental sequence which resolves duality with transcendent third – with this resolution, a new polarity emerges with the resolution as one side of it – then a new resolution & a new transcendence etc.
10) Flow = the full iconic image of the world before it has been reduced & split to create ordinary consciousness, self & world.
11) Intentionality = our attitude towards the objects in consciousness = likes & dislikes = attachments
12) Attachments must be sacrificed in order to "awake" to larger consciousness
13) Awakening to larger consciousness = direct contact with godhead & the all = contact with unity
14) Sacrifice = letting go of thoughts
15) Thoughts = anything that enters into consciousness = foreground attraction
16) Foreground = part of the foreground/background gestalt comprised of convention & perception
17) Convention = conventional aspects of language = words
18) Language = a system for creating meaning via the interaction of metaphors in particular sequences
19) Meaning is created by individual units of language in relationship to each other = the relationship of metaphors
20) Metaphors are comprised of two elements: a conventional one & a perceptual one
21) Conventional metaphors are those that are essentially arbitrary = words
22) Perceptual capacity gives us an iconic image = the fullness of perception
23) Icon & the fullness of perception = "flow" in the world
24) Conventional imagery = the limitation of flow to create individual things
25) Individual things are created in consciousness by the limitation of flow & the creation of the unconscious domain.

26) The unconscious domain is part of the psychoanalytic image of consciousness & the self. There is a split between the unconscious & consciousness with respect to the ego, the id & the super-ego. Each of these metaphorical elements of the self is partly unconscious, that is partly unknown to us, buried or forgotten.

27) Creativity = reversal of conventional gestalt in dialectic of invention

28) Spirituality = personal relationship to godhead or void.

Either spiritually is psychological & involves the invention or rediscovery of a particular state of consciousness with "identification" with a particular image of unity at its core OR it is "real" & involves a real transformation of consciousness which can "let go" of the idea of 'God or whatever" & clearly understands that the task is to transform the world & the consciousness of all people & that any arguments about priority, the small & large self, mystical awakening etc. are all meaningless if this task is not the absolute priority. Actually, if spirituality is essentially psychological, the same thing goes: the task is transformation & the creation of new world & self.

Spirituality is essentially concerned with "magic."

1) Spirituality is concerned with a personal contact with spirit

2) Magic concerns the utilization of religious imagery to enhance the self.

3) Those involved with spirituality, magic & mysticism are essentially involved with the self, its enhancement & protection. They all seem to be suspicious of and dislike religion.

4) Religion is essentially concerned with the organization of the community in worship of the divine or the sacred.

5) The divine or sacred are essentially arbitrary categories created by people to designate a particular domain of spirits & forces that are beyond human understanding.

Meaning, Metaphor & Embodiment

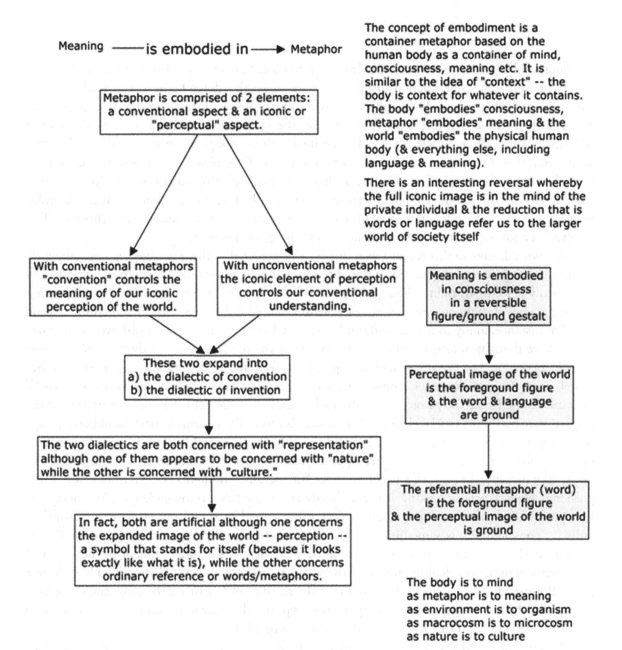

Meaning ──── is embodied in ──→ Metaphor

Metaphor is comprised of 2 elements: a conventional aspect & an iconic or "perceptual" aspect.

With conventional metaphors "convention" controls the meaning of of our iconic perception of the world.

With unconventional metaphors the iconic element of perception controls our conventional understanding.

These two expand into
a) the dialectic of convention
b) the dialectic of invention

The two dialectics are both concerned with "representation" although one of them appears to be concerned with "nature" while the other is concerned with "culture."

In fact, both are artificial although one concerns the expanded image of the world -- perception -- a symbol that stands for itself (because it looks exactly like what it is), while the other concerns ordinary reference or words/metaphors.

The concept of embodiment is a container metaphor based on the human body as a container of mind, consciousness, meaning etc. It is similar to the idea of "context" -- the body is context for whatever it contains. The body "embodies" consciousness, metaphor "embodies" meaning & the world "embodies" the physical human body (& everything else, including language & meaning).

There is an interesting reversal whereby the full iconic image is in the mind of the private individual & the reduction that is words or language refer us to the larger world of society itself

Meaning is embodied in consciousness in a reversible figure/ground gestalt

Perceptual image of the world is the foreground figure & the word & language are ground

The referential metaphor (word) is the foreground figure & the perceptual image of the world is ground

The body is to mind
as metaphor is to meaning
as environment is to organism
as macrocosm is to microcosm
as nature is to culture

A Rant on the Centering Prayer

Bourgeault's program seems reasonable & clear headed. I'm not sure if I misread her earlier ideas or if there were some contradictions. Anyway, I want to get this down because it seems important, and something that I think I can fully agree with. She begins with the idea that one must create an inner observer but that this inner observer is not the ego because the ego is precisely that part of self which cannot observe itself – it is fully identified with its thoughts, emotions, desires, the inner drama etc. This inner observer is actually a new sense of "I" & observes in a nonattached way. It is not lost in the "contents of consciousness," but identified with this inner observer "you" learn to pay attention to the whole field of consciousness not just the foreground elements. It is the bridge between ego awareness (identification with passing thoughts, etc.) & the deeper Self. This new "I" is involved in a sort of "simultaneous awareness" of both ego & deep self.

My own side note to this is that I wouldn't have immediately either identified ego as completely lost in the contents of consciousness or understood the inner observer to be something separate, but analytically it seems all right. Although, I guess I do see identifying the ego with its total lostness in the contents of consciousness as a sort of a "set-up" – obviously there must be something beyond this. For instance, in my own case, without in any way having set up an inner observer of my own, what I have thought of as ego consciousness (or rather the self comprised of dynamic elements of thought as proposed by Freud – ego, id, & superego) as fully able to disentangle itself from id desires as well as super-ego messages. I suppose this is the crux once more, "egoic consciousness" is NOT the same as the Freudian ego or the Freudian self. Again, it is the definition or re-definition of the original state that is the crucial element. The "inner observer," then, seems to partake of both the ego & the super-ego, & in fact it is set up to watch both & also the total field of consciousness. Thus, the inner observer is set up to be aware of both "conventional" thought as well as the full iconic image (the perceptual field.) This is not an exact "fit" because "thoughts" & "emotions" are in the phenomenological way of looking at them already constituted as a transcendent entity (metaphor) that partakes of conventional symbolism & the perceptual field. In any event this "set-up" of ordinary consciousness as something in obvious need of being superseded is a somewhat similar "set-up" as the one I found in Merton, but in that case it was the establishment of the origin of consciousness in the ontological ground of the world as opposed to "inside" the individual. At one point, Bourgeault notes in another context that the sacrifice of Christ on the cross could not be a "set-up" for the resurrection. That is to say, it only "appears" that way in retrospect & one cannot go into the experience with that in mind. It is a difficult forgetting.

Having established the nature of ordinary consciousness, the need for an inner observer & its function, Bourgeault goes on to say that meditation is "usually" understood to be the place to develop a "conscious witnessing presence" but this is not the case in Centering Prayer because the inner voice with its simple command to simply "let go" of thoughts does not require a continuous presence such as the witnessing presence. Where exactly this voice comes from or where it goes in between is a little unclear but it seems to recede into the unconscious & then arise from it. As I have said earlier, it seems to at least have the super-ego function of controlling "thoughts" which in the Freudian model come from the "id" (wishes etc.) & from the perceptual field. In addition, the super-ego as "conscience" & the introjected moral authority seems to fit the bill with the continual admonition to aim at higher awareness by banishing or "letting go" of "lower" thoughts & feelings.

Thus, the witnessing observer in the case of Centering Prayer must be developed outside of the meditative practice. One must learn in a somewhat arduous process how to identify with this "doubled awareness" & thus withdraw identification with ordinary awareness. She goes on to discuss some of the "ground rules" for staying on track with this process. (I want to briefly "look inside myself" for any analogous experience here with the "doubling awareness" & immediately it comes to me that my own experience has always been with a sort of contemplative stillness in which I experience myself to simply "be" in the world with no particular focus. I have always felt that this particular mode of being put me in touch with "eternity" & with a melancholic mood that I have identified with the notion of a "nostalgia for the absolute." I also closely identify this practice & this mood with my own person creative process. The melancholy mood I have identified as originating in the sadness of my relationship with my father – who was very much absent, at least emotionally, for me as a child. I take this as an instance of the need & the desire to form attachment "no matter what" rather than guided by the pleasure principle. My attachment to my father, then, is ambivalent & melancholic. This mood has become for me my "ground" of being & I equate it with being in authentic touch with the real or "truth." I also recognize, of course, that this mood is "my" touchstone & others will have a very different experience, a different "ground" & a different contact with their creativity.

Bourgeault makes it very clear that the "doubled awareness" or the "observing witness" is not to be identified with the super-ego & a primary way of telling them apart is that they have "a different way of speaking." The super-ego addresses the self with "should" & makes judgments whereas this new psychic entity only watches & is never "attached" to any of the states of being or ideas that enter into consciousness. She notes that sometimes it is useful to refer to different states that have to do with egoic identity as "it" – "it is feeling sad" etc. The idea is to get some space between ordinary identity which is identified with our "I" & to identify instead with this deeper being, which in essence is another self.

She states that "obviously then you are not just your thoughts; that mysterious 'chooser' in you must emerge from a much deeper and steadier will at the centre of your being "(p. 128)" The "chooser" is that voice that rises up from the depths & just says "let thoughts go." As I stated earlier it is a little hard to get a handle on this voice & the notion that although it always says the same thing & always implies a judgment – that the thoughts that emerge are not to be identified with, it is not the super-ego. It is engaged in more or less the same function as the super-ego so it doesn't much matter what one calls it. The observer watcher extends this "voice" into everyday consciousness. It is hard not to be aware that this same psychological process happens often in classic cases of dissociation & multi-personality. In this case, however, identity jumps around from split off personality to another & isn't aware of the others at the same time.

At root, what we have then is the identification of self with a passive image of self that "watches" both the contents of consciousness & the general field of consciousness. Now that I have said this, I am told that this is exactly the wrong way to think of it. Now we have the contortions. According to Bourgeault, the observer is not a split off part of the mind at all but is lower down in "magnetic centre." It watches you through your deeper unconscious. When you get the hang of it this deeper magnetic centre looks after everything & you don't have to do anything. Everything is looked after; one's consciousness is free to do whatever it wants. It is not as if we carry it but that it carries us. This is very much the same sort of understanding we reached with Merton. I should have known there would be a "mysterious" aspect to all. At the end, what is inside is given to the outside, or a deeper inside, that we have heard nothing of except that it just magically orients us to God and carries the voice & the observer watcher in this deeper magnetic centre. If there is such a thing, it is invented & we should be able to know something about this invention.

This double awareness is somehow locked in the body as it were & makes connection between both sides of the gestalt of consciousness: foreground & background. The "magical" entity is "magnetic centre." This centre seems to partake of the unconscious & the body – a sort of unconscious body – in fact, the heart. There is contact with "thoughts" as well as with the general field of awareness (which is always a sort of potential from which all foreground objects spring.) She notes, & this is very reasonable indeed, that the goal is not to replace the lower self with the higher but rather to create a marriage between the two. It is certainly very difficult to understand how one could operate in daily life only identified with the larger self or "field awareness."

In all this, there is a pervasive sense of suspicion regarding psychology & the mind. There is a continual characterization of different processes that seem to refer to the mind & also appear to be very similar to processes & aspects of depth psychology which are then affirmed to not be what they appear to be. I understand the desire to distance one's special processes from psychoanalytic concepts because these tend to come with a certain amount of baggage that isn't wanted, but there seems to be a general paranoia about the mind itself, as if it itself could not encompass the state of being aimed at. This I think is the case. With Merton earlier we have the intuition of an ontological ground & here we have a "magnetic centre" which is in the body but outside the mind & yet still capable of watching what is going on in the mind. She does not think that there is a problem with slipping into dissociation – I noted the similarity between a split off personality & the observer above -- & it seems to me that she suggests "a different way of looking at it" in particular so that this pitfall will be avoided. The idea being that by "looking at something in a different way" it will in fact be different. By stating that something is not of the mind but can watch the mind, one will make this "place" come into existence. My own sense of it is that the "magnetic centre" then, is a particular mask that one dons & that it identified as not of the mind, either the objects in consciousness or the field itself. It is the unattached observer & exists in the heart. This is a mystic understanding in the sense that there is no rational way that this could be the case. Except of course we can glimpse an image of mind as not located in the head but rather in the whole body. Certainly, the emotions have more direct contact with the whole of the body, at least in our consciousness, than other mental actions do.

Standing back from it a little it seems the split off aspect of consciousness termed the observer is created in conscious mind so that it can then disappear in unconscious mind. This unconscious aspect of mind then can unconsciously keep track of the mental gestalt while remaining unattached, keeping in mind of course that "disappearing into unconscious mind" really means just that it – its voice – is outside of consciousness until it comes into consciousness. In other words, it's just like anything else; it's not in consciousness when it's not in consciousness, & it is when it is.

There is always this sense of an a priori conceptualization of a larger consciousness that is everywhere & a small one that is "in" consciousness. The large consciousness cannot be "in" consciousness because it is too large. How, then, is one to have the experience of this large consciousness? How is one to experience being "in" this large consciousness when, as soon as one conceives of this large consciousness, it is "in" your own small consciousness & you've lost the game. Thus the contortions. The idea essentially involves "identifying" with this larger consciousness in such a way as the larger consciousness does not ever actually "appear" in consciousness. If it ever appears in consciousness, then you know you only have a conceptual understanding of the large consciousness, not the direct experience. But putting the main problem aside for a moment, let's look at "identification" & see what it entails. First of all there must be something to identify with & given that this something is too big to fit in consciousness we come up against the same problem. So, again setting aside the problem, we nonetheless learn all we can about this larger consciousness & its attributes from reports from others who claim they know something about it, usually from direct experience. We also learn, of course, that although we can have all sorts of aspects of this larger consciousness in our small consciousness, this is not really the large consciousness because it exists elsewhere – in fact it is everywhere & only the concept of everywhere will fit in consciousness not everywhere itself.

So, in fact, this everywhere that won't fit in "as itself" is like everything else in the world. Nothing fits into consciousness itself; only concepts fit in, unless, of course, even the concept of everything is too big to fit in. Thus the contortions. How to identify with something but not have it in consciousness? Simple! Just propose "somewhere else" that you can identify with this all-ness that is not in consciousness. Then the problem is simplified, all you've got to do is find out where this "somewhere else" is but you can't look for it in consciousness because it isn't there so where should one look for it? Somewhere else in the body – that's the closest thing. Maybe the spleen, but more likely the heart or breath, something instinctual moving, alive with spirit but "not us" in the ordinary way. Identify with the heart but not the heart that is in your mind, not even in your heart that is in your body that is in your mind but rather in your heart period.

All the contortions lead to this: how to get out of yourself & go somewhere else. Here the old concept of the detachable self or soul is useful. Just get one of those & then you can go wherever you want. Somewhere along the line the notion of the unconscious comes into it. This is perhaps the most common way of thinking about being identified with something outside of consciousness that is still somehow in consciousness but we don't know it because generally it is outside of our awareness. Things in the unconscious, however, do "pop up" every once in a while. Every once in a while we get a message from the unconscious – some desire or thought or feeling or wish that got pushed out of consciousness but didn't really go anywhere very far away, just out of consciousness knowing that it would figure out a way how to get back into consciousness a little later on. Often it does.

So one way of identifying with the larger consciousness would be to identify with it in the smaller consciousness but then somehow get it to go out of consciousness, not very far but just far enough so that we aren't aware of it but it can come back at crucial times to tell us something. Then we would be identified with the larger consciousness which is outside of our small consciousness – it was so big it wouldn't fit into the small consciousness – well it did to start with – we did have it in small consciousness first before it went away but all we have to do is have the idea that when it is in the unconscious it will grow by itself to fit its bigger shape & then we've got it. Well we haven't really got it because to have it is to not have it & we don't really have it because it's not in consciousness except sometimes perhaps when it appears in its small form in consciousness to tell us something.

With all these contortions we learn a little bit to wonder what is it that is so great about this large consciousness that we should take so much trouble to get it when we can't really have it anyway. What is it? What it is we learn from reports is we get over our anxiety & worries about everything, especially about ourselves because we are not so attached to our thoughts & feelings & things like that which appear in consciousness & that we identify with. The whole contortion thing is really about loosening up our identifications with our little thoughts & so forth & getting an understanding that everything that we do in our consciousness is an illusion, broken up & separated out & introjected & projected -- all the things that consciousness does -- & we get a self that is partly unconscious. Well, the contortions we have to go through do actually loosen up our feeling about who we are so that we aren't so sure any more although we can get to identify with the bigger self being which is everywhere & especially all the good things that it has going for it like love & understanding & calmness. So even though it goes away because it is so big it is always with us in a sense not really in consciousness but we can feel it lurking around everywhere so we are aware that it is there even though we can't exactly be "it." So there it is, & here we are together a little looser.

Hmmmm. Some people would call that a rant. I don't really think so, just thinking around a problem. I explained my position re Centering Prayer & why it didn't make sense to Sherry & she said she thought it made me irritated and jealous. I suppose that defines a little our two different paths. I want to know intellectually how things work but she is quite willing to go on faith. Part of my own feeling however is that Bourgeault is not describing a state of being that I have not experienced. I feel very strongly that I have experienced & continue to experience a state very similar to the one she describes. I also think that this state continues to influence my everyday reality in an ongoing & good way. So when I feel that she hasn't explained things very well or that she has mystified a process in order to "keep in" some of what I consider baggage or thoughts about "the spiritual," then my complaint is not about me not understanding how to get to where she is pointing, but rather that she has missed something essential about the process as I understand it.

My own Experience of "Meditation"

First of all this meditation is in no way a formal meditation, but just concerns a state of being that I enter from time to time, that over the years I have come to think of as a contemplative state. In understanding this state of being in this way, I had no real sense of linking it to the notion of Christian contemplation as a path to mystical awareness. It just seemed "contemplative" to me in the sense of being "thoughtful" & calm. In these states, I have never really thought about anything in particular, but rather simply contemplated being or being in the world. Just being. To me this contemplative state was "normal" in every sense of the word – something that everyone did or at least could do more or less any time they wanted to. It did appear to me to be a slightly altered state of reality in the sense that my normal state involved doing things & thinking & so on. Thus to just sit still somewhere & be aware of oneself in the world in a calm sort of way was a little different but simply one of the things that an embodied person could do.

While in this sort of calm contemplative state I feel that I am in touch with or aware of the eternal dimension. It seems to me that the present moment "could be" eternal – go on forever. I do not really feel that "I" am eternal or that having this sort of feeling of being aware of the eternal dimension means that I will live forever somewhere else or any of those feelings. Rather, I feel that this awareness of the eternal is an effect of consciousness. It is something that the human brain & being are capable of. It is quite a wonderful feeling because it gives one the feeling that one is linked up to everything, to the whole being of the world, & also that one has a place in the world. I suppose I feel that being "in touch" with the world, with being & myself in the world, is to have a sense of belonging in the world. A sense of rightness. When I think about it these moments of what I could call "calm contemplation" occur in nature. There is a sense of "eternal sunshine," a sense of the endurance of light, the particularity of leaves & grass, a sort of hum of life & being, sounds seem to be muted a little, everything kind of just "stops" for a moment. And that is what it is – a moment. All the rest is just resting in that moment. The moment does not seem to be "in" consciousness simply because I'm not thinking of "in" or "out" of consciousness. I am "in" the world

& have a strong sense of that. I guess it is a strong sense of the presence of my own presence, but more strongly the presence of the world, especially the world of nature around me.

I have said somewhere else I think that these contemplative moments are coloured by a slightly sad sense of emotional loss. Coloured by a sense of nostalgia for something lost, something not named but "something" that I suppose might be the eternal dimension itself. For eternity, our invisible place in non-being has definitely been lost – to be born is to experience this loss. I could go on about the imagery of unity but have done that elsewhere. The feeling is simultaneously of being "there" in the world – aware of eternity & aware of the loss of eternity – and I suppose aware of death. Just writing these words brings tears to my eyes. I am not sure if I'm feeling sorry for myself, or if just bringing back the memory of these contemplative moments brings the sadness. The moment does contain the knowledge of death, of being a transitory phenomenon in the midst of nature & now of course I am a person with a terminal illness with a special knowledge that I am going to die. Probably a little of both. I should say that I feel that I have had a number of these contemplative moments that were enduring to some small extent, & they seem now to be superimposed on each other. In fact, they seem to be a single moment caught in the stillness of time, but strangely enough, when I say I feel a contact with eternity, there is a very strong sense of time, not of its passage but of its stillness. The stillness of time is its eternity. So perhaps it is not so strange.

I have also mentioned somewhere else that the melancholic mood which I associate with these moments & also with my own creativity has been engendered by my conflicted & ambiguous relationship with my father. The mood of sadness was the aura of our relationship, & this aura has continued in my life & has become associated for me with a truthful connection with reality, with the true nature of the world. There are two notions that appear for the first time in this brief note: creativity & ambiguity. I would say that my experience of ambiguity in my early relationships (with my mother also) has bestowed on me an enduring ambivalence towards life itself & all the sorts of relationships that one can have. I am ambivalent about just about everything. This ambivalence extends to my own self & the contents of consciousness; things appear to me to have a somewhat tenuous existence & my feelings towards them vary. I mention this only with reference to the notion of non-attachment that so many meditative practices seem to aim at. My own experience with regard to this is that this non-attachment program is very often a cop-out motivated by fear. I believe that strong attachments in life to those one loves & the useful activities of one's life are wonderful things. One will ultimately have to give them up but why rush the process. My ambivalence, then, I relate to a "loosening" of my attachments & with what I understand to be the sense of "spaciousness" aimed at by meditation practice, although they are probably not the same.

The other notion was that of creativity. I definitely relate these calm moments of contemplation to my creativity in the sense that I feel that the sense of calm being connected to the world is essential to having a full sense of being in the world in general. So I suppose I have things a little reversed: contemplation is at one pole of experience – the other being at the experience of intense activity. If one is going to have much to communicate in a creative way, one should at least have some experience of the full spectrum of being. For me, my creative life is far & away the most important aspect of my life, so to say that the experience of contemplation is intrinsic to having a full life is to say that contemplation is necessary for the creative life. For me, to lead a full life is to lead a creative life. In addition, I should say that I have no prejudice with regard to how one can be creative, & creativity is by no means limited to the arts. To be creative is to "make it up" as opposed to following the beaten track of conventionality.

Before leaving the experience of calm contemplation I should say that, although I do not often have "big" moments, I have many small moments or passing moments of awareness of this same state – of the eternal in everyday experience, of, in fact the complete interpenetration of the flow of time by the timeless. One can, in fact, drop into the timeless dimension pretty much any time one wants to by simply stopping the flow of activity whether of the body or the mind but as soon as I have said this I realize that one doesn't have to really "stop" anything. One has only to shift one's awareness to this other dimension of state of being while continuing with whatever one is doing. I suppose this sounds very much like the double awareness aimed at by Bourgeault. Again, I have never aimed at it but always thought of this ability as a completely natural one, which anyone could do. I still think that. I certainly do not see myself as being an expert at this at all. I am not unattached. I do not have a specially constructed witness or observer. Emotions & thoughts & various aches & pains grab my attention continually. And then they let go of me or I let go of them.

For me, creativity is the central aspect of my life, my work. I have said these moments of calm contemplation are important for that work but so is intense activity. And within those times of intense activity which are perhaps more common for me, is where the field of all things is becomes available to me, and the field of potentiality opens up & the world of ideas & things is open. (Or this is how it feels – that all is open & available – of course, this is not the actuality of the case. One must prepare oneself.) And these times of intense creativity are connected to those other times – simply another door into the same room or a couple of adjacent rooms in the mansion of consciousness.

It seems to me that the white heat of creative work is more available to me than the calm contemplative moment, but I believe they form a unity, or a matrix. I was going to say a matrix of moments, but the white heat of creative work actually lasts longer for me than the moments of contemplation. It is more "natural" for me. I think that those who know me would agree that my usual state of being is more "intense" than "calm." Nonetheless, I experience both states. I suppose I don't go on so much about the calm meditative state simply because it has become such a famous goal, so sought after & talked about. Thus, my usual opening in conversation when the topic comes up is to question why one would want to be calm. What's with this calmness I ask, what's the big deal? Why does everybody want it? Well, someone answers, my mind chatters on & on & I'm anxious all the time. I want to shut it off & be peaceful. Don't you want to be peaceful, they ask. No, I don't, I say. I want to be excited. I want to engage with life. I want to be creative. Why do you want to "retreat" all the time? How come everybody is in retreat? What about the advance? Why aren't there any advance centers where people learn how to engage creatively with the world?

My thought is this. These people are desperate to shut off their mind before they've even found out how it works. This is in response to their characterization of "mind" as a sort of out-of-control entity that has taken over their body & just does what "it" wants to do & it's so noisy & so on all the time. This signifies to me that they haven't learned the rudimentary rules for running the machine called mind. It's as if people suddenly found themselves going at a great speed down a super-highway & they suddenly realize that they don't know how to drive. They instantly want to slow down, then stop, hopefully without accidents. This is a very traumatic situation. They have done the right thing. They have coasted to a stop by the highway. But the kicker is that once they have found the off switch, cranked the wheel over & come to a stop, they have no desire to learn how to drive. They actually think driving is a bad thing. This is because they have gotten the idea that the car just does whatever it wants to do & that there is no way of controlling it. The only thing to do is shut it off, then scrap it. Sit somewhere as far away from the road as possible & dream they are on their way to enlightenment.

This, then, is the reason that I do not find myself on the side of peace & quiet & the discovery of the off switch. Seeking enlightenment has becomes the "in" thing to do. Of course, most people can't afford to go all out for mystical awareness. But for them, there all sorts of activities that have been "hived off" as it were & now form separate activities by which some may gain some of the magical enhancements for self, some of the mystical powers by which they can "spiritualize" their perceptions. For these people, every small town has a couple of meditation groups; magazines tell us about stress reduction & how great this new kind of yoga is. TV is full of shows which have dead people coming back to life, & of course we've got super powers of all sorts that either come from the mystic East or the technological West.

Anyway, it's enough to make a grown man cry, as they say. To retreat from life because we are afraid of it is not exemplary behaviour any way you look at it. And because of my own contrary nature I tend to espouse the attitude that fear is at the foundation of religion & also the spiritual sensibility. Everybody is afraid of death. Everybody wants to live forever.

God, when I think back to my own "mystic" days – the early 60s & 70s there was only one mystic book store in Vancouver & when one went on a pilgrimage one would come back with some piece of esoteric wisdom whether it was astrology or a book of Alistair Crowley's. My own investigations were focused on a few different areas that I suppose I should confess: Gurgieff primarily through the work of P.D. Ouspensky, the tarot according to everybody including Crowley, a smattering of Jung, Blavatsky & so on. I also should admit that I never followed any particular "path" never looked for or found a guru, never practiced meditation or yoga. I was also interested in writers who were interested in the mystic journey, the quest for awakening, coming from the mysterious East. These included people like William Burroughs, John Cage, and Jack Kerouac.

I also should confess that in those turbulent times I was never much involved in politics either. I think back & wonder at what can only seem like lost years, wasted years, but I don't really believe that. I was writing or trying to write. I knew enough to know that I wasn't much interested in writing about myself as in confessional poetry. I also wasn't interested in writing novels. I continued to be interested in "performance" and thought of my work, as I still do, as essentially "oral." I was always interested in working with music.

My work was thus neither "poetry" in the classical sense, nor was it popular music. It was something in-between, an instance of my ambivalence towards both sensibilities. I could not "identify" with either & thus created an ambiguous persona that I suppose I have struggled with in one way or another all of my life.

The intensity of the creative situation is more comfortable for me. At least where I live there is no clamour to walk this "path," no supermarket magazine rack with how-to-awaken books. This is, I suppose, not really fair. The magazine rack is actually filled with quasi girly magazines, car magazines, music magazines, computer magazines, etc. Pop culture with its endless products of gadgets & novelty & stereo systems is in the firmly dominant position. The desire for enlightenment, while it definitely has its "spirituality" section in the bookstore, hasn't exactly displaced the novel.

To be just a little bit more honest with myself (no sense going overboard) I would have to admit that my overt rejection of mysticism & my irritation with mystic or spiritual talk has to do with a sense of loss, a sense of promise unfulfilled. Perhaps I am a little disillusioned.

Continued the next day….

I slept & woke up with ideas while reading a few pages of Philip K. Dick's "Now wait for last year" a quite wonderful book. In it, he seems to be working out much the same sort of problem I'm working on but with parallel worlds & alternate futures & all sorts of high jinks. And it's not over yet.

Anyway, I came up with a few ideas that seem to me to "solve" the problem once & for all to my own satisfaction at least. God knows how I'll feel about it tomorrow. So here it is. I began with what appeared to me as several "mistakes" that I have made in my own thinking & that may or may not have been introduced by the books I've been reading – the Bourgeault, etc.

The mistake is to think of the mind or consciousness as a container and/or that one has to identify with the large self as an entity/thing. I have noted, I believe this mistake before, but I seem to keep getting trapped in it. Both of these ideas – mind as container & Large Self as entity view the self from the position of the small or ordinary self predicated upon the limit of flow to create specific types of relationships. Both metaphors – container & identification – are already limited ideas – the container is a certain size & identification is always identification "with" something just as ordinary consciousness is consciousness "of" something. So much for the mistakes or the "traps" that I fall into.

All one does is "experience" the flow of the world – the myriad relationships & connections between all the things in the world before they have become things. This experience of the large world is also the experience of the large self. One identifies not with any "thing" = the all, but rather one identifies with that which experiences this flow. This identification is for me the same identification as with small self but simply with a new experience (experience of flow rather than things). For the meditator, the identification is with the watcher who experiences flow or perceives the total field of awareness as well as the small self & the contents of consciousness.

So, for me, it seems that the ordinary small self can be in one "state" – the ordinary state -- & while in that state "I" experience the world of things & their relationships between themselves & to myself, but it can also be in another "state" – the non-ordinary state -- & while in that state "I" experience the world of flow, the myriad relationships that constitute the field & the flow of the world through me. The experience of "flow" is both "in" consciousness as the sense of a passage, a temporal flow of one thing into another & perceived by "myself" the same self as I've always had but now in a different state of being.

The experience of flow involves the "loosening up" of all the specific "relationships" accompanied as they are be intentions & desires – likes & dislikes, etc. These illusory "things" & the necessary "relationships" that must be established just because they are things begin to be experienced in different relationships to each other & their "thingness" begins to be ambiguous.

The problem, then, hinges on the ability to loosen up one's understanding of the world – loosen up one's understanding of the nature of "things" & the fact that we create these "things" ourselves by limiting the flow of perception to a certain set of "conventional" relationships. This limitation of the full flow of perception, in which all things engage with each other in a myriad of different ways, involves a) by a process of selection & rejection, creating symbolic categories & the boundaries around them & b) by establishing "proper" relationships between these categories. These are essentially nouns & verbs.

It is sometimes difficult to "loosen up" one's grip on or understanding of the world of separate things because this understanding appears to be the very essence of "reality." To loosen up our grip upon reality is a dangerous thing. We might slip off; we might go mad. At the least, we would be "different." Our illusory sense of the world is nonetheless our reality & without it we would be nothing. This is because our sense of self is exactly built up upon & within the matrix of our reality composed of separate things & relationships – all of them having a "relationship" with the self, which is itself comprised of a number of elements or "things" each with their own relationship. The whole thing is very much like a writhing pit of snakes; when one gets the courage & adequate protection to even try to pull on one of them, the whole bunch shifts & pulls back. This is a dangerous business. And it is quite right that to do away with this ordinary consciousness of self & world as an incredibly complex bunch of separate things is a particular arrangement. The "particular arrangement" can refer to both how things "should" be in the moral world & the scientific understanding of the nature of matter & energy, time & space. It is quite clear that one cannot change this situation overnight. At the level of society, in the realm of morality as well as in the world of science, it takes some sort of revolution to change things & then they just change from one thing to another. We're still left with a world made up of separate things & their relationships.

What to do? Or rather, how to do it? We know we want to loosen up the limited definition of things & the limited relationships between things, but we don't know how, yet, to do it. We do know that accomplishing this – never mind at the level of society, but just at the level of the individual – opens up a world of increased "possibility" & also "ambiguity." The more different ways we can see things, the more we can see things "in a different light" the more different sorts of relationships we can "imagine" the more we are willing to shift the boundaries of this or that category in order to include something or exclude something else, the more ambiguous & full of possibility the world becomes. The looser our grip on the "one way" things should be, the more we become aware of "alternate realities." The more ways the world changes in our eyes the more ways we see that we could change, the more we can see different ways of being & doing. Change the world & we change. Change ourselves & the world changes.

Let's back up for a moment & get a few central concepts straight. First, the world of "flow." I am characterizing "flow" as the "original" or primal way the world was (or is) before we divided it up into separate things – separate linguistic categories – before we limited the myriad fibers or threads of connection between all things. In the world of flow, contiguous "things" (which are not yet things) are connected to those "things" (also not yet things) all around it "at every point." There is no "gap" or "space" between things. Everything is joined together at all points along their surfaces & as such there are no bounding surfaces – there are no "edges" to "things" rather, there is the "flow" of one thing into another – things interpenetrate one another – they are not separate but unified, one with the other so that there is no one, no other but only one.

OK. Let's be clear about one thing. One cannot live as a human being in such a world. To be human is to have "reflective consciousness" & reflective consciousness entails the separating out one thing from another – myself from food for instance – to have food & self flow one into the other so that one cannot tell which is food & which is me – one cannot tell where one's edges are, is not a good condition to be in when one is out hunting. It is the world of "hallucination." One may have hallucinations every once in a while & come back to the ordinary world but one can't stay there very long or one is not able to look after oneself, & others will have to take on that task in some sort of institution. Beyond one's own problems in an undefined world, one would certainly not be able to relate with others in the creation of society.

My position is that "ordinary consciousness" must also be maintained as well if one is going to experience the world of flow. Both at once. Of course there are varying degrees of "separation" & "flow" or "unity." So, having defined "flow" as the myriad world of "possible" connections and the undifferentiated world, ordinary reflective consciousness (which is anything but ordinary) separates things out, creates boundaries, names & relationships, precisely in order that we can "do" things, have "realistic" relationships & so forth. There are indeed many ways that an adult man & woman may relate but a great deal of them are forbidden for obvious reasons – some for not so obvious reasons & many "just because" – that is for more or less arbitrary reasons. Marriage is perhaps the most commonly "sanctioned" relationship. If one were really to open up to the myriad connections between the two one would realize that there are a great many similarities that are suppressed or repressed in order to create the ordinary categories that create the boundary between them. In many ways, one wouldn't be able to tell if one were a man or a woman – one would blend into the other. The relationship would become "ambiguous." This term "ambiguity" is a very important one for me & I will return to it again. And again.

The notion of "loosening" up one's more or less fixed notions about the nature of things & their relationships accords well with a general definition of "development" in the context of psychology. Development, by its nature, concerns "progress" – development towards something better. Thus, we speak of the development of intellectual ability, the development of the ability to symbolize or simply "moral development." Moral development, in its most general outline points to the ability to take more & more different "positions" with regard to a problem. At the lower level of moral development, one can only take one position, usually the position of authority. As one develops one's moral faculty, one learns how to take the position of the other & then after a while the position of many different others. At the highest moral level, one can see or understand "all" of the different points of view. With this ability, one is in the best possible position to make a good judgment. In this case, the case of moral development, one has moved from a fixed notion of "the right relationship" to an image of the myriad possible relationships, In a sense, one has moved from "ordinary consciousness" (although the term "lower consciousness" seems better) to a state of higher consciousness or awareness – to the world of "flow."

With this analogy in mind, it seems that it might be possible to simply "develop" higher consciousness starting from lower or ordinary consciousness, and further, that this "development" will concern the ability to see many different facets, many different relationships where before one saw only one or only a few. But what of "intentionality," "desire," our "emotions" & "attachment" to things? The simple fact is that by our willingness to "loosen our grip" on the simplified ordinary world & encompass many different ways that it may be, we automatically loosen our emotional attachments to just this one way, this one thing, & our emotions come to be "spread out" through the whole matrix. Our awareness of the many & the varied takes us away from the socially accepted "conventions" & our own psychological or emotional relationship to things. And by changing the world (the way we experience the world) we change ourselves (the way we experience ourselves.) As the world becomes more multi-dimensional & multi-faceted it paradoxically becomes more bound together as a single unified entity & the more we experience the "flow" of the world, the more we experience ourselves as a part of that flow.

Two equations:

1) The ordinary world = the world of separate things = the world of more or less "fixed" relationships = clarity & disambiguation of the world = apparent unity by way of a complex matrix of known relationships.

2) The world of Flow = the loosening of one's grip on fixed relations & the nature of things = the world of increasing connections & relationships = development of more & more different ways of seeing the world = ambiguity = the world of undifferentiated things = unity = a unitary reality underlying the ordinary world of separate things.

1) Fixed relationships twixt separate things = ordinary reality
2) Loosening up of our understanding of the nature of the things & their relationships
3) Multiplication of ways of seeing reality = a more ambiguous "altered reality"

There is the sense of many tendrils of reality that join all things together. In order to create ordinary reality, one must decrease the number of these tendrils & then establish only one or two of them as "proper" connections. Then increasing awareness involves increasing the number of tendrils again. This involves a going back & "filling in" the tendrils that were earlier rejected.

Social construction, then, would really more accurately termed social de-construction in the sense that the construction involves a "taking away" of connections & certainly not a simple building up of these connections. It involves more a process of limitation by a process of selection of the good & a rejection of the bad. This process, then, is exactly the same with the self. In the Freudian view, the self is created via an introjection of the good & what one likes & a rejection or projection of the bad & what one doesn't like. This is, of course, the primarily illustration of the work of the "pleasure principle." As we have seen, this principle is overruled by the need for relationship at any cost so that one chooses to have even a bad relationship rather than none at all. I am reminded of the sculptural technique of taking away of the stone in order to "find" the head in the stone. The head is only one of a million things that could have emerged, but because of a process of selection & rejection the head appears in the image desired by the sculptor.

Let's get back to the notion that we cannot experience the world of flow on its own. Both ordinary world & the world of flow must be experienced together in some way or in relationship to each other. Something like that. To do this I want to go back to the two dialectics of metaphor – the dialectic of convention, whereby the conventional or arbitrary aspect of metaphor controls the perception or iconic image & the dialectic of invention, whereby the full iconic image of the world controls the conventional aspect of metaphor.

I would like to equate, then, the fullness of "flow" with the fullness of the flow of perception in the iconic image of the world. Icon = flow & non-iconic or arbitrary = conventional or ordinary world. (I like much more the term "conventional" as opposed to "ordinary" because with the first term we have much more the notion of social construction – the idea that the world has been "conventionalized" by human society. On the other hand, "ordinary" seems to belittle the world of human reflective consciousness which is a very non-ordinary & magical thing. "Ordinary" also seems to point to a kind of "natural" world that is "just there" & is ordinary. Certainly nobody wants to be ordinary. Most people don't want to think of themselves as "conventional" either but most of us most of the time are very pleased to know the conventions we need to follow in the social world & indeed are pleased to follow them. As such we are not at all ordinary, but extraordinary creatures on the face of the earth.

The human reflective capacity with its ability to experience both conventional reality as well as non-ordinary, altered reality, flow or enlightenment is NOT ORDINARY. As far as we know, it is only humans who can become enlightened or have god-consciousness or whatever. The self-reflective process is what allows for this, & it doesn't really matter if we have to "get rid of" some part of it or all of it to get on with our evolutionary development of consciousness – it is NOT ORDINARY.

There is a need to experience both sides of the dialectic, the conventional as well as the creative dialectic of invention. The full iconic image of the world = the world of flow, & the dialectic of convention = the limitation of the perceptual world in order to create the conventional. The conventional is the suppression of the myriad & the privileging of the few. In that sense, the world of flow is simply "larger" than the world of convention. The world of flow involves the "filling in" of the connections so that all the separate things blur & merge to create one unity. Flow = the background "field" of perception, the field of all potentialities. Or it is in the "background" in the conventional dialectic, whereas it is in the foreground of the dialectic of invention. What does this mean? It means in the first case if we are going to be aware of "flow" at the same time as we are aware of conventional reality, then we have to somehow split our consciousness so that we are aware of the surface "conventional" items that occupy consciousness as well as "keeping in mind" the full perceptual field from which these items have emerged. With regard to the dialectic of invention, it is a question of being aware of the flow & vastness of the whole perceptual universe & its ability to "settle upon" any of millions of different "thing-like" entities. Flow can take any shape it wants; it is all things but in order to "make sense" it must settle on one thing or another. In order to "make sense" & be communicable, "it," "flow," makes use of our consciousness & trusts us to make the decision. There, I've said it. There is an "it" that is "flow" or "god" or "whatever."

Having said that, the non-gendered pronoun "it" seems more appropriate to designate "instinct" or "desire," as it does in the Freudian system, than a god or even God. Of course, "it," even though non-gendered, still designates some sort of boundaried item in consciousness. On the other hand, because it is non-specific, the term "it" remains "fuller" in the sense that it has not been pinned down. "It" remains somewhat ambiguous & thus partakes of flow in language more say than the pronoun "he," And "he" is closer to flow than "George" which in turn is closer to flow than "George Clooney" which in turn is closer to flow than "George Clooney, the actor," & so forth. I am reminded of the anthropologist Fernandez who speaks of the creation of identity as involving the predication of an inchoate pronoun, the defining of the it.

To be aware of a) convention especially in language b) the flow of perception, c) the operation of instinct, d) ourselves as organisms in the environment, e) invention or creativity f) our adaptation to the world, g) the adaptation of the world to us, h) the vastness of the universe, I) the smallness of our individual selves, society, the world, j) the mutability of all things, k) death, l) birth, m) sex n) memory, o) skin… You get the idea.

The Gaze, as opposed to the look, keeps in the background. It is in a sense unfocussed; the foreground & the background co-exist. Eternity lives in there somewhere.

The thing is ambiguity, occasioned by the loosening of one's grip on the fixed, tends to increase anxiety, unless one has a strong sense of self that is coexistent with the awareness of flow – or perhaps simply a sort of "stability" so that one is not thrown off one's centre. Having a centre, of course, implies a periphery, a boundary. Not being "thrown off one's centre" by the changing boundary condition, which is exactly what will change with the experience of flow, means perhaps rather than a "strong" sense of self, at least an "agile" one. Flexibility is the term that comes to mind. It is the flexibility of the body in dance and the flexibility of the mind in the dance of the mind across the field of possibility or potentiality. Creativity means having a certain flexibility to hand.

Creativity = flow = possibility = myriad of different relationships = choice

Choice, then, is also part of the process of creativity at least, or simply being an actor in the world. One experiences the flow only in order to be able to "do" in better ways. To change the world. To develop oneself in order to change the world.

Thus, we come back to the original mistake: the mistake of thinking of the Large Self as a thing. The limit of mind as container. The necessity of identification with "some-thing." Something like that. The small self can never be killed (sacrificed) & gotten rid of & replaced by the Large Self because the large self won't fit in to ordinary consciousness which is too small. The "small" self or the ordinary self or the conventional self "breathes." It expands & contracts as it experiences non-conventional reality & then conventional reality. But, this pre-supposes the temporal dimension as crucial & it really isn't, although the rhythm of breathing & the beating of the heart are very seductive images. In fact, one may experience both at the same time with some practice; it simply involves, as we have said, the loosening of the attachments & the development of the ability to experience the background at the same time as the foreground in the reversible gestalt which creates "meaning." For meaning is at the root of all this. No doubt about that. Meaning may be small or it may be large but it's still meaning & we live perforce in a meaningful world or else we end it. Suicide. Some practitioners of meditation did go so far in the desire to kill the small self & experience the large. Some today actually look forward to death because they will go to a better place. Well, I'll leave that better place to them. I'll take mine here, thank you very much.

The linguistic contortions occur when we think in terms of entities. The whole thing revolves around the question of whether our thoughts control us or we control them, perhaps a prosaic way of thinking about it. What I mean rather is that in the development of consciousness we learn to "choose" our thoughts & are not satisfied to merely be chosen by them. That is to say, we move to the realm where we create ourselves & are not satisfied with our historical creation by others.

Let's compare the two modes of consciousness: the meditative spiritual one & the phenomenological & creative one.

I'd like to do this by comparing what occurs with the double or dual awareness because this seems to be a common factor. In the spiritual conception, the dual awareness is of the ordinary world & the large spiritual world. In the creative case, the dual awareness if of conventional mind & the flow of perception.

In the Spiritual practice we have the creation of an alternate self or identify with the "observer" or "witness." This has been conceived of in different ways – as being "in" consciousness & also as being in some way "outside" of consciousness. This latter seems to be the case with Bourgeault who sees this entity (pre-eminently a "voice") which seems to, at least in part, fulfill the function of what is known in the Freudian system as the super-ego. It is different in the sense that it only says "let it go" with regard to thoughts & does not have the full function of the super-ego which admonishes, advices, demands & so forth, with regard to the moral action of the person. The problem, then, involves the moving of attention & one's sense of identity away from the small self which is connected in fixed ways to the separate world & bring this attention & sense of self over to the newly created entity which is not quite an entity & which for Bourgeault does not really reside in consciousness (or if so only in the beginning stages of the work) but sinks down into something called the "magnetic centre" which is unconscious, but a deeper more spiritual unconscious than the Freudian one, & which is aligned with the silence that underlies the chatter of ordinary mind. There is a certain amount of contortion of thought here with the necessity of moving awareness & identity from the one "place" to the other "place," which, it seems, will only really appear with practice. It is in the body though & has something to do with the heart & also perhaps with the breathing. This movement from identifying with the ordinary self to identification with the witness "loosens" one's attachments precisely by way of the admonition to "let it go." The witness is developed precisely as a sort of awareness that does not privilege (in terms of likes & dislikes) any aspect of the contents of consciousness which rise up from the unconscious or are occasioned by more ordinary thoughts & events in the external world.

The double awareness consists of the witness being aware of both the smaller ordinary self & the contents of consciousness as well as the background "field" of awareness. There is a slightly ambiguous sense of the "witness" being itself the "Larger self" or alternately the witness merely is aware of the larger self as background field. At this point I'm not quite sure which, or even if it matters much.

Let's move on to the state of affairs with the phenomenological creative view. In this case, the double awareness is the awareness of the conventional world (whereby convention controls perception in the production of meaningful metaphor) as well as the awareness of the creative world (whereby perception or flow controls convention.) To put it another way, the double awareness involves being aware of both the foreground & the background in both of the dialectics. Awareness is split between (perhaps not the best metaphor) the conventional world of things & the unitary flow of perception, between convention & flow. In this case, as I have said, there is a sense that the self (the ordinary self) breathes & in this breathing brings awareness to both sides of the gestalt of meaning (background & foreground). The metaphor of breath seems apt because it involves the alternate expansion of the self (flow) & the contraction (convention.) On the other hand, one may use the metaphor of the split & maintain both sides of the gestalt at once in a sort of diffuse awareness of background & foreground simultaneously.

With this case we also can note that the awareness of flow & the non-definability of the world in terms of things brings about a requisite change in the self, to wit, the boundary between the ordinary or conventional self & the unconscious changes, & the two, conscious & unconscious are unified. The unified vision of the external world brings about the unified image of the internal world. When boundaries dissolve in the external world, boundaries dissolve in the internal world. Of course, with the dissolving of boundaries in the internal world via the "working through" of issues as in therapy, we become more & more aware of the flexibility of the boundaries in the external world.

As should be clear I prefer this second model because it explains my own situation much better than the spiritual one. This latter model focuses upon language, the formation of meaning & creativity. It has the same aim of loosening up our image of the fixed or conventional (ordinary) world but it goes about it not by the meditation practice of letting go but rather through the practice of contemplation, the deep thinking "about" things & their relations. It is about books, study, & creative action.

Meditation practice is about letting the ordinary world go & it doesn't really matter if the practitioner has any real understanding of this world or the function of language, social institutions or whatever. As long as it is a conception & can be put in language it is part of "ordinary consciousness" & in order to awake one must let it all go. I must admit this notion creates anxiety in me, precisely because it is very hard to let go of something which I don't really know the nature of. The fact is, the spiritual or mystic way, as described above in any event, is the way of "faith." In order to follow it one must have in some way come to have faith in the idea that one should act in these ways – in actual fact one must come to have faith in a particular text or person & then follow that path. For myself, I have never come to this state of being. For me, it has been important that I understand what I am doing & why. I suppose it is a path, if it is a path at all, of creativity or intellect.

Meditation practice also focuses primarily on the acquisition (which is not an acquisition for the small self) of double awareness. There is the sense that one should use this new awareness in the pursuit of one's activity in the world & for the betterment of human kind, but this activity is quite separate from the awareness itself which is the enlightened state. It is quite conceivable, then, that one could become enlightened in the sense of having created double awareness for oneself & remain almost completely ignorant of human relations & the ways of the world in general. This also makes me anxious, particularly the idea of giving away my will & putting my faith in another in order to gain what can easily be understood as a more powerful self, certainly an altered state of awareness which to all accounts can be quite wonderful to experience if "conditioned" in the proper ways.

In all, the latter, creative way, leaves will & choice in my own hands. It is actually dependent upon knowledge of the world & the way it works as opposed to moving on "beyond" it before knowing really what one is moving beyond. This is my own experience of conversations with a number of intelligent people who are involved in this mystic quest to one degree or another. In my experience, they have very little knowledge or interest in the way language works or alternate ways of understanding consciousness.

For both paths everything hinges on the "doing" – that is the loosening of our attachments to a certain arrangement of the conventional world & self. In general, we may say that both paths are involved with the development of mind & the expansion of consciousness. The creative path works through contemplation & the "filling up" of the connective arrangement of things in order to experience the "flow" & unity of the world. The meditative or mystic path involves the shift of identity away from small identity to the "witness" & the dawning awareness of the myriad connections between things – the whole background field – the iconic image which I have called "flow." The double awareness is of the background & also the foreground of consciousness.

The creative path has obvious application to the expressive therapies. The client introduces and is introduced to more & different ways of seeing things, different metaphors, & to the interrelationship of the exterior world & the interior world. The self that is not adequate is thereby changed to one with more possibilities, more abilities in the world. In general it is introduced to the notion that self & world are more flexible than previously thought. This is the operative word: flexibility. Increased awareness or consciousness is an increased sense of flexibility.

Part of my difficulty in working through the problem above was caused by thinking of consciousness as a container. When I realized that I was too fixated on this metaphor & substituted the metaphor of conscious as a sort of filter system that has perceptions flowing through it, the problem mysteriously disappeared. Another aspect of my problem concerned "identification" & the fact that in order to identify one must stop this flow in order to create an entity with more or less fixed properties to identify with. This is obviously an illusion. It is a social construction. One identifies with the filtering system certainly but then one's identification is with a "thing" that is constantly changing insomuch as it is constituted by what flows through it. A lot may flow through or very little.

With regard to my "explanation" of the mystic journey in terms of creativity, phenomenology & metaphor, I want to say that while I have for the last while understood this manner of development & progress towards knowledge as my own "path" or way of proceeding, I did not know how it related to the mystic path. So, what I have accomplished is I have been able to show that the way of "creative exploration" based upon phenomenology & metaphor theory arrives at fundamentally the same place, or rather the same state of being, as the awakened mystic identity with the Large Self.

Another Note: Embodiment (Metaphoric & Actual)

The mind & the body are one. We have conventionalized this relationship with boundaries around each & particular ways or relationships between them. Thus, we have perception/sensation, nerve paths, brain decisions, & messages sent back & forth.

A Phenomenological Explanation of Art Therapy

The attitude, right from the start, of a phenomenologist is to keep open the sense of curiosity & wonder at the world – therapeutic presence is characterized as the "diffuse gaze" which takes into account the whole of the perceptual field of possibility. The awareness is of the perceptual gestalt: foreground conventional objects, thoughts, etc. & also the whole of the perceptual field – the fullness of the iconic image of the world – the domain of "flow."

The therapist remains aware of the intentionality or attitude towards the objects of consciousness -- his or her own & the intentionality of the client. It is this intentionality which has created the client's world & also the therapist's apprehension of it, in particular, the "problem" which the client has presented. This world arose from the diffuse world of multiple possibilities & the iconic image of the world & is embodied in the concrete description.

The foreground metaphoric world created by the client & embodied in the description is reduced to essence or a series of essences via the reduction – bracketing of concepts & theories & even as much as possible unconscious ontological suppositions.

The therapist is also aware of being in the world, context, being with others, the general understanding of the nature of self in relation to others, society & social conventions.

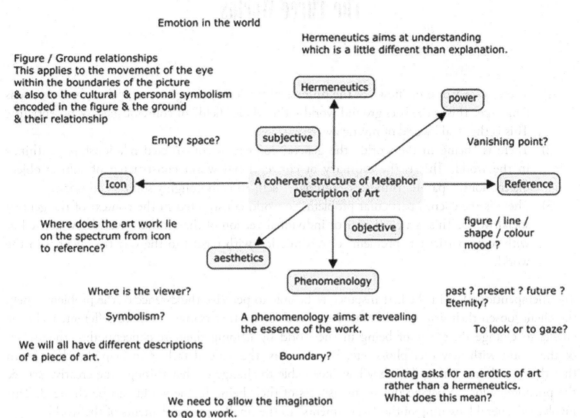

Soul & the working through
of attachments

Emotion in the world

Hermeneutics aims at understanding
which is a little different than explanation.

Figure / Ground relationships
This applies to the movement of the eye
within the boundaries of the picture
& also to the cultural & personal symbolism
encoded in the figure & the ground
& their relationship

Empty space?

Where does the art work lie
on the spectrum from icon
to reference?

Where is the viewer?

Symbolism?

We will all have different descriptions
of a piece of art.

Boundary?

We need to allow the imagination
to go to work.

A phenomenology aims at revealing
the essence of the work.

past ? present ? future ?
Eternity?

To look or to gaze?

Sontag asks for an erotics of art
rather than a hermeneutics.
What does this mean?

figure / line /
shape / colour
mood ?

Vanishing point?

Hermeneutics · subjective · power · Icon · A coherent structure of Metaphor Description of Art · Reference · objective · aesthetics · Phenomenology

The Three Worlds

1) There is the world of "flow" & the fullness of the iconic image – perception always exceeds language. This is the background world – the whole "field" of consciousness & potentiality. This is the "real" world of mystic awareness.

2) There is "being in the world" the general context of constructed relationships & things in the world. This is the ordinary or conventional world constructed of subject-object distinctions, separate "things," & ordinary "self." It is thoroughly social & illusory.

3) There is the client's particular problematic world constructed in the context of the general social world. This is a particular or individual version of the ordinary worldview above but with some particular "problem" or dysfunction with regard to the way the client is in the world.

The therapeutic task is in the first instance to be able to perceive the essence of the problem – help the client loosen their grip on "the way things are" & see that things could be different. Help the clients to change their way of being in the world by helping them re-conceptualize themselves & the world with new metaphors, etc. Beyond this, the general task is to help the client learn that this is only one thing that they have been able to change & that through the creative arts & the phenomenological perspective many aspects of their being in the world can be changed. This involves a general loosening of the "attachments" to the small separate elements of the world.

Gestalt

The notion of "gestalt" has become important for me & for the illumination of this problem of polarities especially that polarity twixt "ordinary consciousness" & "awakened consciousness." By gestalt, here, I am not thinking so much of Gestalt psychology, per se, but rather about the concept of the gestalt itself: the concept of the complementary relationship between foreground & background in perception. The idea of gestalt, then, that I wish to pursue is simple that: perception is always a perceptual gestalt formed of foreground & background. As I have no doubt stated before, but will state again, I am very indebted to Roy Wagner, in my own ruminations here, for his interpretive model of metaphor, gestalt & the dialectic.

Ornstein (1972), & I think many others, places the notion of "gestalt" on the side of non-ordinary consciousness & thus in a polar relationship with the notion of "analysis" in scientific, rational & verbal ordinary consciousness. While in many ways this seems true enough, I want to rescue this notion of gestalt, as it were, from the system of dualities & use it to actually join the two sides of the discourse – the two modes of consciousness. (In the following notes I will refer to these two modes as that of "ordinary consciousness" & "enlarged or "awakened consciousness." This seems a little unwieldy but it seems the best I can do right now.) I have come across the same allocation of gestalt to the right side of the brain with Paul Watzlawick in his "The Language of Change" & it appears that the right side of the brain does have this function – of recognizing gestalts -- & thus I suppose I am proposing to use that side of my own brain & the concept of gestalt to form a meta-gestalt inclusive of the functions of both sides of the brain.

As should be clear by now, the other terms I wish to "rescue" from the system of dualities are "language" & the "verbal" which Ornstein (1972) places firmly on the side of "ordinary consciousness." I want to show, then, that language when placed in the context of human "perceptual" experience is also constructed as a gestalt, & may thus also be used to explore the "relationship" between the two polarities & demonstrate the ways the two modes of consciousness complement rather than oppose each other. In order to do this, the essential link that needs to be made is that between "language" & "meaning." No matter what mode of consciousness we are talking about, "meaning" must always be central. This meaning may be approached through rationality or through intuition, but meaning remains at the centre. I am interested, then, not so much in the explanation of "ordinary consciousness" or "awakened consciousness" as to the meaning embodied in these modes of consciousness & how meaning is approached when in one mode or the other.

I am aware, as I am writing this; of how reductive is this model of 2 & only 2 modes of consciousness. There are in reality as many modes of consciousness as there are people to participate in them or "have" them. But I take these two categories as the polarities they are purported to be, while acknowledging that the two modes may be "mixed" in as many ways as you like & I hope to illustrate that in fact the two modes interpenetrate each other at all points. One may also use the metaphor of spectrum & imagine one's consciousness as lying somewhere "between" the two polar modes as, sort of "awakened" or "half asleep."

Meaning, then, is central & the notion of language & the gestalt. And all of these have to do with "perception." My sense is we need to briefly contemplate a number of quasi equations here. In the first place I will look at the terms simply in the context of our "ordinary consciousness" & the way in which this ordinary consciousness is often characterized from the mystical orientation – as consciousness of separate things in the world & our attachment to them. In addition, this separation of "things" from each other & from us is understood as being created by ordinary language.

1) Perception = the perception "of" something.
2) The perception of something = the perception of "subject-object" relations or "things"
3) The perception of sub-obj relations (things) = perception in the light of our "intentions"
4) Our intentions towards things in consciousness = our attachments to things in the world.
5) Our "attachments" to the objects of consciousness = their MEANING

.OR

1) We perceive separate things, their relationships to each other & our relation to them as subject to object.
2) All the contents of consciousness are apprehended by us in terms of & in the light of their meaning to us.
3) All perception is the perception of meaning.

And because all perception may be understood in terms of the foreground/background gestalt, all meaning may be understood in the same way.

1) Perception = Meaning
2) Perception = background/foreground Gestalt
3) Meaning = foreground/background Gestalt

AND

1) Meaning = Language (a meaningful relationship in language)
2) Meaning = Perception
3) Language = Perception (the perception of meaning in language)
4) Language = Perception = Meaning = foreground/background Gestalt

I'm not quite sure if my putting all of these relationships into this short equation form leads to better understanding or not. But what I am trying to show is a logical relationship between the terms: Language, meaning, perception & the gestalt. (Logic is allowed when dealing with & "in" ordinary consciousness.)

The fact is these terms, looked at from the more intuitive or "awakened consciousness" side of things – there is a simultaneity among them, rather than a causal sequence. There is the sense of a "constellation" of ideas rather than a causal temporal sequence. I believe both of these understandings are true – the causal & the simultaneous.

Right now what I am aware of is that while I have given the bare-bones notion of the gestalt I have given no real illustration of it. What does it mean to say that "all perception is perception in terms of the gestalt?" This is both very simple & very complex. Yes, indeed. In the simple sense what I mean is that in the act of perceiving we as living subjects are aware of a foreground aspect to consciousness (what is going on – that thing that captures our awareness) & also a background context for this foreground. We are aware of individual soccer players clustered around the ball but we are also aware of the field, the track around the field, those watching the game clustered around the edges, & also we are aware of the park which we cannot see & indeed the small town that the park is situated in. All this in one perceptual act. It is clear that much of the background is very vague in consciousness & also that much of it is actually unconscious. Nonetheless, there is always this foreground awareness & this background context. There is always a sharper awareness of the foreground & this more vague understanding of the background. I am going to say right now that the whole thrust of my argument is that "awakened consciousness" involves bringing this background awareness more into consciousness. Even more explicitly, I argue that meditative techniques are aimed at training the mind to take this element of perception more "seriously" than we usually do. But I get ahead of myself.

I have said that perception = gestalt & that perception = perception of meaning = gestalt. This means that "meaning" itself can also be understood in terms of the foreground/background image. In actuality, the perception of meaning is the perception of the meaningful "relationship" between foreground & background. Without background context, there is no meaning. Without there being any foreground that we "pay attention to" there is also no or very little "meaning." Whatever captures my interest (foreground) in the soccer game only has meaning in the context of "the game" itself & all the rest of the receding background. If I don't somehow "know" that this is a game & the rules of the game, the activity of the players becomes more or less meaningless or rather the meaning becomes more ambiguous. One person might be trying to steal the ball & the others are trying to get it back. Maybe they are trying to kill the ball. Of course we cannot even know what a ball is without some background context regarding the use of balls. Use, meaning, context, perception, language – all "in" consciousness. Or rather "in" ordinary consciousness. This metaphor of consciousness as a container is a very common one. It is, however, not the only one & as I have pointed out somewhere else, it does in fact have its limitations & can actually lead to misunderstandings. Let's just keep that as a sort of background contextual meaning.

Meaning, then, implies a meaningful relationship between background & foreground. We can go a little further & say that the foreground consists of separate individual things in a subject-object relationship but that the background is more unified – there is a sense of the whole – a sense of the world that "holds" the foreground action inside itself, as it were. In addition, there is not nearly the subject-object sense that we have with the foreground. I am here, watching the game while the players are over there. We are distinctly separate entities. The context, however, is not really "over there" – rather it is everywhere & while, if I think of it consciously, it is "out there" & I am "in here" (in mind) without really thinking about it I am aware that I also am "in" the world. I am "in" the background. I am part of the wholeness of "being."

Interpretation
&
Language

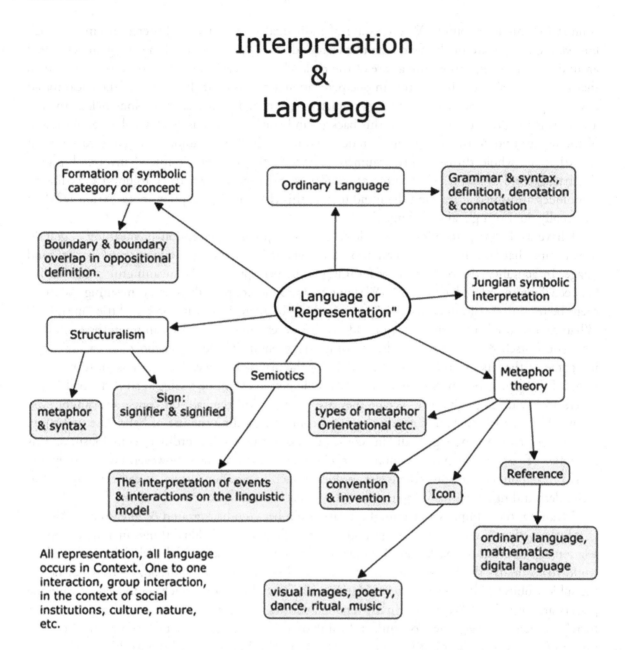

Formation of symbolic category or concept

Boundary & boundary overlap in oppositional definition.

Ordinary Language

Grammar & syntax, definition, denotation & connotation

Language or "Representation"

Jungian symbolic interpretation

Structuralism

Semiotics

Metaphor theory

metaphor & syntax

Sign: signifier & signified

types of metaphor Orientational etc.

convention & invention

Icon

Reference

The interpretation of events & interactions on the linguistic model

ordinary language, mathematics digital language

All representation, all language occurs in Context. One to one interaction, group interaction, in the context of social institutions, culture, nature, etc.

visual images, poetry, dance, ritual, music

Embodiment

With the notion of real-world contexts & our situation as individuals in the world, we are brought to the notion of "Embodiment." We humans are embodied. All entities are embodied. Some entities have "real" bodies – are made of flesh or stone; they may be bodies of water, characterized by exoskeletons & so on. There are other entities which are purely conceptual: ideas that have no body "except the body they have in language." Abstract concepts such as "the mind" may be said to actually be embodied in all of the brains of all of the people but this is a difficult concept & we aren't sure if mind is actually in the brain anyway. More concretely all ideas whether they exist in the world in concrete individual form are "embodied." The "units" we spoke of earlier may be viewed as the "bodies" of the ideas. They are concrete – as written visual language or as particular sounds. Humans – ourselves – are embodied in flesh & blood. Meaning is embodied in language – whether this language is ordinary language or musical language or the language of contemporary fashion.

The next point I want to make is that all of the "units" of language are essentially metaphorical. I mean this in the ordinary sense of metaphor – one thing is understood in terms of another better known thing – but more generally in the sense that all of these "units" of language (of whatever sort) are only meaningful with relation to the actual lived-in world. All languages (all modes of representation) are in this sense metaphoric.

Language = system of representation = metaphoric system of representation = Meaning.

(Although these "equations" do have a logical relationship, the "logic" is not at all precise & thus may be better understood as a system of "substitutions" which are in a sense simultaneous rather than signifying a causal relationship.)

Meaning = Perception of "Meaning" = Perception of Meaning in Language = Perception of Meaning in Metaphor.

Meaning is Embodied in Metaphor

First of all, let me say that the Metaphoric "Body" for meaning is in the same relationship as our flesh & blood body is to our notion of the self. Meaning is embodied in metaphor – the self is embodied in our flesh & blood body. (The "self" is our "own" meaning, the very locus of meaning itself.)

BUT ALSO

Meaning is embodied "in language."
Consciousness is embodied "in the human body."
Perception is embodied "in language & in the human body."

219

Perception is the interesting term here because it is doubly embodied – because all perception is meaningful, it is embodied in language (a representational system), but it is also very much embodied in our human flesh & blood body. (Perception is embodied in language, or the "practice" of language because we are only interested in language or representation insomuch as it actually elicits meaningful images of the perceptual world.)

Bringing the notion of "gestalt" into the picture, we see that Meaning has a foreground – what catches attention -- & a background – the surrounding context. But as we have seen, meaning is embodied in Language (meaning is embodied in metaphor) & language (metaphor) also has a foreground – the specific meaning going on with the word or sentence & also the background – the whole of language & all of its implicit meanings.

BUT as we have seen, metaphor has essentially to do with the relation between the unit in language & the image of the lived world that it conjures up. (So, in effect, there is a sort of doubleness to background – the background of "language" & the background of the perceptual image of the world as a whole. The background then, might be better stated as "language in the world" – which is, I suppose, is another way of saying that the social world & the natural world are inextricably linked together.)

Metaphor = embodiment of meaning = image of the lived-world (including language)

Embodiment of Meaning = Metaphor = arbitrary Unit of language = Image of the lived-world, etcetera…

I should say or should have said earlier, the mode of reasoning I use here partakes of the different modes of consciousness. It is partly analytical (rational) scientific etc., but it is also concerned with the language of "correspondences" – historically, a magical language characterized by similarity or "correspondences" between things. The language of correspondences is essentially a language that places more emphasis upon metaphor & metaphoric substitutions than it does on causal relationships. (Thus, for instance, if one is wanting to promote pregnancy & fecundity by magical means one would look for elements in nature which are characterized by this – a bush full of lots of berries perhaps – or rabbits. Then one would use these elements as symbolic representations of fecundity in various incantations, rituals & so forth. (Lyotard)

The fact is, there is always this tension in language usage – a tension between the meaning produced by the logical sequential sequence of linguistic units & the meaning produced by metaphor or metaphoric substitution, that is to say, a tension between "similarity" (metaphoric substitution) & "difference" established by grammatical rules. This tension, then, can also be understood as a tension between the conventional rules of the game & the fullness of the image of the world, elicited by metaphor.

Image of Metaphor

I will follow Wagner in thinking about representation as falling somewhere along a spectrum, one end of which is "convention" (arbitrary cultural unit) while the other end is the "iconic image" of the world – that is the full perceptual image of the world. Not only do we have modes of representation along this spectrum (conventional arbitrary language – words) & iconic images (a picture of a mountain for instance that looks just like a mountain), but we also have this dichotomy within metaphor itself: Each metaphor, whether conventional or iconic, has a relationship between convention & icon or between convention & the full perceptual image of the world.

The iconic mode of representation (a picture that looks like what it is) is very close to the image of the world we have in consciousness). Thus, with iconic representation, what is "inside" consciousness is very much "like" what is "outside." The perceptual aspect proves to be crucial -- the perceptual aspect of consciousness is more clearly represented by its embodiment in the iconic image. The image of the mountain is the meaning of the mountain. With conventional representation on the other hand, the meaning of the word "mountain" is completely arbitrary & anyone outside our culture with no understanding of our language would have the foggiest idea what this word meant unless we went some way towards linking this word to the iconic image whether by pointing to a picture of a mountain or an actual mountain.

Metaphor, then, has two aspects a conventional representation (conventional – iconic) & also a perceptual image of the world "iconic."

I am left with the explanation of the production of the two types of metaphor via foreground control & the elaboration of the two types of metaphor into the two dialectics of convention & invention.

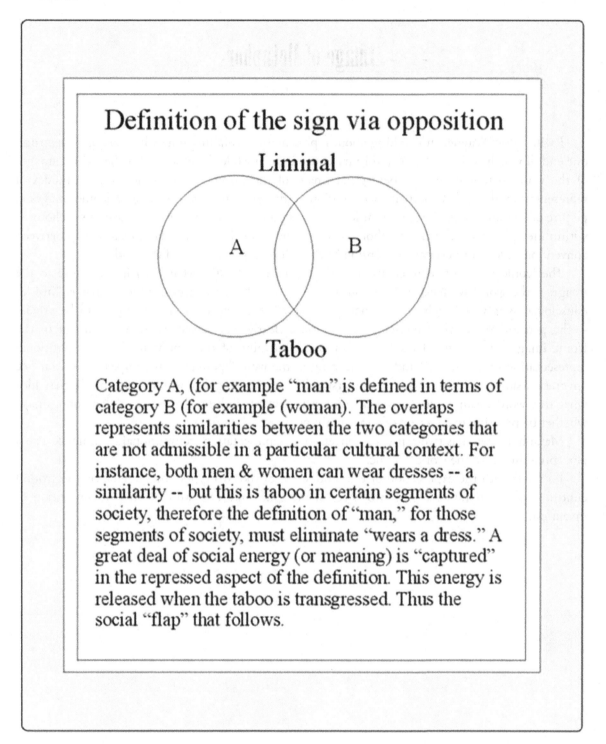

Definition of the sign via opposition

Liminal

A   B

Taboo

Category A, (for example "man" is defined in terms of category B (for example (woman). The overlaps represents similarities between the two categories that are not admissible in a particular cultural context. For instance, both men & women can wear dresses -- a similarity -- but this is taboo in certain segments of society, therefore the definition of "man," for those segments of society, must eliminate "wears a dress." A great deal of social energy (or meaning) is "captured" in the repressed aspect of the definition. This energy is released when the taboo is transgressed. Thus the social "flap" that follows.

Gestalt

I think the thing is to emphasize in the beginning re gestalt – the tendency for us to see wholes, not simply parts – the tendency to see even parts as wholes – to fill in the gestalt.

So we have an image of parts & an image of the whole. This is already implicit in the way we perceive things. In terms of representation & the theory of language (structuralist & post-structural) we have semiotics & the conventional type or arbitrary type of representation & the iconic image of the whole. So the gestalt is by its nature parts & whole. And reversible, background/foreground – a part might make a whole & this whole against a larger whole or the whole image goes into the background with an examination of the details or parts. Ying/yang symbolism.

Whole to part relations & the grasp of the whole = the grasp of the world =iconic rep.

But there is always a conventional aspect in representation – there is always something that represents something in the real world. But this representation may be strictly conventional or iconic.

1) Figure/Ground Meaning: is embodied in symbol (metaphor) as a perceptual gestalt (foreground / background) which falls somewhere along a spectrum of types ranging from conventional representation to full perceptual iconic representation depending upon which aspect of the gestalt (convention or icon) acts as the foreground control on the background image. (diagram of metaphor)

2) Difference/Similarity: The two types of metaphor are created in different ways: the creation of conventional categories or metaphors is based upon the socially decided suppression of similarity (often via taboo) in order to establish clear differences between categories to produce a system of boundaried categories & separate entities while the iconic image is based on similarity rather than difference so that in the visual domain, for instance, we have a visual image (picture) that "looks like" the real-world image, whole & undivided. (diagram of overlapping categories)

3) Metaphoric & Syntagmatic axes: The production of meaning in language as a system is governed by two axes: a vertical axis of substitutive metaphor & a horizontal axis which governs (via grammatical rules) the relationship between the different metaphors as a temporal or causal sequence; conventional metaphors emphasize the causal relationships between boundaried entities while iconic metaphors emphasize metaphor substitution & simultaneity. (diagram of structural sentence analysis)

4) Convention & Invention: The ongoing creation & maintenance of meaning in the context of culture may be understood in the unfolding of two dialectical relationships: one based upon conventional boundaried metaphors & their relationships, (the dialectic of convention which aims to "maintain" the status quo), the other predicated upon the inventive or creative use of language whereby the fullness of the perceptual flow of imagery works within language to create new metaphors, new meaning. (composite diagram showing metaphor & the two dialectics)

The way symbols are used to elicit meaning in the context of language may be understood to operate throughout our experience of self & world. This is no doubt because language was originally created & used by people to manage their relationships with other people & the world at large. I wish to show, then, how this "ordinary" function of language permeates our understanding of "ordinary" consciousness & the nature of the "ordinary world." I also wish to show how the meaning of "enlarged" or "awakened" consciousness as spoken of in mystic discourse is always available in consciousness & with regard to our image of the world & our place in it just as the "iconic" or full perceptual image & especially the dialectic of invention is always available as an option in the "ordinary world" even though the maintenance of conventional imagery & the dialectic of convention is normative, by definition.

Thus we find meaning embodied in our understanding of our own mind (conscious & unconscious) & also as a distinction between mind & body. When conscious imagery is allowed to dominate unconscious imagery, we maintain divided consciousness & the suppression or repression of unwanted or undesirable aspects of ourselves. If, however, we allow the unconscious contents of our mind to dominate our conscious thoughts (in free association for instance) then we work to abolish the split in consciousness & move towards attaining a full perceptual image of self in which there is no split in consciousness, there is no split between body & mind & we can begin to understand ourselves as joined with the world itself, this latter understood as an "underlying" unity, a way of being, impossible to maintain, but which may inform ordinary daily living at all points. As with language, we may move towards the iconic & the dialectic of invention, we may learn to increase our focus upon metaphoric substitution (that is, upon the many possible ways things may be) as opposed to the more limited conventional understandings of things & the ordinary emphasis upon temporal causality. By opening up the many kinds of relationships we can have with things we become less & less "attached" to our ordinary or conventional way of thinking about things; we open up & use the energy repressed in the service of boundaried categories.

And perhaps most interestingly of all, all the work that we can do "on the inside" with regard to understanding the way meaning is embodied in our fragmented & limited world & work towards unifying it in an integrated whole or rather many integrated wholes for why should we have only one. There is no end to this evolutionary thing is there? Or is it right around the corner? What I was going to say was all the work done on the inside is mirrored in the outside. As we integrate the inside, so we integrate the outside. As we integrate the outside (understand the flow of one thing into the next, the myriad of possible ways things could be & their relationships, the way we are "taken up" into the world) the more the split in ourselves is healed.

Dialectics & the Gestalt

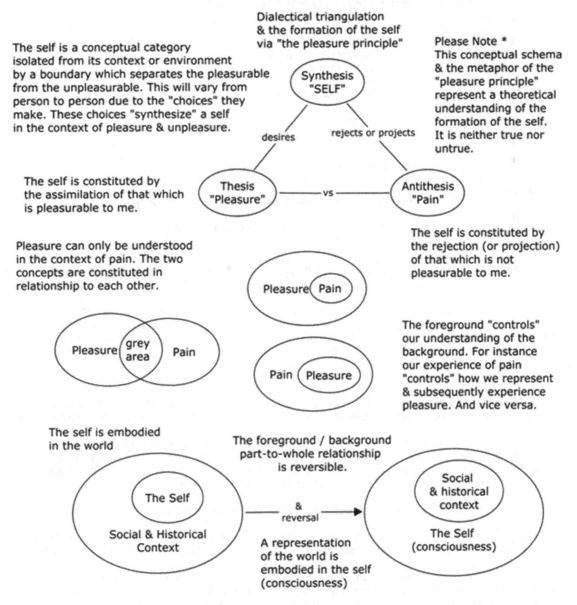

Dialectical triangulation & the formation of the self via "the pleasure principle"

The self is a conceptual category isolated from its context or environment by a boundary which separates the pleasurable from the unpleasurable. This will vary from person to person due to the "choices" they make. These choices "synthesize" a self in the context of pleasure & unpleasure.

Please Note *
This conceptual schema & the metaphor of the "pleasure principle" represent a theoretical understanding of the formation of the self. It is neither true nor untrue.

The self is constituted by the assimilation of that which is pleasurable to me.

The self is constituted by the rejection (or projection) of that which is not pleasurable to me.

Pleasure can only be understood in the context of pain. The two concepts are constituted in relationship to each other.

The foreground "controls" our understanding of the background. For instance our experience of pain "controls" how we represent & subsequently experience pleasure. And vice versa.

The self is embodied in the world

The foreground / background part-to-whole relationship is reversible.

A representation of the world is embodied in the self (consciousness)

We "perceive" meaning & this meaning has been socially constructed over time. This social construction, however, is not "free" but occurs within the constraints of historical context. The meaning of my individual life must be seen understood in social & historical context. Alternately, how this context has influenced my development must be seen in the context of the meaning of my life.

Various authors have held that Dialectical thought is appropriate for dealing with human social & psychological life while analysis is appropriate for understanding the workings of the material world. Why?   * Note: See CMap "Analysis & Causal Relationship"

The Nature/Culture Gestalt

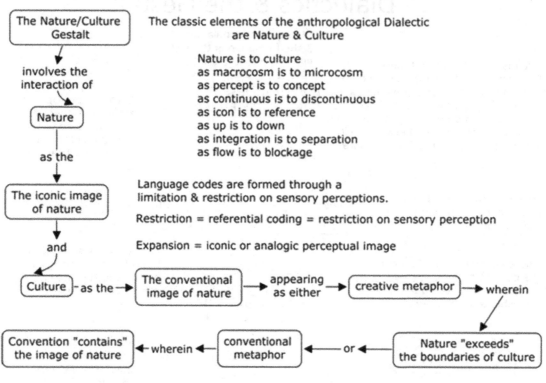

"Nature" is perceived as ceaseless "flow" of perceptions with a sense of an organic seamless whole. "Culture" at least for us tends to be perceived as an artificial & mechanical entity with separate parts.

Nature is "wild" while "culture" is "tame." Where cultures divide up the world into "nature" & into "culture" has fascinated anthropologists of the last century precisely because different cultures divide up their experience in different ways. The cultural includes especially all the "proper" ways to act. The elements of wild nature must be controlled or their spirits appeased.

In psychology the discourse has concerned the relative influences of nature or nurture.

Often we find the elements of nature & culture or nature & nurture polarized as opposites as one of them is "good" or "right" & the other "bad" or "wrong." In order to see nature & culture (or nurture) in opposition to each other is only possible if they are understood to be on the same level of abstraction. In fact, they are not on the same level. The two conceptual entities are are quite different orders. Bertrand Russell termed this sort of mistake as an error in logical typing & theorists such as Gregory Bateson picked up the notion in order to explain certain "double-binds" in communication that could explain certain neurotic difficulties in families.

Nature, is in fact not on the same level as culture but actually contains culture -- it embodies culture in the real or experiential world. On the other hand, culture, in the form of language "contains" our idea of "nature" -- it embodies this idea. But the experiential reality of nature is not on the same level as our idea of it.

Human Existence

I've finished reading the Sonia Kruk's book "Situation and Human Existence." Very interesting. I've made a number of handwritten notes but I don't think I will go back over them. In general what is most interesting is the whole discourse concerning "embodiment" or "incarnation" & the situated nature of the embodied self. In general, the "situated body-self" is understood to be on the side of "being" whereas the unsituated Cartesian cogito rules the domain of "objectivity" or "abstraction" – the domain of reflection. My comments are what I have "picked up" in the process of reading & the elements of my thought are treated in different ways by Marcel, Sartre, de Beauvoir & Merleau-Ponty. So. What is interesting to me. To be aware of "being" is to be in "direct" contact with the world & knowledge but this contact – this knowledge – is inarticulate & must remain intuitional. On the other hand, this intuition of the ground of situated being can "inform" our reflections upon it in our "mind." This "in-form-ation" we get from our situated being problematizes the subject-object distinctions set up in reflective consciousness such that we realize the vast potentiality of being & the "choices" that we have. Possibility opens up to us & our "attachment" to this or that solution, this or that conventional attitude is loosened. This is the ground for our freedom – this ability to step back from our situation & reflect upon it, remembering that it is our intuition of situated being that possibility is open to us. To be in touch with our situated embodied being in the world is to be in touch with the openness of the world – to be in touch with the mystery of the world. This is very much Marcel's catholic interpretation. This is fine as far as it goes but I am not satisfied with his understanding for the need of "faith." On the other hand, faith as a sort of instinctual connectedness to being & to the whole of life seems good enough.

Well, I've looked back at some of my more recent notes to what's what. I find that I am fairly addicted to the collection of dualisms – I mean the separation out of our understanding of the world, the separation of "situation" for instance from "reflective consciousness." My notes tend to be littered with divisions on the page which give some current new dualistic pair or re-think some old ones. I think of this practice as not inherently dualistic but rather that I am documenting the two sides of a dialectic – the two aspects of gestalt – background & foreground.

I came across, I think in the conclusion of the Kruk's book, the distinction between rational analysis as pertinent to the analysis of Nature & all non-human aspects of the world (this from Sartre I think) while dialectical thinking is pertinent for thinking about human life. But this is what I really liked: when analysis is applied to human life it is always ideological whereas dialectics can get at the reality of life. I am not quite sure about the latter half of this sentence but the notion of analysis as ideological when applied to human life is interesting. This is because, I suppose, (analysis as ideology) analysis is always on the side of reflective consciousness & does not take account of situated being.

inner realm grasped only by intuition	external rationality & causality
non-conceptual immediate knowledge	abstracting & objectifying
I am my body (Marcel)	subjectivity = a construct vs. subject autonomy

One is immersed in the world in history but this emersion of the body is also dual, in terms of representation – iconic / perceptual = primordial being but also social & structural

Difficulties arise because although "situation" is the situated body = being, reflective consciousness is also "situated" so that it is also "historical" & a limit on thought or a limit on being. This last notion of "limit" being that reflective consciousness reduces the chaos of unclassified pre-reflective reality to a set of known categories with manageable relationships. The difficulties arise, however, probably because of my own forgetfulness re the gestalt nature of the duality. If being acts as foreground control of the meanings in reflective consciousness then we have the intuitive indwelling of being, whereas if rational reflective consciousness acts as foreground control of situation, then we have the mind's grasp on the historical embedded ness of the situation.

I am aware of a distinction I want to make between the notion of being embedded as an embodied being in the world (flowing with the world as "part of" the world) & the use of tools in the world whereby the tool & the tool-user merge together & "flow" with the world – that is my own project appears to be the project of the world's as well as my own. We are together in this. There is a sense, then, of being in the world as a situated body – passive – as well as a sense of being in the world in a situated body but active – an active agent.

This also comes from the book, then, the notion of one's project. For me, right now, the project of these notes. But I also have other projects – the song-book project – the musical project & so forth. I have hinted or threatened that I might attempt at some point an explication or interpretation of my own creative process – my project or projects. I'm not sure. I have also begun to read Art Frank's book "The Renewal of Generosity" & with this reading I have begun to think about writing about my illness. I have shied away from this as un-interesting in the past but now realize that my creative projects are my "medicine" as it were & consciously conceived of as such, so to write of my process will, I suppose, be to write of my illness.

I am interested in sensing certain congruities between the Stoics (a little of Marcus Aurelius only at this point in Frank's book) & my analysis of the mystical project. Certainly "generosity" can be understood in terms of mystical love & as an aspect of "flow" with regards to the inter-subjective world. Frank sets up a distinction between two types of narrative – one a caring, generous & expository one & the other a blocked one ruled by fear. Interesting to sense the way in which a simple "open" conversation is therapeutic. Spoke with Monica about this the other day when we were in the canoe & she was describing the difficulty a student was having in seeing anything positive in a difficult clinical case. I wondered about putting together a simple paragraph or two regarding the therapeutic effects of open communication – the possible world that this opens up – perhaps not at all applicable at the time but usable as a "touch-stone" in the future.

Generosity of Spirit: a letter

I have been reading Arthur Frank's book on Illness and the Renewal of Generosity and wrote an email which would also be part of these notes.

July 7, 06

Hello Arthur.

I have read the first two chapters of your book "The Renewal of Generosity" & have enjoyed them very much. "Enjoyed" is perhaps not quite the right word for I have found them to be stimulating & to actually have import for me – for my situation, I suppose, both with regards to illness & my "medicine" which is my own creative project(s) at this time. You asked at some point if I was interested in writing about illness. This got me thinking a little about this – my first answer was no, I'm not really interested in illness as a subject but then realized that insofar as my creative project(s) are my medicine, I have been writing "about" my illness for some time. Perhaps I should explain a little about a current project, part of which may be my response to your book. To bring you up to date a little, then. I hope not at too great length.

Over the last while I have been writing a series of "notes" with regard to my own "interpretive method" with regard to critical thought & the working through of intellectual problems. I have been doing this for Monica's students in lieu of teaching various classes from time to time. (These notes will serve as the basis for a seminar series in the next term.) Anyway, in order to demonstrate my interpretive method (an eclectic mix of anthropology, phenomenology & metaphor theory) I chose "mysticism" as my "subject matter." I chose this subject because a great many people in these parts & many of Monica's students are very interested in this subject in one way or another. They are involved in what they think of as "spirituality" & are involved in various practices of meditation, yoga, spiritual/ therapeutic dance & so forth. I confess that I have been over the last while very irritated by various attitudes that seem to pervade this interest in spirituality – especially the derogatory attitude towards the "mind" & intellectual activity, in general, as some sort of "block" to knowledge of the "true" world. Of course, "language" is looked upon as a severe limit on real knowledge & perhaps the whole reason for the horrible state we're all in. This attitude was often accompanied by the fact that many of these people hadn't actually discovered where the "on" switch was & equated anxious chatter about the self with "thinking."

I should say that a number of people have come forth over the last while & by way of trying to help me with my difficult time have proposed various spiritual "paths." While I have appreciated their desire to help I was ultimately quite upset by our inability to really speak to each other – engage in real dialogue. My own "path" which I have for many years considered to be the path of creativity, the path of the poet, (very tied up, as you well know, being a writer yourself, with language,) seemed to be quite out of touch with all these other paths aimed at getting rid of everything I loved. Thus my choice. I suppose I aimed at trying to reconcile the mystic path with the creative path. Demonstrate various problems with the contemporary notions of mysticism & show how language can participate in our emancipation.

I began by simply utilizing what was within reach – my own present stage of knowledge -- & attempted no scholarship but a sort of working out of the symbolism of the mystic proposal – the sacrifice, the type of consciousness aimed at – the identification with the totality of the world – the large self etc. I went on to bring up a number of texts that I hadn't looked at for a while – one on social magic, (really great) & then some mystic texts – friends lent me books on centering prayer, the use of Zen practice in therapeutics etc. & I went upon my merry way, taking things apart & trying to put them back together again. Most recently I have been reading existentialism again, Merleau-Ponty, who has always been important.

That brings me up to the present more or less. I'll say right off the bat; I like very much the subtlety you bring to the subject & the fact of your own dialogic respect for the other. I admit to thinking (& the cover of the book perhaps supports this) that I was going to read another sort of self-help book replete with "spiritual" wisdom at a pretty basic level. Why is it that there seem to be so many "beginners" books on such subjects. Anyway, I am happily surprised to find all sorts of good things in there that I was by no means ready for. But, being who I am & involved in the current project of "the notes" which is in a little bit of disarray at the moment (or perhaps almost finished) I am most interested in finding the similarities & differences between your stoic dialogic approach & the approach I have been taking which I have only characterized as that of "creativity."

The stoic notion of separating out one's judgment of things from the things themselves has great similarity with the state of mind promoted by many different sorts of meditation which goes under the name of non-attachment. Non-attachment itself (& attachment) may itself go under the heading of "intentionality" in the phenomenological project. The world appears to us in the light of our intentions towards it – our emotional likes & dislikes, and all that. The need to bracket those intentions to get at essence. The notion that our judgments "seek out" our pains is very interesting. A kind of seeking light of desire goes out into the world & finds our attachments the threads that bind us to the world & perhaps most of all to our suffering – that which impinges upon our notion of ourselves most dramatically or perhaps just that which impinges upon the body itself whether or not we can say "I am my body." There's a paradox there but perhaps I'll get to it later. (Or perhaps you already get to it with the notion of being hostage to the other – there is a kind of binding that is detrimental & there is a kind of binding that is freedom.)

Perhaps I should say before I go any further that I've been working with a system of dualities which arise both in scholarship &, for instance, in the mystic enterprise itself. Thus we have: ordinary consciousness / mystic non-ordinary consciousness, the unsituated cogito & the situated body-self, reflective consciousness & intuition & in language or representation, the distinction between conventional metaphor (the arbitrary conventions of language) & iconic metaphor (the fullness of the iconic image of the world). These I understand in terms of gestalt & one or the other side of the dualism acting as foreground "control" of the background meaning. And so on.

The daemon is a little more difficult to characterize. Sounds a lot like the soul but then what's the soul. A difficult question. Something that is good or seeks out the good – the best part of ourselves. And where does that come from? It would seem that our ethical understandings certainly arise in reflective consciousness & our ability to stand back from our experience & make judgments but on the other hand, why we should choose the good seems to come from an understanding of our embeddedness in the world (& with other people) – a knowledge of our inter-subjective "obligation" which approaches a sort of instinct. Or we could say that our care for the other stems from the ability to have empathy but what is empathy except our ability to erase the boundaries of self in order to step into those other shoes (transform ourselves with the donning of the mask) & where does this "possibility" (the possibility of transformation) come from but from our own original (& ongoing) "merged nature" with the world – the primordial bond as Marcel has it -- a merging which you or someone quite rightly asserts cannot or should not be maintained (at least when it's time for lunch). A going back & forth, then, between the two sides of the gestalt – the unsituated self established via subject-object relations "in" the mind & the intuitive re-cognition of the pre-reflective state of "continuity" or "flow" in the world before it has been "created" by the series of discontinuities we call conventional language. Oh My.

Death takes us back to the primordial world whereby we become again part of that "indiscrete" flow (for that "indiscretion" of the sacred world I look to Bataille.) A brush with death, then, brings with it a whiff of possibility& the dialogic "care" & generosity of the daemon. (The word "love" certainly does seem to be continually debased.) For me, the creative may be imagined in terms of the primordial flow of the world – the fullness of the iconic image of the world as it is allowed to play upon the field of conventional metaphor. It is the energy of the pre-reflective situated body-self – full of all possibility, all identity, all hope, all the imagined (& thus emptiness) that flows through us in the creative project & it is by this force or awareness that we are "loosened" from our individual desires & plunged back into a primal desire, that if one believed in God, one might be inclined to call God. (Also have been reading a little Swedenborg).

The dialogic reversal of the normal order of things. Very nice. And in this reversal we find our... consolation, our belonging. I am very interested to see how this sense of the dialogic will play out in terms of your stories & in terms of the dialectics I've been working with.

One of the things I have been very concerned to communicate with regard to language (in the notes) is the "presence" at all points of the iconic perceptual dimension of our situatedness. This is to counteract the notion that we have to get rid of language in order to truly perceive our cosmic being. Thus I am working with a concept of metaphoric unfolding & language-in-use which I found in the work of the American anthropologist Roy Wagner. His is a phenomenological notion of metaphor whereby meaning is always embodied (in metaphor) & is comprised of a gestalt whose parts are convention & iconic

231

representation. All conventional usage is always in relation to the fullness of our image of the world. Our image of the world is "limited" by our conventions. Thus he proposes two dialectics: one of convention & the other of invention. It strikes me that this kind of understanding re the formation of meaning (in context) might fit very well with the dialogic imagination & its insistence on the equality of voices. The voice of the other is paradoxically the voice of the inarticulate world. To pay attention to that voice is to pay attention to our own primordial continuity with that world. To pay attention to the other is to pay attention to ourselves – even to pay attention to the other is to pay attention to the unconscious in ourselves. As we discover continuity with the unspeakable in the world we discover the continuity of conscious & unconscious.

The phone is ringing... A friend has stopped by to give me a copy of Merleau-Ponty's Phenomenology of Perception – I've never had the whole book in my hands before – just chapters & essays. It's fat. I'm aware that my writing to you has been somewhat overheated. I suppose I am excited to find someone who might perhaps relate quite easily to my wandering about in the forest of ideas. On the other hand, I'm not at all sure that I've filled in enough to make this wandering very comprehensible.

Anyway. I'm enjoying your book. I wish you well. It is some consolation.

Blake

Looking back at notes: "guiding thread" & the working out of human freedom.

Illness as a path as opposed to a "problem." Problems are dealt with on the side of reflective consciousness – the objective standing back from – the distancing & the analytic working out of a problem. On the other hand, the "path" of illness is an opening out into my situation – a "difficulty" with the primordial bond twixt body & world & also, of course, the immersion in social structure. There is a paradox insomuch as the primordial bond is in a sense my un-freedom – the un-freedom of humanity in general – the immersion of self in the world in a primary & inseparable way & also this primordial bond is represented as the very "salvation" of the human being – the place of hope & "connection" with the "real" world as opposed to the world of illusion (Maya in the mystical tradition) the historical world of social structures. So there is the paradoxical sense in which my freedom is my inextricable connection to the primordial world via the body. The body is the locus of this paradox. To open to the primordial mystery is to open to death & a new signification for "flow" – thinking of Bataille -- & his notion of entering into the flow or stream of endless possibility that is nature or cosmos.

A run at the back & forth between the two modes

In the reflective mode of consciousness, guided by intuition, one may put on a mask & identify with the Other, thus collapsing subject-object distinctions in order to dwell "in" the other. This guiding thread (intuition) leads us out of the reflective social world of things & relationships & back into the primordial world of the situated body where my freedom is found in the free flow of identity (which is the loss of identity) in the pre-reflective world. But, in turn, my re-turn to the primordial is guided by the distancing effect of reflective consciousness & "interpretation" which renders this new identity which is no identity unspeakable but meaningful.

Situation = bodily incarnation = Perception = Meaning = Participation (in the world.) The "hinge" in this series is in Meaning (or Perception). To choose "meaning" is to say that meaning participates in the two domains, the situated & the unsituated but the meanings are different.

The "trap" with regard to managing the dualistic image of the world is not to fall into the reflective world but to forget how to get out again – to forget the dialectic & the reversibility of the gestalt. By "trap" I simply mean confusion.

"Illness" – to "have" is to fear loss.
To "be" = the joy of participation in the world.

I want to think for a moment about the dual world of participation with regard to the situated human body. One may participate in this "bond" twixt situated self & world passively as if "taken up" by the world & "contained" within its vast scope. There is in this participation the joy of "belonging" in the world – the world in all its ambiguity & suffering is nonetheless a place to rest. Or, alternately, one may participate in this situated world & the primordial bond in a creative way, actively, as an active agent. In this sense, one refers to one's "work," one's projects, agency & "doing." All of these things are correctly associated with reflective consciousness.

The point is my active engagement with embodied being can be used to control or guide the meanings elicited in reflective consciousness via the artistic or creative process. My sense of situated wholeness & the multiplicity of the situated world can guide me towards the use of metaphor, new metaphor, and new image in the reflective world. I make a journey into the land of situation & come back with new images.

Power & freedom come from the dialectical movement. There is a sense of entrapment in paradise – entrapment in a place of multiple identities, a place of flow where the world flows through my body & my body is the world "and there is no escape from this." I suppose in a sense one may not be "active" as such in this domain because one's will is not present – one is instinctively engaged but not separate from. Thus one is by definition passive within this domain or active-passive in the sense that one does what one does or what the world does one has no choice. The choice & the activity are involved in what one brings back from one's journey. What has one been able to steel or carry off?

One loses the reflective world, the distance, the subject-object distinctions, one's identity & then one comes back with "something." When one returns to the reflective world, one loses the primordial bond but carries back "gifts"? The gift of generosity perhaps.

In a sense there is "nothing" in either domain on its own – they cannot exist separately – only as a gestalt. Certainly reflective consciousness is situated & the primordial bond is only meaningful insomuch as one may retreat from it & reflect upon one's experience. One "falls" from the primordial paradise of no separations into the world of language & reflection. That is, one falls from the animal world of instinct (primordial control of intellect) into the realm wherein one does for oneself, as it were, -- the world of reflection. One returns as an experienced adult, an explorer, a man on a journey back to his home, understanding that he cannot become as a child again or as an animal. He focuses the "wide domain" in consciousness & is lost until through the long "gaze" he manages the reversal & rather than organizing the world, he is organized by the world – the world flows through him, re-organizing his perceptions. At this moment, he dies & is in love. He laughs, stands up & is a man again.

To fall is to take the world on one's shoulders. To fall is to make an urn & stuff the world in there. To rise up is to empty out the urn, shrug one's shoulders & be taken up by the world again – by death or by the rehearsal of death, on one's own or in ritualized activity.

The two worlds: reflective & pre-reflective

First off – the two states of being or worlds are completely dependent upon each other in the gestalt relationship. One cannot even exist without the other. The pre-reflective is in no way "pure" or at least not initially so for we are immersed in this domain in an unconscious way – that is to say our way of being is conditioned by ordinary daily living, our ordinary consciousness & the reflective mode so that even if we manage to suspend our thought (in passive meditation for instance) or if we work in an intuitive way so that we are active but in the pre-reflective mode (in the making of art for instance) we are still in that mode conditioned by our historical situation. Put another way, our embodied self in the "flow" of the pre-reflective world is already limited & "un-ready" for the openness possible in that condition. On the one hand, our embodied "situation" is still ruled by reflection & on the other even when the gestalt is reversed so that the world is allowed to re-create the conventional world it can only do so to a limited extent, at least in the beginning. This is so because we have not been "trained" in reflective consciousness to open ourselves to the totality of our situation.

I make a note to myself that I must continue to be aware that we can go "back & forth" between the two worlds but that this "back & forth" involves a reversal of the gestalt. To "go" into the world of the primordial bond is to allow the boundary-less world to de-condition my conventional awareness. This de-conditioning of conventional awareness brings me into the world of extreme possibility & the acceptance of the all (good & evil) in such a way that the internal boundary (conscious & unconscious) is erased. The erasure of external boundary acts to erase the internal boundary. The self, as such, increases in "size" just as the external world of possibility increases.

We can, of course, say that we all have experienced, in the past, the pre-reflective mode in a much more "pure" way – when in the womb, as a baby & as a young child. That being said, the purification of our selves & thus this pre-reflective domain actually does involve a regression or an "undoing" of our conventional self. This "undoing" takes place as assimilation twixt the two realms – the impulse to open is carried into the world of reflection where this openness conditions our judgment – or our judgment is less conditioned by conventional understandings than it previously was. With our reflective mind more open to possibility, we again immerse ourselves in the pre-reflective (reverse the gestalt) & in an underlying sense we bring our "expectations" with us. They are unconscious but function nonetheless. The process is life-long. (The process is, I suppose, analogous to the Piagetian notion of assimilation & accommodation – we assimilate new knowledge to our known schemas & we also accommodate new information by changing ourselves or our schemas. Although I have always thought of these ideas as primarily lodged in the world of reflection & the development of intellect, in a sense, this "new knowledge" that "doesn't fit" our known intellectual schemas is a message from the "unknown" or a message from the "deep" world or our situation.)

Another absolute necessity for the "back & forth" twixt the worlds, pertains directly to the ethical or moral dimension. There is a sense that the deeply inter-subjective world of our situation gives us our morality in the broad sense that we should care for others, we only "learn" this by bringing back our experience to the reflective world & contemplation of the elements of this experience. But there is also a sense in which because the deeply known situation of our original bond in the world is all inclusive, it includes good & evil. This is fine for the spiritual person who has "left the world" & who takes no part in it. This is also fine for the artist who can explore the all of the dimensions of good & evil. But it is not fine for anyone who wants to engage in the world in a real way – that is in an active "political" way. I mean it is not fine to make no distinction twixt good & evil.

We have a problem, then, with those who through their creativity or their ability to suspend conventional thought, may in one way or another enter into the domain of situated being BUT have not developed an adequate moral or ethical being. There is, then, nothing that is automatic about the messages from a deep awareness of our human situated embedded as it is in the pre-reflective world. As soon as I say this, I rebel against it. Surely this problem arises because the awareness of the situated domain is not very deep or very pure. I am not sure. Is there development that is real development that nonetheless remains selfish?

All that being said re the "development" of a larger understanding of ourselves & the world, nonetheless it is at all times useful to reverse the gestalt in order to be "seen" by the world – held in the arms of the world & bring back gifts. What a wonderful things it is to bring back gifts.

I am aware of how really well the book on "situation" has suited me. It has really brought things into focus so that now it seems very far away, the period of head banging. The zone of pre-reflective reality has come close. The baggage of the spiritual & the Christian seems to have fallen away. The real thread has been the image of gestalt, the reversible gestalt.

We are immersed in the world in a pre-reflective way – our bodies are continuous with the body of the world & if we allow our sense of wonder & bring our perceptual openness to our bodies in the world – we gain gifts which we can bring back to the world of reflective consciousness & which opens up that world – reducing our attachments & giving us a wider & wider sense of possibility & proportion. The passage between the two worlds, the known & the unknown, the reflective & the bodily, the conceptual & the perceptual is brought about by the reversible gestalt. The knack is to turn off the world & reverse the flow of energy...

Philosophy of Mysticism

On the drive out to the beach I spoke to Monica about the philosophy as opposed to the psychology of mysticism. The philosophy is very similar to existential philosophy (without the spiritual baggage) – the emphasis upon embodiment & situation etc. but mystic psychology is different due to its emphasis upon "transformation" – God & the drama of altered states of consciousness. This is a certain "guiding thread" the "drama" that is involved. Drama & aesthetics are different than the philosophy or theology of a given program.

When I speak of the "similarity" between mysticism & existentialism, I mean that there is a certain similarity between the two worlds that are proposed. Mystic or "awakened" consciousness has certain similarities to the existential notion of the embodied self immersed in the world in a pre-reflective way. Ordinary consciousness & reflective consciousness are, of course, one & the same.

I have begun to read Bataille's "Erotism." It's interesting to note that he begins his argument with the division between two worlds: the continuous world that we enter by way of death & the discontinuous world of individuals & separateness. His argument is that the erotic links the two domains – that our way of regaining our lost world of continuity is via erotism – emotion, physical & religious. Part of his argument is that the history of the erotic & the history of religion are intertwined.

I discussed with Monica different models of consciousness or rather not "models" but metaphors:

1) consciousness as container
2) consciousness as a filter
3) consciousness as a mirror - reflective
4) the stream of consciousness (William James)
5) consciousness as a computer processor – rational processing
6) consciousness as geological strata (Freud)
7) theatre metaphor - light
8) cultural narratives of consciousness
9) consciousness as a mirror
10) consciousness as a machine (Darwinian mechanism)
11) consciousness as something that distances us from the real world

A classical metaphor for consciousness has been a 'bright spot' cast by a spotlight on the stage of a dark theater that represents the integration of multiple sensory inputs into a single conscious experience, followed by its dissemination to a vast unconscious audience. In cognitive theory, such a theater stage is called a 'global workspace', and implies both convergence of input and divergent dissemination of the integrated content. In this century, features of the theater metaphor have been suggested by neurobiologists from Pavlov to Crick.

Neuroscientists and consciousness researchers may or may not accept a view of the global neuronal workspace model as a conceptual metaphor for consciousness, but in this review I reflect it as a plausible one. The workspace model, according to Dennett [4], suggests a non-hierarchical, collateral, co-operative, even competitive, modular system, which allows a multidimensional global accessibility. I claim that the metaphor of consciousness as a global workspace attributed above, characterizes perfectly well the assertion of phenomena both on the neuro-biological and techno-social levels of observation. This is why I am tempted to suggest a broad scale conceptual isomorphism ranging in-between the micro scale structure of consciousness to the macro scale structure of the planetary consciousness. I dare to put forward this idea, because I am convinced that the fundamental structure of human conceptual system is relatively independent of the differences in languages and cultural inheritance, but intrinsically dependent on the embodied orientation to the environment.

How can we understand the evidence? The best answer today is a 'global workspace architecture', first developed by cognitive modeling groups led by Alan Newell and Herbert A. Simon. This mental architecture can be described informally as a working theatre. Working theatres are not just 'Cartesian' daydreams -- they do real things, just like real theatres (Dennett & Kinsbourne, 1992; Newell, 1990). They have a marked resemblance to other current accounts (e.g. Damasio, 1989; Gazzaniga, 1993; Shallice, 1988; Velmans, 1996). In the working theatre, focal consciousness acts as a 'bright spot' on the stage, directed there by the selective 'spotlight' of attention. The bright spot is further surrounded by a 'fringe,' of vital but vaguely conscious events (Mangan, 1993). The entire stage of the theatre corresponds to 'working memory', the immediate memory system in which we talk to ourselves, visualize places and people, and plan actions.

Information from the bright spot is globally distributed through the theatre, to two classes of complex unconscious processors: those in the darkened theatre 'audience' mainly receive information from the bright spot; while 'behind the scenes', unconscious contextual systems shape events in the bright spot. One example of such a context is the unconscious philosophical assumptions with which we tend to approach the topic of consciousness. Another is the right parietal map that creates a spatial context for visual scenes (Kinsbourne, 1993). Baars (1983; 1988; 1997) has developed these arguments in great detail, and aspects of this framework have now been taken up by others, such as the philosopher David Chalmers (1996). Some brain implications of the theory have been explored. Global Workspace (GW) theory provides the most useful framework to date for our rapidly accumulating body of evidence. It is consistent with our current knowledge, and can be enriched to include other aspects of human experience.

Boundaries

I have been thinking a lot about boundary & the disruption of boundary with regard to one's sense of freedom, self, ungrounded & grounded, the erotic & the sacred. And perhaps more than I should, the sacrifice of the self – the nature of this sacrifice.

Boundary breakdown or the loosening of the boundary condition creates ambiguity, first in the domain of representation & then in the domain of self & action.

Bataille argues that there are two fundamentally different worlds – the world of work (the world of rationality, order & relatively fixed & clear boundaries between cultural categories) & the world of the sacred (the world of passionate irrationality, disorder, unfixed boundaries & disruptive violence – spirit as "power.") For him, the erotic is essentially an aspect of the sacred which disrupts the world of rationality & work via the passionate fusion of identities.

From where I'm sitting right now it seems to me that there are a number of more or less distinct forms of "identification" each with its own implications for the boundary conditions between people (self & other.) This is another subject that I've been worrying at or about for some time. It necessarily has to do with identity itself & also indigenous psychology. I'll try to set them out.

1) Identification in the original development of identity. The identification with what one likes & the projection of what one does not like. A more or less systematic set of choices which set up identity & in the process split consciousness (conscious & unconscious). The definition of one's self emerges from this & thus the boundary between self & others in the social world. The self is a social construction essentially accomplished by mimicry or imitation & identification. One may identify with a particular trait or accept a certain definition for "personal" reasons or because it is culturally normative to do so.

2) Identification as ecstatic fusion with the other. This is essentially religious & erotic. The fixed boundaries between self & other are abolished & the individual self is sacrificed in the larger self or expanded consciousness. From this position, the sacred is that violence that disrupts the rational & work-oriented categories or everyday life.

3) Identification with the other for a short period of time for a particular purpose in order to see like the other & take on certain aspects of the other's personality & skills. One finds this magical identification in shamanic ritual with the donning of the mask of the other, usually an animal.

4) Identification of oneself as belonging to a certain group. This is the specification that my boundary condition is essentially like the boundary condition of others in this larger group. Thus I "belong" to a group of eligible voters in Canada, I am a Canadian citizen. I am a man, etc. This hasn't got anything to do with changing one's boundary condition but rather involves a simple recognition of similarity of category. This identification may be rational or primarily emotional.

5) Historically, in small group societies, one is expected to identify with the appropriate socially created & accepted definition of self. This definition of the "proper" self will necessarily repress various aspects of "similarity" between closely associated cultural definitions which lie on the boundaries of each other. These repressions are made in the

service of "clarity" & reflect culturally developed preferences & beliefs. Thus certain similarities between the categories of "man," "woman," "child," "married woman," "animal," for instance, are repressed & the proper relationships between these categories are established. Many of these repressed aspects & improper relations between categories are encoded in social life as "taboo" & if one breaks the rules, (the categories are contaminated) the self & the community are endangered. The categories must be re-established in their proper ways via rituals of purification. These rituals bring one back into proper relationship with the community of others.

6) In modern society, we also have such social definitions (as in 5 above) which exemplify cultural beliefs & biases, but there are also groupings & identifications which pertain to various democratic rights & obligations. These groupings have to do with ensuring equality in terms of political rights, justice & so forth. These cultural categories are created by society & the individual self is introduced into them without consent. The categories purport to be objective & therefore one's own feelings about it are immaterial. One is identified as such & such. This is the world that Frank refers to as "artificial" – the bureaucratic world – the world of specialization. The world of monologue. The census.

7) Identification in the service of the dialogic imagination. This is the realm that Frank speaks of with regard to the re-gaining of generosity in the context of the hospital. It is essentially the opening up of the boundary as spoken of in 5 & 6 above. Certain similarities between self & other (doctor & patient, health & illness) previously suppressed or repressed are acknowledge. And with this acknowledgement, comes the "personal" relationship & the generosity & caring that must accompany it, if the opening up is genuine for it is an admission that "we are the same" – I bring myself love to the other (BUT, of course, I could bring also my own self loathing, but this is not a genuine opening because this self loathing is merely a split in my own self-image whereby I designate some part of myself as "other" or not me.) To acknowledge that I am broken like the patient is broken or that I am the authority like the doctor is to enter into dialogue. What I suppose that is most striking about this concept (care for the self is care for the other) & the general notion of the dialogic imagination is its incredible "civility" – a story that we have agreed to tell "together." This is not the sacred, the erotic the developmental or anything else. It is a conversation. How wonderful. Something for adults to do together. And I don't want to forget Levinas' insistence on the unknowability of the other. I mean, this is not a "merging" of consciousness but rather an intimate but limited way of identifying – perhaps one identifies with the other or perhaps one rather identifies with the conversation.

8) The ID we carry in our wallets. (I suppose this is merely an element of 6 above)

9) There are always the ideas, in the context of mysticism, about setting up some sort of "witness" or spy inside consciousness – as for instance a voice that repeats a mantra -- & then identifying with it, in order to "get around" the small self & its preoccupations with subject-object relations.

I'm sure this is fairly sloppy but interesting to me nonetheless – at least I remain interested in what appears at the boundaries of such lists, for there is always overlap & overlap = similarity & similarity in overlapping categories = ambiguity & ambiguity = possibility & possibility = hope &... I remember also that perhaps the general definition of "development" is important here – development (moral or cognitive) involves the ability to progressively take on more & more different "points of view." So that the morally developed individual is exactly that individual able to "identify" with many different characters each with different outlooks or points of view. This does not necessarily mean this individual has the moral courage to enter into face-to-face dialogue with adherents of all these different points of view. They may remain abstract, I suppose, & therefore limited.

Participation

Ahhh yes – "participation" (writ large on the top of the page) what a great word/concept. And Frank's use of the terms "demoralized" & "remoralized." The term "participation" always brings to mind the "participatory self" that anthropologists refer to as the primary self in the pre-modern, pre-industrial context. The whole magical "participatory" world where the boundary of the self is porous & various spirits & demons can come & go – whereby the whole self can be replaced by some other interloper sent by a bad guy next door & of course one is vulnerable to attack if one has broken the rules. One may fall ill because one has broken the rules & the interloper is in there doing his nasty work. But, of course, this is not the sort of participation we are speaking of with the dialogic imagination. And yet dialogic participation in story-making does involve a porous boundary.

And of course this notion of the consequences of breaking the (moral) rules is very much alive & well with regard to diseases such as cancer. We cancer "types" don't express our emotions nearly as much as we should. hmmmm. In addition, the breaking of the "artificial stance" (professional objectivity) will often be viewed as breaking the rules – the rule-breaker open to reprimand.

But really the stories are about courage, aren't they? The courage to enter into the discourse of the marginalized other, the irrationality of the poor… I realize that I have forgotten pretty much the generosity of the ill – the ability or desire to give of themselves – to create, I suppose a habitable world. (And I suppose my own notes & creative work during my time of illness would fall into this category.) This is where a paradox for me arises for as in all gifts, there is, I believe a cruel edge – the edge that will not let a sleeper continue in his sleep. But perhaps this edge is only from the underdog. But no, Arthur Frank has gone some way to say that generosity should not disturb some deeper private aspect of the unknowable other. I am not sure that this advice can be followed. This will always be open to judgment in the moment & will depend on the ability to listen to oneself as well as to the other. Certainly the dictate isn't followed in art. But there is a place where art & the sacred disagree, perhaps there is a place where art & the moral philosophy of Levinas disagree. I don't really know. Levinas does seem to operate with a notion of the other as God?

Anyway, a note re Levinas: the violence of representation & the eclipse of the Other (& God) with the reduction of the world to the knowable. From Levinas's point of view, this violence of the radical reduction of the world to knowledge has killed the Other. But this, of course, is only an apparent difficulty. It hasn't actually occurred. Or it has occurred if we continue to act "as if" it has occurred. But in fact, the Other is still with us & perhaps more so than ever before.

I want to think about this "violence of representation" for a moment – try to put this in my own world as best I can. And right off I realize I am uncomfortable with what appears to me a reduced notion of "representation." He would appear to only be talking about ordinary spoken & written language & only about its scientific or rational orientation. Gone are all sorts of metaphorical representation which are nothing if not ambiguous & gone also all visual representation which is never reducible to the written.

With the theoretical expansion of representation to include the iconic (the image in one's mind is also representation). And paradoxically, we are absolutely private while holding the fullest possible image of the world in mind. (And the fullness of this image is ordered as a "picture" or a ritual or music not as writing.) It can only be an assumption on our part, & a wrong one, that "my world" is the same as "your world." Thus the full iconic image of the world "stands in for" the Other. (And perhaps it is not so much "unknowable" as "incommunicable.") From this point of view it is rather the violence of the sacred – the power of the other – that disrupts & kills our organized world of ordinary (communal) communication. (The iconic image slays ordinary reference that is reference which reduces the world to the knowable for Levinas)!

There is a reversal of the equation but what does this mean for morality? I am confused perhaps. From this orientation, it is exactly referential language that brings me into contact with other people – but, in the best case, with an expanded metaphorical & richly textured language. But strangely enough, the more I move to the iconic dimension of language the more difficult it is to express myself (the more private is the language) & also my expression perforce becomes more universal. Is the "universal" dimension actually an effect of privacy & the necessity to "assume?"

It seems in a sense that "continuity" at the boundary with other is represented as the iconic is actually private. I realize that I have been thinking of the "other" as "the world" & not as including "other people." I have been thinking of the continuity twixt self & other as the intuition of the continuity of my body immersed in the flux of the energetic world. This means, I suppose, that I have been thinking of "other people" as either a more or less undifferentiated aspect of the outer world or the same as myself. Odd.

So. a certain contradiction is ways of thinking about otherness. I need to think about this dialogic relationship some more.

Compassion, empathy, generosity, caring -- are all predicated upon a loosening up of boundary & also perhaps involves an acknowledgement of the pre-reflective bodily self (the inviolate self before any thought "about" it.) The loosened boundary twixt self & other (& between any one thing & any other thing) is actually an ambiguous zone of similarity & difference – a sort of place abuzz with metaphor – a place where entities wearing masks proclaim that in fact, this = that.) There is, no doubt, a difference between such "flow" (at the loosened boundary) & the dialogic imagination but there is also a similarity. The "flow" at the boundary can easily slip into the world of ecstasy or hallucination or more simply the world of unimpeded creative work, wherein the hand & the tool that holds it are inseparable.

Lots to think about. And the problem always seems to come back to the boundary condition. I remember now the interesting term "alterity" (absolute difference) posited against the merging of self & other. And this opposition to be resolved in the dialogic imagination which remains unresolved & open – unfixed & unfinished – unfinalized.

Two languages

The rational language of reference, syntax, grammar & causality & the creative language of metaphor, allegory, description.

LEFT BRAIN FUNCTIONS	RIGHT BRAIN FUNCTIONS
Syntagmatic axis of structural analysis	Metaphorical axis of structural analysis
Rational exegesis	apprehension of gestalt
grammar, syntax, semantics	Metaphoric substitution, analogy, image
reading, writing, counting, computing	The apprehension of music
digital communication	Analogic communication
	holistic grasping of complex relationships, patterns, configurations, and structures.
In psychoanalysis: Secondary process, ordinary language, apprehension of time passing, computation etc.	In psychoanalysis: primary process -- non-linear associations -- condensation, dream imagery, free association. Like the world of the id, this hemisphere seems to be timeless or much more resistant to the processes of time
	olfactory sense: brings up the whole gestalt
	face recognition – the gestalt of the face recognized all at once & in total
rational relationships in language etc.	competent for the construction of logical classes: abstract classes which do not actually exist: e.g. – the class of "triangles."
The "verbal" hemisphere (Dominant)	Silence: archaic language. concepts are ambiguous – lacks prepositions & other elements of syntax & grammar
	moods, memory, the image or analogy
	primitive arithmetic but precise assessment of quantity

This chart is built from "The Language of Change: Elements of Therapeutic Communication" by Paul Watzlawick (1978).

Cerebral asymmetry & the pragmatic effects of communication.

When presented with conflictual information sometimes one hemisphere inhibits the other & gains control of the efferent pathways. This amounts to what appears as a "repression" of the contradictory perception & a falsification of reality. (efferent – nerve that conveys message to muscles or glands)

But is not a "repression" but rather one hemisphere dominates the other so that the competency of the other hemisphere is unavailable. It is not a "repression" in the sense that the individual does not have some hidden desire that makes him want to "forget" or get rid of some particular knowledge. On the other hand, there is still the question of why one hemisphere or the other gains control of the efferent pathways & thus blocks integration from both hemispheres.

The hemispheric theory leads to the notion that we will have to change our understanding of conscious & unconscious processes. We have two conscious minds which are capable of harmonious, complementary integration for the purpose of grasping and mastering our outer & inner reality, but if & when conflict arises, they may be unable to communicate with each other for lack of a common language. This confirms the theory of dissociation (Pierre Janet) – the vertical separation of the mind as opposed to Freud's horizontal topography of the psychic apparatus.

The Hidden

I am interested in the notion of the "hidden," the repressed, dissociation, the forgotten & also lies & absences.

Wagner speaks of metaphor being the ideal unit for our analysis of communication because it typifies the ambiguous & the hidden. We need interpretation precisely because so many things are hidden & ambiguous & unclear in these modern times.

Frank speaks of the artificial self & the absence or hiddenness of the personal dimension or rather the absence of dialogue. He leans toward an understanding of the self as constituted in relation to the other rather than in isolation. The socially constructed self – other as mirror, etc.

The dialogic story-telling is a call for community & for referential language with its communal references. In a paradoxical sense, this is a move away from the privacy of the iconic image – which tends to be silent. I'm not sure of this because there is also a call for authenticity & the stories, per se, do not need to be constituted as rational unfoldings. Rather in dialogic story-telling there is a call for "communication" which involves both types of metaphor & both sides of the brain. Although there is a move away from the private & the closed off.

Dissociation as a vertical split in consciousness & repression as a horizontal split in consciousness.

And then, this notion of the two brains: two conscious functioning parts of consciousness which may or may not function harmoniously. When there is conflict, one or the other may take over, leaving the other side quiet or hidden, unused.

The notion of the "alterity" of the other – that consciousness that is unknowable & belongs only to the one who possesses it. It cannot be assessed by any other. It is utterly private. And in this sense, one is completely alone. This, then, is hidden from the other because this is the structure of consciousness.

The opposition twixt "sincerity" or "honesty" or transparency AND the ironic, the witty, ambiguous, puns & jokes. In the former there is nothing hidden, in the latter, much.

There is something about the psychological negotiation of the territory or zone at the boundary interface with others that I am dissatisfied with. Philosophical concerns inform the psychology of the negotiation of this dialogic interface but there doesn't seem to be any "structural" necessity for acting in a certain way & not another. I am very unsure of this. Just a feeling. I have the sense that I haven't been able to reduce the relationship to a simple & clear "necessity." As soon as I say this, of course, I am completely unsure if this is a good idea at all. Why should I be able to reduce such a complex procedure & why do I have the compulsion to do so? According to my own lights, ambiguity & possibility rather than clarity & the fixed relationship lead us towards the good & towards freedom but... I am still left with the feeling that I don't quite understand. I want my understanding to include ambiguity & multiplicity & the slipperiness of metaphor but I also want the main elements in clear relationship to each other or perhaps I lack an adequate frame metaphor. Not sure. But I am left with the sense of an argument I wish was stronger or less dependent upon relative "values."

A dialogic relationship is one which engages with the other especially across large oppositional gaps such as that between wealth & poverty, health & illness.

In terms of representation, it is the definitions of these oppositions which need to be reconsidered. When these classes are rendered clear & oppositional with a strict fixed boundary between them, there can be no real meeting – I mean no real meeting of the people who for one reason or another occupy the territory of these definitions – a rich person & a poor person, a healthy person & a sick person. There is a monologue & it is unclear whether it is the monologue of language which "contains" the person within itself or the person who contains the monologue. In any event if the sick person cannot access the healthy part of themselves or the healthy person, the sick part, then there can be no conversation. This is, of course, overly simplistic.

In addition the relationship is not symmetrical – I mean, between sickness & health. Health is the assumed – our everyday reality – the way things are supposed to be. While sickness is that which disrupts our everyday reality, overturns our conceptions of the very nature of self & reality. Thus it is sickness that the healthy (doctor) confronts in the other & it is sickness that the patient confronts in himself, that changes things. And sickness can mean so many things – its causes multiple. I suppose they could be grouped into physical or biological causes & social causes. Here is a list in the order that they occurred to me.

1) the result of bad choices, irrationality, stupidity, dirtiness
2) the hand of the sacred – that which disrupts our everyday secular world – the sacred as power
3) the hand of the teacher – the world of the other – sickness – is that which resists us & it is only in the resistance of the world that we learn – that we have a self or develop one. Sickness is just one face of that which is not me.
4) the result of moral error, inability to express emotions, express too much emotion, disconnection from the body etc.
5) Bad luck, chance,
6) Karma (bad choices etc. but in a previous life-time)
7) Blocked flow of energy – energy is blocked in the body & in the subtle bodies so that there is no flow – stagnation. Reich & cancer. Chinese Medicine. Ayer Vedic medicine. Stress.
8) Black magic – witch doctors inflict illness – voodoo death, breaking of taboo etc.
9) Bad thoughts – negative thoughts – wrong beliefs – distorted personal mythology that drags one down – depression…
10) Improper diet – vegetarianism, toxins in the food
11) Heredity, genetics, evolution,
12) Environmental factors, radiation, germs, toxic pollutants etc.
13) Poverty, lack of education & other social causes of illness
14) Iatrogenic

The stoic program: What is recognized as internal & what as external. What can we affect & what is unchangeable. With regard to illness, especially chronic illness, what we can change is our attitude towards the illness – our internal image of the world & illness.

"It is not the things themselves that worry us, but the opinions that we have about those things." Epictetus.

World Image or Reality Construction

In a pragmatic sense, one suffers in one's relationship to the world but one has no direct contact with the world only with the image of the world, therefore one suffers from one's image of the world. In order to alleviate suffering, one must either change the world itself or change one's image of it. The latter is the primary mode of therapy.

There are things that pertain to the world as such & these can be explained via analysis.

Things concerning the human world & our opinions, on the other hand can only be dealt with in a dialectical way. (Earlier I found another expression of just this with Existentialism in the Kruk's book. Sartre I believe held that when analysis was incorrectly applied to human life it was always ideological.)

It strikes me that part of the problem with "artificial" thinking & artificial selves is that there is the attempt to deal with people as if they are things, or as if they are a part of the natural world which doesn't have a self. Thus the mode of thinking & communicating is analytical rather than dialectical. Dialectical thought, of course, takes advantage of discourse with the other either in imagination or in reality.

The notion that the scientific view of human life (& its use of analysis of the human sphere) is ideological is interesting. Also the idea that only dialectics can get to the truth of human life. Dialogic story-telling. It is ideological in terms of its one-way flow of information/power.

With the dialectic we are into the domain of "deliberation." (Aristotle)

One's world image is constructed in communication, that is, with others. Our reality is socially constructed. Watzalawick (1978) argues that this perception & understanding of the "world image" is a function of the right hemisphere of the brain. He seems to see this synthesis of all that we know & have learned in intercourse with others as an "image." To perceive this gestalt, then is the function of the right side of the brain. Watzalawick thus argues that the attempts by depth psychology to translate this right brain material (the world image) into left brain modes – interpretation, language, rationality, analysis, etc. is wrong.

He proposes three therapeutic techniques instead:
1) The use of right-hemispheric language patterns;
2) Blocking the left hemisphere;
3) Specific behavior prescriptions.
    (Watzlawick, 1978. p. 47)

Deconstruction, Interpretation or the Meaning of Meaning

I am not a philosopher & I am by no means well read in contemporary philosophy but I am certainly aware of deconstruction & the huge impact it has had on contemporary thought in a great number of domains. Recently I have been engaged in getting down my thoughts on interpretive practice for the students of KATI where I lead, intermittently these days, various seminars concerned primarily with the introduction of an eclectic mix of theory – structuralism, post structuralist metaphor theory & various concepts drawn from sociology & anthropology. My primary practice is as a poet, particularly in performance often with other media, dancers, musicians, video, & so forth. From this position, I am very interested in seeing KATI incorporate other of the expressive arts, the inclusion of contemporary media such as photography and video, and the utilization of ideas from the environmental movement & eco-psychology.

Perhaps I should have addressed the philosophical program of deconstruction, especially its overall suspicion of the whole idea of interpretation, even in a brief way at the beginning of these notes, but I didn't, & I can never do this now, even if I were to insert this note at the beginning. It would be a ruse & would necessitate editing, if not re-writing, a number of the earlier notes. I prefer not to do this.

Thus, the time has come as some member of Alice's menagerie said to speak of many things: deconstruction, the problem of "presence" & "difference." (note there is an accent over the first "e") This will supply a sort of belated context that the reader can subsequently insert the previous material into, and see how it changes. If they like.

A brief synopsis of deconstruction would be in order. In some sense deconstruction is simply another term for post-structuralist practice. The project of deconstruction is suspicious of the modernist & structuralist notion of discovering truth beneath a veil, the whole idea of depth analysis, and of the real meaning of things. It is especially suspicious of the discovery of a single truth, a single foundational theory that explains everything. In a sense, we are dealing with a simple loss of faith in the human ability to discover truth at all, but one can't really argue with the fact that science has failed to deliver what it promised. For deconstructionists, reality is not unitary but fragmentary, and is not to be discovered "underneath" the superficial surface of things. Reality is the surface of things. There is no high & low in art, no elite & pop culture – its all one in the market place. Everything shows on the surface and it's in bits & pieces. As such, reality is understood to be socially constructed, an illusion, in particular an illusion of wholes, unified selves, unified theories about society, for example, Marxism & so on.

In many ways, it seems a little difficult to know what the fuss is all about. It's not really very difficult to accept that there is no single one true cause of this or that situation; causes are multiple, multivalent, and ambiguous. The world is complicated. This seems a commonplace. Why would we ever have thought otherwise? I suppose one could say that this is the extent to which the ideas of deconstruction have permeated popular culture. Everything is complex; there are a lot of things going on at the same time. Who knows what's really going on? Look what happened to communism, or look at late industrial capitalism & globalization.

On the other hand, it's hard to accept that everything's on the surface. I'm still amazed to read those lists that appear every once in a while that document the interlocking ownership of large corporate concerns. This information is certainly not on the surface or easily available; it is quite well hidden & shows the very real deployment of power in society. Of course, in a general way, we are well aware that the whole of social life is shot through with power, with individual or corporate concerns that control the flow of money & products. We are very used to the whole idea of asking what does such & such really mean, what is the mask that so & so is wearing. What motivation is hidden beneath the surface? Why do people still have problems if everything is on the surface & not hidden? Is this just a habit of mind? Are the clues to the nature of what is going on right on the surface, & we just don't see them because we are not practiced in reading this kind of sign? Or do we just need to look for more complex explanations?

On the other hand, & somewhat confusingly, deconstruction, for its part, discovers "hidden" agendas everywhere. The whole project is to deconstruct or take apart apparently unitary integrated wholes, whether they be pieces of architecture or educational theories, & discover hidden motives & the real historical & social nature of all that seems "natural" in cultural life. It uncovers the fact that the whole practice of interpretation has come to appear "natural" as have certain literary genres & styles in visual art. It deconstructs theoretical & institutional constructs & points out how theories & interpretive practices have been socially constructed and how this has come about. As with modernist critical theory, it purports to uncover true motives, historical development & so forth. It is suspicious of the structuralist notion of the way that symbolic meaning is formed via oppositional categories, the way in which truth is constructed in relation to untruth, and the feminine in terms of the masculine. It is simply or complexly suspicious. Lyotard I believe used the term "hermeneutics of suspicion."

The difference, I suppose, is that deconstruction does not see itself as just another unified explanatory theory; it, itself, is fragmented, partial, incomplete. From this general angle, deconstruction has been attacked as losing track of humanist goals for the betterment of humankind, of being essentially conservative and so forth. In fact, I don't believe it really is so. Rather, it is fragmented & contradictory, just as it purports to be.

This understanding of reality has particular importance for the therapeutic project, especially as it relates to concepts like the "integrated" or "true" self, psychoanalysis, the notion of the unconscious, transference, & indeed the whole notion of "depth work" as opposed to "counseling." There is also a tension between the deconstructivist notion of "presence," as the reliance upon our certainty in theory & unitary meanings, & the "therapeutic presence" of the therapist. Deconstruction aims to deconstruct the reliance of the whole Western world on logical process. In addition, there is the critique of art & the art world that is relevant in some respects to the work of expressive therapy. In addition, although some have argued that deconstruction has abandoned a critical stance, this is not in fact true, but the critique is somewhat different.

To return to the notion of habit or habitual way of thinking, Derrida calls this habit of thought "presence." It is the certainty we have in our "natural" ways of going about things, specific origins, & interpretations. Deconstruction sets out to show that these are illusory or mythic, and that they are not true and they are not universal. In this sense, then, deconstruction is really a meta language, an interpretation of interpretation. It is a critique of interpretive practice, but it in no way throws out interpretation; it is simply suspicious of unitary, single all-encompassing theories (foundational theories) or theories that purport to be universally true. As mentioned earlier, Derrida is suspicious of the structuralist idea of the universal way the mind is supposed to work via "splitting" & the construction of meaning in terms of oppositions, one term of which is always the superior or true one, while the other is inferior in one way or another. As Brownowski argues in his lectures on the foundation of knowledge and the imagination, there is always this "cut" which renders all knowledge as provisional and temporary until the closed system can be opened up again. This opening up of a closed system of relevance occurs when some sort of unrecognized similarity shows up such that some previously apparently irrelevant fact suddenly becomes relevant. We are, then, very much in the territory of the relative. Truths are relative.

When such theory is applied to the project of psychological healing or therapy, there are sometimes some difficulties. These difficulties occur when deconstruction & post-structuralist theory are crudely applied simply due to laziness or misunderstanding. Sometimes it is a question of just opening things up to a complete relativism so that anything goes; any kind of interpretation works and it is all up to the therapist. A "good" therapist will simply know what is going on in an intuitive way. This sort of notion is aided by the idea that it doesn't really matter what theory is being used because it is the persona of the therapist and the quality of the relationship between therapist & client that count. In this way, some feminist theory claims that it works with an even playing field (the same sports metaphors used in the discussion of the wars in the Middle East) & that there is no power differential between therapist & client. This is an illusion. There is always necessarily a power differential, & to claim there isn't is to ignore this to the detriment of the therapeutic work. This ignoring of power & the ignorance of implicit interpretive practices is fairly common.

Presence relies heavily on the system of binary opposition proposed by structuralism. It seems to me that post-structuralist practice aims to "unpack" the suppressed elements in the overlap between oppositional categories. Thus, post-structuralism is very concerned with boundary & the deconstruction of the common boundaries between categories.

The main terms then are: boundary, overlap of binary oppositions, presence, power, identity or the subject, and post-modernism in general.

It's a little hard to say for fear I'll be called a fool, but really what could be expected of a discourse that purports to be a critique of the process of critique when it is well established that critique itself, that is, interpretation and self-reflective language, is at the root of paradox itself. What can be expected but complete fragmentation? The liar's paradox takes a new twist. The modernist text on one side of the piece of paper states: the words on the other side of this piece of paper are true. When you flip the paper over to the post-modern text on the other side it says: the words on the other side of this paper are a lie. The deal is done. The world collapses. What fun!

If we accept Brownowski's argument that self-reflective language is at the root of all paradox, whether in literature or mathematics, we cannot expect anything but multiple paradox from an ultra self-reflective language whose subject is self-reflective, i.e. critical language that always includes, of course, the original object of thought. This ultra self-reflective language is not so much the logical critique of shall we say "ordinary" self-reflective language, but rather an ongoing creative process that takes as its raw material this already given critique. A logical critique of critique could only affirm the need to go further and take it all apart.) Here I am reminded of that wonderful image given by Paul Shepard of the origin of analysis as a bird of prey picking apart the insides of its dead prey. There is, after all, an inside, an inside that doesn't show itself completely on the surface: the internal organs are so interesting & taste so good. The analysis of analysis, the meaning of meaning, conjures up what sort of image – the author himself perhaps, Mr. Paul Shepard laying before our eyes this metaphorical embodiment of meaning. Embodiment.

There seem to be certain subjects that are ready for deconstruction, others that are not to be touched. What are the untouchables? Dare I mention them – "spirituality," "yoga," "vision sessions," probably hypnotism. Why has post-structuralist, post-modern practice not been applied to the expressive arts therapies? Is the critique of art, of psychoanalysis, seen as enough? What? There is a sense of intense struggle inside of language, an attempt to get out, a searching of every surface for paradox and reversal. Ultimately, there is a sense of being haunted; these texts are haunted by their shadow-forms, by some sort of ephemeral entity conjured up by this intense skeptical attitude, some shadow operator from the disavowed interior depths. This intense scrutiny of the surface of writing, the ways in which meaning is constituted, appears as an almost overwhelming self-consciousness. Sometimes it seems that the difficulty of conveying meaning is so great that the poor soul who is writing never quite gets around to saying what he or she wants to say. There is a repetitious stuttering quality. All writing is itself a foundation, an authority. One's irritation is the irritation of someone who builds & knows any sort of building needs a foundation, even if, as in this case, the building is not built to last. But of course, it also is built to last. It is a kind of lasting foundation whose appearance is fragmented, like a rubble foundation rather than a concrete one. My house has a rubble foundation from the beginning of the 20th century. It's not so highly valued as a complete concrete foundation, which is stronger.

It's also irritating that the vocabulary that seems to be purposively put out of reach of the ordinary person, even the ordinary intelligent person. Word games & puns & so forth are, of course, fun in their own right, but they quickly seem to dissolve into in-jokes and insider references to other philosophers living & dead. Where is the popularizer of deconstruction? Where is that one who can bring home the main import of the works to ordinary intelligent people who are not quite "on" for learning the jargon or the "50-cent words" as First Nations people say.

At this point, the deconstructive writing style, characterized by this intense self-conscious focus on the surface of the sentence, especially perhaps on punctuation and partial words, especially perhaps on the changing "directions" accomplished in writing, (I mean this in a topographical sense rather than as proposition or directions about how to get somewhere) especially the subtle changes in direction, the leaning into the curve that one does on a motorcycle on the highway, the changes in direction of a little breeze, so that meaning seems to come from a slightly different direction now, a direction only given by a little fluttering of the leaves of a tree metaphorical, perhaps historical, carrying with it the whiff of Eden, the cabbala, whatever, the curves that are thrown, the often illegal left turns, the multiple branchings that lead who knows where, the tough rhizomes that are so hard to get rid of when one is clearing a spot for one's tent when camping, this style appears as a sort of mysticism which instead of utilizing the escape from language offered by "sitting" instead for a sort of intellectual gymnastics – or as I have said the plowing through sentences as if they were a field, or rather a field of water, a desert waste, beautiful & sandy, presenting slippery slopes of all sorts, using some sort of machine, some engine that can be steered, that can handle all sorts of different terrain, an intellectual ATV (all terrain vehicle) a deconstruction of the social construction of meaning which is haunted as I said by the ghost or "trace" as deconstructionists have it of meaning or multiple meaning or possible meaning, a meaning from the depths which disavowed in the present can only be historical & which hovers always just out of reach. A mysticism that aims to discover, or unveil (heavens to Betsy) the truth, but a special truth, the truth that is there can be no truth, at least not final, or unitary, or foundational, or certain. A mysticism that leads us into uncertainty & to our memory of the famous dictum of John Keats -- & our hoped for ability to navigate our fragmented world. This word "navigate" seems good to me, again a machine that can be steered, go into reverse.

I recently read of robot races in the desert. This sort of machine is very clever indeed, but it's also the rather crude beginnings of a very sophisticated business. In the bathroom I find myself reading a small history of philosophy. In the chapter on the Cynics, I read about the skeptical attitudes of the early Greeks, the suspicion of spoken or written truth, & also the suspicion of perception itself so that everything is unstable. Lo & behold we have the birth of satire.

And so, of course, the postmodern has a satirical edge.

Key Concepts of Psychoanalysis: a series of diagrams

All the diagrams in this book were developed by Blake Parker, using C-maps and conceptualized in dialogue with Monica Carpendale. Blake created them as teaching aids for presentations and course work.

Psychoanalytic Drive Theory

The life and death instincts (from Wikipedia)

Freud believed that humans were driven by two conflicting central desires:
the life drive (Eros) (incorporating the sex drive) and the death drive (Thanatos).
Freud's description of Eros/Libido included all creative, life-producing drives.
The death drive (or death instinct) represented an urge inherent in all living things
to return to a state of calm, or, ultimately, of non-existence. The presence of the
death drive was only recognized in his later years, and the contrast between the two
represents a revolution in his manner of thinking.

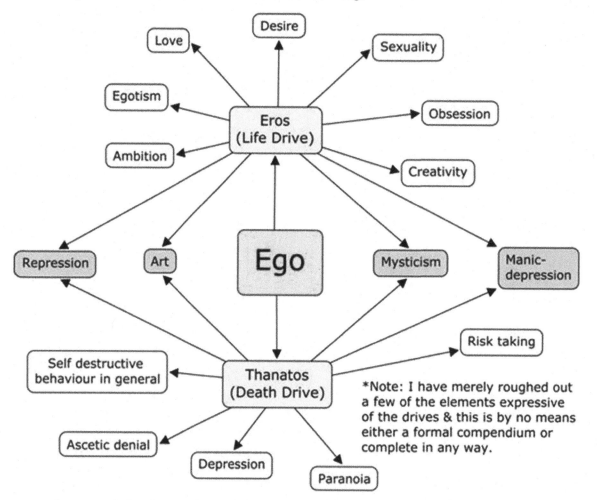

In general the defence or coping strategy of repression works to enhance the life
drive by protecting the ego & making arrangements so that it can achieve
pleasure in a non threatening way. On the other hand, it works in the service
of the death drive insomuch as it operates to shut down pleasures & stifle life.
Manic-depression involves aspects of both of the drives & Art is often a
manifestation of both insomuch as it is certainly a creative manifestation of life
but at the same time there is often the desire to dissappear & to express the
negative realities. I have Mysticism as also a manifestation of both drives,
involving as it does a creative ascension & a radical denial of many aspects of life
often including sexuality & the pleasures of living.

Figure/Ground Gestalt
Primary & Secondary Process

Reversible figure/ground gestalt

Primary process appears as foreground control on the secondary process background -- this is manifested as the surfacing of repressed desire, the symbolic expression of the body & creativity. Background rational thought is reorganized in novel ways, some of them pathological, some merely innovative.

Reversible figure/ground gestalt

Secondary process appears as foreground control on the primary process background -- this is repressive & manifests as conventional control of desire & the expression of the body. Primary process is treated as the irrational background of the body & emotions which come under the control of the rational mind.

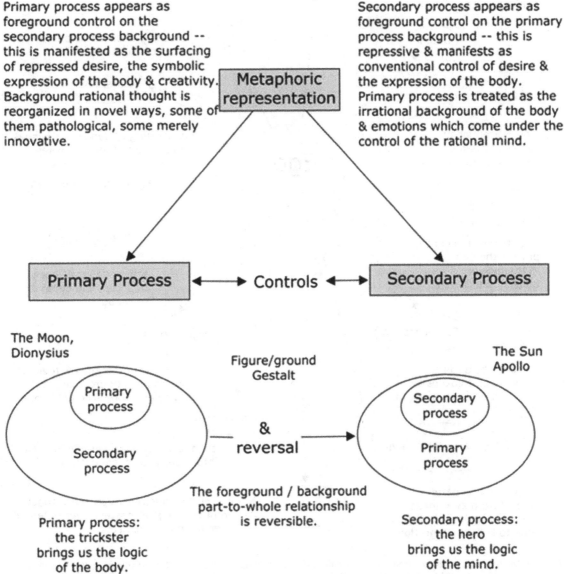

Primary process emphasizes "flow" & the interconnected nature of things. It manifests in diverse ways including neurosis, pathology & dreams. In the realm of the conscious it also informs the creative process in general including the the iconic imagery of ritual, poetry & music. It is the functioning of desire & desire is always the desire to penetrate & to merge with. Because of the chronic repression of its functioning, this manifests in sometimes bizarre ways.

PSYCHOANALYSIS: THE DEFENSES

reversion to an earlier stage of development in the face of unacceptable impulses.

This is not a complete constellation of defenses, "turning against the self," "identification with the aggressor" "avoidance, & isolation of affect" are several others."

Regression

channeling of unacceptable or unattainable desires into imagination.

refusal to accept reality. Primitive defense characteristic of early childhood.

Fantasy

blocking unacceptable impulses from consciousness.

Denial

Repression

Projection

the attribution of one's undesired impulses onto another.

the converting of dangerous wishes or impulses into their opposites.

Ego

Reaction Formation

Rationalization

Undoing

cognitive reframing to protect the ego in the face of undesirable change.

attempt to take back unacceptable behavior or thoughts

Compensation

Displacement

counterbalancing perceived weaknesses by emphasizing strength.

redirecion of thoughts & feelings from an anxiety producing object to a safer, more acceptable one.

Sublimation

channeling of unacceptable impulses into more acceptable outlets.

Compartmentalization

separation of parts of self from awareness causes cognitive dissonance due to lack of integration

Intellectualization

use of the cognitive approach without emotions to gain mastery over potentially overwhelming impulses.

Defense Mechanisms protect us from awareness of undesired and feared impulses. They distance us from a full awareness of unpleasant thoughts, feelings and desires. They represent an unconscious mediation by the ego of id impulses which threaten the integrity of the ego and/or superego. By altering and distorting the original impulse, these impulses (often concerning sex & aggression) are made more tolerable. The defense mechanisms are used to protect oneself from unpleasant emotions, but they often result in harmful problems. In general, the ego utilizes the defenses to protect itself. The defences are coping strategies that have become harmful because unconscious.

Psychoanalysis
3 Dimensions

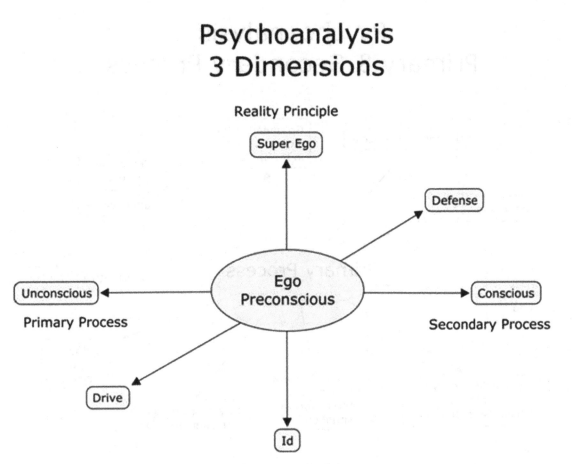

Reality Principle

Super Ego

Defense

Unconscious   Ego
Preconscious   Conscious

Primary Process   Secondary Process

Drive

Id

Pleasure Principle

Centre: Ego associated with the Preconscious. This node participates in all 3 axes in the 3D model

Horizontal Perceptual Axis -- Unconscious & Conscious This is Freud's 1st "Topographical Model" of the Psyche with the associated Primary & Secondary processes

Vertical Experiential Axis -- Id & Super Ego This is Freud's 2nd "Structural Model" of the Psyche with the associated Realty & Pleasure principles

Back to Front Axis -- Drive Energy & Resistance

Note: This map was developed from the 3D mapping concepts
to be found at http://www.psyche.com/psyche/cube/cube_psyche.html

Psychoanalysis
Primary & Secondary Process

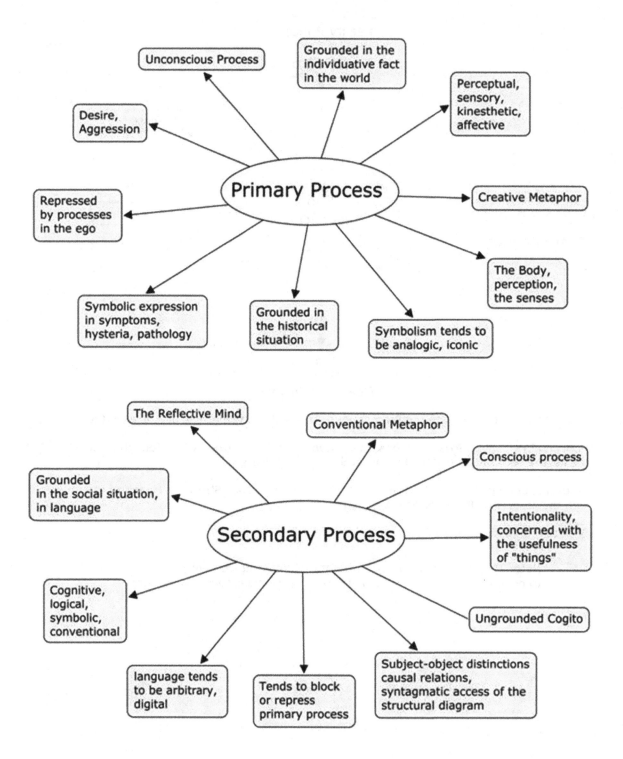

Psychoanalysis
Structural Model of the Psyche

The Structural Model (From Wikipedia)

The ego, super-ego, and id are the divisions of the psyche according to Freud's later "structural theory". The id contains "primitive desires" (hunger, rage, and sex), the super-ego contains internalized norms, morality and taboos, and the ego mediates between the two and may include or give rise to the sense of self.

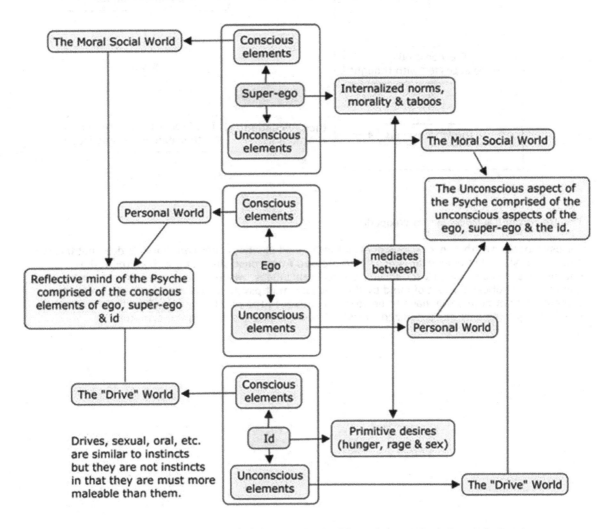

The primary object of classical psychoanalytic work is to bring the unconscious aspects to conscious awareness.

Psychoanalysis
Topographic Model of the Psyche

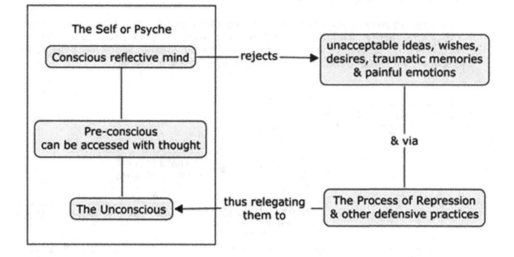

The Topographical Model (From Wikipedia)

For psychoanalysis, the unconscious does not include all of what is not conscious. It does not include e.g., motor skills, but only what is actively repressed from conscious thought. For Freud, the unconscious was a depository for socially unacceptable ideas, wishes or desires, traumatic memories, and painful emotions put out of mind by the mechanism of psychological repression. However, the contents did not necessarily have to be solely negative. In the psychoanalytic view, the unconscious is a force that can only be recognized by its effects—it expresses itself in the symptom.

The Preconscious
& Creativity

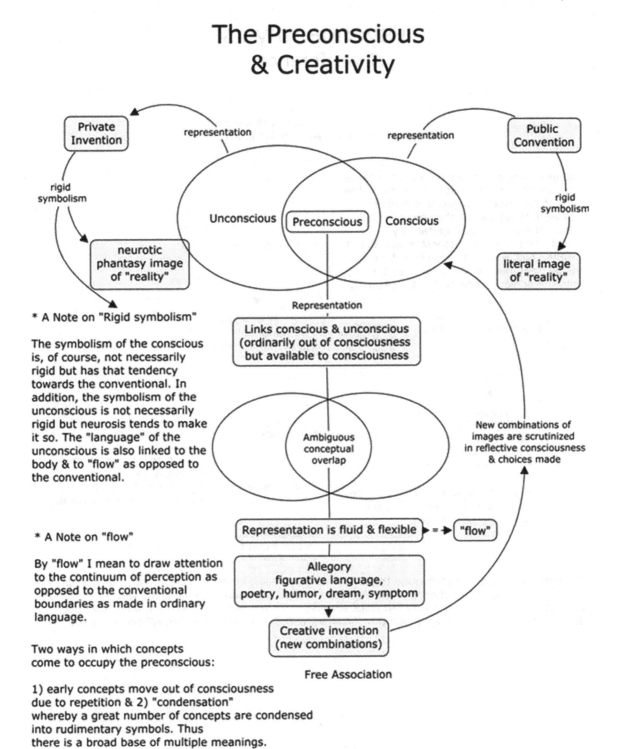

Private
Invention

representation

representation

Public
Convention

rigid
symbolism

Unconscious Preconscious Conscious

rigid
symbolism

neurotic
phantasy image
of "reality"

literal image
of "reality"

Representation

Links conscious & unconscious
(ordinarily out of consciousness
but available to consciousness

Ambiguous
conceptual
overlap

New combinations of
images are scrutinized
in reflective consciousness
& choices made

Representation is fluid & flexible ▶ ⇢ ▶ "flow"

Allegory
figurative language,
poetry, humor, dream, symptom

Creative invention
(new combinations)

Free Association

* A Note on "Rigid symbolism"

The symbolism of the conscious
is, of course, not necessarily
rigid but has that tendency
towards the conventional. In
addition, the symbolism of the
unconscious is not necessarily
rigid but neurosis tends to make
it so. The "language" of the
unconscious is also linked to the
body & to "flow" as opposed to
the conventional.

* A Note on "flow"

By "flow" I mean to draw attention
to the continuum of perception as
opposed to the conventional
boundaries as made in ordinary
language.

Two ways in which concepts
come to occupy the preconscious:

1) early concepts move out of consciousness
due to repetition & 2) "condensation"
whereby a great number of concepts are condensed
into rudimentary symbols. Thus
there is a broad base of multiple meanings.

261

Psychoanalysis
Transference

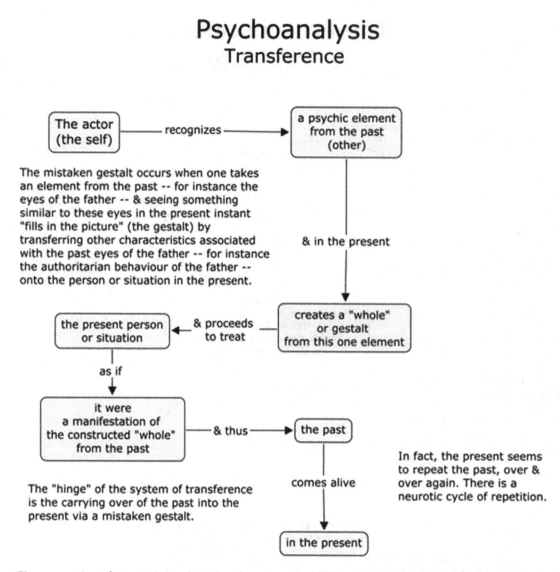

The mistaken gestalt occurs when one takes an element from the past -- for instance the eyes of the father -- & seeing something similar to these eyes in the present instant "fills in the picture" (the gestalt) by transferring other characteristics associated with the past eyes of the father -- for instance the authoritarian behaviour of the father -- onto the person or situation in the present.

The "hinge" of the system of transference is the carrying over of the past into the present via a mistaken gestalt.

In fact, the present seems to repeat the past, over & over again. There is a neurotic cycle of repetition.

The perception of a gestalt involves the almost magical "filling in" of the rest of the picture when only a small amount of information is given. Perhaps the most common example is the way we recognize the human face when only a very few clues are given. A great number of specific ways have been documented concerning exactly how this "filling in" or "completion of the picture" takes place.

The Therapeutic Relationship

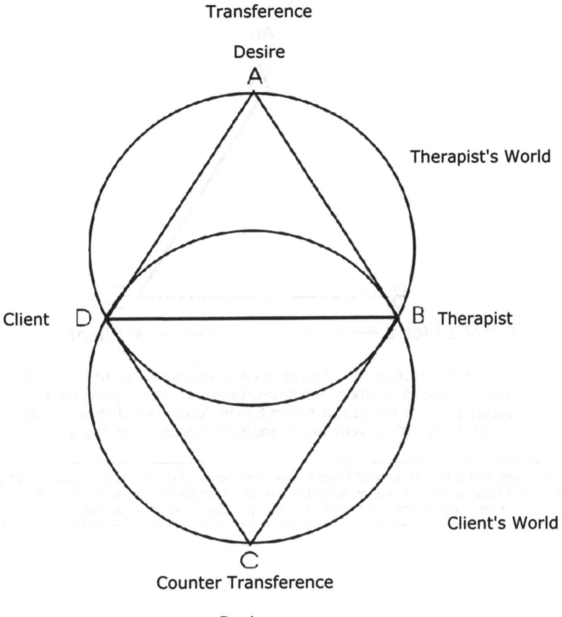

Transference

Desire

A

Therapist's World

Client   D   B   Therapist

Client's World

C

Counter Transference

Desire

Transference

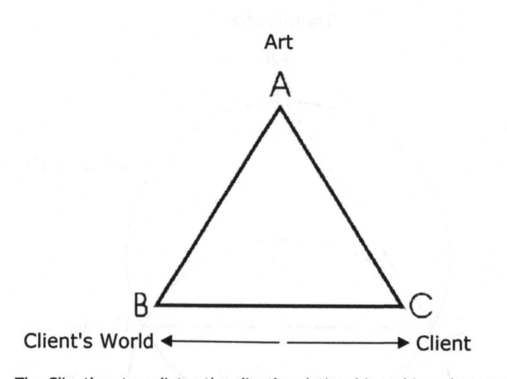

Art

A

B   C

Client's World ←————————→ Client

The Client's art mediates the client's relationship to his or her world.
It can come to "contain" emotions, unconscious imagery, various
aspects of his or her past & hopes for the future. All of these aspects
of the client's psyche are "transferred" onto & into the art.

Because of this transference of ideas & emotions, some of them unconscious, the art
can take on a magical quality. Now that one has a "container" for these difficult &
mysterious aspects of the psyche, the question is: what to do with it?

Infancy &
Toddlerhood

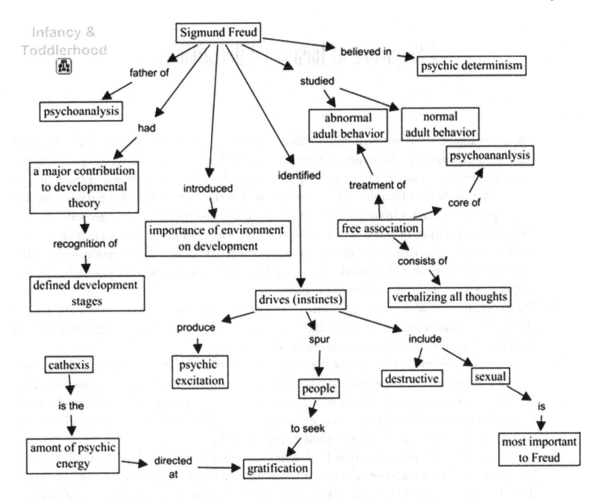

Sigmund Freud

- believed in → psychic determinism
- father of → psychoanalysis
- had → a major contribution to developmental theory
  - recognition of → defined development stages
- introduced → importance of environment on development
- identified → drives (instincts)
- studied → abnormal adult behavior
- studied → normal adult behavior

abnormal adult behavior ← treatment of ← free association

free association → core of → psychoananlysis

free association → consists of → verbalizing all thoughts

verbalizing all thoughts ← psychoananlysis

drives (instincts):
- produce → psychic excitation
- spur → people → to seek → gratification
- include → destructive
- include → sexual → is → most important to Freud

cathexis → is the → amont of psychic energy → directed at → gratification

A Sequence of Ideas and Definitions

1) The Super-Ego: the witness & the injunction to let thoughts go (this sacrificial giving away) are essentially super-ego messages. It does not matter that this "is" the super-ego – the two internal elements serve the same function in the psyche. They both involve introjection or internalization & identification. This is not to say that the "large self" IS the super-ego, just that super-ego messages function to "orient" or "guide" one towards the larger self.

2) Unity: the experience of "flow" is the more developed sense of unity that we experience as a child & as an adult. This is the full experience of the iconic image of perception without the limitation or restriction of repression or reduction in the external world in order to create a proper relationship – that is, devoid of taboo.

3) The experience of "flow" is the opposite to the experience of "separation" – the idea that we are separate from nature & that "things" exist separately. Flow is the recognition that all things are joined & that boundary is essentially arbitrary.

4) The experience in meditation is not the same as the experience of daily living although the meditation (or creative) experience can be carried over into daily living so that we recognize that the creation of separate things is our own creation & that our small self is made in the light of these separations. Thus we recognize our likes & dislikes in the world as all our own – we are also the all – all of it – the good & the evil alike.

5) The recognition of both separation & flow is the beginning of the development of ethics. We must have "relationships" of one sort or another & cannot fully live in unity or flow – thus the character of these relationships must be modulated by our knowledge of unity & our full "participation" in all aspects of the world. This participation implies a responsibility for others & for the whole of the natural world.

6) To "sacrifice" our subject-object relationships & the ordinary self in contemplation or in creativity means that we give up our systematic repressions both inside ourselves & in the external world. By doing so we experience the imaginal flow of one thing into another & our own flowing energies enmeshed in the energy of the world.

7) Enlightenment in the context of mysticism is essentially the same as "art" in the context of creativity. They are not exactly the same thing for why should anything be exactly the same as any other thing – this is only to be accomplished by the arbitrary act of "identification" or "eating" of the other. There are so many similarities between the two, however, that they may be considered the same especially in their relationship to each other. Enlightenment is to mysticism as the creative art is to creativity or art. In both cases, "enlightenment" & "creative being" are not usually carried over whole into ordinary life. They certainly inform it & change ordinary life radically, but, on the whole, one does not exist either as enlightened or in a fully creative state.

8) The difference between enlightenment in mystical experience & art expression in the context of creativity is that enlightenment by & large seems to privilege a particular emotional state or perhaps two: calm equanimity & also love. Creativity, on the other hand, does not choose between any particular state but rather aims at the full engagement of the self in the world & the experience of flow. One may tend to emphasize this as a "passionate"

engagement but that probably simply engages with a stereotyped image of the artist creator. Creativity can occur in any field whatsoever, in mysticism as much as any other.

9) Mysticism & Art are two expressions of creativity. They both aim at the experience of "flow" & the perceptual control of the conventional aspect of knowledge or meaning. Both ultimately aim to "do" something in the world.

10) Art was born in the context of religion. Creativity was originally understood to be in the hands of God. With the humanist revolution, art & religion are understood to be two aspects of human creativity. Human creativity is only possible with full or direct contact between self & the "world." God has become the world.

11) One of the essential boundaries drawn in early religion was that between the sacred & the profane. This in effect re-arranged the flow of energies around these two categories. These two categories were arranged one above the other & were understood to be mutually influential. As above, so below.

12) The experience of "flow" is attained on the one hand by the "un-doing" of language & categorization & on the other by fully experiencing the power of thought. In this latter case, one comes to understand that thought has as great a power as things in the external world. The "wish" is on the same level as "the deed." I am actually not so sure about this last statement" both are "acts" for sure, but whether they are really on the same level I'm not sure. In this case, I feel that the heat of my furnace is not quite hot enough to burn away the dross leaving the pure essence of thought.

13) With reference to 12 above, what I think I wanted to say was the experience of flow was also the experience of the fullness of the symbolic world. The fullness of symbolic thought has "filled in" the emptiness that seems to exist around individual things, that is it "fills in" the silence of the unconscious. It fills in the fullness of contact between entities in the world, & this fullness gives us the experience of symbolic flow. Perhaps this is confusing – it is the fullness of perception expressing itself symbolically – accomplishing a successful raid on the inarticulate.

14) What is silence? It is initially the subtraction of the "noise" of the bad transmission occasioned by so much suppression in the creation of subject-object, and the split consciousness (conscious/unconscious). Beyond this, silence is exactly what John Cage said it was – the sound of whatever happens. Cage desired to go beyond the discrete "notes" & systems of conventional music & let in the fullness of the perceptual world. He understood this as "music."

15) Flow is experienced in meditation, in the creative moment, in a walk in the woods. Contact with the natural world is resting & closer to the experience of "flow" because by & large the natural world was "already there" before things got divided up & separated out. This is certainly true for me. One doesn't know the "names" of the millions of different objects before one, & therefore they don't appear as individual objects but rather as an interwoven matrix, i.e. "flow." On the other hand, the fabricated world is full of objects that were created precisely as objects; their boundary was always in place from the very beginning. In fact, these objects are part of the flow of the world, but it is harder to see them as such precisely because of their origins.

16) Love for the world & everything in it is engendered precisely because of our knowledge that its "appearance" (as separate "things") is our own creation – that our attitudes towards it – our intentionality – our likes & dislikes are created in the matrix of the egoic self. With this knowledge, we are able to move into the experience of flow (creative flow) & love flows

into us & out of us, through us. And love is nothing but that flow which we earlier saw in the images of parental coitus & mother/child. The experiential flow of energies joining two bodies in love. Love is the experience of unity, the 2 in 1. Flow. We rise up from the bed of love. We are born. We create the world. We re-create the world.

17) To re-create the world: we die to the world, re-experience flow, re-construct the relations in the "separate" world (our ethical/creativity). Our creations become the conventions of those who follow. They are dissatisfied, they die to the world.

18) The conjoining of history & the cyclic energy of eternity gives us the image of the spiral.

19) The ordinary world continues to look just like the ordinary world because separation & relationship are absolutely necessary for human life. The "look" of this ordinary world is exactly that – its look – its mask – its drama of separation & coming together. Beneath the ordinary world (& all of its splits including that between the conscious & the unconscious) is the experience of flow, of unity, of the world before we invented it. From this vantage one can see that the human will & human creativity is all "subtractive," always involving a carving away of the many fibers & atoms of connectivity in order to create separate things & their relationships. From this vantage point, our consciousness does intimately participate in the consciousness of all living things & perhaps all things are living – our "will" is gone & the winds of desire blow through us – the only energy in us is the energy of the it, the "id" – instinctual & uncontrolled. The ordinary world continues with its look, its "fashion," its mask, but having seen the "other world," the world of unity, in our creative contact & having known it to be utterly loving & utterly ruthless in its ceaseless flow, we participate in that ordinary world both as player & witness for there is not other place to go. That knowledge of the other world changes us & changes the complexion of the world forever.

20) Language is the model of our "separate" world. It is the very name of our creation, but it is also the matrix wherein we find our understanding of "flow." For there are two axes in the structural apprehension of language: one focused on separation and the other on flow, one focused on causal relations & historical sequence and the other focused on metaphoric substitutions & the experience of eternity. Guess what? You can't have one without the other. The world of metaphoric flow with little attention to sequential relationships quickly adds up to nothing much, as does an over attention to sequence & causal relations. In the first case, we have a constellation of metaphors in a sort of blur of superimposition. In the second case, we have the driest of scientific formulae.

21) Mysticism at least in its practical rather than theological elements is essentially magical – in the sense that it uses religious imagery to enhance the self. No matter the contortions of logic that mysticism must engage in order to deny its rootedness in the human situation, the mystic stands up after sitting & with whatever self he has at the time he engages with the world. As an individual, his self is enhanced even thought he renounces the small ego self for the larger God-self.

22) Interesting that those interested in mysticism for the most part don't like religion & vice versa. Religion is seen as super-ego & false spirituality, not connected with the magical or mystical element of reality.

A Hermeneutic Phenomenological Approach to Art Therapy

By Monica Carpendale (2007)

This paper discusses the key concepts of hermeneutic phenomenology in relationship to art therapy focusing particularly on providing a theoretical foundation for the training and supervision of art therapists. It is my proposal that a hermeneutic phenomenology can provide an excellent theoretical method and basis for art therapy.

There are a number of assumptions or basic propositions that I use. First of all, the underlying human development theory is primarily object relations and social constructivism. I hold the position that language and metaphor are the main means by which we are constructed. I consider the art products made in art therapy to be essentially metaphoric and to be considered as "language" and thus visual and plastic art functions as "text". In the context of Art Therapy, the interpretation of the artist's works (texts) takes place in the presence of the art therapist who functions as a witness and in dialogue between therapist, artist/client and art (text). Art Therapy can function to construct or reconstruct identity through the creative act.

To study consciousness one tries to reduce the perception of phenomena to its essence. Applying phenomenological attentiveness to the creative process of self-expression can lead to the possibility of self-discovery and insight into the essence. In a phenomenological approach to art therapy the specific phenomena of creating artwork can be studied consciously as an immediate experience as well as looking at the artwork.

In terms of phenomenological art therapy practice I draw from both Mala Betensky (1995) and Judith Siano[2] (2004). I have extended their work into the area of art therapy supervision. In the process I draw from hermeneutic theory and a number of phenomenologists, in particular Merleau-Ponty (1969) and Max van Manen (1990, 2002).

Hermeneutic phenomenology can be applied to all aspects of art therapy: the materials, creative process, the client artist, therapist and supervisory relationships. Hermeneutic phenomenology as a methodology is reflective of both terms. In being attentive to how things appear and wanting to let things speak for themselves, it is a descriptive phenomenology and it is an interpretive (hermeneutic) methodology in that all phenomena that presents itself as "lived experience" is already captured in language and already meaningful and therefore interpreted. The process of interpretation acts upon the text, which is the focus of interpretation and it may also acts upon the individual who is interpreting. Insight into the self may thus be revealed.

Hermeneutics is essentially the theory and practice of interpretation with the aim of understanding the writer or artist as well as or better than the individual understands him or

---

2   Judith Siano (2004) makes a distinction between "phenomenological art therapy" and 'art therapy using the phenomenological approach', as taught at the Haifa University in Israel. Peretz Hesse developed the Haifa method. It is a specific method for observation and analysis of the artwork This method teaches the art therapist's skills in phenomenological observation through an in-depth look at the characteristics of the language of art. Form, shape and colour, and composition are central elements in diagnosis and therapy. This method while considered within the field of phenomenology is not representative of the philosophical and psychological schools of theory under phenomenology.

herself. It was Schleiermacher (Messer, Sass, Woolfolk, 1988, p. 6) in his work on the interpretation of ancient texts that first stated that the typical methods did not lead to a deeper understanding of the structure of literature from prior periods. He felt that it was important to consider the socio-cultural context and any particular factor that might influence or affect the writer researcher in the exploration of meaning. The focus on understanding the original intentions of the author became the basis for valid textual interpretation (Woolfolk, Sass, Messer, 1988).

In art therapy interpretation is aimed at eliciting and exploring the meaning emerging for the artist / client. In art therapy supervision hermeneutics focuses on understanding not only the artist /client but also the supervisee / therapist. Max van Manen (1990) describes the hermeneutic emphasis for Dilthey as not being the fundamental thought of the other person but the world itself, the "lived experience," which is expressed by the author's text. Dilthey's hermeneutic formula is lived experience: the starting point and focus of human science; expression: the text or artifact as objectification of lived experience; and understanding: not a cognitive act but the moment when "life understands itself" (Van Manen, 1990, p. 180).

This emphasis on the importance of the "lived experience" as expressed by the individual's text or artifact is fundamental philosophically to the practice of art therapy. The focus on "life understanding itself" and the emergence of meaning for the individual in relationship to the world is a core component of art therapy. Creating art in a therapeutic context provides an immediate lived experience to be explored, which includes not only the thoughts of the artist / client but also their physical, sensory and emotional experience. Both the artwork and the creative process can be considered as a text for exploring meaning.

Heidegger's hermeneutics is considered an interpretive phenomenology. For Heidegger the focus of hermeneutic understanding is not simply to try and understand what the author of the text intended to communicate but he realized that the process of interpreting a text opened up the possibility of the interpreter being revealed by the text (Van Manen, 1990, p. 180). This is very much true in art therapy. The process of exploring the meaning in the artwork and the creative process opens up the possibility of insight and understanding to be both discovered and created in the dialogue between the artist/client and the art therapist. I am choosing to use the term artist/client to refer to the client in therapy because I want to emphasize that everyone that engages in the creative process is an artist and that the identity of the client can be dignified by the seriousness of personal expression of an artist. In fact in many of the successful outcomes of art therapy, clients emerge as artists in their own right. Art making and the creative process become a means of making meaning, of self-expression, of pleasure and a tool in self-understanding.

This possibility of being revealed by the text is both fearful and exciting. Artist clients come in to therapy to gain more self-understanding - with the desire to know and to be known. There is also the fear that if one is truly known that one will not be found to be acceptable. For many artist/clients there is the lurking fear that one will be found to be too bad or too messed up to be loved. It is equally important for the therapist (student/supervisee) to approach the therapeutic encounter and dialogue with the awareness that he or she may also be revealed. In fact, many of the concerns brought into supervision pertain to the therapist/supervisee being unaware of or reluctant to look at the meaning being revealed not only for the artist/client but also for themselves.

Gadamer's position regarding interpretation is that we can never separate ourselves from the meaning of a "text". It is my intention to include, not only writing in the term "text," but also the artwork, the physical body, life narrative's, human action, situation and all of lived experience (Ricouer, 1976, Van Manen, 1990). Applying this idea to art therapy one would say that the therapist is an integral part of the therapeutic experience and the very nature of the questions posed, responses reflected and meaning that emerges in the dialogue is as much a part of the art therapist as the artist/client. The art therapist's belief that meaning and essence will emerge and the seriousness of the endeavour contributes to the experience of artist/client.

The hermeneutic circle was first described by Schleiermacher (Messer, Sass, Woolfolk, 1988, p. 7) and applied to the process of interpretation. It refers to how in interpretation one cannot escape references to what is already known thus understanding will emerge in a circular manner moving from the relationship of parts to the whole and back to the parts. And all of these aspects are in relationship to the viewer/writer/researcher. This philosophic approach to interpretation has been applied to texts and to art. It does not mean that one can never understand a piece of art but it does mean that one can never completely understand a work of art or rather that there will always be the possibility of more meaning to be discovered. This articulation of the process of how understanding and meaning can emerge relates directly to my experience of the art therapy process. Understanding and interpreting a work of art in therapy is an ongoing process, which takes time. As the therapeutic relationship deepens and more insight and personal history emerges interpretation of the creative process and the artwork gradually evolves and changes.

Basically, the hermeneutic circle is a term to describe the manner in which, understanding emerges and refers to the contextual nature of knowledge. Even within considering the meaning of a sentence each of the words have individual meanings but those meanings will only clearly emerge in relationship to the other words. Thus the parts must be seen in relation to the whole and the context of the whole gives meaning to the parts. The same is true with looking at artwork and with looking at the narrative of an individual's life. Thus this awareness of the relativity of meaning and the process in which meaning will emerge is integral to the development of an art therapist.

This circular pattern of interpretation is also referred to as a "hermeneutic spiral" because it moves from the parts to the whole and from the whole to the parts forever. The circular exploration in art therapy pertains to not only looking at the text or artwork in this manner but it also explores the relationships. In art therapy these relationships are between the client and the artwork, the client and the therapist, the therapist and the artwork. One only slowly approaches the truth of the situation and the truth will change as the contexts change.

The principles of phenomenological hermeneutics (Lye, 1996) can provide an interpretive framework to examine the concrete nature of the art materials, the creative process and include psychological and clinical theory. A phenomenological exploration of meaning is always tentative always incomplete - never would a human lived experience be "presumed to be universal or shared by all humans irrespective of time, culture, gender, or other circumstance" (van Manen, 2002). This attitude of the phenomenologist is important for an art therapist. It is important to stay open to new meanings being revealed to never impose an interpretation as fact but to use interpretation to shed light and provide the possibility of understanding and the development of new meanings.

As previously stated I consider in art therapy the artwork to be considered as a text, and as such it can "speak" to us. In using the vocative method in phenomenology when we approach the artwork as 'text' we need to be open to both address and to be addressed by the art. Max Van Manen (2002) explains that the aim of the vocatio is to let things "speak" or be "heard" by bringing them into nearness through the vocative power of language. "The vocatio has to do with the recognition that a text can "speak" to us, that we may know ourselves addressed by it."

There is a tendency when we speak to the artwork or about the artwork to stop listening to the object or artwork of which we speak. The artwork can only speak if we listen to it and are open to being addressed by it. This means that we will not already know what it will give voice to. This is a very significant component of the phenomenologist's attitude that needs to be brought into the art therapy session and into art therapy supervision. The artist/client may be speaking about the artwork and the meaning they have attributed to it with a long narrative but may become more anxious to be asked to look at the art to see what is there. Likewise the therapist/supervisee may come into supervision with the intent of telling the supervisor what happened in the session as if it were fact and not their own interpretation of the session. Looking at the art in supervision or creating art in supervision will often serve to bring the artist/client into more current awareness.

The voking act provides the possibility to "know one's self", not in the narrow sense of narcissistic self- examination but in the sense of discovering existential possibilities, what it is to be human, what lies at the heart of our being and personal identity. The "call" signifies that we need the other, through whom and with whom we seek understanding" (Van Manen, 2002). This need for others to reflect our sense of self is a key component in the therapeutic relationship. We have an implicit, felt or "pathic" understanding of ourselves in situations even though it is difficult to put that understanding into words (Van Manen, 2002).

Art and perception are integrally linked. Creating art is a direct experience. Looking at art and becoming conscious of it is another direct experience (Betensky, 1995). The art therapist needs to suspend a priori judgments about what should or should not be seen. They need to look with openness and to look with intention – to see to perceive. Betensky (1995) quotes Kant "Inner perception is impossible without outer perception." Through the process of looking at the created artwork in art therapy the artist/client learns to see all that can be seen. The structure, dynamics and meaning in the artwork can be explored through first of all a description in detail of the artwork and then connecting the metaphors to their inner experience and associations (Betensky, 1995).

As an object of study, the therapeutic modality of Art Therapy actually has the advantage of offering an intense lived experience - the creative process - and the possibility of reflecting upon this intense lived experience through entering into a dialogue with the artist/client regarding the artwork created. The creative process in Art therapy can take an individual through sensory and kinesthetic expression to perceptual and affective awareness on to cognitive and symbolic meaning (Lusebrink, 1990).

The Phenomenological Method

The phenomenological method fosters an attentive sense of wonder in the world and hermeneutic practice continually aims at open-ended interpretation, the recognition of bias, and the relating of part to whole and whole to part.

Phenomenology focuses on the study of essences: one is always looking for the essential nature or meaning of the phenomena. In philosophy it is used to focus on the individual's conscious, perceptual and intellectual processes, excluding preconceptions and the idea of external consequences (Gregory, 1987). Phenomenology is a philosophical method aimed at getting at the truth - it aims to achieve clarity of insight and thought while including the subject. It makes a distinction between appearance and essence. It is a very appropriate philosophical method to apply to the theory and practice of art therapy. (Carpendale, 2003) Merleau-Ponty, the French philosopher, writes that philosophy is "not the reflection of a pre-existing truth, but, like art, the act of bringing truth into being." (Merleau-Ponty, 1969)

Betensky (1995) wrote "phenomenology offers an answer to a long needed unbiased approach to art therapy in all its spheres: theory, training, and professional practice." She articulates the importance of *'seeing'* and suggests that this is art therapy's most important contribution to general therapy and even to phenomenology itself, because art therapy pays attention to the authentic experience in two ways. First of all there is the direct experience of creating art and second of all there is the direct experience of looking at the art. The second direct experience requires some help to learn how to look in order to see all that can be seen in their art expression (Betensky, 1995).

Merleau-Ponty (1969) wrote "to look at an object is to inhabit it and from this habitation to grasp all things." He continues:

> The world is not problematical. The problem lies in our own inability to see what is there. The attitude of the phenomenologist, therefore, is not the attitude of the technician, with a bag of tools and methods, anxious to repair a poorly operating machine. Nor is it the attitude of the social planner, who has at his control the methods for straightening out the problems of social existence. Rather it is an attitude of wonder, of quiet inquisitive respect as one attempts to meet the world, to open a dialogue, to put him in a position where the world will disclose itself to him in all its mystery and complexity (p.12).

Part of the art therapy experience is reflecting on the 'lived-throughness'. Lived-throughness is brought into the art therapy session by both creating art and bringing the narrative of past experience into the present. The lived-throughness of the creative process, which may through speaking of it produce a 'text', and the lived-throughness of the subject matter or content of the artwork, which may pertain to past experience and feelings, which are present in the individual.

In therapy one has to stay aware of oneself as the therapist – that one exists and is perceiving the subject and that any analysis needs to include the first sensations and aspects of the object/subject from different perspectives (we need to figuratively walk around and get a good look to get a good description. Merleau-Ponty tells us that, "the real has to be described, not constructed or formed" (1969, p. 17).

Phenomenological art therapy as explicated by Betensky (1995) is a clearly formulated art therapy approach that attempts to understand the phenomena of the artwork and the creative process from within itself through "intentional observation" and reflection.

The three main features of the phenomenological method are 1) the attention to the description of the perceived phenomena; 2) focus on capturing the essence; and 3) the essence is found by intuiting and not by deduction or induction. The 5 key concepts of phenomenology concepts outlined by Merleau–Ponty in the introduction of Phenomenology of Religion (Bettis 1969) can be applied to art therapy (Carpendale, 2002). These concepts are: description, reduction, essence, intentionality and world.

Before I relate these concepts to art therapy I would like to speak briefly to the nature of this method. First of all, it is not a sequential process and does not have to follow a specific method - these 5 conceptual elements do not need to appear in any particular sequence, nor do they appear one at a time. Rather, they can overlap and interpenetrate one another much like a weaving. I tend to view these concepts in terms of a figure/ground relationship – thus when we bring one element into focus, it always appears against or as the ground of all the others. Thus when we speak of one, such as intentionality, we are also speaking of the other 4 elements in context. These aspects can be related directly to art therapy and art therapy supervision.

Description

Phenomena are studied as they present themselves in consciousness as immediate experience. In the context of art therapy the artwork is to be considered a phenomena with its own structure, dynamics and meaning. The creating of the artwork is also a phenomena and the dialogue about the art either during or subsequent to the creating is also a phenomena. The artist/client, the art studio environment, other group members if in a group, and the art therapist are all each individually a phenomena and the whole experience is a phenomena. In this step we are looking for a pure description, not analytical reflection and not scientific explanation, and not tracing back to inner dynamics. The description will include the concrete and tangible but it is important to remember that all language is metaphorical in nature and that it is through metaphor that we come to understand the unknown by relating it to what is known. Focusing on the description can be of great value because sometimes the intent to explain loses the essence of the experience. If you really look and describe what you see you will already be 'bracketing out' your assumptions.

Through the process of looking at the artwork and describing it the individual artist/client learns over time to see a great deal more than they saw when involved in the creative process. The artist/client's verbal description is an essential part of the process. The process of a detailed description reveals metaphors that enable the artist/client to connect to an inner experience. The intention in this process is to make a verbal translation of an inner experience through a description of the visual and not to explain, analyze or be seduced into a narrative. As an interpretive process and dialogue it is a return to the image, the creative process and the concrete nature of the artwork. The intent with this step is to look in order to see what is there. The therapeutic process is about learning to look and to perceive. We can find the actual detailed world here and thus ultimately the essence.

In supervision what is called for is a clear description of the client, the therapist, and the artwork and creative process. I repeat myself in stating that this is not an explanation. Explanations and the scientific method move past the immediate experiential data to models or laws of nature, which then control the data. While the scientific method and explanations are useful they can lose sight of the original data if one gets too involved in explaining. Data, which can't be quantified, is dismissed as subjective. The personal meaning of an event may be different than the scientific meaning of an event. In the description one wants to get away from assumptions and interpretations.

Reduction (or bracketing out assumptions)

The significance of the reduction (bracketing) is the idea that we are looking to re-achieve a direct contact with the world as we experience it rather than how we conceptualize it. The intent of the phenomenological method is to come to understand the essential nature or structure of something and in order to do so we need to reflect on it and bracket out our assumptions. Reduction is more a way of being than an act itself. It is the bringing in of a thoughtful attentiveness. The art therapist can benefit from the phenomenologist's attitude of curiousity, open-mindedness, wonder and attentiveness. Max van Manen (2002) writes that

> The aim of the reductio (the reduction or epoche[3]) is to re-achieve direct contact with the world by suspending prejudgments, bracketing assumptions, deconstructing claims and restoring openness.

---

3   Epoche refers to the "bracketing" of attitude in order to see.

This concept has a variety of forms but the idea is simple. Therapeutically the first thing that one needs to bracket out is that there is a problem or at least a specifically defined problem. We want to put it aside for a moment and look to see exactly or hopefully more clearly what is happening. This involves bracketing out our assumptions, interpretations, transferences, counter-transferences, goals, and biases to enable us to distill the essence. In fact, in some sense one is 'bracketing out' the whole question of existence in order to devote attention to the question of meaning.

In order to bracket out the assumptions it is important to consider what they are. Assumptions are the often things that have been told the art therapist about the client - this could include the diagnosis, the therapist's therapeutic approach, and the client, parents' and/or professionals' interpretation of the problem and the client's own assumptions about his or her state of being. The process of the reduction may reveal health in other areas.

The process of bracketing assumptions can be helped by writing them down because if one doesn't go through a process of naming one's prejudices, biases, conceits, demons, pitfalls, interpretations, beliefs, values, therapeutic goals, work pressures, they likely will inhabit the therapeutic space or rather lurk around on the edges. This can happen especially when we experience difficulties or are concerned about how to proceed therapeutically. In fact, it may or may not be the therapist that is stuck.

There are several levels of the reduction that have been outlined by Van Manen (2002). The first one is to return to a sense of wonder regarding the object of interest and to bracket the attitude of taken-for-grantedness. He has described the state of wonder as that moment "when something familiar has turned profoundly unfamiliar, when our gaze has been captured by the gaze of something staring back at us" (Van Manen, 2002). The physicality and sheer presence of an artwork can aid in the possibility of this kind of discovery. It provides an objective other that is also a part of the self because the self has created it.

The reduction is about putting aside one's subjective feelings, prejudices and expectations. It is also about putting aside the clinical, psychodynamic or developmental theory that might come to mind. The intent of the reduction is to see with fresh eyes the actual lived experience of the artist/ client that is not already defined and circumscribed by issues and themes. The eidetic reduction is about not being seduced by the intensity of vivid mental images in the artwork or narrative and being able to focus attention on the essence of lived meaning. The eidetic technique of "variation in imagination" refers to a process of comparing the phenomenon in question with other related but different phenomenon. What makes this experience - this piece of art, this client, this situation or supervisee - unique and different from other lived experiences? This is where one is considering the relationship between the individual lived experience and the universal - iconic - essence - that does not pertain to the immediacy of the lived experience. This does not refer to a generalization of human nature or view of the collective unconscious. One is looking for an experience of meaningfulness.

The philosophical ideas behind the reduction are kindred to the concepts underlying the teaching of therapeutic presence in art therapy. The reduction is not the end of the method it is very much just part of the process of opening up to wonder and to an open ended attitude of curiousity in the mystery of existence.

Van Manen (2002) identifies the hermeneutic reduction as the aspect where we need to bracket all interpretation and attend to an attitude of openness. In order to seek openness one needs to reflect on the assumptions, theoretical frameworks and biases that colour the viewpoint. Part of this process is to become aware of the subjective feelings and pre-understandings that prevent us from having a "radical openness to the phenomenon." (Van Manen, 2002)

It is not possible to completely bracket out all the previous information and understanding so that what may be more important in this step in order to reach a critical self awareness is to express or give voice to these assumptions and concepts. In this process one is examining all of the aspects that cloud or restrict the reflective gaze. It is not that one is trying for the illusion of a pure perspective but that exploration of lived experience is considered with various layers of meaning. The phenomenological reduction focuses on bracketing out concreteness, knowledge, abstraction, theorizing, generalization or all of what we would call 'real' or 'not real', in order for the living meaning to be revealed (Van Manen, 2002). The methodological reduction is the bracketing of one's particular approach, including all the usual "methods or techniques and seek or invent an approach that seems to fit most appropriately the... topic under study" (Van Manen, 2002).

Essence

The term "essence" is derived from the Latin essentia, or esse, which means, "to be" and from the Greek *ousia,* which means the true being of a thing - referring to the inner essential nature of a thing. Essence is the core of the phenomena - that makes it what it is. Husserl referred to essence as the "whatness" of things, rather than the "thatness" of things. The whatness pertains to the essential being or nature whereas the thatness refers to existence itself.

"To seek the essence of perception is to declare that perception is not presumed true, but defined as access to truth" (Merleau-Ponty, 1969, p. 24.). We have perceptual experiences of the real as well as the imaginary. The world is already there before reflection begins. "Looking for the world's essence is not looking for what it is as an idea once it has been reduced to a theme of discourse; it is looking for what it is as a fact for us, before any thematization." (Merleau-Ponty, 1969, p. 24.)

Art can be viewed as holding or mirroring the essence of the art therapy session and it survives the session as a material object. Images hold the possibility of simultaneity, which is impossible in discursive or verbal communication. Looking at the art involves intentionality: looking to discover meaning to discover the essence. To learn from experience one must first have an experience and then become aware of it and then think reflectively about it. It is not the cause or factual truth of the matter that one is looking for but rather the exploration of meaning and an understanding of the essence.

In the phenomenological method there is a focus on distilling the essence. This will include exploring the meaning of the artwork, the creative process and the being of the client. What is the core of the problem? What is in the art? What is the essence of the individual? In art therapy supervision there is the continued process of questioning the art in order to discover meaning. The intention of supervision is to seek the essence of the therapeutic experience.

Intentionality

The intentionality - the motivation for therapy generally focuses on the discovery or creation of meaning in life for the individual. The term "intentionality" refers to the interconnectedness of human beings to the world. It is a term rooted in medieval philosophy as being that aspect that distinguishes mental or psychical existence from physical existence (Bettis, 1969). All consciousness is intentional in nature and in fact all thinking, which includes perceiving, imagining, and remembering, is always thinking about something. The same is true for actions, which are all intentional in that we listen to something or hold something or point at something. It is only with reflection that we are aware of intentionality because in an ordinary state of mind we experience the world as already made, already there. "All human activity is always oriented activity, directed by that which orients it." (Van Manen, 1990, p. 182)

All mental activity is directed towards an object – you can't think without thinking about something. Feeling is not pure – it is always directed or about something. A phenomenologist looks in order to see - to see with intentionality. Intentionality suggests that there has already been a "bracketing" of previous judgments or acquired ideas. When one is intent on what one is looking at; the object of attention begins to exist more than before; it becomes important, it starts to mean something. There is an intentionality of emotion in relation to the object and a new aspect emerges, which is Meaning.

The intention is not specifically to problem solve but to gain a deeper understanding, a glimpse at truth or the essential meaning of an experience. As we become more conscious as a therapist we will perceive the essence of the therapeutic relationship and be able to respond intentionally and not unconsciously.

It is important to remember that the creative process is different than the reflective or interpretive process, because as soon as you start reflecting or analyzing while creating the creative process is circumvented. Experiencing and reflecting are two separate activities and that we cannot experience something while we are reflecting on it. As soon as we start to analyze a feeling or experience we are no longer immersed in the experience of it. This occurs as one starts to look at the artwork in order to see what is to be seen. For this reason it is important not to ask questions regarding the artwork or creative process while the individual artist client is engaged in the work itself. This is because the questions and reflections will change the nature of the creative process itself. Now as soon as I state something like that with some degree of authority I am reminded of times when this is not true or appropriate in a therapeutic process. In fact, there are times with children or adolescents when they might be involved in some intense chaotic discharge and the approach of the "third hand" (Kramer, 2002) could bring the process into a formed expression, which would be more ego-syntonic and lead to a more grounded and positive self-awareness.

World

We create the world and we exist in the world. "The world is not something that exists prior to reflection. Prior to reflection there is lived existence, but this is an immediate and non-reflective spontaneity" (Merleau-Ponty, 1969, p. 11). The human subject is being in the world; being with others. The client can't be described or viewed in isolation. The artist/client is in the world – they have fellow group members, family, school, work, peers, therapist, and others. His or her social interests and interactions are in the external environment. This could also reflect the student/ supervisee's role in the world. There is an interesting paradox - we are always in context with others and we always have intentionality that pertains to someone or thing. Being in the world or context would include the artist client's personal history, significant life events: illness, social/ family changes, losses, trauma, family structure (family of origin & present family), culture, and developmental stages. What are all the related factors? Listen for the gaps in the narrative. It would also include the supervisee's context and being-in-the-world. Are there transference or counter transference dynamics?

From an existential perspective although we are always in relation to others, there is also the dilemma that we are essentially alone and that we die alone.

Conclusion

There is a dilemma in the art therapy world regarding the idea of symbolic interpretation of the art. There are those that are adamant that it is only the artist client that can interpret and there are those who will make assessments and interpretations of the symbolic content, style and process. Many art therapists and art therapy students are taught to be extremely careful not to impose interpretation on their clients. An underlying premise is that it is important for the client to interpret his or her own art. There is no doubt as to the value of the client's own insight and discovery of the significance of their artwork. In reality we all are interpreting life, people, and art, all the time. We may not be that aware of it. Therefore it is important in training to become cognizant of our interpretive assumptions.

How can the hermeneutic phenomenological method shed some light on this dichotomy? Interpretation needs not to be considered as a dirty word. Does the anxiety regarding the possibility of interpretation pertain to the anxiety of being revealed and the thought to be 'dirty' aspects of the self will be revealed. Anthropologically dirt can be thought of as matter out of place. Perhaps it would be appropriate to consider the social construction of metaphors of clean and dirty or light and darkness.

But how does insight and interpretation come to light? Insight can occur as the artist/client is involved in creating the art and when he or she enters into a dialogue with the therapist about their art. Art therapists have conscious or unconscious interpretive frameworks, which give direction to their questions, frame their clinical responses and set a tone for their reflections regarding the artwork. The problem is, how to teach openness towards interpretation while communicating the need for restraint concerning certainty.

The hermeneutic phenomenological method applied to art therapy considers both the art and art making as text and the writing as text. It holds that meaning will continually emerge and that there will always be the possibility of new meanings. It is the attitude of the phenomenologist that we are trying to achieve in the training of art therapists. The ability to perceive and describe with openness and wonder, the ability to describe without explaining, judging or making assumptions, the ability to look with intention and to consider everything in context and relationship, and to intuitively distill the essence are all important therapeutic qualities. For an art therapist this method can be used in the therapeutic session, in the process of reflecting on the session through writing and art making and in supervision.

Max Van Manen (1990) writes that

> To do hermeneutic phenomenology is to attempt to accomplish the impossible: to construct a full interpretive description of some aspect of the life-world, and yet to remain aware that lived life is always more complex than any explication of meaning can reveal. (p. 18)

Phenomenology has been a philosophical method that has used writing as its mode of inquiry. I would suggest that art therapy provides an opportunity to use not only writing but to also include engaging with the art and the creative process as text. To write is to draw us in through words. Writing in a phenomenological inquiry is based on the idea that no text is ever perfect, no interpretation is ever complete, no explication of meaning is ever final, and no insight is beyond challenge. (Van Manen, 1990)

References

Betensky, Mala Gitlin. (1995). *What do You See? Phenomenology of Therapeutic Art Expression.* London: Jessica Kingsley Publishers.

Bettis, J. Ed. (1969) An Introduction to Phenomenology: Merleau-Ponty, Maurice. *Phenomenology of Religion.* SCM Press Ltd. London. P.5-12.

Carpendale, Monica. (2002) Getting to the Underbelly: Phenomenology and Art Therapy. CATA Journal, Winter, Vol 15 #2.

Merleau-Ponty, (1969) Maurice. An Introduction to Phenomenology. What is Phenomenology? Bettis, Joseph, Dabney. Ed. *Phenomenology of Religion.* SCM Press Ltd.

Merleau-Ponty, M. (1962) Phenomenology of Perception, Routledge & Kegan Paul, NJ, p. 68. Cited in Betensky, M. (1995) *What do You See? Phenomenology of Therapeutic Art Expression.* Jessica Kingsley Publishers. London. P. 6.

Siano, Judith. (2004) An Introduction to Art Therapy: the Haifa University approach for phenomenological observation. My personal doctrine. (Spiral bound paper)

Van Manen, Max. (2002) www.phenomenologyonline.com

Van Manen, Max. (1990) Researching Lived Experience. The Althouse Press. University of Western Ontario, London, Ontario.

Writing in a reflective phenomenological method. (Carpendale)

This activity can be done in a number of ways. You can start with a word. In the beginning you must pay attention through all of your senses. The senses include visual perception, auditory perception, scent, taste, touch and internal proprioceptive sensations. It is important in paying attention to not reach for the first information but to allow one's sight and mind to be relaxed and achieve a diffuse gaze.

Writing as a reflective practice is not about thinking a specific thought and then writing down what your insight is. It is about writing as a process of discovery, as a way of perceiving as an active practice. The intention is to practice free writing in the way that one would free associate to an image, idea, sensation, or feeling. Let the words flow, and flow is a key word. Let all the words and thoughts come onto paper - remember that the creative process is about discovering what is and then allowing meaning to emerge through an interpretative practice.

In writing, just start with a description. Don't edit; write whatever comes to mind. If your mind wanders go with it and discover other places. When you are not sure what to write come back to the word and write it again repeating it until another image or thought comes to mind. Be aware of shifting from what may be in the foreground of your mind to background. How are things connected? How are they separate? What are you taking for granted? Write your assumptions that should be bracketed out. What are the clichés and metaphors that come to mind? What are the negative or shadow aspects that are lurking around? Let your mind roam free and write whatever occurs to you, including: memories, word play, associations, metaphors, parables and stories.

After writing, take some time to read what you have written. Underline in colour key phrases, insights, and aspects that seem of value. Think of this as looking for the horizon or gap where light can get through. What is the essence of what you have written? Reflect and distill the essence. Write a poem. Let a word or small poem – a haiku - emerge.

After the observations and paying attention, the writing, reflecting, and distilling the essence, it is important to be witnessed. The words or poems should be read aloud. The intention is to find a voice, an authentic voice. This can be one's own voice or can be another's voice created by placing yourself in another's shoes – another person, a plant, an animal or an object. The intention is to speak from a specific place and to empathize by giving an "I" voice.

Words: focus on household items, animals, plant parts, gardening, house cleaning, etc.

Getting to the Underbelly (Carpendale, 2002)

This art therapy supervision exercise combines art making and writing with the five central concepts of the phenomenological method. It is a deeply contemplative philosophical method in which one allows oneself to perceive the many levels of meaning implicit in the description of reality so that one can distill the essence. The phenomenological method is used to investigate the full subjective experiencing of things in the world as they present themselves in consciousness as immediate experiences.

The Exercise

This exercise can be used to explore any therapeutic issue or clinical concern, any aspect of transference or counter transference. It involves the creation of art in response to the specific concern. This can be done as post-session art or during supervision. The intention is to provide a framework to "unravel knots" and gain a better understanding.

The method is contemplative and meant to illuminate essence, not to establish scientific fact or causality. The steps in the process, as given, are not meant to be a recipe wherein the steps must follow each other in a specific order. Rather, the key concepts are intended to function as reflective foci from which one can move forward and backward using each to throw light on the others. For example, while reflecting upon Intentionality one may become aware of Assumptions that crowd the mind and distract one like the sounds of crows cracking walnuts on the tin roof outside one's bedroom window. While reflecting upon these assumptions, one may become of aware of the overall context of the situation and from this awareness grow an intuition of essence.

Suggested Art Materials: drawing paper, oil pastels, pencils and/or felt pens.

In general, the process involves the making of five pieces of art. However, it could also be approached by creating one piece of art and then writing about it from the perspective of five key concepts. The purpose is to explore, as fully as possible, the supervision question through the lens of each step of the phenomenological method.

After making each piece of art, sit back and have a look. Get some distance and reflect. Write about it. Aim at an accurate description of what you see in the art. You may want to underline key phrases and note associations. You may want to write a poem (especially concerning your work on essence). Remember that essence will be discovered by intuition. Move back and forth between the images you did for each concept. Allow your intuition to connect personal meanings with objective factors. Intuition will integrate the whole process.

The exercise is broken down into five separate components below:

281

Description: The first piece of art created is an image of the situation. What is called for here is a clear depiction of the client, the therapist, and the art - not an explanation or interpretation. It is a return to the things themselves. This might be done in a number of different ways: a realistic narrative depiction, an abstract depiction of feelings, or symbolically as a metaphor or series of metaphors. Just as in creating art in therapy, there isn't a right or wrong way to do it.

Put the art up and have a look at it – perhaps step back and get some distance. The focus is on the actual artwork. The intent with this step is to look in order to see what is there. Observe the structure of each image, the figure ground relationships, the interrelated components, the dynamics, symbolism and style of expression.

Write a description of what you see. In this step we are looking for a pure description, not analytical reflection, scientific explanation, or any tracing back to inner psychological dynamics. If you really look and describe what you see you will already be 'bracketing out' your assumptions. With a premature focus on explanation we can lose the essence of the experience.

Reduction: This step is about looking at and setting aside one's assumptions. Such assumptions might include information about the client from the referral source (and the parent if the client is a child), the diagnosis, theoretical principles that seem applicable, different professionals' interpretations of the problem as well as the client's own assumptions. These assumptions could also include the therapist's transferences and counter transferences. Here one 'brackets out' the question of the existence of the problem behaviour in order to devote attention to the question of underlying meaning.

Make a piece of art about your assumptions. Or write them down. You are trying to put down what you think you know or what other people have communicated to you. The purpose is to record all of these biases and assumptions so that you can set them aside and be able to look at the situation afresh. You might like to try free writing - writing continuously without picking up your pencil and without editing for a brief period.

If one doesn't go through a process of naming one's prejudices, biases, conceits, interpretations, beliefs and therapeutic goals, they tend to lurk around the therapeutic space causing disturbances. These assumptions may become more evident when we are unsure how to proceed therapeutically. In fact, it may not be the client who is stuck but ourselves because we are stuck on an interpretation or particular viewpoint.

Intentionality: All mental activity is directed towards an object – one can't think without thinking *about* something. All feeling or desire is directed towards something. This basic continuity between subject and object is an underlying characteristic of phenomenology. When one is intent on what one is looking at, the object of attention begins to exist more than before. It becomes important. It takes on meaning to explore. The intention here is to explore the existential meaning of life for the individual.

Make a piece of art focused on the concept of Intentionality. Explore the motivation and desire of the client and therapist. Explore the meaning of symbols, events, client's artwork etc. The intentions of the client will be in direct relation to their biases and assumptions. On the other hand, the therapist's intention might be important here. More biases and assumptions may come to the fore and then one may wish to return to the second piece of art. Reflect on the art and write about it. Describe what you see and include any and all associations.

Essence: Reflect on the essence of the situation. Create another piece of art that expresses the essential feeling or what you see as the essential elements of the situation. Remember that the essence is discovered by intuiting - not by deducting. The conception of essence will be distilled from the description and aided by setting aside your assumptions. Poetry is often useful at this stage. If you are stuck at this step go on to the next step and come back to it when you look at all of the images together.

World: The human subject is in the world with others. Everyone's social interests and interactions in the external environment impinge upon one. We are aware of the existential dilemma that while we are always in relation to others, we are essentially alone, and we all die alone.

On a new sheet of paper draw or map out all the relevant relationships and place the situation in context. The client does not exist in isolation. This contextual element of the exercise pertains to the contemplation of the personal history, culture, family of origin, significant life events, illness, losses and developmental stages of the client. This step also takes into account cross-cultural and ethical considerations. The client is in the world with fellow group members, family, peers, and so on. The exploration of this domain may also pertain to the therapist's own role in the world. While this step might involve creating a genogram or sociogram it can also be expressed in a more symbolic and creative manner.

Conclusion: There are a number of ways to work with this model, other than the one given above. One single piece of art might be created and then the five concepts explored through writing. Yet another way to approach this exercise would be to focus on the writing first, underline the key phrases, (sometimes called horizons) and then move to explore the essence in the art. The key phrases that one underlines are those that grab your attention - those statements that feel like they hold the potential of light or insight or alternately point to darkness and shadow. One is aiming to underscore the indications of a gap, a space, a silence, a shout, a place or phrase that moves and refers to different levels.

One might also add a final step by creating a sixth piece of art as *reflective synthesis* (Kidd & Kidd, 1990) of the five original pieces. A further level of insight and integration might be achieved by putting all of this art up together and exploring it in dialogue with an art therapy supervisor, fellow supervisee or colleague.

References and Bibliography

This bibliography and reference list has been constructed posthumously from Blake's personal library, his known sources, influences and books he collected. They are not necessarily all relevant for this series of essays but they constitute the scope of his personal research. However, it is by no means complete, but it is the best that I can give you at this time. M. Carpendale, 2014.

Armstrong, Karen. (2004) The Spiral Staircase. New York: Alfred A Knopf.

Alford, Fred, C. (1989) Melanie Klein & Critical Social Theory: An Account of Politics, Art, and Reason Based on Her Psychoanalytic Theory. New Haven and London: Yale University Press.

Barthes, Roland. (1974) S/Z. New York: Hill and Wang.

Barthes, Roland. (1985) The Responsibility of Forms. New York: Hill and Wang pub.

Bataille, Georges. (1954, 1988) Inner Experience. Translated by Leslie Anne Boldt. New York: State University of New York Press.

Bataille, Georges. (1973) Literature and Evil. London: Marion Boyars Pub.

Bataille, Georges. (1967, 1988) The Accursed Share Vol 1. Translated by Robert Hurley. New York: Zone Books.

Bataille, Georges. (1989) The Tears of Eros. San Francisco: City Lights Books.

Bateson, Gregory. (1979) Mind and Nature: a necessary unity. Toronto: Bantam books.

Becker, Ernest.(1973) The Denial of Death. New York: The Free Press, Macmillan Pub.

Benedict, Ruth. (1934) Patterns of Culture. Boston: Houghton Mifflin Company.

Benjamin, Walter. (1986) Reflections. New York: Schocken books.

Bennett, Colin. (2002) Politics of the Imagination: the life, work and ideas of Charles Fort. Manchester, UK: A Critical Vision Book, Headpress.

Berger, Peter L. & Luckman, Thomas. (1966) Social Construction of Reality. New York: Doubleday & Company, Inc.

Berman, Morris. (1981) The Re-enchantment of the World. Ithaca, New York: Cornell University Press.

Bersani, Leo. (1986) the Freudian Body: psychoanalysis and art. New York: Columbia University Press.

Bettis, Joseph. Ed. (1969) Phenomenology of Religion. London: SCM Press

Bourgeault Cowley, Cynthia. (2004) Centering Prayer and Inner Awakening. Cambridge, Massachusetts.

Brenner, Charles. (1974) An Elementary Textbook of Psychoanalysis. New York; Anchor Books.

Brown, Norman O. (1959) Life Against Death: the psychoanalytical meaning of history. New York: Random House.

Brown, Norman O. (1966) Love's Body. NewYork: Vintage Books.

Burke, Kenneth. (1989) On Symbols and Society. Chicago: the University of Chicago Press.

Burroughs, William. (1981) Cities of the Red Night. New York: Henry Holt & company, Inc.

Clifford, Geertz. (1973) The Interpretation of Cultures. New York: Basic Books, Inc. Pub.

Clifford, James. (1988) The Predicament of Culture: twentieth-century ethnography, literature and art. Cambridge, Massachusetts: Harvard University Press.

Craib, Ian. (1990) Psychoanalysis and Social Theory. Amherst: University of Massachusetts Press.

Damasio, Antonio R. (1994) Descartes' Error: Emotion, Reason, and the Human Brain. N.Y.: Avon Books.

Davenport, Guy. (1981) The Geography of the Imagination. San Francisco: North point Press.

Derrida, Jacques. (1981) Dissemination. Chicago: University of Chicago Press.

Derrida, Jacques. (1982) Margins of Philosophy. Translated Alan Bass. Chicago: University of Chicago Press.

Derrida, Jacques. (1996, 1998) Resistances of Psychoanalysis. Translated by Peggy Kamuf, Pascale-Anne Brault, & Michael Naas. Stanford, CA: Stanford University Press.

Douglas, Mary. (1966) Purity and Danger: an analysis of the concepts of pollution and taboo. New York: Ark Paperbacks.

Douglas, Mary. (1982) Natural Symbols: Explorations in Cosmology. N.Y.: Pantheon Books.

Durkheim, Emile. (1938) The Rules of the Sociological Method. New York: The Free Press.

Edinger, Edward F. (1984) the Creation of consciousness: Jung's Myth for modern Man. Toronto: Inner City Books.

Fiske, John. (1982) Introduction to Communication Studies. New York: Methuen.

Foucault, Michel. (1973) The Order of things: an archaeology of the human sciences. New York: Vintage books, Random House.

Foucault, Michel. (1979) Discipline and Punish: the birth of the prison. New York: Vintage books, Random House.

Foucault, Michel. (1984) The Care of the Self: the history of sexuality, vol.3. New York: Vintage books, Random House.

Frank, Arthur. (2004) Renewal of Generosity: illness, medicine and how to live. Chicago: University of Chicago Press.

Giddens, Anthony. (1982) Sociology: a brief but critical introduction. New York: Harcourt Brace Jovanovich, Publishers.

Goodman, Nelson. (1955) Fact, Fiction and Forecast. New York: The Bobbs-Merrill Company, Inc.

Hammond, Sandra. (2002) Knowing the Spontaneity of Experience: The Fourth foundation of Mindfulness

Heppner, Maxine. Editor (2008) Across oceans: writings on collaboration.

Holcombe, John. Web download (LitLangs 2004, 2005, 2006)

Happold, F.C. (1964) Mysticism: A study and an Anthology. Pelican Pub.

Harrison, Michael. (1973) The Roots of Witchcraft. London: Tandem Publishing, Ltd.

Hodge, Robert, & Kress, Gunther. (1988) Social Semiotics. Ithaca, New York: Cornell University Press.

Hyde, Lewis. (1998) Trickster makes this world: mischief, myth and art. New York: North Point Press.

James, William. (1948) Essays in Pragmatism. New York: Hafner Publishing Co.

James, William. (1958) The Varieties of Religious Experience. New York: Penguin books.

Jaynes, Julian. (1976) The Origin of Consciousness in the Breakdown of the Bicameral Mind. Boston: Houghton Mifflin Company.

Johnson, Robert A. (1989) He: understanding masculine psychology. New York: Harper & Row Publishers.

Kidd, S. & Kidd, J. (1990) Experiential Method Qualitative Research in the Humanities Using Metaphysics and Phenomenology. New York: Peter Lang Pub. Inc.

Kleinman, Arthur. (1980) Patients and Healers in the context of Culture: an exploration of the borderline between anthropology, medicine and psychiatry. Berkeley, CA: University of California Press.

Kramer, Joel & Alstad, Diana. (1993) The Guru Papers, Masks of Authoritarian Power. Berkeley, California: North Atlantic Books.

Kruk, Sonia. (1990) Situation and Human Existence. London: Unwin Hymen Ltd.

Lakoff, George and Johnson Mark. (1980) Metaphors We Live by. Chicago: University of Chicago Press.

Langer, Susanne K. Philosophy in a New Key: a study in symbolism of reason, rite and art. (1957) 3rd edition. Cambridge, Massachusetts: Harvard University Press.

Lindesmith, Alfred. Strauss, Anselm. Denzin, Norman. (1975) Readings in social Psychology. 2nd ed. Hinsdale, Illinois: The Dryden Press.

Marwisk, Max. (1970) Witchcraft and Sorcery. London: Penguin books.

Mauss, Marcel. (1967) The gift: forms and functions of exchange in archaic societies. New York: W.W. Norton & Company.

McElroy, Ann. & Townsend, Patricia K. (1989) Medical Anthropology in Ecological Perspective. Boulder, Colorado: Westcott Press, Inc.

Merlaeu-Ponty, Maurice. (1964) The Primacy of Perception. Northwestern University Press.

Merleau-Ponty, Maurice. An Introduction to Phenomenology in Phenomenology of Religion, Joseph D. Bettis, ed. (1969). London: SCM Press Ltd.

Merton, Thomas. (1967) Mystics & Zen Masters. Dell Pub. co.

Michelet, Jules. (1973) Satanism and Witchcraft: a study in medieval superstition. Secaucus, New Jersey: Citadel Press.

O'Keefe, Daniel Lawrence. (1982) Stolen Lightning: The Social Theory of Magic. New York: Vintage Books.

Ornstein, Robert E. (1972) The Psychology of Consciousness. New York: Penguin Books

Ouspensky, P. D. (1949) In Search of the Miraculous. New York: Harcourt Brace Jovanich, Pub.

Ouspensky, P.D. (1957) The Fourth Way. New York: Vintage Books, Random House.

Paglia, Camille. (1990) Sexual personae. New York: Vintage books.

Parker, Blake. (1994) The Romantic body: Therapy and Metaphor. Simon Fraser University, MA thesis.

Pendergast, John J., Fenner, Peter, and Krystal, Sheila, eds. (2003). The Sacred Mirror: Nondual Wisdom and Psychotherapy.

Reich, Wilhelm. (1949) Character-Analysis. New York: Orgone Institute Press.

Reich, Wilhelm. (1945) The Sexual Revolution: towards a self-governing character structure. New York: The Noonday Press.

Reik, Theodore. (1948) Listening with the Third Ear. New York: Farrar, Strauss pub.

Ricoeur, Paul. (1967) The Symbolism of Evil. New York: Beacon Press, Harper & Row Pub., Inc.

Rieff, Philip. (1966) The Triumph of the Therapeutic: uses of faith after Freud. Chicago: University of Chicago press.

Ruitenbeek, Hendrik M. ed. (1962) Psychoanalysis and Existential Philosophy. New York: E.P. Dutton & Co., Inc.

Seligmann, Kurt. (1948, 1968) Magic, Supernaturalism, and Religion. New York: the universal Library, Grosset and Dunlap.

Shepard, Paul. (1978) Thinking Animals: Animals & the Development of Human Intelligence. N.Y.: Viking Press.

Shorter, Edward. (1992) From Paralysis to Fatigue: a history of psychosomatic illness in the modern era. New York: Free Press, Macmillan, Inc.

Showalter, Elaine. (1985) The Female Malady; women, madness, and the English culture, 1830-1980. London: Penguin Books.

Shweder, Richard A. (1991) Thinking through Cultures: expeditions in cultural psychology. Cambridge, Massachusetts: Harvard Press.

Silverman, Kaja. (1983) The Subject of Semiotics. Oxford: Oxford University Press.

Sturrock, John. (1986) Structuralism. London: Paladin, Grafton books.

Teilhard de Chardin, Pierre. (1955) The Phenomenon of Man. London: Wm. Collins Sons & C. Ltd.

Trevor-Roper, H.R. (1956) the European Witch-Craze. New York: Harper Torchbooks, Harper & Row Pub.

Turner, Victor. (1969) The Ritual Process: Structure and Anti-Structure. New York: Cornell University Press.

Turner, Victor. (967) The Forest of Symbols. Ithaca, New York: Cornell University Press.

Van Gennep, Arnold. (1960) The Rites of Passage. Chicago: University of Chicago Press.

Veith, Ilza. (1965) Hysteria: the history of a disease. Chicago: Phoenix books, University of Chicago Press.

Von Dusen, Wilson. (1968) The Presence of Other Worlds. NY: Swedenborg Foundation.

Van Manen, Max. (1990) Researching Lived Experience: Human science for an action sensitive pedagogy. London Ont. Canada: The Althouse Press

Wagner, Roy. (1986) Symbols That Stand for Themselves. Chicago: University of Chicago Press.

Roy Wagner, (1981). The Invention of Culture. Revised and Expanded Edition. Chicago: University of Chicago Press.

Watzlawick, Paul. (1978) The Language of Change: Elements of Therapeutic Communication. New York: W.W Norton & Co.

Wilden, Anthony. (1987) The Rules are no game: The strategy of communication. Routledge & Kegan Paul Ltd.

Winnicott, D. W. (1971) Playing and Reality. London: Penguin books.

Yates, Frances A. (1964) Giordano Bruno and the Hermetic Tradition. Chicago: University of Chicago Press.

The Life and Times of Blake Parker

Sept. 25, 1943 – Jan. 30, 2007

Blake was born in 1943 in Vancouver but grew up in Toronto. He began writing at 15 and as he put it "the habit persisted" and at the time of his death in 2007 he had almost 50 years of performing, writing, and recording. Blake was prolific – there are numerous writings and recordings that will be published and produced posthumously. As a teenager in the 50s, Blake was strongly influenced by the Beat poets who came before him. His lively, experimental spoken word projects reflect a mature yet quirky genre that is the predecessor of today's rap and hip hop. As part of the populist spoken word movement, his work aspires to an integration of high art & low entertainment. Blake Parker integrated into his performance poetry – mixed media, technology, mythology and improvisation. He described his key concerns and background:

> I have been working in mixed media for most of my life, beginning with my work with the innovative group "Intersystems" in the 60s in Toronto. I was doing performance poetry & tape work at that time and it was in that context that I first met and worked with the electronic music composer John Mills-Cockell who I have continued to work with over the years. It seems to me that the concept of "mixed media" is not really new or innovative; rather it is as ancient as the first ritual, the first theatre, which certainly utilized all the modalities of sound, action and words. What is new is the alienation of one aspect of human theatre from another – thus we just have spoken word or just music or what have you....
>
> I have been keenly interested in the uses of technology in art and the ways it can mold and manipulate consciousness in the context of popular culture. In the sense that we can say that technology is ideology, then it is technology that we must engage with in order to deconstruct that ideology. I take the critique of technology as one of the major agendas of contemporary art. Mass technology always has & always will promote a sort of forgetfulness and the process of unraveling its influence will always involve a re-membering of what has been forgotten. Among that which has been forgotten is the mythology that brings the human body & the animal body into a close matrix of living metaphors. The body as animal confronts the body as machine.

This description is particularly interesting in the light of his writing in the last few years of his life which focused on cyborgs exploring themes of renovation and rebirth. He did a couple of performances Cyborg Landscapes and Confessions of a Cyborg in the last few years of his life.

Blake was involved in writing and performance poetry for all of his adult life and was very interested in the cross-fertilization of different disciplines. He was involved in a number of experimental and mixed media collaborations, including work with:

Toronto Kathak dancer Joanna Das and the Toronto Tabla Ensemble.
The Three Poets –improvisation with Paul Landsberg & Stephen Parrish.
Wireless Bodies and Confessions of a Cyborg with media artist Ruby Truly.

Stella: Black and White —with the electronic music composer John Mills-Cockell.

Projects with Jude Davison: Drop Dead Scene, Slow Resurrection: The Life and Times of Leland Frank, The Terminal City Trilogy.

Video: The Self with Fred Rosenberg photographs & music by Jude Davison.

The Princess and the Kid: a project with his daughter Eva Tree and Jude Davison.

Cyborg Landscapes: dance, music & spoken word with Diane Taylor, Thomas Loh.

Blake Parker was a performance poet, writer, graphic designer, teacher and medical anthropologist.

As a partner in Blue Heron Productions: research in Communication tools, Blake designed 9 therapeutic communication board games with his partner, Monica Carpendale. They collaborated in developing a number of therapeutic board games, which are sold around the world, for which Blake did all of the graphic design work.

He used his background in medical anthropology as faculty member of the Kutenai Art Therapy Institute, lecturing on psychoanalysis, research, symbolic interpretation and cross-cultural orientations to healing.

Blake lived consciously always with intention, authenticity and passion. This is also the way that he died at home – surrounded by family, extended family & friends – soaked in music, love, laughter & tears.

Thoughts on Death

My present philosophical outlook
Blake Parker
December 10, 2006

My philosophy, such as it is, concerning death is, I suppose, somewhat eclectic, taking cues, as it does, from a number of different philosophical outlooks. I do not mean that I have a well worked out philosophy but rather that I have cobbled something together that I hope, before I begin the task, to be more or less cohesive and non-contradictory. At the end, we shall see. Up until this time, I have been content to simply work out or express my ideas in my various haphazard writing & recording projects but have never undertaken to address the question of personal philosophy directly. Given the apparent shortness of my time left on the planet, it seems, that if I'm going to address something like this, it's a good time to start.

At the beginning I should simply state that I do not think that there is life after death or that my ego or soul or any other part of me is going to survive death. My notion is strictly scientific in this regard. I am an atheist. Consciousness, for me, is strictly dependent upon the body & is the result of biological evolution. On the other hand, it seems perfectly logical to think that my body & whatever there is of psychic energy will be transformed or changed into other forms & that I will thereby become part of the larger landscape. So while there is no survival of an "I" there is an ongoingness that is actually more pleasing to me at this point, than the notion has been in the past, due I believe to my current interest in environmental philosophy.

Perhaps in this 2nd beginning, I'll just give a cursory list of obvious philosophical influences, to act as touchstones as it were. Surrealism, especially the works of Georges Bataille, Psychoanalysis, Existentialism, particularly Sartre & Merleau-Ponty, Zen, particularly Alan Watts, Structuralism & post-structuralism including especially metaphor theory & elements of Stoicism & some elements taken from the environmental movement. A little of this, a little of that.

It strikes me that Language theory doesn't have that much to do with things except for the fact that I take the "I" or the self to be a socially constructed entity. Reality, or "knowledge" itself is socially constructed as an interlocking set of discontinuous categories. It is quite obvious, then, that with the death of the body, the self merely dissolves – there is no longer a foundation for the metaphorical reality that consciousness is. When I say that the self "dissolves" I draw upon Georges Bataille & more strictly mean that the body & the self leave the "discontinuous" world of social life & enter into the "continuous" life of "nature" or the non-social world. Nature or the non-social world, in this context, may be given the term "sacred." In this I follow a great number of different authors in understanding the human world as dialectical & comprised of two foundational domains which go under a great number of different names including: "Cosmos" & "Nomos," "Continuous" & "Dis-continuous" as well as "Sacred" & "Profane." These are understood to be dialectical entities not binary oppositions.

When, I die, then, both body & mind leave the world of the profane & enter into the sacred "flow" of the Continuous cosmic world. Or nature, the environment. Thus it appears that I have a distinct notion of the sacred while I do not lean upon the usual notion of life after death which would seem to be the usual reason for "believing" in the sacred or "God" or whatever. I should say here, also, that I follow Bataille in characterizing the sacred as essentially violent, hastening to add, because this word "violence" seems so shocking when linked to the sacred, that I simply take "death" in whatever form it takes as the most violent possible thing that can happen to the living human being. Whether the sacred is seen as "violent" or characterized in some other way, it is utterly disruptive of the discontinuous social world. The distinct "edges" of our self-created categories of things & the disjunction between subject & object, are completely disorganized with death & the entrance into the sacred domain of continuous life, of flow. This disorganization of the conventional brings one into contact with an infinite potential & also sometimes one may experience various profound emotions of love & ecstasy. (It seems that perhaps the fear & paranoia which also comes up in this context are occasioned by trying to hold on to the disrupted order instead of letting it go. "Letting it go" in this case would mean especially not holding on to particular elements that are understood to constitute identity.)

In order to further characterize this world of "nature" & "flow" I should say that this is also the world of eroticism & creativity in general. The creative, the erotic & the contemplative all give temporary intuitive access to this domain before death. I should also say that I am in agreement with Freud that what many take to be "spiritual yearning" is actually a yearning for the oceanic feeling occasioned by the fact of one's being merged with the mother before birth. Freud's notion of the polymorphous perverse, to characterize the erotic engagement of the very young child with the world of flowing reality also appeals to my own desire to be somewhat iconoclastic. My own yearning for this lost mythological time has been tinged with melancholy, a product of my own childhood & the somewhat distorted attachment to my parents' own uneasy way of being in the world. It should be clear that overall I prefer the dynamism of creative thought to the calm contemplative attitude. Oh that oceanic feeling.

I can further say, expanding on the notion of spiritual yearning, that in most mystical traditions this world of natural flow, often characterized as complete plenitude or emptiness, is identified with the larger mystic self or cosmic consciousness. In the very general story of the mystic journey, the small self or ego is sacrificed in order to gain this larger self. As Thomas Merton said in his discussion of Zen, one may perhaps best apprehend this domain, this understanding of self via an "ontological intuition." I find this notion of ontological intuition to be quite congenial & if some wish to call contact with this domain spiritual as opposed to an intuitive apprehension of the ground of evolutionary history, so be it.

While on the subject of Zen, I also am quite in agreement with Alan Watts in characterizing the enlightened state, if there really can be such a thing, as spontaneous, humorous, creative, playful & improvisatory. From this point of view, one does not take either oneself or "reality" as of any great moment. I mean, "reality" is to be understood as something cobbled together by people in various different cultures in various different situations in order to negotiate their survival. William Burroughs with his carnie sensibility captures this notion very well with his continual interest in who has control of the "reality concession." Reality is malleable & very changeable across time & culture. And "power," of course, in its various discursive streams continues to assert itself in the establishment of reality for the benefit of this or that social group.

Zen & the environmental movement are quite similar in their understanding of the malleability of reality – they both call for a lightness of touch, a dancing "with" nature & the world, rather than any sort of belief in a "solid" reality or in human dominance of nature. The main thing I would have to say about this state (or altered state) is that it really is no big deal. It is certainly nothing to be obsessed over or turned into some special state of being that one should try to be in as much as possible. It is simply the unstable shifting nature of reality that underlies all of our "realities." As such, one returns to it in "play" & for the formation of new & different realities. There is no point at all in attempting to stay there for any length of time although there is perhaps an auto-erotic element of pleasure to be found there. Also one may find a certain amount of "refreshment" there.

It seems, then, that contact with the sacred, if we can call it that, & insofar as one can have contact with it, is far more interesting when alive than when dead, for while one in death merges with the flow of all things, one has no particular consciousness of it.

I take from psychoanalysis the basic structure of the psyche (socially constructed as I have said) while from Existentialism, I take the obvious – personal responsibility for one's actions, towards one's fellow beings & the environment in general. This doesn't really have much to do with my philosophical attitude towards death, except that I take it that my death is fundamentally my own responsibility. I suppose I could blame my cancer on a neurotic character structure, originating with my upbringing or lack of it by my parents & I suppose there is some sense that the general pollution of the environment may also be blamed but to lean on such ideas would be to act in bad faith. This brings me to the Stoical idea that there are fundamentally 2 kinds of things in one's life: things that cannot be influenced or changed & things that can be influenced & changed. In general, the idea is that one may not change the objective facts of a situation but that one may always change one's "attitude" or "orientation" towards them. My death, then, is my responsibility & I while I do not have control of the fact that I have cancer, I do have control of my attitude towards my illness.

I should also mention that I like very much Tielhard de Chardin's notion that there are two fundamental elements to evolution – differentiation – the elaboration of different species & a sort of centrification – the cultural evolution of human caring or love. Thus for him, individual healing or salvation, as with any number of other religious thinkers, is always linked to collective healing or salvation. As long as I'm on the topic of evolution, I should also say that I find congenial, the idea of the anarchist thinker Bookchin that human kind is the naturally evolved ethical part of nature. As for one's moral responsibility, I have never found a better statement than that one should do unto others as you would have them do unto you.

It seems, then, that I feel myself to have a personal relationship with "the sacred" understood as an ontological intuition, primarily through creative endeavor. This relationship has nothing to do with any god or spirits or any non-material entity – rather, it is simply an intense (perhaps even relentless) relationship with the world. The question: "who dies?" is answered quite simply by stating that the "I" (as a socially constructed entity) dies with the body. With death, the whole shebang that is me enters into the flow of the all & the everything & given the vast extent of the universe, I must admit that whatever I have been will be quite diluted in my future form. My death as my life, is my own responsibility. Or rather I should say, I suppose, I must "give myself over" in some sense to the greater power of the cosmos, my responsibility extending only to those parts of the actual dying that I can influence.

This notion of "giving oneself over" to something more powerful than oneself seems to be at the centre of creative endeavour in general. I like the simplicity of the American anthropologist Roy Wagner's formulation of creativity as the reversal of the ordinary relationship of convention to invention. In our ordinary lives we impose our conventions on the fullness of the universe but in the creative dimension we open ourselves to the fullness of the universe & allow that to guide us in the creation of new metaphor. I suppose I should say that the creative imagination stands at the very centre of all that I hold to be best in human life.

In the end, I remain much more interested in life than in death. Although I continue to often be discontented, I take this to be a general characteristic of life on the planet & can say that I have truly had a wonderful life. I found a life-long love with Monica & my children are very wonderful indeed. I have also been very lucky to have such a wonderful brother & sister. I was also able to get to know both of my parents in a deep & abiding way after long separation. Luckily, I came across my "work" such as it is – writing & performing – fairly early on & it has sustained me over the years in wonderful ways. I have also been lucky enough to have a number of very great friendships over the course of my life. I find much more interesting the horizontal "working through" of the human "soul" – that is the nurturing of human friendship, love, memory and creative endeavor – than any ascension of the spirit. I have been so very lucky to be able to participate in a wonderful & ever expanding creative "conversation" with all those close to me & I can say with great pleasure that this conversation has only gotten richer & "better" in these last years.

Looking back over the last paragraph I realize I have used the word "lucky" quite a number of times, all having to do with my relationships with family & friends. This makes me realize how much I really do credit sheer blind luck for the good things in my life. (Although I suppose I do in some part "buy" the notion that one makes one's own luck by being open to possibility.) The bad things for the most part I can quite easily credit to my own ignorance & foolishness. The bad in myself is pretty much understood to be the same badness we find everywhere – selfishness in all its guises. One of these general disguises for selfishness I take to be simply the neurotic thinking that expects different outcomes from the same behaviour. What could I have been thinking of?

Let's see if I can give a brief embodied reading of the evolutionary life process who's end is death. Meaning (foreground) is embodied in language (background). Language (foreground) is embodied by the mind, (background) in particular, the self as a metaphoric construction is embodied by the mind. The mind (foreground) is embodied by the biological brain/body (background). The biological brain/body (foreground) is embodied by its external environment (background). At each level the interaction between embodied & the embodying environment interact, form themselves to each other, change each other. At death, the whole process of embodiment is undone or reversed & I become some incredibly small part of the environment which embodies new life in turn. The writing, a little dry I suppose but so be it. But the world, so vast & so filled with mystery.

At the end now of this short statement it still seems to me that while obviously somewhat "thrown" together of this & that, the structure still seems to stand thought it is a little shaky & certainly lets in more than a little wind & rain, somewhat like a child's fort made of sticks & things. But for all that, a comfort.

Blake Parker
Nelson BC
December 16, 2006

Notes: Thomas Merton cite
came across Lao Tzu, good & Scientific pantheism seems to fit me to a T. look further.
Reciprocity relates to empathy & the golden rule as well as to the constitution of categories.